NEW TESTAMENT INTRODUCTION
HEBREWS TO REVELATION

HEBREWS TO REVELATION

New Testament
Introduction

by

DONALD GUTHRIE, B.D., M.Th., Ph.D.

Lecturer in New Testament Language and Literature,
The London Bible College

LONDON

THE TYNDALE PRESS

39 BEDFORD SQUARE WC1

PRINTED AND BOUND IN ENGLAND BY
HAZELL WATSON AND VINEY LTD
AYLESBURY AND SLOUGH

CONTENTS

CONTENTS

6

ABBREVIATIONS

ATR   Anglican Theological Review.

AV   Authorized Version (King James').

BJRL   Bulletin of the John Rylands Library.

CB   Century Bible.

CBS   Cambridge Bible for Schools and Colleges.

CGT   Cambridge Greek Testament.

Clar B   Clarendon Bible.

CNT   Commentaire du Nouveau Testament.

DSB   Daily Study Bible.

Enc. Bib. Encyclopaedia Biblica.

EB   Etudes Bibliques.

EC   Epworth Preacher's Commentary.

EGT   Expositor's Greek Testament.

EQ   Evangelical Quarterly.

ET   Expository Times.

Eng. Tr. English Translation.

Exp.   Expositor.

Exp. Bib. Expositor's Bible.

HDB   Hastings' Dictionary of the Bible.

HE   Eusebius' Historia Ecclesia.

IB   Interpreter's Bible.

ICC   International Critical Commentary.

ILNT   Introduction to the Literature of the New Testament.

INT   Introduction to the New Testament.

JBL   Journal of Biblical Literature.

JPTh   Jahrbücher für protestantische Theologie.

JR   Journal of Religion.

JTS   Journal of Theological Studies.

KEK	Kritisch-exegetischer Kommentar.
LHB	Lietzmann's Handbuch zum Neuen Testament.
LNT	Literature of the New Testament.
LXX	Septuagint.
MC	Moffatt's New Testament Commentary.
NkZ	Neue kirchliche Zeitschrift.
NLC	New London Commentary.
NTD	Neue Testament Deutsch.
NTS	New Testament Studies.
RB	Revue Biblique.
RHR	Revue de l'Histoire des Religions.
RV	Revised Version.
RSV	Revised Standard Version.
TC	Torch Commentary.
ThBl	Theologische Blätter.
ThLZ	Theologische Literaturzeitung.
ThZ	Theologische Zeitschrift.
TNT	Tyndale New Testament Commentary.
TR	Theologische Rundschau.
TSK	Theologische Studien und Kritiken.
TU	Texte und Untersuchungen.
WC	Westminster Commentary.
ZNTW	Zeitschrift für die neutestamentliche Wissenschaft.
ZTK	Zeitschrift für Theologie und Kirche.

PREFACE

The non-Pauline Epistles of the New Testament and the book of Revelation present a deeply interesting field of study, although they pose many problems for the critical student. They may be said to provide a fascinating cross-section of early Christian life and thought and will well repay careful investigation.

As in the volume on the Pauline Epistles, I have mainly kept in mind the needs of theological students, but the same plan adopted in that volume will, I hope, prove of value to many others. The footnotes will again give guidance to those who intend to pursue their studies further, but may be readily passed over by the general reader.

It will be noted that the amount of discussion on some of the Epistles is disproportionate to their length, but I have followed the same principle which I adopted in the former book of giving full consideration to critical problems where they arise. As before, detailed summaries of the contents of the various books have been included. It is my hope that this book will lead many into a fuller appreciation of those books which all too often receive less than their due share of attention.

I wish to acknowledge indebtedness to my colleagues Ralph P. Martin, M.A., and J. Clement Connell, M.A. The former read through the manuscript and made helpful suggestions and the latter assisted in the preparation of the Index. I am also indebted to the Principal and Governors of my college for granting me a term's leave of absence from college duties, without which this book would have been considerably delayed.

D. G.

CHAPTER ONE

THE EPISTLE TO THE HEBREWS

This Epistle raises several problems, for not only is it anonymous, but its destination and purpose are both obscure. The importance of careful examination of all these problems, even if no dogmatic conclusions can be reached, cannot be exaggerated since they affect both the approach to the Epistle as a whole and the understanding of the argument. Moreover, its modern relevance clearly depends on a right appreciation of its original setting.

I. AUTHORSHIP

a. External evidence

A review of the early history of this Epistle at once places in its true perspective the discussion on authorship, for it becomes immediately evident that there was no firm tradition on this matter in the earliest period.

There are remarkable parallels between this Epistle and the Epistle sent by Clement of Rome to the Corinthians (cf. Heb. xi. 7 and *1 Clement*, ix. 4 and xii. 1; Heb. i. 3f. and *1 Clement*, xxxvi. 1f.) which make it certain that Clement was in possession of the Epistle. Suggestions that trace both to a common source[1] or suppose that the author of Hebrews was acquainted with *1 Clement* cannot seriously be maintained.

The sequence of thoughts which are parallel to the Epistle, especially in *1 Clement*, xxxvi, supports the contention that Clement had the Epistle before him, although he uses some freedom in his citations. This latter fact does not detract from the authority which for Clement was clearly invested in the Epistle, for he uses the same freedom in citations from other New Testament Epistles.[2] Yet he gives no hint of authorship.[3]

[1] A. Nairne mentioned the idea, but admitted it to be in the realm of fancy, that both authors were influenced by the Roman liturgy (*The Epistle to the Hebrews*, 1917, p. xxxix). He thought that Clement had read the Epistle.

[2] It has been suggested that Clement assumes that the Corinthians would know of Hebrews and regard it as authoritative. (Cf. K. Endemann, *NkZ*, 21, 1910, p. 103.)

[3] This by itself would not be decisive since he cites Pauline letters without indication of Pauline origin (except in the case of 1 Cor.). (Cf. B. F. Westcott, *On the Canon of the New Testament*,[4] 1875, p. 50.)

There is little other positive evidence about the Epistle until the end of the second century.[1] It was excluded from Marcion's Canon, but the Epistle would certainly not have appealed to him with his aversion to the idea of any continuity between the Old Testament and Christianity, which forms so integral a part of the thought-structure of the Epistle. It is further omitted from the Muratorian Canon, although this may be due to the corrupt state of the text of that Canon. In any case it was definitely not included in the Pauline Epistles, for these are restricted to seven churches. At the end of the century, however, more specific references are made to it, but these at once reveal a divergent tradition. In the East the Epistle was probably regarded as Pauline, at least from the time of Pantaenus. Clement of Alexandria, who described the Epistle as Paul's (Eusebius, *HE*, vi. 14), derived this opinion from 'the blessed presbyter', who is generally supposed to be his predecessor at Alexandria, Pantaenus. Origen was equally certain that the thoughts were Pauline, but he could not imagine the style to be his. His own supposition was that one of the pupils of the apostle wrote down from memory what he had heard. For this reason he not only did not quarrel with any church which regarded it as Paul's but even himself cited it similarly. Yet he added his famous caution, 'But who wrote the Epistle God only knows certainly.' At the same time he mentions that some held 'Clement, who became bishop of Rome', and others Luke, to be the author.[2]

Subsequent to Origen, the Eastern Church generally did not doubt the canonicity of the Epistle and indeed assumed its Pauline authorship. In the Chester Beatty papyrus (P46), the Epistle appears among the Pauline Epistles, being placed after Romans,[3] and this represents the position not later than the mid-third century. In the majority of early Greek manuscripts it is placed after 2 Thessalonians and before the personal letters of Paul.[4]

In the West the only early evidence of views on authorship comes

---

[1] Van Unnik, *The Jung Codex* (ed. F. L. Cross, 1955), pp. 115ff., finds traces in the *Gospel of Truth*. Cf. the further study of S. Giversen, *Studia Theologica*, XIII, fasc. II (1959), pp. 87–96, who finds parallels but many differences.

[2] Origen obviously regarded the idea of Pauline authorship as of some antiquity, for he mentions that the tradition was handed down by 'men of old' (Eusebius, *HE*, vi. 25, 11–14).

[3] Cf. F. G. Kenyon, *The Chester Beatty Biblical Papyri* (1936), fasc. III, p. viii. Cf. also his *The Story of the Bible* (1936), p. 116.

[4] Cf. Feine-Behm, *Einleitung in das Neue Testament*[11] (1956), p. 221.

from Tertullian who attributed it to Barnabas in the only place where he mentioned it.[1] This isolated use of the Epistle suggests that it did not possess the same authority as the Epistles of Paul which were extensively cited by the same writer.[2] As already mentioned, the Muratorian Canon omits it, but this cannot be cited as evidence for its definite rejection from the Roman Canon. Eusebius,[3] who follows the general eastern tradition in including this Epistle among the Pauline Epistles, mentions that in his time the Roman Church disputed the Pauline authorship and that on the grounds of this some others were rejecting the Epistle. It was similarly omitted from the later African Canon, while Cyprian never mentions it. This reflects the prevailing approach of the West towards this Epistle until the time of Hilary, Jerome and Augustine.[4] These writers show the impact of eastern ideas on the western churches, but it is significant that, although Hilary regarded the Epistle as canonical, he does not specifically cite it as Paul's.[5] The other writers are similarly witnesses to a compromise affecting the Western Church, for neither seems convinced of Pauline authorship and yet both cite it as Paul's. It was their willingness to do this that finally settled the matter in the West and secured for Pauline authorship an unchallenged position until the Reformation, when Erasmus, Luther and Calvin all questioned it.[6] For Luther this involved its relegation to the end of the Bible with other books considered by him to be of lesser value. His own theory was that Apollos wrote it. Later Grotius returned to the earlier theory of Lucan authorship, while subsequent investigators have devoted themselves to pressing the claims of a wide variety of possibilities.

[1] *De pudicitia*, 20. Cf. Westcott, *op. cit.*, p. 367. J. V. Bartlet (*Exp.*, VI, v, 1902, p. 423) maintained that Tertullian was magnifying Hebrews at the expense of *Hermas* (the reverse procedure from what he imagined is found in the Muratorian Canon).

[2] T. Zahn cites some evidence which suggests that both Hippolytus and Irenaeus might have known and quoted Hebrews, although not regarding it as Pauline (*Introduction to the New Testament*, Eng. Tr. 1909, II, pp. 295, 310).

[3] *HE*, iii. 3.

[4] There is something to be said for the view that early Western opinion, in its rejection of Pauline authorship, was more consistent than the Eastern Church with its vacillations over Pauline authorship (cf. K. Endemann, *NkZ*, 21, 1910, pp. 102ff.).

[5] Cf. A. Souter, *The Text and Canon of New Testament* (1913), p. 190. Hilary uses the introductory formula, *maxime cum Scriptum sit.*

[6] Cf. *Ibid.*, pp. 198ff.

The divergent early views and the later speculations do not suggest that discussion of various theories is likely to be very profitable, but the process is worth while if only to illustrate many facets of the author's background, which are necessarily brought to the fore in such discussions.

b. Various suggestions

Investigations will commence with those names which commanded some ancient respect and the most notable of these is clearly Paul.
(i) *Paul.* Most modern writers find more difficulty in imagining how this Epistle was ever attributed to Paul[1] than in disposing of the theory. The grounds for dispute may be set out as follows:

1. Its anonymity would not conform to Paul's style, although this fact did not deter nineteenth-century[2] supporters of Pauline authorship, who regarded it rather as confirmatory than damaging, since an apostle to the Gentiles could hardly have addressed an Epistle to the Hebrews without incurring the resentment of the readers. But this attaches too much weight to the title. Clement of Alexandria, who expresses a similar opinion, cites with some approval the view of Pantaenus that the absence of Paul's name was occasioned by respect for the Lord, whom he presumably regarded as the Apostle to the Hebrews, and by the fact that Paul regarded this Epistle as a work of supererogation. But these explanations are clearly unconvincing in helping to remove what is an obvious difficulty for the acceptance of Pauline authorship. Moreover, nowhere in the Epistle does the author lay claim to any apostolic authority, which would certainly be strange for Paul.

2. But difference of style is even more apparent and would seem to make the theory of Pauline authorship inconceivable. The language, as Origen noted, is more Greek, with its more polished periods, its more designed argumentation and its absence of the usual Pauline abruptness, digressions and even disorderliness.[3] Where breaks in the

---

[1] Cf. F. D. V. Narborough, *The Epistle to the Hebrews* (1930), p. 9.

[2] Cf. Bishop C. Wordsworth, *St. Paul's Epistles* (1872), p. 370. For the most recent advocacy of Pauline authorship, cf. W. Leonard, *The Authorship of the Epistle to the Hebrews* (1939). H. C. Thiessen (*INT,*[4] 1956, p. 301) considers that rejection of Pauline authorship is not absolutely certain.

[3] Feine-Behm (*op. cit.,* p. 222) maintain that this Epistle is one of the best Greek writings in the New Testament and most scholars would agree with this judgment.

argument occur, the writer always picks up the threads in a deliberate, almost leisurely, manner, in strong contrast to Paul's habit of losing his line of argument altogether.[1] This clear difference cannot be mitigated by the difference of form, assuming this Epistle to be more an oration than an Epistle in the sense of Paul's letters. The most that could be supposed is that a member of the Pauline circle wrote down such an oration as he had heard Paul preach it, but, if so, much of the oratorical effects must be due to the reporter rather than to the orator.[2]

3. An even more damaging objection is the absence of the characteristic Pauline spiritual experience.[3] There is no suggestion of the author being dominated by a spiritual crisis comparable to the Damascus experience and there is consequently an absence of that tension so characteristic of Paul. It need not, of course, be supposed that similar background experiences must be brought into every writing of an author, but in spite of some personal allusions this author does not project himself into his writing as Paul habitually does.

4. There are undoubtedly theological differences between this Epistle and the Epistles of Paul, in spite of the many similarities (for these latter see p. 48f.). Whereas Paul makes much of the resurrection, our author concentrates on the exaltation. Whereas Paul calls special attention to the redemptive aspect of the work of Christ, this Epistle deals more with His cleansing, sanctifying and perfecting work. This Epistle also makes more of the idea of the new covenant, but lacks the familiar Pauline tension between flesh and spirit and the believer's mystic union with Christ. A rather different approach to the law is also suggested, since our author appears to regard it as an instrument for the attainment of man's highest end and never, as Paul does, as a possible scene of conflict. Most significant of all, there is no mention in Paul of the High-Priesthood of Christ, which forms the central theme of this Epistle.[4]

While full weight must be given to these differences in discussing

[1] F. W. Farrar (*The Epistle to the Hebrews*, 1888, p. xxxviii) well said of this writer, 'He has less of burning passion and more of conscious literary control.'

[2] See the discussion on the literary form on pp. 50ff.

[3] E. F. Scott (*The Literature of the New Testament*, 1932, p. 198) went so far as to suggest that the author does not even seem to be acquainted with Paul's teaching.

[4] Cf. Feine-Behm (*op. cit.*, pp. 222, 223) for a statement on these differences. In connection with Christ's High-Priesthood, it should be noted that certain hints suggest that Paul at times thought along these lines, as did Peter and John (cf. O. Moe's discussion in *ThLZ*, 72, 1947, cols. 335–338).

the problem of authorship, it should be noted that differences from Paul do not amount to disagreements with Paul (see discussion on Paulinism on pp. 48f.). Nor must it be supposed that these doctrinal differences necessarily exclude Pauline authorship. Yet if they do not *require* its rejection, it must be admitted that they appear to suggest it. Some allowance must be made for the different reader-circle that would be involved if Paul were author (but see objection 1 above). It may not be a fair comparison to set writings directed to Gentiles over against a writing which appears to have been sent to Jews (see later discussion pp. 24ff.). There is no certain knowledge, moreover, as to how Paul would have dealt with the high-priest theme had he applied himself to it. Too much emphasis should not, perhaps, be laid upon these doctrinal differences. After all, that acute scholar, Origen of Alexandria, recognized here the thoughts of Paul.

5. The different historical position of the author is generally considered to be conclusive against Pauline authorship. In ii. 3 it is evident that the author had received his Christian instruction directly from those who had heard the Lord,[1] whereas Paul was particularly insistent that he was brought into salvation by a supernatural revelation (cf. Gal. i. 12). On occasions Paul identified himself with the experience of his readers rather than allowing his own to predominate, but it is questionable whether he would ever have set himself so definitely in contrast to those who had personally heard Jesus Christ in the flesh.

There seems little doubt from these considerations and from the uncertainty of early Christian attestation that Paul was not the author of this Epistle. This is not to deny the possibility, but rather to confirm the improbability. But if not Paul, who was the author?

(ii) *Barnabas*. This suggestion deserves second place in our considerations because it is the only other one which has early ecclesiastical support. In fact it may possibly be the oldest attested since Tertullian does not attribute it to Barnabas as if it were his own conjecture and it is reasonable to suppose that it was current at a still earlier period.[2]

---

[1] Cf. F. D. V. Narborough (*op. cit.*, p. 10) who argues that the author had been converted in the ordinary course of evangelization.

[2] J. Moffatt (*ILNT*,[2] 1912, p. 437) suggested that Tertullian may be reflecting a Roman tradition. But A. Harnack (*Das Neue Testament um das Jahr* 200, 1889, pp. 79ff.) thought there was no reason to suppose that any churches with whom Tertullian was in touch regarded Hebrews as by Barnabas. A. Nairne (*The Epistle of Priesthood*,[2] 1915, pp. 3, 4) thought the idea was a guess on the part of simple Christians.

Yet, because the evidence is restricted to Africa, it cannot be claimed that this suggestion commanded much general consent. But Westcott suggested[1] that the Epistle may have been mentioned in the Claromontanus List under the name of Barnabas, since stichometry (i.e. measurement by number of lines) appears to lend support to that conjecture, and if so, this second witness would extend the area of attestation. Moreover, two other witnesses to the same idea are the fourth-century *Tractatus de Libris* and the comment of Philastrius (fourth-century bishop of Brescia).[2] But all these would still restrict it to the Western Church.

The strongest basis for this claim is the certainty that Barnabas as a Levite would have been intimately acquainted with the temple ritual. Nevertheless this detail must not be overstressed since the author's main obsession seems to be the biblical cultus rather than contemporary ritual procedure. At the same time there is nothing in the Epistle to condemn the suggestion, even if there is similarly nothing to commend it. It may be added that the description of him as a son of consolation (Acts iv. 36) and the author's description of his work as 'a word of consolation' (Heb. xiii. 22) furnishes an ingenious parallel, which would support the general suitability of Barnabas as the possible author.[3] Barnabas might well have been capable of such a literary production, but the data for determining that he did produce it are practically non-existent.

Because of the generally assumed Hellenism of the Epistle it is an important question whether or not a man whose known connections were with Jerusalem and Cyprus would have sufficiently imbibed the Greek outlook to produce an Epistle with Alexandrian colouring. Apart from the fact that the Alexandrian background has probably been over-stressed (see later discussion), it is not improbable that some Hellenistic speculation of the Philonic type had penetrated into Cyprus.[4]

---

[1] *The Epistle to the Hebrews* (1889), pp. xxviii, xxix. The number of *stichoi* (lines) cited would not fit the *Epistle of Barnabas*, but would suit the Epistle to the Hebrews.

[2] Cf. J. V. Bartlet, *Exp.*, VI, v (1902), p. 426.

[3] K. Endemann, *NkZ*, 21 (1910), pp. 121, 122, pointed out in addition the sevenfold use of παρακαλειν—παράκλησις.

[4] Among those who have favoured Barnabas as author may be mentioned Salmon, Bartlet, Wickham, Riggenbach, Bornhäuser and Badcock; E. C. Wickham (*The Epistle to the Hebrews*, 1910, p. xii) maintained that the Epistle

But two considerations are not very favourable to this theory. If Barnabas had been the author, would he have described his own introduction to the gospel in the terms of ii. 3? And if it had been known that he was the author, is the rise of the Pauline tradition capable of any explanation? It might be contended in answer to the latter that Barnabas' name alone was not sufficiently authoritative to command canonical acceptance for the Epistle, as is evident in the case of the spurious Epistle which circulated under his name, but it is not conceivable that the substitution of Paul's name for that of Barnabas could have secured canonicity if any other tradition were already established or at least in some circulation.[1] In connection with the first consideration, it is not absolutely certain that ii. 3 would necessarily exclude Barnabas, unless, of course, it is interpreted as indicating a second generation situation. The early Acts narrative does not give any concrete data about the way that Barnabas became a Christian, although it is difficult to believe that he had never personally heard the Lord if he were a resident in Jerusalem.[2] Moreover, Barnabas, as an early member of the Jerusalem church, was presumably in sympathy with the general approach of those first Jewish Christians.[3] But the approach in this Epistle is very different, with its broader Hellenistic outlook.[4]

The comparison of this Epistle with the so-called *Epistle of Barnabas* proves conclusively that the same writer could not have written both Epistles, although there are some common features. Both deal with the Old Testament and both appear to write against a background of

suits Barnabas' character as a Hellenist by birthplace, but a Hebrew by race. K. Endemann (*op. cit.*, pp. 102–126) went so far as to claim that Barnabas alone fitted all the evidence. H. Strathmann (*Der Brief an die Hebräer,*[6] 1953, p. 71) is favourable, but admits its conjectural character.

[1] Cf. McNeile-Williams, *INT*[2] (1953), p. 237. It is not an altogether convincing suggestion of Renan's that it was Barnabas' lot to be lost in the greater glory of the apostle Paul, although J. V. Bartlet (*op. cit.*, p. 427) favoured this idea.

[2] Tertullian (*De Pudicitia*, 20) says of Barnabas, *qui ab apostolis didicit*, which would agree with ii. 3, but on the other hand it was probably no more than a deduction from the Epistle itself.

[3] J. V. Bartlet (*op. cit.*, p. 420) regarded ii. 3 simply as an instance in which the author identifies himself with his readers and which does not require the author to have received his Christian teaching secondhand. In fact, Bartlet maintained that all the New Testament evidence shows that Barnabas was a man of considerable influence in Jerusalem, which, he thought, strongly suggested that he was a personal hearer of the Lord (pp. 411ff.).

[4] Cf. Feine-Behm, *op. cit.*, p. 230.

Alexandrian rather than Judaistic ideas. Both mention levitical insti-
tutions and both contain teaching about the temple (or tabernacle).
But there the resemblances end.[1] The *Epistle of Barnabas* is greatly
inferior in spiritual grasp, in historical appreciation and in breadth of
understanding of the problems with which it deals. It is sufficient to
remark that if Barnabas were the genuine author of this *Epistle of
Barnabas*, he could not possibly be regarded as author of the Epistle to
the Hebrews. But the former *Epistle*, which is strictly anonymous,
appears to have been spuriously attributed to the illustrious name of
Paul's companion.[2] When compared with the Epistle to the Hebrews
it can only be said that the ascription of the latter to Barnabas has much
more to commend it than is the case with the former, but beyond that
we cannot go.

(iii) *Luke*. There were some in Origen's day who attributed the Epistle
to Luke, while Clement of Alexandria regarded him as translator from
Paul's Hebrew original and this notion of Luke's connection with the
Epistle has found supporters among modern critics.[3] The main prop
for the theory is the literary affinities of this Epistle with the Lucan
writings.[4] In addition to verbal and stylistic similarities, there are some
features which have been supposed to connect the Epistle closely with
Acts and especially with Stephen's speech. F. D. V. Narborough brings
out the following similarities: both contain reviews of Hebrew history;
both stress the call of Abraham and mention Abraham's non-possession
of the land; both describe the tabernacle as divinely ordered; and in
both the tradition that the law was mediated by angels finds a place.[5]

[1] Cf. B. F. Westcott's comparison, *op. cit.*, pp. lxxx–lxxxiv.

[2] Cf. K. Lake, *The Apostolic Fathers* (1912), I, p. 337.

[3] J. Moffatt gives a list of authors who have supported this contention (*ILNT*,
p. 435). A compromise suggestion was made by F. J. Badcock in his book *The
Pauline Epistles and the Epistle to the Hebrews in their historical setting* (1937), p. 198.
He considered that the voice was Barnabas', but the hand was Luke's. He also
thought that Philip might have had something to do with it, thus accounting for
similarities with Stephen's speech. All these were, of course, acquainted with
Timothy.

[4] The arguments were clearly brought out by A. R. Eager, *Exp.*, VI, x (1904),
pp. 74–80, 110–123. Cf. also Moffatt, *op. cit.*, pp. 435, 436. Cf. the article by
C. P. M. Jones, 'The Epistle to the Hebrews and the Lucan Writings', in *Studies
in the Gospels* (ed. D. E. Nineham, 1957), pp. 113–143.

[5] *Op. cit.*, p. 11. W. Manson (*The Epistle to the Hebrews*, 1951, p. 36) mentioned
in addition the distinctive call to 'go out'; the idea of the 'living Word'; the incidental allusion to Joshua; and the heavenward direction of the eyes.

The force of these comparisons naturally depends on the theory that Stephen's speech was composed by Luke, but if Luke is reproducing an independent genuine tradition the comparisons have less weight. It may well be that the author was acquainted with Luke's writings and was greatly influenced by them in ideas and phraseology,[1] but this is a mere conjecture and there is little more that can be said in support of Lucan authorship. Moffatt wisely concluded that all that can fairly be postulated is community of atmosphere.[2] But even this would be questionable if the essentially Jewish background of the Epistle be admitted.[3]

(iv) *Clement*. The remarkable parallels which exist between the Epistle and Clement's epistle, as already mentioned, no doubt led to the early notion of common authorship,[4] or at least to the theory of Clement as translator.[5] But Westcott[6] has sufficiently demonstrated that the differences outweigh the similarities. Clement's language and style, method of citation, range of thought and insight are all removed from those of the author of Hebrews. There is in Clement an absence of that creative contribution to Christian theology which is so evident a feature of the canonical Epistle. The parallels and similarities are well accounted for by Clement's acquaintance with this Epistle.

(v) *Silvanus*. The most that can be said in support of this suggestion[7] is that Silvanus was a member of the Pauline circle and was associated with the writing of 1 Peter. The latter consideration is thought to have some relevance because of certain literary resemblances between 1 Peter and Hebrews. There is no disputing these similarities, but the mere fact of verbal similarities cannot establish identity of authorship without

---

[1] Cf. Westcott, *op. cit.*, p. lxxvi.

[2] *ILNT*, p. 437. W. H. Simcox (*Exp.*, III, viii, 1888) drew attention to the verbal and theological similarities between Hebrews, the Pastoral Epistles and the Lucan writings, but suggested three different writers all belonging to the same circle.

[3] Cf. Feine-Behm, *op. cit.*, p. 229.

[4] Cf. Eusebius, *HE*, iii. 38. This view was revived by Erasmus and has been held by various more recent scholars (cf. Moffatt, *op. cit.*, p. 438, for details). K and S. Lake (*INT*, 1938, p. 158) mention the theory favourably, but do not commit themselves to it.

[5] As, for instance, by Jerome (cf. Eusebius, *HE*, iii. 37).

[6] *Op. cit.*, p. lxxvii.

[7] Cf. F. Godet, *Exp.*, III, vii (1888), pp. 264, 265. It had previously been maintained by Mynster (1825) and Boehme (1825) (mentioned by Wohlenberg, *NkZ*, 24, 1913, p. 760).

other corroborating evidence.[1] It must remain, therefore, an unsupported hypothesis, especially in view of the uncertainty of the precise part played by Silvanus in the production of 1 Peter. Moreover, the differences outweigh the similarities, for there is no evidence in 1 Peter of a similar method of citation and Alexandrian background of thought. It must be remembered that Silvanus was a Jerusalem Jew.[2]

(vi) *Apollos*. Ever since Luther[3] embraced the idea of Apollos as author of the Epistle, this conjecture has won adherents,[4] particularly among those who emphasize the Alexandrian background. The main arguments in support are:

1. Apollos' close acquaintance with Paul, thus accounting for Pauline influences.

2. His connection with Alexandria, which would account for the Alexandrian colouring.

3. His knowledge of the Scriptures, which would explain the biblical content of the argument and the use of the LXX version.

4. His eloquence, which well suits the oratorical form of the Epistle.[5]

5. His contacts with Timothy.

6. His considerable influence in various churches.

---

[1] G. Wohlenberg (*NkZ*, 24, 1913, pp. 742–762) examined these similarities very thoroughly and argued that common authorship better explained the relationship than use of Hebrews by the author of 1 Peter, or a common milieu theory (as von Soden proposed).

[2] Recently T. Hewitt (*The Epistle to the Hebrews*, TNT, 1960, pp. 26–32) has favoured Silvanus, following Selwyn's claims for such a close relationship between this Epistle and 1 Peter, which goes beyond common sources, traditions or circumstances. Since Selwyn regarded Silvanus as the real author of 1 Peter, it is, therefore, proposed that he also wrote Hebrews. Four lines of evidence are said to support this.

  1. Silas was known at Rome (1 Pet. v. 13) and at Jerusalem.

  2. Timothy and Silas were well known to each other.

  3. Silas, when attached to the Jerusalem church, would be well acquainted with the temple cultus.

  4. The writers of both 1 Peter and Hebrews were steeped in the LXX.

But too little is known about Silas to be certain.

[3] Moffatt does not regard Luther as the originator of the idea (cf. *ILNT*, p. 438).

[4] Among recent advocates are T. W. Manson, Ketter, Howard, Spicq and Lo Bue. It was also favoured by Zahn, *INT*, II, p. 356, hesitatingly.

[5] See Moffatt, *The Epistle to the Hebrews* (ICC, 1924), pp. lviff., for a discussion of the author's rhetorical tendencies. Cf. also Narborough, *op. cit.*, p. 15.

There is no doubt that this hypothesis is a happy one in many respects and there are no data which can be brought against it.[1] Yet the absence of any early tradition in support is a serious difficulty, especially as it might have been expected that the Alexandrian church would have preserved such a fact, if fact it was. Moreover, Acts xviii. 24ff. tells nothing about Apollos' Philonic education. Neither is there any knowledge of literary activity on his part.[2] The most that can be said is that this is a plausible conjecture, but even if established it would add little or nothing to our understanding of the historical situation of the letter apart from making a Roman destination (see later discussion) less probable.[3] Nevertheless there is something to be said for the view that if some famous unknown did not write the Epistle, Apollos fits the requirements as well as any.

(vii) *Philip.* It was Sir William M. Ramsay[4] who maintained a Caesarean origin for this Epistle and postulated that Philip the deacon sent it to Jerusalem to commend Paulinism to the Jewish Christians there. Since it was sent, in Ramsay's opinion, after Philip had conversed with Paul, this would well account for the Pauline influences in the writing. But why should Philip have couched his approach in so Hellenistic a form if this were his purpose? And why was the Pauline influence not considerably greater than it is?

(viii) *Priscilla.* Harnack[5] proposed that Priscilla, with the assistance of her husband, might have written the letter, and he supported his contention by appealing to the enigma of anonymity. The name of a woman as author would have been so prejudicial to its acceptance that it would be omitted for reasons of prudence. That this pair were illustrious teachers is indicated by their ability to instruct such a man as

---

[1] This was strongly maintained by F. W. Farrar, *The Epistle to the Hebrews* (1888), p. lviii.

[2] A rather fanciful theory was proposed by E. H. Plumptre (*Exp.*, 1, i, 1875, pp. 329–348, 409–435) that Apollos was not only author of this Epistle, but, before his enlightenment by Aquila and Priscilla, author of the Book of Wisdom also.

[3] T. W. Manson has avoided this difficulty by postulating a Colossian destination (see p. 36).

[4] *Exp.*, v, ix (1909) pp. 407–422; *Luke the Physician and other studies* (1908), pp. 301–308.

[5] *ZNTW*, 1 (1900), pp. 16–41. This idea was favourably regarded by J. Rendle Harris in the appendix of his *Side Lights on New Testament Research* (1908).

Apollos. The writer, like these two, had close associations with Timothy and had come under the influence of Paul. Another point made by Harnack was that Paul seems now to be dead and had in his last letter specially mentioned both Timothy and Aquila and Priscilla, and this will fit the circumstances of the Epistle. Moreover, since the author is so closely identified with his readers and hopes to return to them, this would be intelligible if the group were the church in Aquila and Priscilla's house. Moreover, in the list of heroes in Hebrews xi, certain women are mentioned and this is supposed to indicate a woman's interest. But those mentioned are not particularly prominent and one of the most renowned of early women heroes,[1] Deborah, is omitted altogether. The use of the plural in xiii. 18[2] cannot seriously be claimed as support for joint authorship, since xiii. 19 is emphatically in the singular, as also xi. 32 and xiii. 22, 23.[3] In further support of this view can be cited the pilgrim approach (xi. 13–16); the reference to nautical terms (iii. 6, 14, vi. 19, xiii. 9); the interest in the tabernacle, since Aquila and Priscilla were tent-makers; and the interest in childhood (v. 12, xi. 23, xii. 7) and parenthood (vii. 3, xi. 23).[4]

There are no reasons for supposing that the Epistle shows such signs of femininity as would warrant this hypothesis, especially in view of Paul's own declared opinion against women teachers (1 Cor. xiv. 34f.). It can hardly be supposed that Priscilla with her close connections with the apostle would have proceeded so contrary to his policy.[5] It is true that she assisted her husband in instructing Apollos in the Christian truth, but this was a private action. It need not indicate, as Harnack supposed,[6] that Priscilla, who is mentioned first in Acts xviii. 26, must have been of high intelligence to instruct the educated Apollos, for the way of God was understood not by intellectual but by spiritual intelligence.

[1] Harnack (op. cit., pp. 40, 41, n. 6) placed little weight on this.

[2] The plural in v. 11 appears to be an epistolary usage.

[3] Harnack supposed one author, who is at times joined by another in exhortations (op. cit., p. 37).

[4] Cf. F. B. Clogg, INT[3] (1948), pp. 138, 139.

[5] F. D. V. Narborough also points out that the authoritative tone of the Epistle does not accord with the idea of feminine authorship, in view of other New Testament teaching (op. cit., p. 12). Cf. also the criticisms of C. C. Torrey, JBL, xxx (1911), pp. 142ff.

[6] Op. cit., p. 36.

c. Conclusion

In the light of the preceding discussions,[1] an open verdict is clearly the safest course and in this the opinion of Origen can hardly be improved upon. It may not appeal to the mind to admit that a thinker of so profound a type should remain anonymous and yet, as A. Nairne pointed out, the precision of a name would not much illuminate the background.[2] Of greater importance is the situation which the Epistle was intended to answer.

II. THE READERS

In discussing the addressees, it is necessary to examine the title, 'To the Hebrews', since this in modern times has often been summarily dismissed, because it did not belong to the original text and because the earliest definite attestation for it is early third century.[3] Thus E. F.

---

[1] No mention has been made in these discussions of the proposal of A. M. Dubarle, *RB*, xLvIII (1939), pp. 506–529, that Jude was the author. He finds similarities in vocabulary, syntax, stylistic processes, mentality and culture between Hebrews and the Epistle of Jude. But similarities of this kind may be accounted for by the common background of Jewish Christianity.

[2] *The Epistle to the Hebrews* (1917), p. lvii. Moffatt, (*ILNT*, p. 442), Michaelis (*Einleitung in das Neue Testament*,[3] 1961, p. 272), Michel (*Der Brief an die Hebräer*,[11] 1960, p. 11), Meinertz (*Einleitung*,[5] 1950, pp. 144, 145), Dibelius (*A Fresh Approach to the New Testament and Early Christian Literature*, 1937, p. 197) and W. Neil (*The Epistle to the Hebrews*, 1955, pp. 14ff.) all decline to propose any definite name. A. S. Peake (*Hebrews*, n.d., p. 10) suggestively inferred that since the writer knew the community so well (see next section), he was probably one of their leaders, who was for a time separated from them. E. J. Goodspeed's idea that Hebrews may have been originally pseudonymous, rather than anonymous (*INT*, 1939, p. 257), may at once be dismissed, for had the letter originally borne an ascription to Paul, it is impossible to envisage any situation in which it would lose its ascription and still continue to be regarded with some favour. There are no parallels to this kind of thing among the pseudepigrapha.

[3] It is so described by Tertullian and was probably the traditional title before his time (*De Pudicitia*, 20). Pantaenus seems to have known it under this title also (Zahn, *INT*, II, p. 294). Zahn considered that the very brief title was added for ease of reference when Hebrews was bound with various other letters (*ibid.*, p. 295). But this could only have happened to the original autograph and must, therefore, have occurred at a very early date. It is an interesting conjecture, but no more. H. Thyen (*Der Stil der jüdisch-hellenistischen Homilie*, 1955, p. 16) thinks that the title was attached on the incorporation of the Epistle into the Pauline Epistles.

Scott describes it as a guess,[1] while F. D. V. Narborough regards it as suspiciously vague.[2] Yet while admitting that the title may not be authentic,[3] we ought not to dismiss it too lightly since there is no evidence that the Epistle bore any other address.[4] It expressed at least the common belief at an early period concerning the destination.[5]

Yet 'the Hebrews' would not naturally describe a local group since it is a national title and, in order to define the readers more closely, it is necessary to take careful account of the internal evidence.

a. Internal evidence in support of a particular community

There are several indications which dispose of any idea of a general address and lead to the definite conclusion that a specific local community was in mind.

(i) *It has a definite history.* The author mentions 'former days' (x. 32) and persecutions which have been endured (x. 32, xii. 4). The description of these trials is sufficiently detailed to require the assumption of definite knowledge by the author of the readers' past circumstances. He speaks of their public exposure to abuse, of their sympathy with others so treated, of their joyful resignation to the plundering of their property in the cause of Christ (x. 33, 34) and of their generosity in ministering to other Christians (vi. 10). He knows the circumstances under which they became Christians (ii. 3), and he knows their present state of mind (cf. v. 11ff., vi. 9f.). Their attitude towards their leaders is evidently needing correction (xiii. 17).

(ii) *It has definite links with the writer.* In addition to the evidence just adduced, it is clear that he knows them personally and hopes soon to revisit them (xiii. 19, 23). He urges prayer on his behalf (xiii. 18) and mentions the release of Timothy as an item of news in which they would be personally interested, especially as the writer hopes to have Timothy with him on the visit.

[1] *The Literature of the New Testament*, p. 200.

[2] *Op. cit.*, p. 20.

[3] F. Godet (*Exp.*, III, vii, 1888, p. 242) was disposed to regard the superscription as the author's own, because of the way the Epistle begins.

[4] The evidence is well collated by B. F. Westcott, *The Epistle to the Hebrews*, pp. xxviiff. Cf. G. Hoennicke's suggestion that the absence of an address may be due to persecution circumstances, or may be due to later intentional omission. *NkZ*, 29 (1918), p. 350.

[5] In spite of Moffatt's opinion that at the time of the affixing of the title, the circumstances of its origin had been lost sight of (*ILNT*, p. 432).

(iii) *It was a section of a larger community.* Not only does the Epistle narrow down the addressees to a local community, but implies that only part of that group is mainly in mind. The statement in v. 12 that the readers ought by now to be teachers contains the implication that they are capable of a teaching ministry, and this could hardly apply in general to the rank and file members of the church. At the same time they are not the most prominent members of the community, since in that case they would not be urged to submit to their leaders.[1] Moreover, the readers appear to form a homogeneous group, which is more likely in a small community than in a larger.[2] So there is much to support the contention that they were a small house-community, which had broken away from and was at least acting independently of the main group of Christians to which they were attached. This may well be why they are urged not to forsake the general Christian assembly (x. 25), i.e. in favour of their own house-group. Such groups are known to have existed, for Paul mentions no less than three in Rome (Rom. xvi. 5, 14, 15) and there may have been many more, not only at Rome but in all large cities.[3]

All that has so far been established does not indicate the nationality of the readers, for which the general argument of the Epistle is the only source of information available and this will next be discussed. The further question of the locality cannot be dealt with until the nationality question has been settled. There are three main possibilities: Jewish Christians, Gentile Christians or Christians irrespective of race.

b. Internal evidence in support of a Jewish Christian destination

The most obvious support for this view is the wide appeal made to the Old Testament and the author's assumption that his readers will be acquainted with the details of the levitical cultus. Furthermore, the whole argument of the Epistle would have obvious relevance to Jewish Christians, with its stress on the necessity for Messiah's sufferings, the reasons for the supersession of the levitical priesthood, the notion of a spiritual instead of a material sanctuary and the fulfilment of the pro-

---

[1] N.B. that in xiii. 24 they are urged not only to greet their own leaders, but also all Christians generally, which suggests that they had separatist tendencies.

[2] So A. Harnack, *op. cit.*, p. 21.

[3] A. Nairne (*The Epistle of Priesthood,*[2] 1915, p. 10) declined to see in the readers a house-church with a general membership, but preferred rather to think of some scholarly men who were accustomed to meet as a group.

mise of a new covenant in Christ.[1] There is a significant, although almost incidental, reference in ii. 16 to the descendants of Abraham which would make a direct appeal to Jewish Christians. Moreover, the author's argument proceeds in a manner which would well fit the background of Jewish readers with its references to Moses, Joshua and the Aaronic order.[2]

Against this has been placed the language of the Epistle, which is claimed to be a more literary and polished Greek than could be expected from a Jewish writer.[3] Yet this in itself does not rule out a Jewish Christian destination since all the Jews of the Dispersion used Greek and there is no need to suppose that the language and style of the author represent the language and style of the readers. Similarly the citations from the LXX instead of the Hebrew Old Testament admittedly disfavour a Palestinian destination, but do not altogether exclude Jewish Christian readers. Again, it has been maintained that the Epistle deals with biblical ritual, not with Judaism, as might be expected if Jewish Christians were specifically in mind.

These objections and others[4] have been used to support the theory of a Gentile destination, which will next be discussed.

c. Evidence claimed to support a Gentile destination

Some scholars have strongly argued for Gentile readers on the grounds that there is nothing in the Epistle which demands a Jewish destination. The traditional view is said to have arisen under the influence of the

---

[1] Cf. E. C. Wickham (*op. cit.*, p. xvi) for an elucidation of these points.

[2] Riggenbach strongly argued that many of the statements of the Epistle would be unintelligible unless addressed to those who were born Jews (e.g. ix. 15, xiii. 13). The appeal to the fleshly weakness of Jesus, His sufferings and His transference to another world would cause offence only to Jews (*Der Brief an die Hebräer*, 1913, pp. xxiii–xxv). V. Burch (*The Epistle to the Hebrews*, 1936, pp. 1ff.) brought further arguments in support of a Jewish destination by maintaining that the author has been influenced by the synagogue lectionaries and by the Maccabean story, both in his choice of themes and in the structure of his Epistle. If Burch's thesis is admitted, a Gentile destination would be impossible to imagine. But J. Héring (*L'Epître aux Hébreux*, 1954, p. 129) criticizes Burch on the grounds that many passages from the Jewish liturgies, to which Burch appeals, are not used in this Epistle.

[3] Cf. E. F. Scott, *op. cit.*, p. 200.

[4] K. Endemann (*NkZ*, 21, 1910, p. 122) pointed to the explanation of Hebrew words in Heb. vii. 2 and to the details in ix. 1–10 as evidence that the Epistle was not intended for Hebrews.

title, which is regarded as erroneous.[1] Gentiles as well as Jews would be
acquainted with the Old Testament when they became Christians, as
the LXX was regarded as authoritative Scripture by all Gentile churches.
The idea of Gentiles inheriting much from Israel's past history is further
supported by the New Testament conception of Christians as the New
Israel. The argument of the Epistle, although difficult, was not more
difficult for Gentiles than the Epistle to the Romans.[2] There is, moreover, no mention of the Jewish-Gentile controversy, which is usually
taken to indicate a time when the controversy was settled,[3] or else to
point to a community which was not troubled by it. But this omission of
the controversy would, on the whole, favour Jewish Christians rather
than Gentiles, since it was for the latter that the controversy was acute.
It has also been maintained that the stress on the humanity and fleshly
weakness of Jesus would well offset any Docetic-like claims,[4] in which
a distinction was made between the heavenly Christ and the human
Jesus.

The fact that the writer does not mention the temple must not be
pressed too far, but it would certainly be more strange for Jewish than
for Gentile readers, assuming for the present argument that the temple
in Jerusalem is still standing. Yet the writer goes back to first principles
as the basis of his argument and this is better demonstrated from the
tabernacle. This factor is, therefore, neutral, for arguments based on the
Pentateuch would have relevance for both Jews and Gentiles. The further argument that iii. 12 (falling away from the living God) would be
appropriate only for Gentiles must be given little weight, since the
Epistle presents all apostasy as an abandonment of the living God.[5] Some
stress has been laid on the mention of 'dead works' (vi. 1, ix. 14) as in-
applicable to Jews, as well as the elementary principles listed in vi. 1ff.[6]
But it is doubtful whether there is evidence enough to conclude with
E. F. Scott[7] that the writer did not understand Judaism, because its
central feature was law and not sacrificial ritual. That may very well
be true, but all that can safely be deduced from the Epistle is that the

[1] So J. Moffatt, *ILNT*, p. 432; E. F. Scott, *op. cit.*; R. H. Strachan, *The Historic
Jesus in the New Testament* (1931), p. 90; F. D. V. Narborough, *op. cit.*, pp. 20ff.
A more recent advocate of a Gentile destination is G. Vos, *The Teaching of the
Epistle to the Hebrews* (1956), pp. 14ff.

[2] Cf. Feine-Behm, *op. cit.*, p. 227.

[3] Cf. McNeile-Williams, *INT*, p. 231.   [4] Cf. Feine-Behm, *loc. cit.*

[5] Cf. M. Dods, *The Epistle to the Hebrews* (*EGT*, 1910), p. 232.

[6] Cf. G. Vos, *op. cit.*, pp. 14–18.   [7] *Op. cit.*, p. 200.

author deals not with Judaism but with the Old Testament, a fact which provides no determining evidence in the discussion of destination.[1]

d. Evidence for a mixed community of readers

Since none of the evidence so far educed compels a Jewish Christian destination and none leads to any positive conclusion regarding a wholly Gentile destination, a compromise has been suggested.[2] Neither Jews nor Gentiles are in mind, but Christians generally, who had become discouraged and needed challenging to renewed effort. But Westcott[3] rejected the notion of a mixed community on the grounds that the letter betrays no such mixture, nor does it touch on points of heathen controversy.

It is clear that no dogmatic conclusion can be reached on the grounds of internal evidence, yet a definite balance in favour of a Jewish Christian destination must be admitted, if any credence at all is to be attached to the traditional title.[4] The problem of the readers is, on the other hand, so intimately connected with the problem of the purpose that any decision must await the result of investigations on this matter. That type of reader which best accounts for the method of argument and general aim of the Epistle will naturally carry most weight.[5]

III. PURPOSE

There is almost as much difference of opinion about the writer's aims as about his own identity and that of his readers. This problem is nevertheless of greater importance, since it affects the interpretation of the Epistle. The writer describes his writing as 'a word of consolation' (xiii. 22) and full attention must be given to this before proposing other

[1] After reviewing the evidence for destination, A. Wikenhauser (*New Testament Introduction*, 1958, p. 465) maintains that the balance of evidence is against a Jewish Christian destination.

[2] Cf. E. F. Scott, *op. cit.*, pp. 200, 201; also Feine-Behm, *loc. cit.*

[3] *The Epistle to the Hebrews*, p. xxxvi.

[4] A. B. Davidson (*The Epistle to the Hebrews*, n.d., p. 9) was so sure of a Jewish destination that he said of the title, 'Anyone reading the Epistle now would stamp it with the same title, apart from all tradition respecting its origin or destination.'

[5] The suggestion has even been made that the readers are not Christians at all, but Jews as yet undecided about Christianity. Cf. P. Stather Hunt, *Primitive Gospel Sources* (1951), p. 291 and F. C. Synge, *Hebrews and the Scriptures* (1959), pp. 44ff., who take πρός to mean 'against' and not 'to' the Hebrews.

aims. That there are many hortatory passages scattered throughout the Epistle cannot be denied. These would well conform to the idea of 'consolation', although some (especially chapters vi and x) contain serious warnings. But the problem is to find the purpose of the doctrinal sections. These cannot be so easily fitted into the 'consolation' theme. Perhaps the author wished to remind his readers of his essentially pastoral and practical purpose and, if so, the carefully worked out passages on the theme of Christ as High Priest must be interpreted in the light of xiii. 22 and not vice versa.[1] That is to say, the writer's arguments are not to be regarded as a theological treatise or an intellectual exercise, but as a burning issue of vital practical importance. But what was this issue? There have been various suggestions which will now be outlined.

a. To warn Jewish Christians against apostasy to Judaism

This is the most widely held view and is supported by the assumption that chapters vi and x suggest that the readers are tempted to apostatize. Since the argument of the Epistle is designed to show Christ's superiority over the old order, it is further assumed that the apostasy in question must involve a return to Judaism. In xiii. 13 the readers are exhorted to make a clear break and to come outside 'the camp', which may reasonably be interpreted as the camp of Israel. The challenge of the hour for Jewish Christians is to sever connections with their ancient faith, since Christianity is of a different and higher order.[2]

The main problem of these Christians was dissatisfaction, not with

---

[1] Th. Haering ('Gedankengang und Grundgedanken des Hebräerbriefs', *ZNTW*, 18, 1917–18, pp. 145–164) drew attention to the close relationship between the statements regarding the faith and the admonitions as part of the basic sequence of thought in the Epistle, similar to the framework of ancient admonition discourses. Some have considered the possibility that Hebrews was designed for catechetical purposes, which would agree with the writer's description in xiii. 22 (cf. G. Schille's article, 'Die Basis des Hebräerbriefes', *ZNTW*, 47, 1957, pp. 270–280).

E. Käsemann (*Das wandernde Gottesvolk, Eine Untersuchung zum Hebräerbrief*, 1939, pp. 10, 11) suggested that the 'word of encouragement' was to Christians whose hope was wavering in the same way as that of the wandering Israelites. Cf. V. Burch (*op. cit.*, pp. 113ff.) for a similar idea, but without the Gnostic background which Käsemann brings in. Cf. also G. Bornkamm (*Studien zu Antike und Urchristentum*, 1959, pp. 188–203), who regards the High Priest theme as an interpretation of the Church's baptismal confession of Christ as Son of God.

[2] Cf. A. Nairne, *The Epistle to the Hebrews*, p. lxxiv.

true Christianity but with Christianity as it was as yet imperfectly understood by them. It was little more than a reformed Judaism, which in the end was not regarded as in the ancient camp of Israel, for their compatriots would ostracize them for their professed Christian connections. Nor was it in the new 'camp' of the Church. The hankering after the old must have been very real, for the new camp had no prestige comparable to that which Judaism derived from Moses, and the danger of apostasy was correspondingly great.[1] In place of the grandeur of the ritual of the old order was substituted a spiritual conception centred entirely in a Person and no longer in a splendid temple. It must have caused much perplexity in the minds of the recently converted Jews. Now, if this be a true picture of the situation, the writer would aim to show the incomparable superiority of Christianity in fulfilment of all the glories of the old order and by this means would encourage the readers to resist any temptation to return to Judaism. Such an apostasy he describes in very severe terms, but there is no hint that any had as yet fallen a prey to this temptation. In spite of the fact that some modern scholars[2] have disputed the traditional interpretation, it does at least account for the main drift of the argument and, in this respect, has much to commend it.

At the same time the apostasy in vi. 1ff. need not be a turning back to Judaism, since no indication is given there of its nature. This applies also to the statement in x. 29. The fact is, the identification of the apostasy with an act of deliberate turning away from Christianity to Judaism is an inference drawn from the author's preoccupation with the levitical cultus. But the inference may, nonetheless, be a true one.

Some difference of opinion exists among the advocates of this theory as to the more precise identification of the Jewish Christians in mind. The idea that the Epistle was a general circular[3] cannot be seriously entertained in view of the evidence already cited that a definite community was in mind. This hypothesis involves some editorial processes for which there seems to be no warrant within the Epistle itself. More

[1] Cf. C. Spicq, *L'Epître aux Hébreux* (1952), pp. 221, 222; M. Dods, *The Epistle to the Hebrews (EGT,* 1910), pp. 237ff.
[2] Notably J. Moffatt and E. F. Scott.
[3] Cf. M. Dibelius, 'Der himmlische Kultus nach dem Hebräerbrief', *ThBl,* 21 (1942), pp. 1–11. In his book *A fresh approach to the New Testament and early Christian Literature* (1936), p. 196, Dibelius regarded the letter as a written speech with a conventional letter conclusion. He disputed that the Epistle related to a specific occasion.

to the point is the theory that a house-community of Jewish Christian intellectuals is being addressed. A. Nairne thought of these people as a group of the author's friends, who, like himself, had received an Alexandrian education.[1] They would be Hellenistic Jews by birth and training who had embraced Christianity, but were finding it hard to give up Judaism.

An alternative view is that the small community consisted of converted Jerusalem priests.[2] It is stated in Acts vi. 7 that a great many priests were obedient to the faith as a result of the preaching of Stephen, and it is an attractive hypothesis that some of these had formed into a separate group and were strongly tempted to return to their former dignity in connection with the temple ritual. With their Jewish experience and ability they ought by now to be teachers (v. 12), but their Christianity was as yet elementary and immature (vi. 1, 2). It may be objected against this hypothesis that no other New Testament evidence supports the idea of an exclusively priestly community, but the smallness of the number involved in this case may well be the reason for the absence of corroborative evidence. This must remain a conjecture, although a conjecture which deserves careful consideration.

Another modification of this view which might be a possible solution is the hypothesis that the readers were formerly connected with a Jewish movement akin to the Qumran sect known to us from the Dead Sea Scrolls and were weighing the advantages of their former allegiance against their new faith. The severance of the Covenanters from the Jerusalem temple and the repudiation of the current sacrificial system might lend some support to this idea. These Covenanters were diligent students of the Old Testament Scriptures and endeavoured to interpret them in the light of contemporary events.[3] Might it not be that the author of this Epistle is giving a Christian interpretation of the Old Testament to rectify false methods of exegesis and to show that the hope of the future lies, not in the restoration of the old covenant as the sectaries believed, but in the establishment of a new covenant in

---

[1] *Op. cit.*, p. lxxii.

[2] So K. Bornhäuser, *Empfänger und Verfasser des Hebräerbriefes* (1932); M. E. Clarkson, *ATR*, xxix (1947), pp. 89–95; and C. Sandegren, *EQ*, xxvii (Oct. 1955), pp. 221–224. C. Spicq speaks favourably of the theory and connects the community with Jerusalem (*op. cit.*, pp. 226–231). Sandegren suggests that the original address may have been 'To Priests' instead of 'To Hebrews', since the two words are similar in Greek uncial writing.

[3] Cf. F. F. Bruce, *Biblical Exegesis in the Qumran Texts* (1960), pp. 7ff.

which all the ritual of the old is seen to be fulfilled in Christ? The greatest tragedy would be to forsake the new for the old, an action which would amount to re-crucifying the Son of God. Another common element is the priestly emphasis in both the Qumran Community[1] and in the argument of the Epistle to the Hebrews, while a further interesting feature is the continuance of 'instruction about ablutions' (Heb. vi. 2, RSV), which finds a parallel in the constant lustrations of the Covenanters.[2] The esoteric doctrines of the sect might also be alluded to in Hebrews xiii. 9, especially the idea of cultic foods.

Yet the evidence for such an hypothesis is not strong and must remain no more than a conjecture. The existence of such a Jewish Christian group converted from the Essenes is not otherwise attested, although it is not impossible that such a group existed. The main problem would seem to be the absence of any positive treatment of the ancient law, which loomed large in Qumran thought.

b. To challenge restricted Jewish Christians to embrace the world mission

This is the most recent proposal, ably advocated by William Manson.[3] While admitting that the readers were Jewish Christian, he was not satisfied that the threatened danger was apostasy from Christianity to Judaism. To him it was a failure to embrace the world-mission purpose of God. The readers shared the restricted approach of the Jerusalem church and were content to regard Christianity as little more than a sect of Judaism. It may be that they were anxious to retain the advantage of sheltering under a *religio licita*, which was only available so long as they were classed as Jews. According to Manson, the writer's absorbing interest in the Old Testament ritual was to reassure these Christians, who were missing the cultus of Judaism, that the universal truths of Christianity were of far greater consequence. He further claimed that the antecedents of the Epistle are to be sought in the speech of Stephen where a similar approach to the cultus is found.[4] Although

---

[1] Cf. J. T. Milik, *Ten Years of Discovery in the Wilderness of Judaea* (1959), pp. 99ff.

[2] *Ibid.*, p. 101.

[3] *The Epistle to the Hebrews* (1951). His theory is taken up by W. Neil, *The Epistle to the Hebrews* (*TC*, 1955).

[4] Details are stated above, pp. 19f. in the section on the theory of Lucan authorship of this Epistle.

not all would agree that the writer's view of history coincides with Stephen's,[1] yet there seems little doubt that his universalism finds an echo in Stephen's declaration that the Most High dwells not in houses made with hands.

While there is much insight in this hypothesis, it is difficult to imagine that such strong words concerning apostasy could apply to a failure to appreciate the world mission of Christianity. The terminology of vi. 6 and x. 29 seems to imply a definite act of apostasy against Christ Himself, and, while a denial of universalism would certainly be a denial of Christ's expressed purpose to redeem men of all nations, it is open to question whether such an attitude constitutes re-crucifying Christ and exposing Him to contempt. These terms point rather to a positive renunciation of Christianity.

c. To announce the absolute character of Christianity to mainly Gentile Christians

Christian believers, surrounded as they were by many other faiths, would require an assurance of the greatness and superiority of Christianity over all other religions. They would want to know that it presented a method of worship which was not one of many, but was unique because none other taught the perfect way of worship.[2] The writer would, therefore, appeal to the Old Testament in order to prove the glory of Christianity and for this reason would not specifically deal with Judaism. The author's knowledge of the latter is not first hand. It is book-knowledge or even, in E. F. Scott's opinion, no true knowledge at all.[3] In order to account for the great emphasis on the cultus, Moffatt suggested that the Gentile Christians were perhaps affected by speculative or theoretical Judaism.[4]

But the most damaging criticism of this hypothesis is the absence of any references to pagan rites or mysteries or to tables and cups of demons,[5] as, for instance, are suggested by Paul's treatment of the Corinthian situation. Nor can a case be made out for regarding this

---

[1] E.g. J. P. Alexander (*A Priest for Ever*, 1937, p. 17) finds Paul nearer to Stephen than the author of Hebrews.

[2] Advocated by J. Moffatt, *ILNT*, pp. 444ff.; *The Epistle to the Hebrews* (*ICC*), pp. xxivff.; and R. H. Strachan, *op. cit.*, pp. 74ff.

[3] Cf. *op. cit.*, p. 200, where he maintains that the author misunderstood what Judaism meant.

[4] *Op. cit.*, p. 445.   [5] Cf. the criticisms by W. Manson, *op. cit.*, p. 22

Epistle as a Christian Gnosis,[1] for there are no traces of Gnostic tendencies. On the other hand, due weight must be given to the fact that the author betrays no consciousness of any distinction between Jewish and Gentile Christianity and this *may* be evidence that Gentiles were included in the author's purpose. At the same time it is difficult to believe that the detailed and elaborate argument based on levitical ritual would have convinced Gentile Christians of the absolute character of Christianity. Only those who were already convinced of the greatness of Judaism would see the point of the author's attempts to show the supreme worth of Christianity by means of its superiority to Judaism. This line of argument might have had relevance to former proselytes, but hardly to those who had had no former connection with the Jewish cultus.[2]

d. To counteract an early type of heresy

This suggestion has been maintained in two forms:

1. As an answer to a sect of Jewish Gnostics,[3] or
2. An answer to the specific Colossian heresy.[4]

The two suggestions are clearly closely allied, especially if the Jewish character of the Colossian heresy is maintained. Under the hypothesis that Gnosticism is being combated, the threatened apostasy is understood as a forsaking of Christianity in preference for an incipient Gnosticism, which not only maintained the mediation of angels and thus depreciated the unique mediatorial work of Christ, but also tended towards asceticism on the one hand and immorality on the other. This theory would account for the prominence of 'angels' in the argument at the commencement of the Epistle, for the mention of strange teachings and salvation by meats (xiii. 9) and for the reference to meats and

---

[1] Cf. E. F. Scott, *The Epistle to the Hebrews* (1922), p. 41.

[2] A. C. Purdy, in his article, 'The purpose of the Epistle to the Hebrews in the Light of Recent Studies in Judaism', *Amiticiae Corolla* (ed. H. G. Wood, 1953), pp. 253–264, partially sides with Moffatt in rejecting the idea of an apostasy to Judaism. But he also rejects the notion that speculative Judaism is in mind and considers that the problems behind Hebrews were normative to first-century Judaism.

[3] F. D. V. Narborough, *op. cit.*, pp. 20–27.

[4] T. W. Manson, 'The Problem of the Epistle to the Hebrews', *BJRL*, xxxii (1949), pp. 1–17.

washings in ix. 10. The uncompromising rigorism of the author is claimed to be more intelligible when seen against such a background. Deliberate wrongdoing of the kind which some Jewish Gnosticism allowed could obtain no forgiveness (vi. 4–8, x. 26–31). Immorality is, in fact, specifically mentioned in xii. 16.

This Jewish Gnostic theory has been further modified in T. W. Manson's attempt to set the argument of the Epistle against the background of the Colossian heresy. He suggested that chapters i–iv answered the doctrine of intermediaries as reflected in Colossians ii. 18, and chapters v–x the ritual tendencies which also formed part of the same heresy (cf. Col. ii. 14ff.). His theory is that Apollos sent the Epistle to the Colossian church before Paul wrote his own Epistle, which was not, in fact, produced until after he had seen and read the former. But the theory seems to demand that Apollos wrote only to the Jewish section of the Colossian false teachers, since the Epistle to the Hebrews completely ignores the other element in the Colossian heresy, i.e. the Gnostic philosophy. This is an interesting suggestion, however, and may be linked with the suggestion mentioned earlier that Jewish Christians influenced by the Qumran type of Judaism may have been in mind. It is not impossible that this type of heresy was more widely diffused than is generally recognized and, therefore, the need to locate the heresy in Colossae is not immediately apparent, nor, in fact, is the need to postulate Apollos as author.[1]

What all of these theories of the author's purpose make abundantly clear is that the readers needed to be warned against turning away from Christianity, but it is impossible to be quite certain by what they were tempted. The positive knowledge that the author aims to show the all-sufficiency and supremacy of Christ over other agencies and His complete fulfilment of the Jewish ritual system enables an intelligent interpretation of the argument,[2] even if a more precise understanding of the readers' circumstances would throw added light upon certain obscurities in the statements made.

---

[1] McNeile-Williams criticize Manson's view on the ground that Clement of Rome acknowledged the Epistle as authoritative and yet it was known as non-Pauline. They find it difficult to see how Clement came to possess a copy with such an unchallenged status twenty or thirty years later (*INT*, p. 238).

[2] A recent writer, A. Wikgren ('Patterns of Perfection in the Epistle to the Hebrews', *NTS*, 6, 1960, pp. 159–167), suggests that the author is presenting a kind of philosophy of history through symbolic patterns of perfection.

IV. DESTINATION

It may seem futile to pin down to any definite locality a community of whose circumstances so little definite information can be gathered, and it will not be surprising that several suggestions have been made. The following brief review of them will once again focus attention on the extraordinary complexity of the attempt to reconstruct the historical situation.

a. Palestine

Many have maintained a Jerusalem or Palestinian destination, but most of these have done so in the belief that Jewish Christians, who were tempted to apostatize to Judaism, are in mind.[1] One of the most important considerations is the existence or otherwise of the temple, a problem which also influences the dating. Westcott[2] found no difficulty in the author's use of 'tabernacle' for 'temple' and maintained that the Jerusalem temple was still standing and that the readers must have lived in its vicinity.[3] He supported this from patristic evidence that 'Hebrews' was used as a description for the Jerusalem church, but this will carry no weight for those who regard the title as no more than an early guess. There is the further evidence that a crisis is imminent (i. 2, iii. 13, x. 25, xii. 27) and this might be understood as the approaching siege of Jerusalem. The former sufferings which the readers endured (x. 32, xii. 4) would be accounted for by the known persecuting zeal of the Jerusalem Jews against the early Christians (Acts *passim*). Other corroborating evidence which might seem to support the Jerusalem destination[4] is the absence of the Gentile-Jewish controversy, which would not have affected an all-Jewish church, and the fact that no church ever laid claim to this Epistle, which is readily understandable after Jerusalem was destroyed. Another factor which has predisposed some scholars to prefer a Jerusalem destination has been their accept-

[1] F. Delitzsch (*Commentary on the Epistle to the Hebrews*, 1868, p. 20) maintained that the title must indicate Palestinians, since in Palestine alone was a distinction made between Hellenists and Hebrews. But the Epistle contains no such contrast.

[2] *The Epistle to the Hebrews*, p. xl.

[3] G. A. Barton (*JBL*, LVII, 1938, pp. 199, 200) argues that in every case where the author mentions the performance of parts of the ritual he uses the present tense. This, he thinks, is intentional and points to the continuity of the temple ritual with the old tabernacle ritual.

[4] Cf. G. Salmon, *INT*⁶ (1892), pp. 427ff.

ance of Barnabas as the author. But, apart from the fact that the author problem is indecisive, very little is known about the movements of Barnabas to be certain of his continued connection with the Jerusalem church, although this is quite probable.[1]

Several objections have been lodged against this hypothesis, the most damaging of which appears to be the improbability of any author addressing a Jerusalem group in the terms of ii. 3[2]; the difficulty of the Hellenistic approach if Jerusalem Jews are in mind (unless, of course, a small Hellenistic section of the predominantly Hebrew church is visualized); the apparent discrepancy between the generosity of the community to which the Epistle is addressed (vi. 10, x. 34, xiii. 16; cf. also xiii. 2, 5) and the poverty of the Jerusalem church[3]; the seeming inappropriateness of v. 12 as a reference to Jerusalem Hebrew Christians, and the use of the LXX. Moreover, the description of the leaders in xiii. 7 would seem strange if the Jerusalem leaders were in mind.[4] It is further thought that the situation in x. 32ff. supposes *one* previous persecution which would not fit the Jerusalem church in Acts,[5] while if xii. 4 means that the church had as yet suffered no martyrdoms, this would not be true of Jerusalem. Most of these objections would, however, be removed if the destination were more generally Palestine, or some adjoining district where the Greek language was dominant, but where the Jewish Christians still maintained close contact with the Jerusalem church.

b. Rome

The majority of modern scholars favour Rome as the destination mainly on the strength of the following evidence.

[1] There is little ground for the opinion of G. Edmundson (*The Church in Rome in the first century*, 1913, pp. 80–82) that Barnabas was for a time in Rome. The evidence cited was the Clementine Recognitions, which Edmundson thought might here have preserved a genuine tradition.

[2] Cf. Moffatt, *ILNT*, p. 446. If the whole of the Jerusalem church was in mind, ii. 3 would be inconceivable, but if a small group only was in view, it is not entirely impossible that none of them had heard the Lord personally. (Cf. A. Nairne, *The Epistle of Priesthood*, 1915, p. 20.)

[3] Peake (*op. cit.*, p. 23) discounted this argument on the ground that poverty would not exclude kindness to fellow Christians, and it must be admitted that none of the references mentioned above absolutely demands the idea of material generosity. At the same time xiii. 5 would have little relevance to poverty-stricken people.

[4] Cf. Feine-Behm, *op. cit.*, p. 226.   [5] *Ibid., loc. cit.*

1. The fact that it was at Rome that the Epistle was first known, as early in fact as the first century, for it must have been authoritative some time before Clement of Rome cites it in AD 95 in his Corinthian Epistle.

2. The concluding salutation in xiii. 24 (οἱ ἀπὸ τῆς Ἰταλίας) seems more naturally understood of Italians who are away from Italy and are sending greetings home, than of Italians sending greetings to some other non-Italian destination.[1] Yet the phrase is ambiguous and cannot sustain too much weight.[2]

3. Timothy, who is mentioned in xiii. 24, was known to the Roman Christians (cf. Col. i. 1, Phm. 1).

4. The description of the leaders in xiii. 7, 17, 24 is similar to that in *1 Clem.* i. 3 (ἡγούμενοι; cf. *1 Clem.* xxi. 6 and Hermas, *Vis.* ii. 2, 6, iii. 9, 7, where προηγούμενοι is used).[3]

5. The allusions to the generosity of the readers in vi. 10ff., x. 32ff., would agree with the known history of the Roman church from other sources.[4]

6. The reference to meats in xiii. 9 suggests a tendency which is similar to that seen in Romans xiv.[5]

7. The spoliation of goods referred to in x. 32 could be explained either by Claudius' edict (AD 49) or by Nero's persecution, both of which affected the Roman Christians (assuming that other Jewish

---

[1] 'They of Italy' would in that case need to describe the whole Italian church, but this is improbable. Michaelis (*op. cit.*, p. 270) points out a parallel in the reference to Asiatic churches in 1 Cor. xvi. 19.

F. J. Badcock (*The Pauline Epistles and the Epistle to the Hebrews in their historical setting*, 1937, p. 192) maintained a third alternative, i.e. Italians on the way home from Jerusalem sending greetings to a Hellenistic group in Jerusalem from Caesarea.

[2] McNeile-Williams prefer the former meaning (*INT*, p. 233), but Narborough feels similarly about the alternative (*op. cit.*, p. 27). F. Lo Bue (*JBL*, lxxv, 1956, pp. 52–57) suggested that 'they of Italy' were Aquila and Priscilla, which is not entirely improbable. Michel (*op. cit.*, p. 368) admits an ambiguity, but understands the phrase to point to an Italian colony outside the Italian peninsula.

[3] A. Harnack (*ZNTW*, 1, 1900, p. 21) made the further comparison of Heb. xiii. 7 with *1 Clem.* v. The latter describes Peter and Paul as examples and Harnack thought that these apostles were the 'leaders' referred to in Hebrews. But this rather vague description of them is most unlikely.

[4] So Feine-Behm, *op. cit.*, p. 228. A. Harnack (*op. cit.*, p. 20) refers to the letter of Dionysius of Corinth in this connection.

[5] Cf. Davidson, *op. cit.*, p. 16.

Christians, like Aquila, would be caught up in a general expulsion of Jews).

But on the other hand, ii. 3 is difficult if Rome was in mind, for there could have been few who had been evangelized by eye-witnesses, especially accompanied by signs and miracles, unless the community in question consisted of those who had infiltrated to Rome in the course of commerce or trade. The difficulty is not insuperable, and in view of the external evidence this destination has much to commend it. Owing to the scarcity of extant data about the circulation of the New Testament writings in the sub-apostolic period during the latter part of the first century, it is not possible to put too much stress on Clement's knowledge of the Epistle. He appears to be acquainted with I Corinthians and Ephesians and probably many other of Paul's Epistles which were not sent to Rome. That Christian writings were being exchanged at this period is, therefore, indisputable and it is impossible to dogmatize about the circulation of the Epistle to the Hebrews. A period of twenty to thirty years (if Hebrews is dated early) would be ample for the Epistle to reach Rome if it was elsewhere regarded as authoritative. It is further difficult to pin down the particular troubles, which are reflected in x. 32f., to any specific event in Rome. The Neronian persecutions would appear to be much too severe, unless the group addressed in this Epistle was unobtrusive enough to escape the worst of the onslaught. Moreover, these troubles were in 'former days', which suggests some interval, and this would only be possible if the Epistle were dated much later (see discussion on the date). Perhaps a more weighty objection is the different type of Judaism which seems to be reflected in the Epistle to the Hebrews as compared with that in the Epistle to the Romans, the latter showing little evidence of the Hellenism which seems to influence the former. But again the solution may be found in the restricted number to whom the Hebrews was probably sent. If addressed to the whole church at Rome, the absence of any reference to Gentiles in the Epistle would also be inconceivable, but the difficulty would be less acute for a smaller house-group.[1] All that can safely be claimed, however, is that we know that it *was* used in Rome in the first century, but insufficient literature is preserved from other

---

[1] E. Nestlé (*ET*, x, 1899, p. 422) pointed out that the title, 'To the Hebrews', would not be surprising for Rome, since inscriptions record a synagogue there known simply as Ἑβραίων.

districts to enable us to pronounce more confidently on any alternative
theory.

c. Other suggestions

The Alexandrian colouring has suggested an Alexandrian destination,
but this seems dubious because the church at Alexandria not only laid no
claim to it, but the early Alexandrian Fathers assumed it was addressed
to the Hebrew people of Palestine by Paul. Furthermore, Alexandrian
ideas were so widely diffused that almost any place in the Hellenistic
world would be equally suitable on this score. T. W. Manson's idea of
Colossae has already been discussed (p. 36), while Asia Minor has been
represented by an Ephesian destination (F. W. Farrar),[1] or Galatian
destination (A. M. Dubarle),[2] and more vaguely by an Asiatic Centre
(Perdelwitz).[3] F. Rendall ventured to propose Syria (perhaps Antioch),
but without any special considerations which would not equally well
apply to other proposed Jewish Christian destinations.[4] V. Burch,[5]
however, on the basis of the Maccabean background which he claims
for the Epistle, concludes more confidently for Antioch as its destination because this was the 'Shrine of the Maccabees'. But his arguments
here are too tortuous to admit of certainty.

The claims of Corinth have recently been advocated,[6] but this suggestion is not likely to receive wide support because of the difficulty of
ii. 3. Still others have proposed Cyprus on the supposition that Barnabas was the author,[7] while A. Klostermann[8] proposed that the title was
a scribal error for 'to the Bereans'.

[1] *Op. cit.*, p. xxxiv, largely on the grounds that Apollos, whom he thought
was author, and Timothy were connected with it.

[2] *RB*, XLVIII (1939), pp. 506–529.

[3] *ZNTW*, 11 (1910), pp. 105–110. Cf. also A. B. Davidson's still vaguer, 'Some
community of the Dispersion in the East' (*op. cit.*, p. 18).

[4] *The Epistle to the Hebrews* (1883), pp. xvii, xviii. His main argument was
based on the title, which, he thought, must indicate Hebrew-speaking Jewish
Christians, but this is a rather more restricted usage than is necessary.

[5] *Op. cit.*, pp. 137ff.

[6] F. Lo Bue, *op. cit.*, pp. 52–57. It was earlier suggested by H. Appel, *Der
Hebräerbrief ein Schreiben des Apollos an Judenchristen der Korinthischen Gemeinde*
(1918), cited by Feine-Behm, *op. cit.*, p. 227.

[7] Cf. Riggenbach, *op. cit.*, pp. xlv, xlvi; A. Snell, *New and Living Way: An
Explanation of the Epistle to the Hebrews* (1959), p. 18.

[8] *Zur Theorie der biblischen Weissagung und zur Charakteristik des Hebräerbriefes*
(1889), p. 55, cited by O. Michel, *op. cit.*, p. 12.

V. DATE

The difficulty of settling the precise circumstances of the readers and the identity of the author naturally affects the dating. But the *terminus ad quem* is certainly fixed by Clement's epistle, which is generally dated at AD 95.[1] The *terminus a quo* is determined by the answer to the problem of the relationship of the Epistle to the fall of Jerusalem (AD 70). Was the temple still standing? The only information we have is the use of present tenses in references to the ritual (cf. vii. 8, ix. 6f., 9, 13, xiii. 10), but these need not mean that the temple ritual is still continued, since Clement also used present tenses to describe similar ritual (*1 Clem.* xli).[2] In these cases the present tenses describe what Moses had established and are a natural literary device. Of greater weight would seem to be the absence of any indication in the Epistle of the catastrophe for, if it had already happened, it would have been a conclusive argument for the cessation of the old cultus.[3] For this reason many scholars date the Epistle before AD 70, either in the early part of the decade or when the trials of the siege had become imminent.[4] These considerations will naturally have little weight for those who deny that the author has any interest in the temple, but is wholly absorbed with the tabernacle.

Quite apart from this, however, there are certain other indications which support a date before the fall of the city. The tone of the Epistle and the call to 'come out' would have particular point if the doom of the city was imminent, especially in view of the warning of Jesus in Mark xiii. 14f. E. C. Wickham[5] argues that the appeal to the heroes of

---

[1] Cf. E. T. Merrill (*Essays in Early Christian History*, 1924, pp. 217ff.) who denies authorship by a bishop named Clement and dates it *c.* AD 140. But this dating is not usually followed.

[2] Wickham (*op. cit.*, p. xviii) draws a distinction between Clement's use and that of the author of Hebrews, for it makes no difference to his argument whether the ritual was discontinued or not. But the present is found also in Josephus, Justin and the Talmud. (Cf. Farrar, *op. cit.*, p. xxv.)

[3] Cf. T. W. Manson (*BJRL*, XXXII, 1949, pp. 1–17), who maintained a date prior to Paul's letter to Colossae, considered that the use of the Melchizedek high-priesthood argument rather than an appeal to the destruction of the temple makes it most probable that the temple still stands.

[4] Cf. G. A. Barton, *JBL*, LVII (1938), pp. 205–207. A. Nairne (*The Epistle of Priesthood*, p. 22) suggested that the clash of the Jews with Rome imposed a claim to loyalty on the part of the readers, who had only imperfectly understood Christianity.

[5] *Op. cit.*, p. xix.

the past in chapter xi becomes more significant if there still existed the possibility of their return to the faith of their fathers in the form of the historic ritual. The reference to Timothy, which supports the view that the Epistle was written by a member of the Pauline circle, is perhaps more intelligible if placed as near as possible to Paul's time, but this cannot be pressed since the later history of Timothy is unknown. The ecclesiastical situation appears to be primitive, for no church officials are mentioned by name, but only 'leaders' generally (xiii. 7, 17).

Time must be allowed for the 'former days' during which the readers had been persecuted. If this former persecution was Nero's, that would at once date the Epistle later than the fall of Jerusalem. But destination enters into this discussion, for if Palestinians are in mind the Neronic persecutions would have no relevance. In fact it seems almost unnecessary to assign the persecution mentioned to any specified historic occasion, for Jewish Christians must have been constantly under fire from Jewish enemies of the gospel (cf. Acts). Even if Jewish Christians at Rome are in mind, it is not impossible that a certain amount of ill-treatment and confiscation took place in the execution of Claudius' edict for the expulsion of Jews from the Imperial City (cf. Acts xviii. 2), and this would undoubtedly have involved Christian Jews (compare the case of Aquila).[1] If Hebrews x. 32ff. refers to this, an interval of some fifteen years separated the two persecutions and this would allow and, in fact, require a date previous to AD 64. But it seems a fair inference from chapter xiii that Paul is no longer alive, in which case the Epistle must not be dated long before AD 64.

Advocates for a later date base their contentions on the imminence of the persecution subsequent to Nero's, i.e. Domitian's,[2] and on the later development of the thought. Thus sometime in the decade

---

[1] It is significant that the references to persecution in Heb. x are comparatively mild. Moffatt suggested that they may amount to no more than mob violence (*ILNT*, p. 453).

[2] D. W. Riddle (*JBL*, XLIII, 1924, pp. 329–348), on the grounds of a comparison between Hebrews and *1 Clement*, concluded that the former could only recently have been received by the author of the latter and must, therefore, belong to the same period. But his assumption here is without foundation. Cf. also Goodspeed's view that *1 Clement* was written in response to Heb. v. 12, the latter Epistle having only recently been produced subsequent to Paul's letter-collection (*INT*, pp. 258, 259); cf. also his article in *JBL*, xxx (1911), pp. 157–160. H. Windisch (*Der Hebräerbrief*,[2] 1931, p. 126) claimed that at least ten years must separate Hebrews and *1 Clement*, but, if so, it might as well be thirty years.

AD 80–90[1] is chosen by those for whom this line of evidence carries any weight. Unfavourable to this hypothesis is the statement that the readers have not yet 'resisted unto blood', which would not fit Nero's persecution unless the small group addressed had been treated less severely than most. The alleged use of some of Paul's Epistles is also claimed to support this later date, since time would be required for the circulation of these Epistles.[2] Yet literary affinities are unreliable in settling questions of date, unless they indicate literary dependence so certainly that some chronological arrangement of the writings is possible. Those who maintain an earlier date place little emphasis on Paul's literary influence on the author, for the fact that he belonged to the Pauline circle is sufficient explanation of many parallels with Pauline thought and phraseology. Another argument for a later date is based on the supposition that ii. 3 implies second generation Christianity, but no weight can be attached to this since the statement may perfectly well be understood of the original members of the community.[3]

In view of all the data available, it would seem reasonable to regard this Epistle as having been sent either just before the fall of Jerusalem, if Jerusalem was the destination, or just before the Neronic persecutions if it was sent to Rome.

VI. BACKGROUND

Interest in the theological affinities of the Epistle was only aroused when Pauline authorship became widely disputed. Until then it was treated as part of the Pauline Corpus and integrated into the Pauline theology. But in recent times there have been several different attempts to reorientate the Epistle and to put it in its rightful place in the development of Christianity. The first strong reaction was towards Philonism and a strongly Hellenistic interpretation of the Epistle, but there have

[1] Cf. E. F. Scott, *The Literature of the New Testament*, p. 199; Feine-Behm, *op. cit.*, p. 231. Feine-Behm reject the view of M. S. Enslin, who arbitrarily dates it about AD 110. McNeile-Williams narrow the date down to c. AD 80–85 (*INT*, p. 235) and Michaelis to soon after AD 80 (*op. cit.*, p. 273).

[2] H. von Soden (*JPTh*, 10, 1884, p. 493) argued for a period of time subsequent to the end of Paul's Jewish-Gentile conflict.

[3] Cf. A. S. Peake, *op. cit.*, p. 9. A. Harnack (*ZNTW*, 1, 1900, p. 29) agreed that 'second generation Christians' must be understood genealogically, not chronologically.

been other attempts to define more closely the author's relationship to the primitive tradition, to Paulinism and to Johannine thought.

a. Philonism

The movement which treated the Epistle as a Philonic interpretation of Christianity reached its peak at the end of the nineteenth century in the complete denial of any Paulinism. Ménégoz,[1] for instance, denied the possibility of any conciliation between the point of view of Paul and that of Hebrews, and refuted any idea of the author's dependence on Paul's Epistles.

That there are certain similarities between the two authors no-one would deny. In both there is a tendency towards allegory, a reverence for the text of the LXX, similar formulae of citation, a readiness to attach importance even to the silence of Scripture (cf. Heb. vii. 3), the appeal to Melchizedek as a type,[2] a similar interpretation of the apparent in the light of the real and many significant words and phrases common to both.[3] A few other features might be mentioned, such as the attaching of meaning to individual names (vii. 2), the contrast between the earthly and the heavenly (cf. ix. 23f., viii. 1ff.), the created and the uncreated (ix. 11), the past and the future (ii. 5, ix. 1ff., xiii. 14), the transitory and the abiding (vii. 3, 24, x. 34, xii. 27, xiii. 14).[4] There may be here, as in Alexandrian Judaism, a trace of the background of the Platonic theory of ideas,[5] but antitheses were not the sole property of the philosophers and were, in fact, inherent in the transference from Judaism to Christianity. Yet inferences drawn from these data have given rise to different opinions. There is at the present time less inclination to conclude that the author shows a direct dependence on Philo's works,[6] since literary similarities cannot prove conscious use by one author of another's work. They may, however, indicate a similar

---

[1] La Théologie de l'Epître aux Hébreux (1894), pp. 249, 250.

[2] Until Philo, the Melchizedek theme seems to have held little interest among the Jews. (Cf. the study of G. Wuttke, Melchisedech, der Priesterkönig von Salem, 1927, Beihefte ZNTW).

[3] Cf. C. Spicq, L'Epître aux Hébreux, pp. 39–91, for a thorough examination of these Philonic connections.

[4] Cf. Feine-Behm, op. cit., p. 223.

[5] J. Héring (op. cit., p. 10) maintains that the author's thoughts are nearer a Platonic than a biblical framework, although he admits a difference in outlook.

[6] Cf. W. Manson, op. cit., p. 184.

background, and may further suggest in the case of Hebrews that the author had been educated under Philonic influence.[1] Caution is nevertheless needed in drawing even this inference since religious phraseology and ideas cannot be regarded as the property of one man, and, even if language and style show some close affinities with Philo's writings, there are marked differences in the author's methods and outlook. As compared with the allegorization of Philo, which is integral to his whole approach to Old Testament exegesis, the writer to the Hebrews does not strictly allegorize, although he comes near to it in dealing with Melchizedek.[2] The long section on the levitical cultus proceeds on the assumption that Christ brings out its full implications in His own fulfilment of it, and in this respect the writer is much closer to primitive tradition than to Philo. This leads up to another fundamental difference. Philo does not treat the Old Testament history as history, but as a framework for his philosophical ideas. But for the writer to the Hebrews the history is treated literally, as the catalogue in chapter xi shows. The force of his argument would be considerably weakened if he were assumed to have Philo's view of history. E. F. Scott[3] has pointed out another difference in that Philo dispenses with ceremonial in favour of inward communion, whereas the author of this Epistle still thinks of worship in terms of sacrifice. In other words, his approach is more thoroughly biblical. He does not, as Philo, bring certain philosophical presuppositions to his understanding of the Old Testament, but approaches it with the sole key that Christ has fulfilled the old order. If this appears to have any affinities with Philo's theory of ideas, it is little more than superficial, for the early Christians generally regarded the Christian fulfilment as essentially 'better' than the old. Although all had not reached the same complete appreciation of it as the author of this Epistle, there is nothing imported into this approach from Hellenism, which could not have been a development from the primitive Christian tradition. At the same time the author's Hellenistic background would have equipped him thoroughly to express in an adequate form what was, in fact, inherent in the tradition.[4]

[1] C. Spicq agrees with Ménégoz that the author is a Philonist converted to Christianity (*op. cit.*, p. 198).

[2] V. Burch (*op. cit.*, 1936, p. 84) vigorously disputes any dependence of the author on Philo for his Melchizedekian theme.

[3] *The Epistle to the Hebrews*, p. 56.

[4] Cf. C. K. Barrett in *The Background of the New Testament and its Eschatology* (ed. W. D. Davies and D. Daube, 1956), pp. 363–393, for a similar view.

But although many scholars[1] would still maintain in general an Alexandrian exegetical approach, there are indications of a movement away from this position towards a greater stress on the eschatological outlook of the writer and this will be considered under our next heading.

b. Primitive tradition

A parallel, yet later, reaction against treating the Epistle as Paulinist is the attempt to trace its origin in the primitive tradition. This movement is of the utmost importance in establishing the modern relevance of the Epistle, for it implies that the author is no mere antiquarian divorced from the main current of Christian development. Details have already been given of the remarkable similarities between Hebrews and Stephen's speech[2] and, on the basis of this, the Epistle has been interpreted. The author shows a close acquaintance with the facts of Jesus' earthly life and this has been supposed to provide evidence of acquaintance with the Synoptic Gospels. It is not certain that dependence can be established, but it is significant that the author reflects in his argument three allusions to the Synoptic tradition: the temptation of Christ, the cleansing of the temple and the rent veil.[3] Yet there is little about priesthood in the earliest traditions of primitive preaching, as preserved for us in the Acts, and as this forms so central a part of the author's argument, it must be considered a development, though a perfectly natural one, from that primitive tradition.[4]

W. Manson has pointed out that the author shares the predominant eschatological approach which Jewish Christianity inherited from Judaism.[5] The 'two-age' theology can be traced behind the doctrine of the Epistle, with the implication that the 'age to come' has already come.[6] R. H. Strachan,[7] while maintaining that the author's views are

---

[1] E.g. R. H. Strachan, *op. cit.*, p. 78; F. D. V. Narborough, *op. cit.*, pp. 20ff. E. Käsemann (*op. cit.*, pp. 52–116) makes much of the Gnostic background of the Epistle, but few other scholars give much weight to this aspect of the author's Greek background (cf. Käsemann's review of Michel's commentary, *ThLZ*, 75, 1950, cols. 427–430).

[2] See pp. 19f.   [3] Cf. C. Spicq, *op. cit.*, pp. 99–109.

[4] Cf. L. O. Bristol, 'Primitive Christian Preaching and the Epistle to the Hebrews', *JBL*, LXVIII (1949), pp. 89–97. See also V. Taylor, *The Atonement in New Testament teaching*[2] (1945), pp. 111ff. and R. V. G. Tasker, *The Gospel in the Epistle to the Hebrews* (1950).

[5] *Op. cit.*, pp. 184f.   [6] Cf. C. K. Barrett, *op. cit.*, p. 391.   [7] *Op. cit.*, p. 79.

based on the Platonic doctrine of the two worlds, nevertheless agreed that his mind is still governed by the Jewish apocalyptic view of history.

c. Paulinism

In spite of the swing away from Pauline influences in the interpretation of the Epistle, the problem of the relation of the Epistle to Pauline doctrine remains. In general, those inclined to stress either of the preceding influences tend to deny or else reduce to a minimum the impact of Paul upon the author.[1] Yet there are many parallels which cannot be lightly passed over, and which imply a much closer liaison in thought between the two writers than is often imagined.

H. Windisch[2] has listed a number of similarities between Paul and this Epistle, of which the following are the most striking:

A similar doctrine of Christ, His previous glory and part in creation (Heb. i. 2, 3, 6: 1 Cor. viii. 6; 2 Cor. iv. 4; Col. i. 15–17).

His self-humbling (Heb. ii. 14–17: Rom. viii. 3; Gal. iv. 4; Phil. ii. 7).

His obedience (Heb. v. 8: Rom. v. 19; Phil. ii. 8).

His self-offering for us (Heb. ix. 28: 1 Cor. v. 7; Eph. v. 2).

A similar view of the new covenant (Heb. viii. 6: 2 Cor. iii. 9ff.).

A similar view of Abraham's faith as an example (Heb. xi. 11, 12, 17–19: Rom. iv. 17–20).

A similar view of the distribution of gifts by the Spirit (Heb. ii. 4: 1 Cor. xii. 11).

An appeal to the same Old Testament passages (e.g. Ps. viii. in Heb. ii. 6–9 and 1 Cor. xv. 27; Deut. xxxii. 35 in Heb. x. 30 and Rom. xii. 19; Hab. ii. 4 in Heb. x. 38, Rom. i. 17 and Gal. iii. 11).

A similar use of the athletic metaphor of the Christian life (Heb. xii. 1: 1 Cor. ix. 24).

[1] Cf. Ménégoz, op. cit., p. 184, in contrast to Philonism, and E. F. Scott, op. cit., pp. 49ff. The latter admits it to be perplexing that the author, although having some contacts with the Pauline circle (e.g. Timothy), was so unaffected by Paul's work—an evidence, he thinks, that Paul's influence in his own age was not as wide as is often supposed.

[2] Op. cit., pp. 128, 129.

It can hardly be maintained, therefore, that the author shares no affinities with the apostle Paul. Indeed, Windisch himself considered this must indicate either a Pauline disciple or else a writer who, in common with Paul, had reproduced similar elements in the tradition.[1]

At the same time differences in approach have already been noted see p. 15), and many scholars have drawn a strong antithesis between the two writers. If the writer of Hebrews is dealing with Judaism he deals with it in a different way from Paul,[2] although, as already noted, he deals with biblical data rather than Judaism. His approach to the law is different, for he never appears to wrestle with the law after Paul's manner,[3] although it must be recognized that Paul never disputed the validity of the law. The real question is whether there are any fundamental positions which the author assumes to which Paul would have taken strong exception and the answer must surely be in the negative. If it may reasonably be maintained that Paul would have said them in a different way, it may not be deduced that he would not have consented to the expression of them. Our conclusion must be that, while showing independence, the writer of this Epistle is as much in line with Paulinism as with the primitive tradition.

d. Johannine thought

Not much attention has been paid to affinities with the Johannine literature, but it has generally been supposed that this Epistle represents a position midway between the Pauline and the Johannine theology.[4] C. Spicq[5] cites many parallels and concludes that the author was dependent on the Johannine catechesis, which was later crystallized into the Gospel and Epistles. The result of these different lines of investigation is really to demonstrate the remarkable affinity of this Epistle with all phases of early Christian development. It may necessitate a revision of much modern theory about that development, for criticism has tended to think too rigidly of straight-line development in terms of sequence, as if this Epistle must be fitted into a scheme dominated by chronology. A truer appreciation of the facts would seem to require

[1] It is significant that Windisch, although he paid full attention to the Philonic background, nevertheless considered the author of this Epistle to be nearer to Paul than is any other New Testament writer (cf. A. Nairne, *The Epistle to the Hebrews*, p. lxiii, for an appraisal of Windisch's approach).

[2] Cf. R. H. Strachan, *op. cit.*, p. 87; E. F. Scott, *op. cit.*, pp. 93ff.

[3] Cf. J. P. Alexander, *op. cit.*, p. 58.   [4] Cf. R. H. Strachan, *op. cit.*, p. 103.

[5] *Op. cit.*, pp. 109–138.

a theory of co-lateral development in which Pauline thought, the theology of Hebrews and the catechesis of John could all find a place contemporaneously.

e. The Old Testament

In the course of the previous discussions many references have been made to the author's use of the Old Testament and it goes almost without saying that this formed a dominant characteristic of his background. He cites the LXX version and for the most part adheres to it more closely than does the apostle Paul. His citations from it are introduced by formulae which indicate great reverence for the sacred text and a belief in its divine origin. He treats it both literally and symbolically.[1] The whole Epistle is a classic example of an authoritative answer to the question, How are Christians to regard the Old Testament revelation? The emphasis on the cultus may well have been given because, in the author's own mind, this was the most difficult material to which to ascribe a contemporary Christian relevance, and the author's skilful interpretation of the fulfilment of the Old Testament in Christ must have been of immense value to many who had either to rethink their approach (as the Jews) or to grapple with unfamiliar Scripture (as the Gentiles). If it were for no other reason but this, the inclusion of this Epistle in the Christian Canon would be amply justified.

VII. LITERARY FORM

The possession of a conclusion without an introductory greeting and without address raises a problem as to the form of the letter. Its conclusion and its personal allusions to the readers mark it out as a letter, whereas its style, method of argument and various incidental indications (e.g. 'time would fail me to tell', xi. 32) point rather to a sermon. Theories which have postulated a lost introduction, whether accidental or intentional, are quite unconvincing in view of the absence of any textual evidence.[2] Similarly, attempts to regard chapter xiii, or parts of it, as a postscript added to a homily are also faced with lack of

---

[1] Cf. R. Rendall, *EQ*, XXVII (1955), pp. 214–220, for the author's method in using Old Testament quotations and J. van der Ploeg, *RB*, LIV (1947), pp. 187–228. F. C. Synge (*op. cit.*, pp. 53, 54) disputes that the Old Testament context had any significance for the author of this Epistle, but this is probably an exaggeration.

[2] Cf. Moffatt, *ILNT*, pp. 428, 429, for details. Cf. also Feine-Behm, *op. cit.*, p. 225.

textual support. Nevertheless, the form of the Epistle presents certain problems.

A. Deissmann regarded the Epistle as the first example of Christian art-literature,[1] but this must not be pressed in view of the definite historic situation which the Epistle was clearly designed to meet. It does not read like 'a mere literary exercise'.[2] In the same way the historical situation disposes of the circular view of its origin.[3]

Yet its oratorical character almost demands that it was originally a spoken sermon, or at least was prepared for delivery to some community.[4] Was it a sermon prepared by the author but read to the community by another?[5] Or was it first a delivered sermon which the hearers and especially the leaders urged the preacher to preserve in permanent form?[6] In the former case some epistolary conclusion must have been added to give personal greetings from the absent writer to the congregation he hopes soon to visit, and in the latter case the preacher would have added the greetings as a kind of covering letter at the time of supplying the church with the written copy. But the problem is not easy to solve.[7] There is no doubt that the writer has his readers in mind

[1] *The New Testament in the light of modern research* (1929), p. 51.

[2] To quote W. Manson, *op. cit.*, p. 5. O. Roller (*Das Formular der paulinischen Briefe*, 1933, pp. 213ff.) has shown that during the first century AD a form of letter was prevalent that did not belong to the general category of Greek letters, although written in Greek. The formulae used in these were oriental rather than Greek. It may be that this Epistle was never intended to conform to the normal Greek literary practice, hence the omission of the normal introduction.

[3] As M. Dibelius maintained, *ThBl* (1942), pp. 1–11.

[4] Many writers have advanced this view. Cf. P. Wendland, *Die urchristlichen Literaturformen* (LHB, 1912), pp. 306–309; E. Burggaller, *ZNTW*, 9 (1908), pp. 110–113; R. Perdelwitz, *ZNTW*, 11 (1910), pp. 59–78; H. Windisch, *op. cit.*, p. 122; Moffatt, *ILNT*, p. 428; E. F. Scott (see footnote [5]); G. Salmon (see footnote [6]). A. B. Bruce (*The Epistle to the Hebrews*, 1899, p. 10) maintained that this Epistle is too long and abstruse to be a sermon, but he thought that parts (e.g. chapter xi) might have been. P. Carrington, *The Primitive Christian Calendar* (1952), pp. 43, 44, has made the interesting suggestion that the Epistle may have been a *megillah* ('roll') for the Day of Atonement.

[5] E. F. Scott, *The Literature of the New Testament*, p. 199.

[6] G. Salmon, *INT*, p. 429. In his view it was a sermon of Barnabas' preached at Jerusalem.

[7] A. Nairne rejected the sermon theory and was inclined to regard the title as a playful subtlety meaning, 'To those who are Hebrews indeed' (*The Epistle to the Hebrews*, p. lxxiii). C. Spicq (*op. cit.*, p. 21) regarded the Epistle as an apologetic tractate. But cf. W. Nauck, article 'Zum Aufbau des Hebräerbriefes' in *Judentum Urchristentum Kirche* (Festschrift für Joachim Jeremias, ed. W. Eltester, 1960), pp. 199–206.

throughout his composition because he punctuates his doctrinal argument with direct moral exhortations to them.

A comparison with 1 John is instructive as a parallel case in which no author's name is stated, nor any addressees defined. This would seem to support the contention that Hebrews had no other introduction than that which it now possesses, yet it has been objected that the parallel is not close since in 1 John i. 4 the writing makes clear that the author is purposing to *write* to the readers, whereas Hebrews contains no reference to writing until xiii. 22.[1] But if the author urges the readers to 'bear with' his 'word of exhortation', 'for I have written to you briefly' (RSV), it is most natural to suppose that the whole was originally composed as a letter.

Assuming, however, that it was originally a homily, the question of the purpose and extent of the epistolary conclusion at once arises. Some have treated xiii. 22–25 as a later addition on the strength of which, because of its Pauline flavour, the whole Epistle was included in the Pauline canon.[2] Others have regarded the addition as a fictitious device of the author, especially framed to give the impression of Pauline origin.[3] The former of these alternatives is excluded by the common outlook, purpose and style to be found in both i–xii and xiii.[4] The latter is most improbable since no author wishing to suggest

[1] Cf. Moffatt, *ILNT*, p. 429.

[2] Feine-Behm (*op. cit.*, p. 224) cite Overbeck, *Zur Geschichte des Kanons* (1880), for this view.

[3] Cf. P. Wendland, *loc. cit.* W. Wrede (*Das literarische Rätsel des Hebräerbriefe*, 1906, pp. 1–5) gives a useful survey of theories of a similar nature. He mentions the view of Berger, de Wette, Overbeck, Weizsäcker and Perdelwitz, who all regarded xiii. 22–25 (or 18–25) as an addition to the homily. Wrede himself thought that the writer changed his mind. His first intention was a homily. Then he began to turn it into an Epistle in chapter xiii, and finally decided to give it a Pauline flavour in verses 22–25. In the latter portion he was influenced by Phm. 22 and Phil. ii. 19–24 (cf. *ibid.*, pp. 39–43). C. C. Torrey (*JBL*, xxx, 1911, pp. 137–156) has a similar theory, but extends the additions to include xiii. 1–7, 16–19.

[4] This is strongly maintained by C. Spicq in his article 'L'authenticité du chapitre xiii de l'Epître aux Hébreux' in *Coniectanea Neotestamentica XI in honorem Antonii Fridrichsen* (1947), pp. 226–236. Spicq finds in Heb. xiii four major themes from the body of the Epistle; the elimination of Mosaism which obliged Christians to break with the levitical cultus; the analogy between our Lord and the levitical sacrifices; life on earth as a pilgrimage; and perseverance in the faith assured by a docile attitude towards the leaders. The first three may be admitted, but there is no basis for the fourth in either part. Spicq adds many other parallels affecting style and articulation. For a linguistic comparison between i–xii and xiii, cf. C. R.

Pauline origin would have been foolish enough to neglect the use of an introductory formula in chapter i announcing authorship. A third view is that the concluding three verses were added by Paul to an Epistle written by one of his associates.[1] The description, 'our brother Timothy' and the word 'grace' in the greetings are claimed to support this.[2] But it is strange that Paul gives no hint of his identity and three verses are, after all, a very narrow basis on which to form an estimate of authorship.

Yet another and highly improbable view is that Hebrews xiii is part of the 'severe letter' of Paul to Corinth.[3] Some similarities may suggestively be found, but the processes by which such an ending came to be attached to an anonymous letter like Hebrews are too baffling to be readily credible.

VIII. LITERARY AFFINITIES

Because so much stress is placed on literary affinities some attention must be paid to those affecting this Epistle, although considerable reserve is necessary before making any deductions from these data. Of the Pauline Epistles the parallels with Romans are most marked, but other less striking parallels are found in 1 and 2 Corinthians, Colossians and Philippians.[4] There are similarly parallels with 1 Peter and many of these are common only to Hebrews and 1 Peter in the New Testament.[5] Again the Lucan writings furnish many parallels, although these are mostly in vocabulary.[6] Attention has already been drawn to Johannine parallels (see pp. 49f.), but in this case it is the underlying catechesis and not the written Gospel which is in mind.

In the case of the Pauline Epistles, 1 Peter and the Lucan writings, various inferences regarding authorship have been made, based on the

Williams (*JBL*, xxx, 1911, pp. 129–136) who considered one author wrote both parts. Cf. also H. Strathmann, *Der Brief an die Hebräer* (1953), p. 68.

[1] Cf. F. J. Badcock, *op. cit.*, pp. 199, 200, for this view. As he maintained in any case a composite authorship (Barnabas/Luke), an appended postscript by Paul presented no difficulty to him.

[2] G. A. Simcox made a comparison between Heb. xiii. 20, 21 and 2 Tim. iv. 5–8 and concluded that both passages were Pauline (*ET*, x, 1899, pp. 430ff.).

[3] Cf. E. D. Jones, *ET*, XLVI (1935), pp. 562–567.

[4] Cf. F. D. V. Narborough, *op. cit.*, p. 16, for details. E. J. Goodspeed (*INT*, p. 256) and A. E. Barnett (*Paul becomes a Literary Influence*, 1941, pp. 69–88) maintain that Hebrews reflects all of Paul's Epistles, except 2 Thessalonians and Philemon.

[5] Cf. Moffatt, *ILNT*, p. 440; Narborough, *op. cit.*, p. 12.

[6] Cf. Moffatt, *op. cit.*, p. 436. See comments on pp. 19f.

supposition that strong literary parallels point to identity of authorship. Yet none of these inferences has very widely commended itself. Alternatively, theories of literary dependence have been proposed. The author's use of some or all of the above-mentioned writings may at least be considered a possibility, but beyond that we cannot go. It is notably difficult to establish the direction in which literary dependence took place and this inevitably leads to difference of opinion. For instance, if 1 Peter is Petrine, it probably preceded Hebrews,[1] but if it is not apostolic (see pp. 98ff.) and Hebrews is dated early, Hebrews must have preceded 1 Peter. If both are late, who can determine the direction of dependence? It is probably better to leave out any appeal to literary parallels altogether, until some more objective method of determining dependence can be devised.

IX. ITS MODERN RELEVANCE

If the Epistle has been relatively neglected, it is because the argument seems obscure to those unfamiliar with the Old Testament background. Old Testament criticism has had its repercussions on the influence of this Epistle for, so long as much of the Old Testament remains under suspicion, the relevance of this Epistle cannot possibly be appreciated. Yet it gives to our contemporary age the same message as it gave to its original readers, an assurance of the superiority and finality of Christ and a clear insight into the Christian interpretation of Old Testament history and forms of worship. It is no wonder that the language of this Epistle has become the language of devotion, moulding the expression of praise and petition, for it meets the fundamental need of man; it speaks of a way of approach and a method of worship which is superior to all others, and which is unaffected by the march of time.

CONTENTS

I. THE SUPERIORITY OF CHRISTIANITY (i. 1–x. 18)

This is contrasted with several different methods of approach and culminates in the doctrinal exposition of Christ as the eternal High Priest.

[1] F. J. Badcock (op. cit., pp. 191, 192) maintained the reverse in view of the originality of the Epistle to the Hebrews, and he thought that Peter might easily have become acquainted with it through Mark or Silvanus.

a. Superiority to the old revelation (i. 1–3)

The divine character of the prophetical messages is at once admitted but the vital difference in Christianity is in the glorious Person who has become God's medium. This opening statement sets the tone for the whole Epistle, for Christ is introduced both in His royal dignity and in His fulfilled Priesthood.

b. Superiority to angels (i. 4–ii. 18)

This contrast derives particular force from the belief that angels were messengers of the old revelation and Christ is seen to be greater than both the revelation itself and also its messengers. The writer in the course of this explanation digresses to exhort the readers to heed this great revelation declared through Christ (ii. 1–4). In view of this superiority to angels, some explanation is required of Christ's humiliation and this next occupies the writer's thoughts leading him to explain why the incarnation was not only necessary but fitting (see verse 10). In becoming man, like His brethren, He was qualified to perform His high-priestly work (verse 17) and this is another incidental indication of the main exposition to follow. His seeming inferiority to angels was therefore only temporary and was an essential part of His redeeming activity.

c. Superiority to Moses (iii. 1–19)

It was equally important to settle the relationship of Christ to Moses and the writer makes clear that Moses was only the representative of the house of Israel in the rôle of a servant whereas Christ, as Son, held a superior office. The readers are identified with the house and thus Christ's authority over them is emphasized (verses 1–6).

The greatness of Moses could not prevent many of the Israelites from losing their inheritance and this fact is used by the writer to exhort the readers to hold fast (iii. 7–19). As in the preceding sections the Old Testament is used to support the argument and the word 'today' from Psalm xcv is interpreted of the present day of grace.

d. Superiority to Joshua (iv. 1–13)

The mention of 'rest' from Psalm xcv recalls to the writer's mind the parallel between the rest offered to Israelites and that available for Christians. Even if some Israelites lost their inheritance, others did enter the promised land under Joshua (see verse 8, RSV), but the inheritance did not amount to 'rest'. *That* still remained and is identified by the writer as the rest given to believers. In pondering this theme of rest he thinks of God resting after creation and implies that the Christian's rest is of the same quality (verses 1–10). Because of this some resolve is required if the inheritance is not to be lost, and the seriousness of this warning is brought home by the living character of God's word (verses 11–13).

e. *The superior Priesthood of Christ* (iv. 14–vii. 28)

1. The writer has now reached the point of discussing more fully what he has adumbrated already in ii. 17ff., that Christ is a High Priest of superior qualifications to any other. He fulfils the two fundamental requirements of sympathy and divine appointment (iv. 14–v. 10). In order to demonstrate the first the writer alludes to Christ's agony in the garden, and to prove the second he draws from two Old Testament testimonia, in one of which he introduces the order of Melchizedek to which he declares that Christ was designated. This latter theme is of such importance that the author intends to develop it, but at this stage he skilfully introduces a searching challenge (v. 11–vi. 20).

2. The next section is an interlude in the doctrinal argument containing warnings and encouragements. The writer becomes suddenly conscious of the difficulty of his exposition (verse 11) and remembering the dulness of the readers he takes the opportunity of challenging them to strive for greater maturity (verse 14). It was time they grew up and left behind the elementary doctrines (vi. 1–3). The alternative to advancement is going back and the thought of apostasy strikes the writer so forcefully that he issues a solemn warning as to its consequences (vi. 4–8). He is not meaning to suggest that his readers have actually turned back, however, for he commends them for their love and then encourages them to press on to inherit the promises (vi. 9–12). The thought of promises reminds him of Abraham and his experience of God's immutable word as a guarantee of great security, like a good anchorage. But Christians have a further Guarantor in the person of their High Priest, who belongs to the order of Melchizedek (vi. 13–20).

3. The expression 'after the order of Melchisedec' clearly needs explaining, so the writer appeals to the Genesis story (Gn. xiv) to bring out certain features in Christ's Priesthood which he intends to demon-

strate as being superior to Aaron's. Melchizedek's names are suggestive (peace and righteousness), as is also the strange way in which he appears and disappears from the story (illustrative of Christ's eternal existence), and his evident superiority to Abraham and thus to the later levitical order (vii. 1–10). But this type of argument must be brought into concrete relationship to the levitical priesthood and the first difficulty is that Christ belonged to a different tribe from what the law prescribed for the priesthood (vii. 11–14). Yet the law cannot be considered perfect and the qualification of the superior High Priest is not therefore genealogical but spiritual (indestructible life; verse 16). This makes possible the High-Priesthood of Christ, which is seen to be superior in its solemn divine attestation, its permanence and the sinlessness and perfection of the Holder (vii. 15–28).

f. The superiority of the priestly work of Christ (viii. 1–x. 18)

The real crux of the argument is now reached. A high priest must have functions; what then are Christ's? He obviously cannot minister on earth, so He is shown to have a superior sanctuary, heaven itself (viii. 1–6). Moreover, the covenant under which Christ ministers is a new covenant foreshadowed by Jeremiah, which makes the old obsolete (viii. 7–13). This leads the writer to describe some of the ritual of this obsolete covenant in order to bring out more clearly the greater glory of the new. The new order of sacrifice needs no continuous repetition. Whereas the Aaronic high priest entered once a year, Christ not only entered once for all but entered a heavenly and not an earthly sanctuary. He took no animal blood, but offered His own through the Spirit. This demonstrates the superiority of Christian atonement (ix. 1–14) and leads to a further development in the argument, since Christ becomes Mediator of the new covenant through His death (ix. 15).

But the death of an eternal High Priest seems paradoxical and is explained by analogy with a legal testament, which becomes valid only on the death of the testator (ix. 16–22). The uniqueness of the sacrifice of Christ is then reiterated in order to emphasize its timelessness and its effectiveness for the removal of sin (ix. 23–28). The whole argument for the superiority of Christ's atonement is now summed up in contrast to the levitical system (x. 1–18) and the completeness of His act is particularly demonstrated by His enthronement in heaven (x. 12), the same conception as that with which the discussion began (i. 3).

II. EXHORTATIONS BASED ON THE PRECEDING
ARGUMENTS (x. 19–xiii. 17)

a. The superior method of approach should be used (x. 19–25)

All that is necessary is faith in this High Priest and this will affect our approach, not only to ourselves but to others. Mutual encouragement is so valuable that assemblies of Christians should not be neglected.

b. The dangers of apostasy must be noted (x. 26–31)

The possibility of those who have understood the privileges of the Christian way spurning the truth they know causes the writer to issue another warning similar to that of chapter vi.

c. Yet memory of past days is cause for encouragement (x. 32–39)

The writer recalls their former steadfastness and does not wish them to think he is censuring them too severely, but emphasizes their need to hold on to their confidence.

d. Examples of historic endurance are cited to illustrate the triumph of faith (xi. 1–40)

The need for endurance stated in the last chapter leads to the introduction of illustrations. Faith in this case is not used in the same way as in Paul for it describes here an attitude of trust with a strong element of hope and fortitude. Most attention is paid to the patriarchs, but the whole history of the past could furnish examples.

e. But the greatest example of all is Jesus Christ (xii. 1–11)

If the readers are at present suffering they should look at Jesus Christ in His endurance upon the cross and should remember that discipline is necessary for God's sons.

f. Moral inconsistencies must be avoided (xii. 12–17)

There is need for resolution in pursuing the right path and certain specific injunctions are given for the avoidance of bitterness and immorality. Esau's example is cited as a warning.

g. The superiority of the new covenant is again maintained (xii. 18–29)

Its great glory, its great Mediator and its great stability are all mentioned, together with another exhortation to take advantage of this new way of worship, remembering the awesomeness of God.

h. Practical results must follow from these considerations (xiii. 1–17)

There are exhortations affecting social life (1–3), private life (4–6) and religious life (7–9, 17) interspersed with a concluding doctrinal section explaining the Christians' new altar (10–16).

III. CONCLUSION (xiii. 18–25)

The author requests prayer on his behalf, especially that he might the sooner be able to return to the readers, and follows this with a moving benediction, which passes into a doxology. A final appeal to the readers, a reference to Timothy, greetings from some Italian Christians and a brief benediction then close the Epistle.

CHAPTER TWO

THE EPISTLE OF JAMES

This is the first of the Catholic or general Epistles, so called because they lack indications of a specific address. It is consequently more difficult in these cases to reconstruct the historical situation to which they belong, which in itself opens the way for a variety of conjectures. Yet a careful criticism is not left without some indication of their circumstances of origin and the effort involved in ascertaining these will be repaid by the greater clarity with which the books will be understood. With the exception of 1 Peter and 1 John the Catholic Epistles have played only a minor part in moulding the thought of the Christian Church and have been largely overshadowed by their more illustrious companion Epistles in the New Testament, notably by the Epistles of Paul. If this is true in the modern Church, it will be no great surprise to find that a similar phenomenon occurred in the ancient Church. This must be borne in mind when surveying the external evidence.

The Epistle of James has suffered much through misunderstandings, the most notable example of which was Martin Luther's oft-quoted description of it as an Epistle of straw. The course of nineteenth-century criticism dealt a further blow against the Epistle and has left in its wake a general inclination to regard James as a product of an inferior Christian outlook in contrast to the strong meat of Pauline theology. Yet while attention to the differences is invaluable for demonstrating the wide variety of early Christian religious experiences, the Epistle of James can be rightly understood only within the context of the whole New Testament Scriptures. Its contribution is very different from that of Paul's letters and yet it was a true instinct that led the Church to include it in its Canon, for it represents an age of transition, without knowledge of which our appreciation of early Christian history would be the poorer and our grasp of ethical Christianity incomplete.

I. AUTHORSHIP

a. The external evidence for the Epistle

The earliest Christian writer to mention this Epistle as the work of James was Origen, who also clearly recognized the Epistle as Scripture.

In one of his citations Origen has been thought to imply some doubt,[1] but since on numerous occasions he cites it as Scripture without hesitation,[2] it is highly questionable whether he himself felt any reserve over accepting it. It is to be noted that there is no mention of it in the Muratorian Canon (which also makes no mention of Hebrews and the Petrine Epistles), but this may be due to the obviously corrupt state of the text of that Canon and little weight may, therefore, be attached to it as an evidence of exclusion from the Canon of the Roman Church. Yet it may be significant that the African Canon also omits this Epistle.

The evidence of Eusebius is interesting, for, although he classes it among the disputed books (*Antilegomena*), he cites it as if it were genuine.[3] He mentions that the Epistle of James was said to be by the Lord's brother, but that some regarded it as 'spurious'.[4] All that may certainly be deduced from this is that not all Christians of Eusebius' acquaintance regarded it as authentic. His own practice would seem to reveal his personal approach to the Epistle, but it is just possible that in citing it as James', he is merely following conventional procedure,[5] for he says, 'But nevertheless we know that these have been publicly used with the rest in most churches.' What hesitancy there was at this time may well be accounted for by uncertainty over the identification of 'James'.[6] Jerome similarly voices some uncertainty over it and in one place regards it as published by another in the name of James, the Lord's brother,[7] and yet he also cites from it as from Scripture. Another evidence unfavourable to the authenticity of James is its omission from the early Syriac Canon.[8]

The problem is to know what inferences to draw from this evidence. There are two possibilities. It may either be supposed that the doubts

[1] In his commentary on the Gospel of John, he mentions James with the formula, ὡς ἐν τῇ φερομένῃ Ἰακώβου ἐπιστολῇ ἀνέγνωμεν (on Jn. xix. 6).

[2] Cf. *Ad Rom.* iv. 1 and *Hom. in Lev.* ii. 4. Cf. also *Hom. in Josh.* vii. 1.

[3] J. B. Mayor (Epistle of James,[3] 1913, p. xlix) cites *Eccl. Theol.* ii. 25, iii. 2; *Comm. in Psalm*, p. 648 Montf. (as Scripture) and p. 247 (as by the holy apostle).

[4] Eusebius, *HE*, ii. 23.

[5] Cf. W. O. E. Oesterley, *The General Epistle of James* (*EGT*, 1910), p. 387.

[6] Cf. R. V. G. Tasker, *The General Epistle of James* (1956), p. 19.

[7] In *De Vir. Ill.* ii: 'Jacobus qui appellatur frater Domini . . . unam tantum scripsit epistolam . . . quae et ipsa ab alio quodam sub nomine ejus edita asseritur.' (Cf. Westcott, *On the Canon of the New Testament*,[4] 1875, p. 448.)

[8] It formed a part of the Peshitta but was not included in the statement in the Doctrine of the Addai (cf. Souter, *The Text and Canon of the New Testament*, 1913, pp. 225f.) nor in the Syriac Canonical list dated about AD 400 (*ibid.*, p. 226).

regarding the Epistle are evidence of non-apostolic authorship, in which case the other evidence on this disputed question will be viewed with a disposition against the authenticity of the Epistle. Or else some explanation of the phenomenon may be sought and, if an adequate answer can be given, not only will the internal evidence be more favourably considered, but there will also be a greater inclination to include the traces of the Epistle found before AD 200. These traces have been fully examined by J. B. Mayor,[1] who claimed to find quotations or allusions in Clement of Rome, Pseudo-Clement (2 Clement), the Didache, Barnabas, the Testaments of the XII Patriarchs, Ignatius, Polycarp, Hermas and some of the later second-century Fathers. Even if Mayor's evidence were admitted in detail, this list would need to be adjusted, since few scholars would now date the Testaments in the Christian era. But Mayor's allusions have not commended themselves generally.[2] At the same time, it is probable that much more weight should be given to some, at least, of this evidence than is the usual practice. Especially does this seem true of Clement and Hermas. Yet those who on other grounds conclude for a second-century date for James are bound by that very fact to find some other explanation for the similarities. Some resort to the theory of a common milieu to which James and the other writers are indebted,[3] while others reverse the dependence and maintain that 'James' was acquainted with Clement and Hermas.[4]

The real crux lies in the treatment of this second-century evidence.

[1] Op. cit., pp. li–lxiii. Cf. also G. Kittel, ZNTW, 43 (1950–51), pp. 55–112 for a more recent full examination.

[2] Oesterley (op. cit., p. 386) does not deny the possibility of indebtedness, but considers the similarities are not sufficient to prove it. But many writers, such as J. H. Ropes (A critical and exegetical commentary on the Epistle of St. James, ICC, 1916, pp. 43ff.), neglect this line of evidence altogether. See also E. C. Blackman, The Epistle of James (1957), p. 31, and K. Aland, ThLZ, 69 (1944), col. 102.

[3] Cf. J. Moffatt, ILNT, p. 467; K. Aland, loc. cit.; O. J. F. Seitz (JBL, LXIII, 1944, pp. 131–140; LXVI, 1947, pp. 211–219) explained the connection between James, 1 and 2 Clement and Hermas by the common use of an apocryphal work (probably the same source which is behind 1 Cor. ii. 9).

[4] Moffatt cites Pfleiderer for this view. More recently F. W. Young (JBL, LXVII, 1948, pp. 339–345) has suggested that in the similar treatment of the Rahab story in James and 1 Clement it seems probable that James is the borrower. But even if literary dependence could be established, it could equally well be the other way round. G. H. Rendall's opinion that Clement is a 'born quoter, with little originative gift' (The Epistle of James and Judaistic Christianity, 1927, p. 102) is much to the point here. Cf. also R. J. Knowling, The Epistle of St. James (1904), pp. xlix–li.

Before citing his detailed lists of indirect parallels, J. B. Mayor makes the following comment on the direct evidence for the authenticity of the Epistle (i.e. in more or less formal catalogues) and on the difference in approach between the East and West, the latter being much more tardy in its recognition than the former. 'The difference is easily explained from the fact that the Epistle was probably written at Jerusalem and addressed to the Jews of the East Dispersion; it did not profess to be written by an apostle or to be addressed to Gentile churches and it seemed to contradict the teaching of the great apostle to the Gentiles.'[1] Among others who have maintained the authenticity of the Epistle, the opinion of two may be noted on this point. R. J. Knowling[2] considered that the circumstances of writing presuppose a Jewish Christian reader-circle which would partly explain the obscurity which surrounded the letter in its earlier history, together with the fact that it does not claim apostolic authority. R. V. G. Tasker[3] has drawn attention to the lesser interest in the reproduction of the general Epistles as compared with the specific church Epistles, because the latter were indisputably apostolic. On the whole it is not altogether surprising that this brief Epistle of James was not much quoted in the earliest period, for it did not possess such wide appeal as the more dynamic Epistles of Paul. It is the kind of letter which could easily be neglected as, in fact, the treatment of it in the modern Church abundantly shows and, once neglected, a fertile soil was provided for future doubts, especially at a time when spurious productions were being attributed to apostolic names.

b. The traditional view of authorship

After this brief survey of external attestation it is possible to examine the internal data for the traditional view of authorship with an open

---

[1] *Op. cit.*, p. li.

[2] *Op. cit.*, p. liii. In a similar vein H. F. D. Sparks (*The Formation of the New Testament*, 1952, p. 129) writes, 'The fact that the Epistle is a Jewish-Christian document, whoever wrote it, may have been in itself sufficient to discredit it in the eyes of Gentile Christians; while its essentially practical attitude would inevitably make it seem of little consequence to those whose main interests were theological. Accordingly, its neglect by the early Church is by no means an insuperable barrier to accepting the Lord's brother as the author.'

[3] *Op. cit.*, p. 19. A. Carr (*The General Epistle of St. James*, CGT, 1896, p. ix) regarded the absence of citation as capable of satisfactory explanation on the grounds of the letter's freedom from controversial subjects and its address to a group (i.e. Jewish Christians) which soon lost its specific identity.

mind. There is no conclusive evidence for the late appearance of the Epistle and possibly even some evidence for its early influence.

(i) *The author's self-identification.* The writer introduces himself quite simply as 'James, a servant of God and of the Lord Jesus Christ', but his very simplicity has turned out to be ambiguous; for James is a common name and the accompanying description is not sufficiently distinctive to assist the identification. Any man called James who was engaged in Christian work would fit the description, except for the obvious authority which the writer assumes. Moreover, the Epistle itself does nothing to alleviate this ambiguity. Nevertheless, assuming for the present that this opening address is authentic, there are only two New Testament people known as James who could with much credence come into the picture and even these can be fairly easily narrowed down to one. James, the son of Zebedee, of the apostolic band, has found many supporters in the course of Church history, but he would be ruled out almost certainly by the fact that he was killed by Herod in AD 44 and it is reasonably certain that the Epistle was written later than that. However, there is now general agreement that the opening greeting is intended to point to James, the Lord's brother, who became leader of the church at Jerusalem. The simplicity of the description is in support of this, for it is evident that a well-known James must have been intended, and as far as the biblical record is concerned, the Lord's brother is the only James who appears to have played a sufficiently prominent part in early Christian history.

Thus far there is general agreement, but at this point opinions diverge, for there have been various theories based on the assumption that the James mentioned in the opening greeting was not the true author of the Epistle. Some theories assume that the name is no more than a pseudonym attached to the letter to add a note of authority, while others regard the salutation as a later interpolation and, therefore, as no part of the original writer's design. These alternative theories will be dealt with below,[1] but for the present the not unreasonable assumption will be made that the writer intended to indicate that he really was James, the Lord's brother.[2] To discover whether this is a true assumption, it is necessary to examine carefully the other evidences which support it.

---

[1] See pp. 77ff..

[2] K. Baltzer and H. Köster (*ZNTW*, 46, 1955, pp. 141f.) suggest, on the basis of a reference in Hegesippus, that James was called Obadiah, that 'the servant' clause in Jas. i. 1 may have some connection with Ob. i. 1 (LXX).

(ii) *The author's Jewish background.* That the author's mind has drawn much from the Old Testament can hardly be denied. Admittedly the direct quotations number only five (cf. i. 11, ii. 8, 11, 23, iv. 6), three from the Pentateuch, one from Isaiah and one from Proverbs. Yet the indirect allusions are innumerable (cf., e.g., i. 10, ii. 21, 23, 25, iii. 9, iv. 6, v. 2, 11, 17, 18).[1] When the writer requires illustrations for prayer and patience he turns to Old Testament characters. His approach to ethical problems and his denunciations and warnings find striking parallels in the Old Testament prophetical books. He appears as a kind of Christian prophet.

There are many other less obvious indications of a Jewish mind. There are traces of Hebrew idioms behind the Greek forms of language; there are instances of the well-known Hebrew love of assonance; there are expressions which are reminiscent of Hebrew fullness of speech; and there are instances of the Hebrew prophetic style.[2] To cite this as evidence of Jewish background is not to prejudge the further question of the Epistle's original language (see discussion below, p. 90). It merely shows that the author's mind was fully at home with Jewish methods of thought and expression.

The description of the addressees in terms of the Jewish Diaspora is a further corroboration of the view that the author was a Jew, whatever be the meaning of James' expression, which is further discussed in the section dealing with destination. Certain other terms such as 'Lord of Sabaoth' (v. 4) would come much more naturally to a Jew than to a Greek. Moreover, the author refers to Jewish formulae when writing about oaths, stresses the Jewish law (ii. 9–11, iv. 11, 12) and mentions the major constituent of the Jewish creed, i.e. the unity of God (ii. 19).

From this evidence, it seems conclusive that the author was a Jew, and that there is no reason to suppose that James, the Lord's brother,

---

[1] Mayor (*op. cit.*, pp. lxix ff.) finds parallels from the following books: Genesis, Exodus, Leviticus, Numbers, Deuteronomy, Joshua, 1 Kings, Job, Psalms, Proverbs, Ecclesiastes, Isaiah, Jeremiah, Ezekiel, Daniel and seven minor prophets. In addition there are parallels with the Wisdom literature. Some scholars have maintained the author's literary dependence on these latter books (particularly Wisdom and Ecclesiasticus). Cf. A. Plummer, *St. James* (*Exp. Bib.*, 1891), p. 74 and R. J. Knowling, *op. cit.*, pp. xv, xvi. It must, however, be recognized that James' spiritual standpoint is much superior to that of the authors of these Wisdom books. Cf. G. Salmon (*INT*, p. 465) and J. H. Ropes (*op. cit.*, pp. 18, 19) against James' close knowledge of these books.

[2] For details of all these characteristics, see Oesterley, *op. cit.*, pp. 393–397.

must be excluded. But the following considerations are more posi-
tively in support of the traditional theory of authorship.

(iii) *Similarities between James and the Acts.* That there are some parallels
between this Epistle and the speech and letter attributed to James in the
Acts is indisputable. These deserve mention in detail because of their
significance. Χαίρειν ('greeting') is used both in James i. 1 and in the
letter recorded in Acts xv. 23 and elsewhere only in Acts xxiii. 26.
'The honourable name by which you are called' (Jas. ii. 7) reminds us
of Acts xv. 17. The exhortation to the 'brethren' (ἀδελφοί) to hear is
found in both James ii. 5 and Acts xv. 13. Parallels are found in the
case of isolated words such as:

ἐπισκέπτεσθε (Jas. i. 27; Acts xv. 14)
ἐπιστρέφειν (Jas. v. 19, 20; Acts xv. 19)
τηρεῖν (or διατηρεῖν) ἑαυτόν (Jas. i. 27; Acts xv. 29)
ἀγαπητός (Jas. i. 16, 19, ii. 5; Acts xv. 25).

These parallels are remarkable in that they all occur within so short a
passage attributed to James in Acts and because they are of such a
character that they cannot be explained by the common accidents of
speech.[1]

Yet these data cannot at once be claimed as conclusive evidence of a
common mind behind the respective passages, since all scholars would
not admit the verbal correctness of the Acts speeches, and if what is
preserved in Acts xv is composed in the author's own words (i.e. Luke's)
it could not support our present argument. To discuss the Acts speeches
at this point is not possible, but even on the supposition that Luke is not
giving the *ipsissima verba* of James, it still remains remarkable that he
has happened to preserve these parallels. It is, of course, a possible
explanation that the author of Acts has reproduced echoes from James,
which would necessitate the theory that he attempted to conform his
speeches and letters to the style of known models, but the parallels are
of too incidental a kind to make this at all likely. It is no more probable

[1] Tasker (*op. cit.*, p. 26) is cautious against placing too much weight on these
resemblances, because resemblances between James' speech and other New
Testament books could be cited where similarity of authorship is not in question.
But if, on other grounds, similarity of authorship may be presupposed, as for
instance in tradition, the resemblances would naturally possess more weight. On
the other hand, not all scholars admit the force of the parallels at all (e.g. McNeile-
Williams, *INT*, p. 209, explain them away).

that the author of James (assuming now a later writer) included in his pseudonymous Epistle echoes from the letter of James in Acts, for this was generally contrary to pseudepigraphic procedure. It may reasonably be maintained, therefore, that this evidence from Acts, while not conclusive, is yet corroborative of the traditional view of authorship.

(iv) *Similarities with the teaching of Jesus*. Again the parallels are of such a character that the more notable of them deserve special mention, particularly as there are more parallels in this Epistle than in any other New Testament book to the teaching of our Lord in the Gospels. The following passages are compared with the Sermon on the Mount:

    i. 2. Joy in the midst of trials (cf. Mt. v. 10–12).

    i. 4. Exhortation to perfection (cf. Mt. v. 48).

    i. 5. Asking for good gifts (cf. Mt. vii. 7ff.).

    i. 20. Against anger (cf. Mt. v. 22).

    i. 22. Hearers and doers of the Word (cf. Mt. vii. 24ff.).

    ii. 10. The whole law to be kept (cf. Mt. v. 19).

    ii. 13. Blessings of mercifulness (cf. Mt. v. 7).

    iii. 18. Blessings of peacemakers (cf. Mt. v. 9).

    iv. 4. Friendship of the world as enmity against God (cf. Mt. vi. 24).

    iv. 10. Blessing of the humble (cf. Mt. v. 5).

    iv. 11, 12. Against judging others (cf. Mt. vii. 1–5).

    v. 2ff. Moth and rust spoiling riches (cf. Mt. vi. 19).

    v. 10. The prophets as examples (cf. Mt. v. 12).

    v. 12. Against oaths (cf. Mt. v. 33–37).

In these instances the common ideas are obvious enough, but it is noticeable that nowhere does James cite the words of the Lord. There is no proof, therefore, of dependence on the Gospel of Matthew.[1] The parallels suggest rather that James is reproducing reminiscences of oral teaching which he had previously heard.[2]

[1] M. H. Shepherd (*JBL*, LXXV, 1956, pp. 40–51) disagrees with this judgment. He finds eight main discourses in James, all of which show parallels with, although no citations from, Matthew. He concludes that the author (a second-century writer) knew Matthew probably through hearing it read in church.

[2] Cf. Feine-Behm, *op. cit.*, p. 239; G. Kittel, *ZNTW*, 41 (1942), pp. 91ff. Owing to the omission of the chief motives which produced the Synoptic Gospels, Ropes (*op. cit.*, p. 39) maintained that James in religious ideas is nearer to the collectors of the sayings of Jesus than to the Gospel authors themselves. But his distinction is somewhat arbitrary. E. Lohse (*ZNTW*, 47, 1956, pp. 1–22) disagrees with Kittel and maintains that the method of making allusions to the Lord's words is similar

In addition to these parallels there are others from different parts of our Lord's teaching, such as the following:

i. 6. Exercise of faith without doubting (cf. Mt. xxi. 21).

ii. 8. Love to one's neighbour as a great commandment (cf. Mt. xxii. 39).

iii. 1. On the desire to be called teacher (cf. Mt. xxiii. 8–12).

iii. 2f. On the dangers of hasty speech (cf. Mt. xii. 36, 37).

v. 9. The Divine Judge at the doors (cf. Mt. xxiv. 33).

It will be noted that all the parallels so far quoted are from Matthew's Gospel, and this fact must be given due weight in discussions on the relationship between the two books, but some of these parallels are found also in Mark and still others might be cited from Luke.[1] The cumulative effect of this evidence must be in favour of the presumption that the author was in close touch with the teaching of Jesus.[2] It should, moreover, be observed that these parallels are not produced in any mechanical way, but with a real understanding of the point of view from which our Lord proclaimed His teaching.[3] This means that they are more than merely linguistic similarities, which would in themselves prove inconclusive.

to that found in the *Didache* and is no evidence, therefore, for an early dating (similarly K. Aland, *op. cit.*, cols. 103, 104). But it certainly does not exclude an early dating.

[1] K. Aland (*op. cit.*, cols. 99, 100) maintains that James is indebted to Lk. iv. 25f. for his reference to the three and a half years of rainlessness in Elijah's time, but he uses this as an argument for a late date. But who is to say that James did not hear our Lord speak these words? After all, they are set in the synagogue of Nazareth. B. H. Streeter (*The Primitive Church*, 1929, p. 193) suggested that James in his Sermon on the Mount allusions is nearer Luke than Matthew, and probably used the same recension of Q as did Luke.

[2] The view of O. Cone ('James (Epistle)', *Enc. Bib.*, 1914, col. 2322) that the evangelic tradition had made only an indistinct impression upon the writer's mind is clearly refuted by the facts. McNeile-Williams (*INT*, p. 208) minimize the closeness of the connections even with the Sermon on the Mount and suggest dependence on some variant oral tradition.

[3] Knowling has an illuminative comment on this fact. He writes of the Sermon on the Mount, 'In the Sermon and in the Epistle, the meaning of the old Law is deepened and spiritualised and the principle of love is emphasised as its fulfilment; in each, righteousness is set forth as the doing of the Divine Will in contrast to the saying, "Lord, Lord!"; . . . in each, God is the Father, Who gives liberally every good and perfect gift, the God Who answers prayer, Who delivers us from evil, Who would have men merciful as their Father is merciful; in each, Jesus is Lord and Judge . . .' (*op. cit.*, pp. xxi, xxii).

(v) *Agreements with the New Testament account of James.* Our first introduction to James, the Lord's brother, is as an unbeliever in the claims
of Jesus (cf. Mk. iii. 21; Jn. vii. 5). But it was not a hostile unbelief. He
probably had great respect for Jesus, but could not agree with His
methods and as yet had no understanding of the significance of His
mission.[1] It was the resurrection which caused the change, for not only
do we find that the Lord's brethren were mentioned among the disciples (Acts i. 14), but that James was specially singled out for a resurrection appearance (1 Cor. xv. 7). Probably James told Paul about it
when they met (Gal. i. 19). It is significant that Paul, in referring to him,
implies that James was numbered among the apostles; in fact he names
him among the three pillars of the Jerusalem church.

When he presided at the all-important Jerusalem Council, there is no
doubt that he held a commanding position in the local church, taking
precedence even over Peter. Yet, at the same time, no specific office is
ascribed to him and it is probably an anachronism to call him bishop of
Jerusalem. Nonetheless the authority with which he addressed the
church on that occasion (Acts xv. 13ff.) is in full agreement with the
tone of authority which the author of the Epistle assumes in his salutation.[2] The same is true of the account of Paul's final visit to Jerusalem,
when James alone is mentioned by name among the elders of the church.
Moreover, Paul accedes to James' request (or was it a command?) to
observe a Jewish vow.

These incidents point to an important characteristic about James,
which became elaborated in Christian tradition.[3] He was still devoted
to the law and zealous for the continuance of Jewish ritual requirements.
His outlook was correspondingly limited. The full freedom of the
gospel had not yet reached him. He lived in an age of transition.[4] It is

[1] See Mayor, *op. cit.*, pp. xlv, xlvi.

[2] T. Henshaw (*New Testament Literature in the Light of Modern Scholarship*, 1952,
p. 359) denies that the author writes with authority, for he claims that he says
nothing for which he could not find warrant in previous authorities.

[3] For the evidence from tradition, cf. Tasker, *op. cit.*, pp. 27, 28.

[4] Cf. G. H. Rendall, *op. cit.*, pp. 110ff. for a concise account of James' position.
G. Kittel (*ZNTW*, 30, 1931, pp. 145–157) considered that James was not a fanatical
Jew and that he disagreed with the ritualistic Jewish Christian party. He was a
moderate, as the account of the Apostolic Council shows and was not, therefore,
a zealous opponent of Paul. (Cf. also *ZNTW*, 43, 1950–51, pp. 109–112.) But K.
Aland (*op. cit.*, cols. 101–102) disagreed with this opinion on the strength of Acts
xxi and the early Christian tradition.

not surprising, therefore, to find him the author of an Epistle in which many of the cardinal Christian doctrines are not mentioned (see later discussion on this). Nor is it surprising to find him addressing himself in a general manner to Jewish Christians.

(vi) *The conditions within the community*. The problem of the circumstances of the readers will be discussed later, but one aspect of it needs to be mentioned here. The community appears to belong to the period before the fall of Jerusalem. The oppressors are wealthy landowners, who, after the siege of Jerusalem, virtually ceased to exist in Judaea, to which district the Epistle is generally thought to have been sent. It was evidently a pressing social evil for the wealthy to extort from the poor and to live luxuriously on the proceeds, a condition of affairs which is well attested in the period leading up to the siege. Certainly the position described in James v. 1–6 would well fit this period[1] and, if so, would be in harmony with the hypothesis that the author was James, the Lord's brother.

Arguments along these lines are bound to be mainly negative, but they can demonstrate that no social conditions are implied in the Epistle which belong to a period later than the life of James, and thus indirectly they may lend support to the traditional authorship. Not all have agreed on the interpretation of these conditions and their objections will be considered below. But there is nothing anachronistic in assigning this Epistle to an early date. In fact, in addition to the social surroundings of the community, the internal conditions of quarrelsomeness among the Christians may well point to an early stage in the history of the community before much maturity had been reached.[2]

Two other considerations point in the direction of an early Jewish origin. The rather abrupt reference to 'wars and fightings' (iv. 1) would have been highly relevant to the explosive conditions of internecine strife in the period just before the siege of Jerusalem. And again the thoroughly Jewish background of the letter is evidenced by the absence of any allusion to masters and slaves and by the omission of any denun-

---

[1] Rendall (*op. cit.*, p. 32) remarked, 'As a mark of time it should be noted that these economic conditions, the day of large land-holders preying upon a burdened peasantry, came to an end with the Jewish War, and point decisively to an earlier date.'

[2] Ropes (*op. cit.*, p. 41), who rejects the traditional view, nevertheless recognizes that the conditions of life indicated in the Epistle need not imply a long lapse since the formation of the churches.

ciation of idolatry, both of which would have been inappropriate in an epistle attributed to such a devoted Jewish Christian as James.[1]

c. Arguments against the traditional view

In spite of the strong tradition, which appears to have early roots, and the many indications from internal data which support the tradition that James, the Lord's brother, was the author, there is a strong body of opinion which rejects this view. The grounds of these objections will now be considered.

(i) *The Greek is too good for a Galilaean peasant.* The style of Greek is generally good and cultured and this fact has been regarded as conclusive against the traditional view. Thus Dibelius makes the categorical statement, 'The style is frequently cultured, the Greek vocabulary large, the entire diction not that of a man whose real language was Aramaic.'[2] While admitting the good quality of the Greek, which has been pronounced by competent authorities to be among the best in the New Testament,[3] some modifications are necessary. Oesterley[4] has drawn attention to some indications of a Hebrew background to the language, while Ropes[5] admitted that the language was Koiné with a biblical tinge. Rendall[6] went so far as to maintain with some cogency that the author's hand 'is not that of a skilled or practised writer, with easy command of his resources or his pen'.

With these modifications regarding the Greek style, the fact still remains that it is paradoxical that one of the most Jewish letters in the New Testament should have been written by an author apparently so much at home in the Greek language, and some sympathy must be felt for the objection that a Galilaean could not have acquired such facility,

---

[1] Cf. on this point, Knowling, *op. cit.*, pp. xii, xiii.

[2] *A Fresh Approach to the New Testament and Early Christian Literature* (1937), pp. 229, 230.

[3] Cf. J. H. Moulton and W. F. Howard, *A Grammar of New Testament Greek*, II (1929), p. 27.

[4] *Op. cit.*, pp. 393–397. Cf. also A. Wikenhauser, *New Testament Introduction*, p. 483.

[5] *Op. cit.*, pp. 24f. A. Wifstrand (*Studia Theologica*, II, 1948, pp. 170–182) considers the language to be that of the hellenized synagogue.

[6] *Op. cit.*, p. 34. In his chapter on 'Form, Style and Composition', Rendall maintained that these indications are fully in keeping with what we know of James.

since his native tongue was Aramaic.[1] Yet this appears to be largely an
a priori argument. It clearly can neither be proved nor disproved that
James, a Galilaean, was incapable of writing this Epistle. It has been
maintained that there was nothing to induce James to learn Greek since
all his dealings appear to have been with Jewish Christians.[2] But this
opinion takes insufficient account of the known bilingual character of
Galilee.[3] There were many Greek towns in that district, and because of
this it must surely be assumed that it was in the power of any Galilaean
to gain a knowledge of Greek.[4] If *a priori* arguments are to be used, it
would be more reasonable to assume that James was bilingual than the
reverse.

Yet the problem still remains whether a peasant could have acquired
sufficient education to write the type of Greek found in the Epistle,
even supposing him to have been bilingual from early years.[5] Rendall
answered emphatically in the affirmative, maintaining that the Jewish
people were the most literary of all the Mediterranean nations and
citing the LXX as evidence of the Jewish adoption of Hellenism.[6]
Oesterley[7] on the other hand admitted the possibility of such learning,
but denied the probability. The question cannot be decided conclusively on *a priori* suppositions. But one consideration would appear to
tip the balance in favour of James being bilingual, and that is his position as leader of the Jerusalem church. Constant travellers to and from
Jerusalem would bring him in touch with people from various parts[8]

---

[1] McNeile-Williams (*INT*, p. 205) put it too strongly when they say, 'Anyone
who knew the early conditions knew that St. James could not have written the
Epistle in its Greek shape and yet it gradually acquired "apostolic" repute.' This
assumes that those responsible for its 'apostolic' status must have been entirely
ignorant of the early conditions, in spite of the fact that most of them were
Greek speaking.

[2] So Oesterley, *op. cit.*, p. 400.

[3] Moffatt (*ILNT*, p. 474) cites J. Hadley, *Essays Philological and Critical* (1873),
pp. 403f., as the best statement of the case known to him. Cf. also Zahn, *INT*, I
(1909), pp. 34–72; J. H. Moulton, *A Grammar of New Testament Greek*, I (1908),
pp. 6ff.; and more recently S. Liebermann, *Hellenism in Jewish Palestine* (1950), pp.
100ff.

[4] J. B. Mayor, *op. cit.*, p. ccxxxvi. A. T. Cadoux's comparison with Burns'
mastery of English is not an exact parallel, but is, at least, suggestive (*The Thought
of St. James*, 1944, p. 37).

[5] Cf. E. Lohse, *ZNTW*, 47 (1956), pp. 19, 20.

[6] *Op. cit.*, p. 39.   [7] *Op. cit.*, p. 399.

[8] Cf. R. V. G. Tasker, *op. cit.*, p. 29; A. Ross, *The Epistles of James and John*
(1954), p. 19.

and the majority of them would undoubtedly be Greek speaking. It may even be argued with some cogency that opportunities for public speaking and debate would develop in him some mastery of the rhetorical style such as vivid illustrations and rhetorical questions.[1] Again there is a reasonable possibility that James may have employed a Greek amanuensis.[2] On the whole, it would seem that not much importance should be attached to the objections based on language and it is significant that most weight is now placed on other considerations.[3]

(ii) *The author does not claim to be the Lord's brother.* It has been maintained that James would surely have described himself in this way in order to add to the authority with which the Epistle would go out to Jewish Christians.[4] But this type of argument is not as valid as at first appears. For the apostle Paul recognized that knowledge of Jesus Christ in the flesh was no longer important (2 Cor. v. 16) and the same consideration would lead the Lord's kinsmen to refrain from claiming any advantages due to family ties with Him. Oesterley[5] imagined that this argument was weakened by the mention in John xix. 25–27 of our Lord's concern for His mother, but the parallel is not obvious. Our Lord's reference to His mother was due to compassion, but a very different motive would have operated if James had mentioned his relationship. His reference to himself as a 'servant' is far more becoming.

(iii) *The author makes no reference to the great events of our Lord's life.* Particularly surprising is the omission of any reference to the death or resurrection of Jesus.[6] Since James is specially mentioned by Paul as a witness of the risen Christ (1 Cor. xv. 7), it might reasonably be expected

[1] Cf. Tasker, *loc. cit.*

[2] G. Kittel (*ZNTW*, 43, 1950–51, p. 79) suggested that James wrote through a Hellenistic Jewish Christian belonging to the primitive Church, possibly from the Stephen circle.

[3] E. C. Blackman (*op. cit.*, p. 26) mentions the excellence of the Greek as a difficulty, but does not discuss. J. H. Ropes (*op. cit.*) laid no weight upon it. But M. Dibelius (*Der Brief des Jakobus*,[10] 1958, pp. 15f.) regarded the Greek as a conclusive objection to an author brought up as a Jew in Palestine.

[4] So Oesterley (*op. cit.*, p. 397), who argues that, for the Dispersion Jews, the more authoritative the author the more effective the letter.

[5] *Ibid.*

[6] On the absence of reference to Christ's death, cf. Ropes, *op. cit.*, p. 33; and on the resurrection, Oesterley, *op. cit.*, p. 398. McNeile-Williams (*INT*, pp. 203, 204) find this a particular difficulty, for they note the absence of the 'personal spell' of Jesus upon the author.

that this event would have made so deep an impression on his mind that he could not have written an epistle of this kind without reference to it. The relevance of this argument must at once be admitted, but there are certain considerations which considerably lessen its weight. In the epistle ascribed to James in Acts xv, there is no reference to any theological tenet, but that letter was sent for a more restricted purpose than this and the parallel is, therefore, somewhat loose. At the same time it is easy to assume that in every Christian communication the great Christian doctrines must appear, without examining sufficiently the basis for this assumption. The author, in this case, obviously assumes his readers' cognizance with these doctrines, otherwise he would have made a point of mentioning them.[1] But the real problem is whether an early Christian writer like James would ever have made such an assumption when writing a general circular.

To explain this phenomenon, reference must be made to the purpose of the letter, which may fairly simply be described as ethical and not doctrinal. It may of course be maintained that for the Christian Church doctrine and practical exhortation are inseparable, but it must be remembered that this view of the matter is drawn mostly from Paul. It is not absolutely certain that all moral exhortations were invariably backed by theological considerations, although it is unquestionable that the dynamic for behaviour proceeded from the Christian's experience of Christ. A fair conclusion of this matter would be that, although it might have been expected that James would have mentioned the death and resurrection of Jesus in his ethical Epistle, it cannot be said to be entirely incomprehensible for him not to have done so.

(iv) *The conception of the law in this Epistle is said to differ from what might be expected from James.* It has been maintained that James' conception of law may be summarized as moral law, whereas from Acts and Galatians we are led to expect that the law for him would involve ritual as well as moral requirements.[2] There is a curious silence regarding the burning question of circumcision with which James was so deeply involved. Yet this will be an embarrassment only if the Epistle is dated during the intensity of the conflict. If the Epistle is dated before the Apos-

---

[1] Unless, of course, he was ignorant of them, but this is highly improbable.

[2] Cf. Blackman, *op. cit.*, pp. 25f. O. Cone ('James (Epistle)', *Enc. Bib.*, 1914, col. 2322) thought that it was very improbable that a writer to Jewish Christians would so entirely ignore the Mosaic law and ritual, but his argument is not self-evident if James' purpose was wholly ethical.

tolic Council (see discussion below), it is not surprising that circumcision is not mentioned, for until then it seems to have been taken for granted.[1] The picture of James drawn from Acts and Galatians is naturally influenced by the conflict over Hellenistic Christianity, but it must be remembered that in both sources James is represented as a leader of conciliatory action and by no means as a bigot for Jewish ritualistic demands. That James' position was misrepresented in tradition is not surprising since Peter's clash with Paul seems to have been occasioned by 'certain men from James' (Gal. ii. 12), and it is not altogether improbable that these men were more zealous for legal observances than their leader. Even in the account of Paul's meeting with James in Acts xxi. 18ff., James suggests the vow, not on the grounds of strong personal conviction, but because of avoiding offence among the many thousands of Jews who had become Christians. It was a matter of expediency.

In view of this it should occasion no surprise that James does not raise the matter in an epistle which is almost wholly ethical. Moreover, the approach of James to the moral law is closely linked to the teaching of Jesus on the same theme. It is precisely the type of ethical instruction to be expected from a Jewish Christian about the mid-first century, especially from a man so closely acquainted with the moral teaching of Jesus as James must have been.[2]

(v) *The author's relation to other New Testament books is said to be unfavourable to James, the Lord's brother.* There are parallels between this Epistle and some of Paul's Epistles (1 Corinthians, Galatians, Romans)[3] and 1 Peter. Only those who maintain literary dependence on the part of the author of this Epistle find difficulty here over the authorship, mainly on the grounds of dating, on the assumption that James must be considerably later than the Epistles he is citing, particularly if the Pauline Corpus

---

[1] K. Aland (*op. cit.*, p. 100) considers that the absence of ritualism from a Jewish Christian before the mid-first century is unthinkable. But the omission of allusions to it need not mean that James has dispensed with it entirely.

[2] Cf. Feine-Behm, *op. cit.*, p. 244. It is interesting to note that earlier critics of authenticity often based their late dating of James on the mistaken grounds that it presents Christianity as a *nova lex* (cf. Knowling's criticisms, *op. cit.*, p. lxii).

[3] Cf. J. Moffatt, *ILNT*, p. 466; W. Sanday and A. C. Headlam, *The Epistle to the Romans* (1895), p. lxxviii. J. B. Mayor (*op. cit.*, p. lxxxix) also adds some parallels with 1 Thessalonians, 2 Corinthians, Philippians, Colossians, Ephesians, and the Pastorals.

of letters is already in existence. In the case of Paul, the most notable parallel is the faith versus works debate and much will clearly depend on whether Paul corrects James (or a misunderstanding of him) or vice versa. Many notable names may be cited in support of both these possibilities, for the whole subject has been very thoroughly discussed.[1] It is both impossible and unnecessary to repeat the main points of the discussion, but, on the whole, probability favours rather more the view that Paul is acquainted with a perversion of the kind of teaching proposed by James than that James is safeguarding against a perversion of Paul. If this view is correct, any objection to James' authorship would at once be removed, but since the alternative is not impossible, it needs to be considered whether such a viewpoint must exclude the possibility of James' authorship.

There are no sure grounds for supposing that James could not have known Paul's teaching on faith as the sole means of salvation, nor even that he could not have been acquainted with the Epistle to the Romans. The data available do not allow any such conclusion to be reached. The same may be said of allusions to other Pauline Epistles, although, if James' dependence on these could be established, it would support a later date for James and make authorship by the Lord's brother more difficult.

In short, the arguments based on literary dependence are really arguments which are assumed to prove a late date and would support the assignment of the Epistle to the sub-apostolic period. A case in point is the alleged dependence of James on 1 Peter, which, if established, would make an early date for James difficult to maintain on the basis of the authenticity of 1 Peter. But it would naturally be impossible for those who hold to the non-apostolic authorship of Peter to maintain the apostolic authorship of James. The dependence of James on 1 Peter is by no means certain, but there are undoubtedly several parallels as the following will show:

James i. 1; 1 Peter i. 1	James iii. 13; 1 Peter iii. 2, 4
James i. 2f.; 1 Peter i. 6f.	James iv. 1; 1 Peter ii. 11
James i. 12; 1 Peter v. 4	James iv. 6f.; 1 Peter v. 5f.
James i. 18; 1 Peter i. 23	James iv. 10; 1 Peter v. 6.
James i. 21; 1 Peter ii. 1f.	

[1] For details of some representative treatments, see footnote [1] on p. 89.

But although the majority of scholars favour the priority of 1 Peter,[1] some, such as J. B. Mayor,[2] argue strongly for the reverse, while yet others, such as J. H. Ropes,[3] prefer to appeal to a common spiritual atmosphere.

It is better not to depend on arguments based on literary use of other Epistles in cases where the evidence leaves room for wide variations of opinion, and little real weight can, therefore, be put on the objection under consideration.[4] The same may be said regarding parallels with *Clement* and *Hermas*, but in these cases probability is certainly more on the side of the priority of James than vice versa, as has already been seen.[5] The theory that James is based almost wholly on secondary material is highly questionable[6] and even if it be held that James echoes other New Testament books, the most that could be supposed with certainty is that the author possessed a mind receptive of common Christian ideas. It would help very little in deciding the question of authorship.

(vi) *The external evidence is said to raise suspicions against the tradition.* This objection has been left until last, although it is invariably the jumping-off ground for criticism of the tradition. But it has already been discussed and some plausible explanations of the tardy reception of the Epistles suggested (see p. 63). Because of this, the argument cannot be considered conclusive either way, like so many of the other details, although it would naturally carry weight if the cumulative effect of other evidence should be felt to point towards non-authenticity.

d. Alternative theories regarding the origin of the Epistle

Some account must now be given of the ideas advanced by those who dispute the traditional ascription of the Epistle. There are six different theories which come to our notice.

(i) *That the Epistle is pseudonymous.* It has been proposed that the ascription to James is a literary device used by the original writer, who

---

[1] Cf. Moffatt, *ILNT*, p. 338; McNeile-Williams, *INT*, p. 211.

[2] *Op. cit.*, pp. xcviii f. Cf. R. J. Knowling (*op. cit.*, p. xlvi) and F. Spitta (*Der Jakobbrief*, in *Zur Geschichte und Literatur des Urchristentums*, II, 1896, pp. 183–202), who even suggested that 1 Peter has used James as a model.

[3] *Op. cit.*, p. 22. Many scholars, not surprisingly, admit uncertainty about the relationship.

[4] Mayor (*op. cit.*, p. xciii) suggested that Heb. xi was written with the Epistle of James in mind, and if this view is correct it would support an early date.

[5] See p. 62.   [6] As T. Henshaw, *op. cit.*, pp. 352ff., appears to hold.

was an unknown teacher of the sub-apostolic age. In support of this the widespread practice of using pseudonymous ascriptions in the early Christian period is usually appealed to, or else the unknown writer is supposed to have had the same relation to James as had the author of Mark's Gospel to Peter.[1] The former alternative is defective because of the lack of any close epistolary parallels,[2] while the latter may be questioned as an inaccurate analogy. Mark's connection with Peter is well attested and his position as 'interpreter' unquestionable, but even so his work was not issued under Peter's pseudonym, nor was it ever later ascribed to him. The most damaging criticism of this kind of theory lies in the simplicity of the description of the author and in the lack of an adequate motive. Had the real author wished to indicate beyond dispute that he was interpreting or recording the actual teaching of James, the Lord's brother, why did he leave the title so ambiguous? Ropes[3] attempted an answer by supposing that during the first and second centuries a letter in the name of James would seem to the Christian public to be claiming the authority of the great James, and no further identity would, therefore, be needed. But it was not the usual practice of pseudonymous writers to play down their heroes—rather the reverse.[4]

The absence of motive for a pseudonymous production such as James is a strong argument against it. If the letter is merely a moralizing tract, why did it need James' authority and why should he be chosen?[5]

[1] So McNeile-Williams, *INT*, p. 205: 'If he was the "interpreter" of St. James it is easy to understand how the latter's name was adopted by the writer.'

[2] See the present writer's *New Testament Introduction: The Pauline Epistles* (1961), pp. 282ff. Cf. also his article on the general dilemma confronting hypotheses of pseudonymity in *Vox Evangelica* (ed. R. P. Martin, 1962).

[3] *Op. cit.*, p. 51.

[4] Rendall (*op. cit.*, p. 106) argued against the pseudonymous theory on the grounds that no-one would have issued an epistle under James' name unless he was already known as a letter-writer. Knowling (*op. cit.*, p. xxiv) cites a spurious epistle which commenced, 'James, bishop of Jerusalem'. J. Marty (*L'Epître de Jacques*, 1935, p. 249), who upheld the pseudonymity theory, explained the absence of any other identification allusions by appealing to the paraenetic nature of the contents (as in the *Epistle of Barnabas*).

[5] A. T. Cadoux rightly mentioned that James' name would not have retained interest among Gentiles for long and this must constitute a difficulty for any pseudonymity theory (*op. cit.*, p. 38). The best that H. von Soden could suggest was that the author may have known and venerated James, the Lord's brother, or perhaps the orthodox had to reclaim James from the Ebionite appeal to his authority (*JPTh*, 10, 1884, p. 192).

And if James intends to oppose Paul, why is there no greater stress on his authority?

(ii) *That the Epistle was an anonymous production later attributed to James.* To avoid the difficulties of an intentional pseudonymity, some scholars have proposed that the attribution to James belongs to a later stage in the history of the Epistle.[1] While this theory is more conceivable than the theory of pure pseudonymity, it avoids few of the difficulties of the latter, and creates new difficulties of its own. It now becomes necessary to account for the ascription. The best that can be done is to imagine that certain Christians thought the anonymous tract was of such value that the Church ought to class it among its apostolic books and the only way possible was to attach to it an apostolic name. But this whole theory is highly artificial, for it is difficult to believe that the churches generally would have been prepared to receive a work merely because it bore a name which could be apostolic. In the period when spurious apostolic works began to be prolific, particularly in support of Gnostic ideas, the vigilance of the Church was much too intense to allow such a work as James to slip through its net. The mere fact that doubts were expressed over James in the third century is evidence enough that many were very guarded about the books to be authorized.

(iii) *That the Epistle was by some other 'James'.* This is closely akin to the last, but rather more plausible. James was a common name and it might well have happened that some later James wrote the Epistle and that he was subsequently mistaken for James of Jerusalem. This theory was mooted by Erasmus[2] and has been maintained by many since.[3] But the absence of any early evidence for it seems distinctly unfavourable to it. An unknown writer, whose name was James, would surely have realized that his readers would confuse him with the well-known James and, unless he intended such confusion, would have given more specific description of his own identity. This type of theory does not carry with it much conviction.

[1] For instance A. C. McGiffert, *A History of Christianity in the Apostolic Age* (1897), p. 585. He thought the form of ascription was influenced by Jude. L. E. Elliot-Binns (*Galilean Christianity*, 1956, pp. 47ff.) maintains this type of theory although claiming a very early date for the Epistle. He thinks that the ascription was added in Jewish Christian and Ebionite quarters to exalt James at Peter's expense.

[2] Cited by Moffatt, *ILNT*, p. 472.

[3] A modern treatment of this view may be found in D. W. Riddle and H. H. Hutson's *New Testament Life and Literature* (1946), pp. 198ff.

(iv) *That the Epistle was originally a Jewish document.* Because of the strong Jewish background of the Epistle, it has been maintained by F. Spitta[1] and L. Massebieau[2] that the major part of the letter is pre-Christian. A later author has Christianized this material by the addition of the name of Christ in i. 1 and ii. 1. But this theory may be criticized on the following grounds:

1. It is incredible that the Christianizing process would have been confined to such meagre modifications and, in any case, the text in both these instances does not lead us to suppose an interpolation.[3]

2. It is a forcing of the evidence to maintain, as Spitta does, that it is more reasonable to find the antecedents of James' teaching in Jewish moral teaching than in the Sermon on the Mount. As Mayor[4] has cogently pointed out, in most of Spitta's parallels the Jewish material shows far less resemblance to James than the Christian material, but the reverse would be necessary if Spitta's theory were right.

3. The Epistle is not marked by distinctively Jewish teaching. In other words it does not require a non-Christian Jew as its author. A Jewish Christian could quite well have written it and there is, therefore, no evidence to support the theory of pre-Christian origin.

4. The whole Epistle breathes a Christian spirit, in spite of the absence of specific Christian doctrine. Had Spitta given more attention to this, he would not have conceived an interpolator who was content with two brief insertions.

Many scholars who have not shared Spitta's viewpoint have nevertheless been indebted to him for drawing attention to the Jewish background of James' thought.

(v) *That the Epistle was patterned on the twelve patriarchs.* This is the theory proposed by Arnold Meyer.[5] The idea is that an earlier author had produced an allegory on Jacob's farewell address to his twelve sons

---

[1] *Op. cit.*, pp. 1ff.

[2] 'L'Epître de Jacques, est-elle l'oeuvre d'un Chrétien?' in *RHR* (1895), pp. 249–283. *N.B.* More recently M. E. Boismard (*RB*, LXIV, 1957, p. 176n.) writes rather favourably of a Jewish origin. He maintains that in this letter Κύριος always refers to God, not Christ.

[3] Cf. Ropes, *op. cit.*, p. 32; and Tasker, *op. cit.*, p. 34.   [4] *Op. cit.*, pp. clxxv ff.

[5] *Das Rätsel des Jakobusbriefes* (1930). Cf. also W. K. Lowther Clarke's comparison of James with the *Testament of the XII Patriarchs*, *Concise Bible Commentary* (1952), pp. 914, 915. H. Thyen (*Der Stil der jüdisch-hellenistischen Homilie*, 1955, pp. 14–16), who favours Meyer's view, supposes that a Jew has summarized a synagogue homily on the theme of Jacob's address to his sons.

and that this has been adapted for Christian purposes. The ascription to James is traced to 'Jacob', who addresses the twelve tribes. The moral teaching of the Epistle is then connected with the various patriarchs. One or two examples will illustrate. The theme of joy (i. 2) is connected with Isaac, patience (i. 3, 4) with Rebecca, the passage on hearing (i. 19–24) with Simeon. These connections of thought are not only generally far from obvious, but in most cases so extremely subtle that the point of them would never be conceived by any but devotees of the allegorical method.

Ingenious as the theory is, its very ingenuity is its greatest barrier. As Tasker[1] aptly remarks, 'At least we might have expected that the author would have given his readers some clue as to what he was really doing; and how strange it is that Christendom should have had to wait so long for the key to the understanding of his purpose!' There are far easier ways to account for the ascription to James than this connection with Jacob, and it would be wiser to leave allegory alone when attempting to discover the origin of the Epistle, unless there is some indisputable indication that it was intended so to be understood. But such certain hints are lacking.[2] Moreover, it would be strange indeed to discover allusions to Job and Elijah in a testament of Jacob, although such anachronistic lapses are not entirely unknown in Jewish pseudepigrapha.[3] But it is not to be expected in such a writing as this Epistle, which does not look ahead as all the Jewish apocalypses did.

(vi) *That the Epistle incorporates some genuine material.* An attempt to mediate between the traditional view and the various alternatives so far outlined is found in the idea that an editor has worked over, adapted and added to an original core of genuine material. The genuine core may have been either written or oral, and perhaps consisted of some homily (or homilies) of James, the Lord's brother, which had made an impression upon the editor's mind.[4]

[1] *Op. cit.*, p. 36.

[2] Blackman (*op. cit.*, p. 29), who does not find Meyer's theory convincing, nevertheless considers it a merit that it attempts to indicate a unity in James. But it is hardly a merit if the unity proposed is an artificial one.

[3] Marty (*op. cit.*, p. 255 n.) cites as a parallel the *Testament of Adam* in which David and Judas Maccabaeus are mentioned.

[4] Cf. Rendall (*op. cit.*, p. 33) for one presentation of this type of theory, although it should be noted that he does not fully commit himself on the question of whether James himself or a reporter penned the Epistle.

W. Bieder (*ThZ*, v, 1949, p. 94 n. 2) inclines to a similar view. A more thorough-

This type of theory has many advantages over the previously mentioned proposals, for it can account both for the somewhat disjointed character of the contents and for the tradition connecting the Epistle with James, the Lord's brother. But it cannot adequately account for the adaptation of the material into a letter-form. It is, of course, conceivable that someone recognized the general value of James' homilies and was prompted, therefore, to edit them into a kind of circular under the name of James who, after all, was the true author of the material used. But a thing is not true because it is conceivable, but because the evidence requires it, and this can hardly be said in this case. If the editor was working under the supervision of James himself, this would amount almost to the traditional view. But if he is editing some time later than James' lifetime[1] the problem of motive becomes acute, for why a later editor should suddenly have conceived such a publication plan when the great majority of the intended readers must have known that James was already dead is difficult to see, and it is even more difficult to understand how the letter came to be received. If some real connection with James would have been generally recognized, why the need for this theory at all, since it would possess no advantage over the traditional view? It would furnish no better explanation for the tardiness of recognition among the Church's orthodox writers.

e. Conclusion

It would seem preferable to incline to the traditional view on the principle that the tradition has a right to stand until proved wrong. Although some of the arguments for alternative views are strong, yet none of these views has any better claim to credibility than the tradition. In these circumstances the authorship of James, the Lord's brother, must still be considered more probable than any rival.

II. THE ADDRESSEES

During the course of the discussion on authorship, many other questions have been partially answered, and this is one of them. Not only
going editorial theory is advanced by Oesterley, *op. cit.*, p. 405. Cf. also C. M. Edsman (*ZNTW*, 38, 1939, pp. 11–44), who suggested that the author has taken over and combined disparate material, much of it of a Hellenistic provenance (he cites parallels from the Hermetic literature and Clement and Origen of Alexandria). But a Jewish basis is much more probable (cf. L. E. Elliott-Binns, *NTS*, 3, 1957, pp. 148–161, on the background of Jas. i. 18).

[1] So Oesterley, *op. cit.* His tentative suggestion was that a genuine text of James was enlarged by a process of comments upon it.

does the Epistle presuppose an author with a Jewish background, but also readers with the same background. Yet on this latter point some considerable caution must be exercised, for wide differences of opinion exist. There are several possibilities: that the readers were unconverted Jews, or else Christian Jews, or else Hellenists, or else Christians generally, both Jew and Gentile. The most probable of these can be decided only from a discussion of the address of the letter and the circumstances of the readers.

a. The meaning of Diaspora in i. 1

At first sight 'the twelve tribes in the dispersion' (RSV) would seem to point fairly conclusively to Jews. Such an interpretation would be in full accord with the technical Jewish use of the term to describe those of their number living outside Palestine. In this case the addressees would be Jewish Christians scattered throughout the Empire. This interpretation would, of course, fit in well with authorship by James of Jerusalem, and is, in fact, the traditional interpretation.

Yet since in 1 Peter it is necessary to attach a spiritual and not a literal meaning to 'dispersion' (see discussion on pp. 118f.), is it not reasonable to suppose a similar interpretation here? The idea of the Christian Church as the new Israel would make a strong appeal to the early Christians and would arise naturally out of the conviction that the Christian teaching was a continuation of the Old Testament.[1] Moreover it has been pointed out that the twelve tribal divisions of Israel had long since disappeared and must, therefore, be understood metaphorically.[2] But caution must enter here in view of Acts xxvi. 7 and Matthew xix. 28, where the twelve tribes would seem to describe the Jewish people. The difficulty is to decide whether James and 1 Peter both mean the same thing by the word 'dispersion'. While it would be more natural to suppose that they do, it need not necessarily follow, for, unlike James, 1 Peter makes no mention of the twelve tribes. That the idea of a Christian Diaspora was current seems undeniable, but that James thought of it in this sense is not beyond challenge. What other factors, therefore, may be deduced to settle the matter?

[1] J. H. Ropes (*op. cit.*, p. 40) interpreted the word as a reference to the dispersion of Christians generally. So also Moffatt, *ILNT*, p. 464; Marty, *op. cit., ad loc.* J. Schneider (*Die Kirchenbriefe, NTD*, 1961, pp. 3, 4) understands the addressees as Jewish Christians outside Palestine who came under James' jurisdiction.
[2] Cf. E. F. Scott, *The Literature of the New Testament* (1932), p. 211.

b. The circumstances of the readers

The regular meeting-place of the addressees is styled a 'synagogue' (ii. 2) and this at once suggests Jewish Christian groups.[1] The view that Jews and not Christians are being addressed has already been discussed and dismissed, but it is difficult to avoid the impression that the Christians have a Jewish background. James mentions nothing about Christ as Messiah, but this seems to be assumed. Nor does he mention circumcision, which, as already pointed out, would be understandable if the readers were Jewish and the letter was sent before the Council of Jerusalem. Even if sent later, the omission of any reference to circumcision would certainly favour a Jewish, rather than a mixed Jewish-Gentile, group of Christians, unless, of course, the Epistle were dated so late that the controversy was by then forgotten.

It would seem from this Epistle that the believers were mainly poor. The allusions to the rich are more intelligible if these were unbelievers who were on the fringe of the church and were taking advantage of their wealth and influence to intimidate the poor Christians.[2] At the same time rich men must at times have attended the Christian synagogues, otherwise the discussion in chapter ii would not be relevant.

Little is said about church organization, but two allusions are significant. Elders are referred to in v. 14, 15, although in connection with faith healing, not church rule. There also appears to have been a group of people known as teachers (cf. iii. 1), whose duties may have overlapped, but were distinct from, those of the elders. Nevertheless the reference may have nothing to do with a teacher's office, but may merely allude to the process of teaching.

The Christians were people of weak faith, who needed strong exhortations to more consistent Christian living, which accounts for the ethical content of the Epistle. It cannot be denied that the general outlook of the believers was immature, as must often have happened in the primitive period both among Jews and Gentiles. This theory of Jewish Christian immaturity is supported by the apparent zealousness for the law coupled with a failure to practise it (cf. i. 22ff., ii. 8ff.). They had in fact brought into the church many of the failings of Judaism.

---

[1] H. von Soden (*JPTh*, 10, 1884, p. 179) maintained that this word was widespread in the Greek world for gatherings. But the Jewish sense is more natural.

[2] Mayor (*op. cit.*, p. cxvi) considered that oppression by the rich is more intelligible for a Jewish community than a Gentile.

To sum up, it seems better to regard the letter as addressed to Jewish Christians, but the alternative view that Christians generally may be in mind has much to be said for it.[1] (See the discussion on the destination of 1 Peter, pp. 116ff.)

III. DATE

It is obvious that decisions about the authorship will affect opinions about the date. The alternatives are easily stated. If the Epistle was by James, the Lord's brother, it must have been before AD 62,[2] the most likely date for his martyrdom, whereas if some other author wrote it, the only certain fact is that it must have been produced after an interval of some years from James' death. But within each of these alternatives there is room for difference of opinion. Advocates of the traditional authorship may be subdivided into two groups in respect of dating: those who prefer a date before AD 50[3] and those who date it towards the end of James' life.[4] Those who take any other view of authorship vary between late first century and late second century, the majority preferring a date about AD 125. With such wide variation in the results of different investigations, it must be expected that the processes by which these results are attained will in themselves prove somewhat inconclusive. The main evidence appealed to in discussions of dating is as follows:

a. The absence of reference to the fall of Jerusalem

This is naturally a pivotal point in any chronology affecting Jewish people. It has been maintained[5] that any author writing after the event must have made some allusion to it, but this may be questioned on the ground that Christians were not as deeply affected by it as were

[1] Von Soden (loc. cit.) argued that none of the references which appear to indicate Jews can be considered conclusive, since similar evidence would result in the readers of Paul's letters to the Galatians, Corinthians and Romans being declared Jewish.

[2] According to Josephus (Antiquities, xx. 9. 1), although Hegesippus less probably has AD 68 (cf. Eusebius, HE, ii. 23. 18).

[3] Recently by G. Kittel, ZNTW, 41 (1942), following Zahn and Schlatter; H. C. Thiessen, INT, p. 278 (AD 45–48); and A. Ross, op. cit., p. 20. Earlier by J. B. Mayor, op. cit., pp. cxxi ff.; and J. V. Bartlet, The Apostolic Age (1907), pp. 203ff.

[4] The majority of those accepting authorship by the Lord's brother.

[5] So J. B. Mayor, op. cit., p. cxxii.

non-Christian Jews. Nevertheless a Christian Jewish writer (and particularly a Palestinian writer) could hardly have remained entirely unaffected.

In further support of this contention, it may be said that the social conditions reflected in the Epistle distinctly favour a date prior to the siege, after which landowning Palestinian Jews virtually ceased to exist.[1] If the addressees were farther afield this factor would not be so relevant, but even then some reference to the siege might be expected if Jews were being addressed.

b. The absence of reference to the Jewish-Gentile controversy

The author either intentionally ignores this or else is unaware of it and both are inconceivable after it had become a burning issue. This consideration not only favours a date before the fall of Jerusalem, but before the rise of the controversy (i.e. before AD 50). This is admittedly an argument from silence[2] and a perfectly natural explanation might be possible if more data were available. If, for instance, some community were addressed that was exclusively Jewish Christian, the Gentile problem would not yet have arisen. Nevertheless, such a circumstance could hardly be postponed long after the Jerusalem Council.

c. The primitive character of church order

This has already been mentioned above (see p. 84) and it is necessary here to do no more than draw attention to the fact that this favours an early dating. It would support a date within James' lifetime better than a later period.

d. The Jewish tone of the letter

This again has already been discussed. It was used as an argument for an early date by J. B. Mayor,[3] who maintained that it pointed to the earliest possible date after Pentecost. It would certainly be more natural in an early letter and to this extent may be cited in support of a date before AD 50, although it need not exclude a date in the seventh decade.

e. The state of the Christians

The addressees do not appear to be very recent converts. Indeed the condition of the Christians has been thought to point to a date much

---

[1] Cf. Rendall, op. cit., p. 32.   [2] Cf. Tasker, op. cit., p. 31.   [3] Op. cit., pp. cxxiv f.

later than James' lifetime, because the Church has been invaded to such an extent by worldliness.[1] There is, however, bound to be a large subjective element entering into any assessment of this kind of evidence. It has not been unknown for churches to develop the kind of errors to which James alludes after a very brief history and this consideration can really lead us nowhere in determining chronological questions.[2] Moreover, as pointed out already (see pp. 84f.), the social conditions within the community favour an early rather than a late date.

f. Exposure of Christians to persecution

This may at first sight exclude the earliest date mentioned and may, in fact, seem to point to a second-century date (i.e. during Trajan's perse-cution). But the allusions in the Epistle do not require anything differ-ent from the persecution which followed Stephen's death, and the conditions which prompted that Jewish hostility must often have been repeated. Clearly this is another factor that can help little in fixing the date.

g. The relation to other New Testament letters

Here again differences of opinion over the order of priority of James, Paul's Epistles and 1 Peter in particular almost entirely cancel out literary affinities as useful data in fixing the period of publication. If James is used by Paul and Peter, an early date is clearly demanded, but if James is the user, an early date is almost as certainly excluded.[3] In fact it could be argued that time would be needed for copies of Paul's Epistles and 1 Peter to reach James. In cases like this any decisions are almost bound to be influenced by prior considerations and can contri-bute very little on their own merit. It can safely be said that nothing in the parallels with other New Testament books excludes the possibility of a date within James' lifetime, although the evidence might be used in theories of later dating.

h. The relation to the Apostolic Fathers

Some resemblances between James and 1 Clement may be cited as throwing light on dating. The latter appears to cite the former,[4] but

---

[1] Cf. E. F. Scott, op. cit., p. 211.

[2] Mayor (op. cit., p. cxxviii) used as a parallel the fact that faults seem to have existed in most of the primitive churches.

[3] Cf. McNeile-Williams, INT, p. 211.   [4] So Rendall, op. cit., p. 102.

many scholars who date James in Hadrian's reign naturally cannot agree to this order of dependence.[1] Presuppositions again influence decisions and the same may be said of the relation of James to the *Shepherd of Hermas*, although the majority of scholars would agree that James is prior to *Hermas*.[2] It is significant, therefore, that *Hermas* may well be citing James, in which case this would be evidence for the circulation of James in the early second century and for its origin long before *Hermas*. It supplies a further indication of a first-century date.[3]

i. Conclusion

The general drift of these considerations is more in the direction of an early date than a later one and this accords with what has already been said on the subject of authorship. But it is less easy to decide between AD 50 and AD 62 as to the most likely early date. The former has much to be said for it and is probably to be preferred.

IV. PURPOSE

Since there is so little evidence about the precise circumstances of the readers, it is not easy to arrive at any definite conclusion regarding the purpose. One thing, however, is clear. The Epistle is essentially practical and would appear to be designed to correct certain known tendencies in behaviour. Such problems as the true attitude to wealth, the control of the tongue, the approach to oaths, Christian prayer and other practical themes are discussed. They appear to come out of the author's own pastoral experience.

But what light does the faith versus works passage (Jas. ii) throw on the author's purpose? This has already been touched upon above (p. 76) and the suggestion made that Paul in his approach to the matter is counteracting a misunderstanding of James and, if this is correct, it must be clearly understood that James is exposing the fallacy of a dead orthodoxy, i.e. a piety in which profession produces no results. If, on the other hand, James is subsequent to Paul, various other

---

[1] Cf. McNeile-Williams, *op. cit.*, p. 212. Cf. also F. W. Young, *JBL*, LXVII (1948), pp. 339–345.

[2] Cf. Moffatt's discussion, *ILNT*, p. 467. Dibelius (*A Fresh Approach to the New Testament and Early Christian Literature*, 1937, pp. 226f.) classes James in the same literary *genre* as *Hermas*. Cf. also Knowling, *op. cit.*, pp. 1ff.

[3] A very full survey of the relation of James to the Apostolic Fathers will be found in the article of G. Kittel, *ZNTW*, 43 (1950–51), pp. 55–112.

considerations enter into his purpose. Either James writes to counteract a misunderstanding of Paul on the part of some Christians or else he writes independently of Paul and happens to touch upon a matter of burning importance with which Paul had also had to deal.[1] The former encounters difficulties, since James' treatment would not adequately clarify Paul's own teaching. There is, for instance, no reference to the 'works of the law', which would be of special interest to any Jewish Christians affected by Paul's teaching. The second view is possible and should not lightly be dismissed, but some sort of acquaintance of one with the other's teaching would almost be expected, particularly since both Galatians and Acts point to the association of the two men.

Another theory which has recently come to the fore is that James has an anti-Gnostic purpose, the advocates of which theory obviously prefer a second-century date. The main representative of this view is H. J. Schoeps,[2] who finds certain Gnostic catchwords taken up by the author. But the improbability of so late a date has already been shown, while the catchwords might have been partially culled from James' letter.

V. LITERARY FORM AND STYLE

J. H. Ropes made much of the similarity of James to the form of the Greek diatribe, the form used by popular moralists. Characteristics of this style, which he claimed to find in this Epistle, are truncated dialogue with an imaginary interlocutor, the question and answer method, the use of certain set formulae, frequent imperatives, rhetorical questions, apostrophes and many other literary devices to add vividness.[3]

---

[1] On the faith versus works controversy, cf. the following works: for the priority of James to Paul, Mayor, *op. cit.*, pp. lxxxix–xcviii; Rendall, *op. cit.*, pp. 71–83; Carr, *op. cit.*, p. xxxvii; for the view that James corrects a misunderstanding of Paul, P. Feine, *Theologie des Neuen Testaments*[7] (1936), pp. 407f.; G. Kittel, *ZNTW*, 41 (1942), pp. 94ff.; Dibelius, *op. cit.*, pp. 227, 228; against this view, cf. Knowling, *op. cit.*, p. xliv; for the use by both of a common stock of language, cf. Knowling, *op. cit.*, p. xlvi. J. Tielemann (*NkZ*, 44, 1933, pp. 256–270) maintained with much probability that had James written to different readers he might have approximated more closely to Paul.

[2] *Theologie und Geschichte des Judenchristentums* (1949), Excursus I on 'Die Stellung des Jakobusbriefes', pp. 343–349. Cf. also C. M. Edsman, *ZNTW*, 38 (1939), pp. 11–44.

[3] Ropes, *op. cit.*, pp. 12ff. Blackman (*op. cit.*, pp. 23, 24) assumes that the influence of diatribe is now generally admitted.

That certain rhetorical devices are used cannot be gainsaid, but it is another matter to classify the work on this score alone with the Greek diatribe. Indeed, the strong Jewish background, which has already been noted, would exclude the probability of Ropes' view.[1]

The question has been raised whether this Epistle was originally written in Aramaic and was later translated into Greek. It was F. C. Burkitt[2] who strongly advocated this view, but in order to maintain it he had to regard the Greek text as a free translation, in view of its freedom from Aramaisms. The theory was an attempt to provide a *via media* between the traditional view and the alternatives. The language difficulty in the traditional view of authorship is overcome, but the theory puts rather more onus than one would expect on the translator and for that reason has not commended itself. The same is true of W. L. Knox's[3] basic Aramaic document, plus oral reminiscences, plus Hellenistic cultural influences. The editor must have been a man of genius to weld all this together into a unity, which never gives the impression of translation-Greek in any of its parts.

It is worth observing the poetical element in this Epistle, for this may provide an offset to the theory of overmuch Greek influence. Certain features typical of Hebrew poetic style (such as parallelism) are found in the Epistle,[4] and it may be supposed that such poetic forms had made a deep impression on the author long before he wrote his Epistle. It is significant that this same feature is apparent in our Lord's teaching, and it is an interesting conjecture that a love for Hebrew poetic forms may have been particularly encouraged in that Nazareth home.

Some notice must also be taken of the way this letter fits into current New Testament forms of teaching. It is widely held that the early Church made use of contemporary ethical codes for its moral teaching. This is not impossible provided ample allowance is made for Christian interpretation. No doubt some patterns of moral instruction were developed for catechetical purposes and it is highly probable that traces

---

[1] Rendall (*op. cit.*, p. 33) maintained that Ropes pressed his evidence too far Cf. also A. Wifstrand (*Studia Theologica*, II, 1948, pp. 177, 178), who calls Ropes' view 'a grotesque overstatement'. He finds many instances of what he calls 'spontaneous semiticisms', which are quite foreign to the diatribe.

[2] *Christian Beginnings* (1924), pp. 65–70.

[3] *JTS*, XLVI (1945), pp. 10–17. Knox treats the Epistle as a 'collection of Genizah fragments from the church of Pella or even of Jerusalem'.

[4] Cf. A. Carr, *op. cit.*, pp. xli–xlv.

of these have survived in the New Testament writings. What marks James off from the rest is that its ethical teaching occupies the whole Epistle and is not, as in other cases, linked with doctrinal passages. It may well be that some of the types of ethical material which formed an important aspect of catechesis have here been more fully preserved. In other words James is writing as he was in the habit of teaching.[1]

Closely akin to this idea of ethical catechetical patterns is the further idea that traces of a primitive baptismal liturgy may be found. This has been particularly worked out by M. E. Boismard[2] in a comparison between James and 1 Peter, in which he claims to find evidence that both are influenced by earlier, baptismal, stereotyped forms, including hymns.[3] More will be said about this kind of hypothesis in dealing with 1 Peter, but the matter is not easy to assess owing to the lack of data about early liturgies. There is a tendency to read back later practices into the primitive period, and special caution is needed to ensure that this does not happen in this case.

CONTENTS

An analysis of this Epistle is difficult because of the lack of any clearly defined thread of thought running through it. The following scheme merely describes the sections in the order in which they occur.

a. Greeting (i. 1)

James introduces himself and very generally defines his readers.

b. Trials and how to meet them (i. 2–4)

Trials are to be faced joyfully, for they will then have a stabilizing effect on character.

---

[1] Cf. Blackman, *op. cit.*, pp. 13–23. P. Carrington (*The Primitive Christian Catechism*, 1940) and E. G. Selwyn (*The First Epistle of Peter*, 1947, pp. 365–466) have developed the idea of patterns of ethical instruction.

[2] 'Une liturgie baptismale dans la prima Petri: II. Son influence sur l'épître de Jacques', *RB*, LXIV (1957), pp. 161–183. Cf. also J. Cantinat in Robert-Feuillet, *Introduction à la Bible* (1959), II, p. 563.

[3] E.g. Boismard cites Jas. i. 12 as a fragment of such a hymn; also Jas. iv. 6–10, where there is a fairly close parallel to 1 Pet. v. 5–9.

c. Wisdom and how to obtain it (i. 5–8)

James assumes that all true wisdom comes from God and can be received in response to faith. Doubt can lead only to instability.

d. Wealth and how to regard it (i. 9–11)

Its transitory character is insisted upon and therefore it becomes irrelevant for the Christian. Rich and poor arrive at a common level.

e. Temptation and trial distinguished (i. 12–15)

Trials are used of God to develop endurance and lead to reward. But temptation springs not from God but from a man's own evil desires.

f. Good gifts (i. 16–18)

Not only does God send trials, but all perfect gifts. The basic gift of life is provided by His unchangeable will.

g. Hearing and doing (i. 19–27)

When the word is heard and received all that is opposed to God's righteousness must be put away. Hearers of the word are warned of the dangers of not doing and a special explanation is given of the difference between vain and pure religion.

h. Against partiality (ii. 1–13)

The theme of rich and poor recurs, although now it is the Christian attitude towards them that is emphasized. God has chosen the poor to be rich in faith, whereas so often it is the rich who are the oppressors. The royal law of love is in any case opposed to partiality, and those who do not fulfil this law fail in respect of the whole law.

i. Against a barren faith (ii. 14–26)

In this well-known passage James exposes the fallacy of an inoperative orthodoxy. He illustrates from both Abraham and Rahab that the faith which is commended is that which is linked with works. On the other hand, James is not decrying the need for faith, for he assumes this as a basis. He will show his faith in fact by his works.

j. Qualities required in teachers (iii. 1–18)

(i) *Control of speech* (iii. 1–12). A teacher has a great responsibility and should not rush into the task without contemplating the dangers of uncontrolled speech. The tongue is liable to become the most undisciplined member of the body, with the result that the whole is affected. By means of various illustrations James shows the deadly danger of untamed speech and the extraordinary inconsistency with which the same lips can utter blessings and cursings.

(ii) *True wisdom* (iii. 13–18). There is a distinct contrast between a wisdom which results in jealousy and bitterness and that which produces good fruits and which is from above. Those who have the latter are truly the wise and understanding.

k. Dangers (iv. 1–17)

(i) *Human passions* (iv. 1–10). One of the worst manifestations of false wisdom is the unloosing of passion, seen in the outbreak of strife and the tendency to compromise with the world. The antidote is humiliation and submission to God who will exalt those who are truly repentant.

(ii) *Evil speaking* (iv. 11, 12). James attacks the general human failing of being critical of others and points out that those who do this are being critical of the law.

(iii) *Rash confidence* (iv. 13–17). The folly of planning apart from the will of God is vividly described and its tendency to arrogance noted.

l. Warnings to wealthy oppressors (v. 1–6)

James thinks next of those who put all their confidence in riches and who use their wealth as an opportunity to oppress those less fortunate. Such men are denounced in language which recalls the Old Testament prophets.

m. Encouragements to the oppressed (v. 7–11)

The quality most needed is patience, and this is enjoined by reference to the Lord's coming. The farmer awaiting the harvest illustrates the quality, while the prophets and the patriarch Job show how to be patient in the midst of suffering. But its real basis is the compassion of the Lord.

n. Against oaths (v. 12)

The Christian's word should be so unequivocal that oaths become redundant.

o. The power of prayer (v. 13–18)

If a Christian is sick, prayer is enjoined upon the elders of the Church, and the power of such a method is illustrated by appeal to the fervently effectual prayer of Elijah when he prayed for rain.

p. Help for the backslider (v. 19, 20)

A special commendation and reward is promised to those who help others to turn back from the errors of their ways.

CHAPTER THREE

THE FIRST EPISTLE OF PETER

I. THE EPISTLE IN THE ANCIENT CHURCH

No discussion of the value of this Epistle for today can proceed without first establishing its position in the ancient Church. It is against such a background that examination of the problem of authorship must be made, and this in turn affects the dating of the Epistle and the historical situation that it was originally intended to meet.

So strong is the evidence for the use of this Epistle in the early Church that C. Bigg[1] regarded it as proved and maintained that it was considered to be canonical as early as this word had a meaning. There are clear parallels in Clement of Rome's *Epistle to the Corinthians*[2] which would appear to indicate his knowledge and use of this Epistle. Some scholars do not admit the certainty of Clement's borrowing, but J. W. C. Wand[3] has no doubt about it and uses this fact as a basis for his discussions on the date of the Epistle. The traces in Ignatius, *Barnabas* and *Hermas* are more open to dispute, but Polycarp's definite citations from the Epistle can hardly be challenged. Yet he does not cite it as Peter's nor does he mention Peter in his epistle, and this has been taken to infer that he knew it only as an anonymous work, since in the case of Paul's Epistles he twice names the apostle in citations. But it was not Polycarp's normal habit to name his authorities when quoting, and it must therefore be assumed that when he did so there was some special reason. Nor is the reason far to seek, for Paul, unlike Peter, had in fact written to the same church to which Polycarp now addresses his letter and this fact is used as a basis for special appeal. As F. H. Chase[4] has pointed out, the citations from 1 Peter are of a general hortatory type, whereas in the Pauline citations epigrammatic, axiomatic statements are introduced. This may be accounted for by the probability that Polycarp echoes 1 Peter from memory, but in some cases cites Paul's words from manu-

---

[1] *The Epistles of St. Peter and St. Jude* (1901), p. 15.

[2] Cf. Bigg's list of citations, *op. cit.*, p. 8. The authors of *The New Testament in the Apostolic Fathers* (1905), p. 137, however, consider these parallels as not worthy of serious attention.

[3] *The General Epistles of St. Peter and St. Jude* (1934), p. 9.   [4] *HDB*, III, p. 781.

scripts in his possession. Whether this conjecture is probable or not does not, however, alter the fact that Polycarp's omission to cite this Epistle as Peter's is no evidence that he knew it only without its opening address,[1] for it is inconceivable that subsequent to Polycarp's time an epistle already so widely revered and used would have 'acquired' a Petrine authority which it did not previously possess.[2]

By the time of Irenaeus it was often quoted as Petrine. Tertullian and Clement of Alexandria have examples of the same procedure. Others who during the same period witness to the authority of the Epistle are Theophilus of Antioch, the author of the *Letter of the Churches of Vienne and Lugdunum* (Lyons) and the writer to Diognetus.[3] From this evidence it may justly be concluded that the attestation for this Epistle is as strong as for the majority of the New Testament writings. Yet one gap remains to be filled. The Muratorian Fragment omits reference to both Epistles of Peter, and some scholars have supposed that this could only mean that the church of Rome towards the close of the second century did not regard the Epistles as canonical. But at this point the text of the fragment is open to doubt and Westcott's conjecture that we have here a chasm is probably correct.[4] At least the

[1] As A. Harnack maintained, *Die Chronologie der altchristlichen Literatur* (1897), I, p. 463. Cf. also his *1 Clemensbrief*, p. 57n. Wand (*op. cit.*, p. 11) points out the fallacy of Harnack's argument, since *1 Clement* cites the opening greeting of 1 Peter (Introduction to *Ad Cor.*).

[2] There are possibly echoes in the Valentinian *Gospel of Truth*; cf. W. C. van Unnik, *The Jung Codex* (ed. F. L. Cross, 1955), pp. 115ff. It is just possible that Papias knew the Epistle under the name of Peter, but the evidence cannot be regarded as conclusive (cf. F. H. Chase, *HDB*, III, p. 780). Eusebius expressly states that Papias quoted the former Epistle of John and that of Peter (*HE*, iii. 39. 17), and if he is here reflecting a true tradition there is no question that 1 Peter was named as Peter's at a much earlier period than Irenaeus. In view of the fact that no evidence exists to the contrary, it seems reasonable to regard this as authentic tradition.

[3] For details of these witnesses, cf. C. Bigg, *op. cit.*, p. 11.

[4] *On the Canon of the New Testament*[4] (1875), pp. 216, 217. Zahn's conjecture that the reference to the *Apocalypse of Peter* should be omitted and a reference be inserted indicating acceptance of both Epistles of Peter (*Geschichte des neutestamentlichen Kanons*, 1, 1888, pp. 315f.), was strongly criticized by Harnack (*Das Neue Testament um das Jahr 200*, 1889, p. 84) on the grounds that no other evidence exists in the West for 2 Peter being named at this period. But neither Zahn's emendation nor Harnack's criticism is relevant here, since no importance can be attached to an emended text in the history of the Canon, while the omission of any earlier citation of 2 Peter in the West contributes nothing to the evidence for 1 Peter.

clearly corrupted state of the text makes any certain inferences from omissions precarious, and this evidence, or rather lack of it, can hardly offset the widespread authority which the Epistle enjoyed as the foregoing data have proved. Although it may not have been used as freely in the West as in the East, there is no evidence that it was ever disputed.

In spite of the fact that this attestation seems conclusive enough for the authenticity of this Epistle, B. H. Streeter[1] challenged it on the grounds that, if the Epistle was written by Peter in Rome, it would be expected that the Latin churches would most quote it, but this type of argument is fallacious, since it was not sent to the West but to the East.

Our conclusion must be that this Epistle not only exerted a wide influence on early Christian writings, but that it also possessed for them apostolic authority. This makes clear that the primitive Church, as far back as any evidence exists, regarded it as a genuine Epistle of Peter, and thus any discussion of objections to Petrine authorship must sufficiently take account of this fact.

II. AUTHORSHIP

The very great weight of patristic evidence in favour of Petrine authorship and the absence of any dissentient voice raises so strong a presupposition in favour of the correctness of the claims of the Epistle to be Peter's own work that it is surprising that this has been questioned. Yet because some scholars either have wholly rejected the genuineness of the opening address or else have proposed various theories to get over the difficulties which are thought to be involved in the traditional view, it will be necessary to examine these difficulties. The main objections will first be given and then the possible answers to these objections from the point of view of Petrine authorship.[2] Finally, certain

---

[1] *The Primitive Church* (1929), p. 119.

[2] In common with many other parts of the New Testament, 1 Peter came under the fire of criticism in the early nineteenth century mainly on the grounds of its relationship to the Pauline Epistles. (For details, cf. A. F. Walls' Introduction to A. M. Stibbs' *The First Epistle General of Peter*, TNT, 1959, p. 18.) But many other grounds of objection have been raised by such critics as Holtzmann, Jülicher, von Soden, Streeter, Goodspeed, E. F. Scott and F. W. Beare. At the same time the traditional position has been maintained by a steady stream of scholars among whom have been such notable names as Chase, Salmon, Hort, Zahn, Bigg, Selwyn, Michaelis, McNeile-Williams. For this reason it is surprising to find Beare asserting so confidently that the case against the attribution to Peter is

considerations will be mentioned about the difficulties of alternative theories.

a. The objections to apostolic authorship

(i) *Linguistic and stylistic objections.* That the writer was thoroughly at home in the Greek language is admitted by all. The Epistle has a fairly polished style which has been influenced by the Greek of the LXX with which he is intimately acquainted, as is evident not only from his direct citations but also from the many instances where his language is moulded by Old Testament forms. This very fact has proved to some scholars to be a stumbling-block to the acceptance of Petrine authorship. It is suggested that the writer's acquaintance with the LXX is a literary knowledge and not the kind of knowledge that a practising Jew would possess, for he shows no evidence of his religious inheritance such as Paul so clearly shows.[1] The writer's vocabulary is extensive and varied and his command of Greek syntactical usages not inconsiderable.[2] Indeed, his Greek is smoother than that of Paul, who was highly trained in comparison with Peter. And herein lies the main difficulty.

Can such facility in the Greek language be imagined in a Galilaean fisherman, whose native tongue was Aramaic and whose educational background would not dispose towards linguistic ability? F. W. Beare[3] feels the difficulty so keenly that he answers emphatically in the negative. The incidental description of Peter in Acts iv. 13 as 'illiterate' ἀγράμματος is claimed to add weight to this objection, although it should be noted that the more probable meaning of this word in the context is 'not formally trained'.[4] In fact, in the traditional allusions to Peter, he is depicted as needing an interpreter when addressing people whose mother tongue was Greek. The tradition may, of course, be

overwhelming (*The First Epistle of Peter,*[2] 1958, p. 29). This overstatement is justly criticized by J. W. C. Wand ('The Lessons of First Peter', *Interpretation,* IX, 1955, pp. 387–399).

[1] Cf. F. W. Beare, *op. cit.,* p. 27.

[2] Cf. F. H. Chase, *HDB,* III, p. 782, for details. Cf. also J. H. Moulton and W. F. Howard, *A Grammar of New Testament Greek* (1929), II; p. 26; R. Knopf, *Die Briefe Petri und Judä*[7] (1912), p. 16, that only Luke and the author of the Epistle to the Hebrews compares with this author's feeling for Greek style. There are a number of *Hapaxes* in this Epistle.

[3] *Op. cit.,* pp. 28f.

[4] Cf. A. F. Walls, *op. cit.,* p. 24 n. 3.

wrong, but it is strong enough to raise doubts about Peter's facility in the Greek tongue.[1]

(ii) *Historical objections.* A major crux in the attack on Petrine author-ship is the historical situation presupposed in the Epistle. The author is writing to persecuted Christians (cf. 1 Pet. i. 6, ii. 12, 15, iv. 12, 14–16, v. 8, 9), and particularly mentions reproach suffered for the name of Christ. It is therefore supposed that Christianity has now become a crime in itself, as distinct from the mere social nuisance which it was considered to be at an earlier time. This cannot, it is claimed, be out-breaks of mob violence, but official organized opposition to Christi-anity. Yet although the Neronian persecutions were directed against Christians in Rome there is no evidence that such persecution spread to the provinces to which this letter is addressed (i.e. Pontus, Galatia, Cappadocia, Asia and Bithynia). But if the Neronian persecution is ruled out, the Epistle must be dated during either the Domitianic or Trajanic persecutions and in either case this would dispose of apostolic authorship, since Peter, according to tradition, was martyred in the time of Nero.[2]

Moreover, parallels between the situation described in Pliny's correspondence with the Emperor Trajan and that suggested by this Epistle lead some scholars to conclude that the same occasion is in mind.[3]

[1] Cf. R. Knopf, *op. cit.*, p. 17.

[2] Cf. O. Cullmann, *Peter: Disciple, Apostle, and Martyr*, 1953, pp. 89–152, for the evidence of Peter's martyrdom. W. M. Ramsay's view that Peter lived on until near the end of Vespasian's reign (*The Church in the Roman Empire*, 1893, pp. 209f.) has gained no support (but cf. P. Gardner-Smith's article 'I Peter' in *Encyclopaedia Britannica*[14]).

[3] E.g. H. J. Holtzmann, *Lehrbuch der historisch-kritischen Einleitung in das Neue Testament*[2] (1886), p. 494; F. W. Beare, *op. cit.*, pp. 13ff. Cf. J. W. C. Wand (*op. cit.*, p. 15) for details of these parallels. He admits that they are 'powerfully attrac-tive'. No doubt the enquiry of Pliny as to whether the name or the crimes associa-ted with the name was to be the subject of punishment strongly disposes the minds of some scholars to accept a dating of the Epistle in Trajan's reign, as also the fact that Pliny was Governor of one of the very provinces to which 1 Peter was addressed. The most recent advocates of a Trajanic date are J. Knox, 'Pliny and 1 Peter: A note on 1 Pet. iv. 14–16 and iii. 15', *JBL*, LXXII (1953), pp. 187–189, and F. W. Beare, *op. cit.*, pp. 9–19. Knox maintains that 1 Peter was written to urge Christians to refuse to be condemned on any other charge than their pro-fession of Christianity. He thinks they were being condemned for 'inflexible obstinacy' and hence needed to be exhorted to make their defence with gentleness and reverence (1 Pet. iii. 15). But any refusal to recant, in whatever spirit, would surely have been regarded as 'inflexible obstinacy'!

Some form of this theory is held by many[1] who dispute the unity of the Epistle and who draw attention to the different approach towards persecutions after iv. 12 (but see the discussion on the Unity, pp. 121ff).

Another objection which may be mentioned here is the want of any known connection of Peter with any of the Asian churches among which the Epistle was designed to be circulated. Furthermore, these Gentile districts would more naturally come under the supervision of the apostle Paul, in which case it is thought to be strange to find Peter addressing them after Paul's death, since his ministry was concerned with the circumcision.

A different kind of historical objection is that raised by B. H. Streeter[2] over the use of such a term as 'fellow-elder' (v. 1) by an apostle, and the author's claim to be an eyewitness of the sufferings of Christ which, he thought, could not have been written by Peter, who was not present during the whole period of the passion. Moreover, it is maintained that an apostolic author such as Peter would have reflected in his writing far more reminiscences of his personal contacts with Jesus,[3] and of his knowledge of the sayings of his Master. But this objection cannot be regarded as serious since the presence of such reminiscences in the case of 2 Peter is regarded by some as an objection against apostolic authorship,[4] and there is no sure canon of criticism which can pronounce on the validity of either.

(iii) *Doctrinal objections.* Opponents of Petrine authorship place much emphasis on the affinities in thought between this Epistle and the Pauline letters.[5] It is maintained that the author has borrowed from

[1] For example, R. Perdelwitz, *Die Mysterienreligionen und das Problem des ersten Petrusbriefes* (1911); B. H. Streeter, *The Primitive Church*, pp. 122ff.; H. Windisch-H. Preisker, *Die katholischen Briefe*[3] (1951), pp. 76, 77, 159. W. Nauck (*ZNTW*, 46, 1955, pp. 68–80) rejects any distinction between hypothetical and real persecutions because both are essential to the whole picture.

[2] *Op. cit.*, pp. 120, 121.

[3] Cf. F. H. Chase, *HDB*, iii, p. 787, for details. R. Knopf (*op. cit.*, p. 15) makes much of this objection, particularly because of the tradition that Peter was behind Mark's Gospel, as a result of which it might be expected that some evidence of Peter's discipleship with the Lord would be included in an epistle under his name.

[4] Cf. Bigg, *op. cit.*, p. 232.

[5] Cf. E. F. Scott (*The Literature of the New Testament*, p. 220), who goes so far as to maintain that the writer must have studied several of Paul's Epistles. Similarly, F. W. Beare (*op. cit.*, p. 25) writes of the author as 'a man who is steeped in the Pauline letters'.

some of these, particularly Romans and Ephesians.[1] But even apart from literary connections the author's theological background is so much akin to Paul's that he has been regarded as a member of the school of Paul.[2] Yet how could this have happened to Peter? Some scholars[3] feel that this is too much to ask of the elder apostle, who had never had any close connections with Paul, and who had in fact ranged himself against him.[4]

A corollary to the alleged borrowing from Paul's Epistles is the supposed want of any originality in this Epistle. In other words it is considered that there is nothing characteristically unPauline in it.[5] Even the absence of reference to the question of the law has been regarded as a difficulty in a letter written by the leader of Jewish Christianity.[6] In other words, this difference from Paulinism is rather evidence of Pauline influence than the reverse. Such an objection depends for its weight on the assumption that no apostle of Peter's stamp could have lacked originality. Indeed it assumes that all apostles must have been creative. A different objection of an almost opposite kind is the alleged maturity of the author's thought and its kinship with the Old Roman Creed,[7] in particular the doctrine of the descent into Hades.

When all these objections are cumulatively considered, they will appeal to different minds with different force, but the fact that they have seemed to some scholars sufficiently conclusive against Petrine

[1] Quite apart from the problem of Peter borrowing from Paul, the parallels with Ephesians have been used as further evidence for a late date for 1 Peter by those who already reject the Pauline authorship of Ephesians (cf. C. L. Mitton, *The Epistle to the Ephesians*, 1951). In his first edition (pp. 9, 10) Beare could assert that since most scholars now regard Ephesians as a second generation work, 1 Peter must be even later. But Beare is here exaggerating the support for the late dating of Ephesians. For the parallels with Romans, cf. W. Sanday and A. C. Headlam, *The Epistle to the Romans* (*ICC*, 1895), pp. lxxiv ff.; but note Wand's strictures about accepting all these as evidence of literary dependence (*op. cit.*, p. 19). Cf. the further remarks on Literary Affinities on pp. 127ff..

[2] Cf. M. Dibelius, *A Fresh Approach to the New Testament and Early Christian Literature* (1936), p. 188.

[3] Cf. F. W. Beare, *op. cit.*, p. 25.

[4] Cf. E. F. Scott, *op. cit.*, p. 220; R. Knopf, *op. cit.*, p. 18.

[5] Cf. A. Jülicher-E. Fascher, *Einleitung*[7] (1931), pp. 193ff. F. W. Beare (*op. cit.*, p. 25) slightly modifies this position by admitting that the writer has a mind of his own, but 'has formed himself on Paul's writings'.

[6] Cf. Knopf, *op. cit.*, p. 17.

[7] Mentioned by McNeile-Williams, *INT*, p. 223.

authorship is reason enough for carefully examining their validity. In considering this, it is as well to recognize that those swayed by these objections generally pay no heed to the external evidence, although they have at times been caused no small embarrassment when they have attempted to explain it.

b. An examination of the objections to apostolic authorship

(i) *Linguistic and stylistic objections.* It is a difficult matter to decide whether any man could or could not attain to fluency in a language other than his own, when so little is known about the personal capacities of the man in question. More stress may have been given to Peter's former occupation of fishing than is really justified, for at the most conservative dating of this Epistle an interval of more than thirty years separated Peter the writer from Peter the fisherman, and who can measure what facility he might have achieved over so long a period? Even if Aramaic had been his native tongue, he lived in a bilingual area[1] and would not only have used Greek of a colloquial kind before his Christian ministry, but would regularly have used it in his conversations with Hellenistic Jews, even at Jerusalem or Antioch.[2] Moulton and Howard,[3] in fact, suggest that Peter's Greek may have been better than his Aramaic.[4]

The widespread use of the LXX version by a Palestinian Jew is not extraordinary when he is addressing himself to Gentile areas, for the Greek version of the Scriptures was the Bible of the Gentile Churches, and Peter could hardly have been unacquainted with it when working among Hellenistic Jews.[5]

But do the words of Papias about Peter's interpreter being Mark really support the contention that Peter's Greek was so poor that he needed the services of an interpreter? Clearly the words are intended to authenticate Mark's Gospel, and it is straining the language to suppose that Papias meant to imply Peter's linguistic inability.

We must conclude, therefore, that it cannot be asserted that Peter *could* not have written this Epistle on the grounds of language and style.

---

[1] See discussion on pp. 71ff. in connection with the Epistle of James.

[2] Cf. Moulton and Howard, *op. cit.*, p. 26.   [3] *Ibid., loc. cit.*

[4] Knopf (*op. cit.*, pp. 16, 17) admitted that a Galilaean might know Greek sufficiently well to make himself intelligible, but thought that there is a great difference between this and the Greek of 1 Peter. Similarly, Beare, *op. cit.*, p. 28.

[5] Cf. A. F. Walls (*op. cit.*, p. 25), who mentions that in James' speech in Acts a point is reinforced by a citation from the LXX.

At most we may note its extraordinary character, and at least we may maintain that no conclusive barrier to apostolic authorship exists on this score. Yet in order to meet the difficulty felt by many scholars, an alternative view has been postulated suggesting that an amanuensis, Silvanus, has either himself been responsible for the stylistic character-istics, or was in fact the author of the Epistle, writing under Peter's direction.[1]

We are left in no doubt that Peter employed Silvanus as his scribe or secretary, for he tells us so in v. 12. But did this amount to co-author-ship, and if it did not, what degree of latitude did Peter allow Silvanus in expressing his thoughts? It is well known that ancient secretaries were at times allowed considerable freedom in writing down their master's ideas. Indeed, in certain cases the secretary would be given only the barest outline of the contents and would then produce the letter in conformity with the outline.[2] The master would, of course, check over the finished product and it would be assumed that the contents were authenticated by him. Although the language would be that of the amanuensis the fundamental ideas would be those of the master.

In the case of 1 Peter, Silvanus would well fill the bill, for if he is to be identified with the Silas of Acts[3] he was well acquainted with Paul and was, in fact, associated with him in the address of both the Thessa-lonian letters. Some have suggested co-authorship with Paul in the production of these letters, and if this is a valid deduction it is not improbable that a similar combination with Peter resulted in the production of 1 Peter. Selwyn[4] has strongly argued for this probability

[1] This assumes that 1 Pet. v. 12 means that Silvanus was Peter's scribe and not merely the bearer of the Epistle.

[2] Cf. the instructive discussion of J. A. Eschlimann, 'La Rédaction des Epîtres Pauliniennes', *RB*, LIII (1946), pp. 185ff.

[3] Most scholars incline to this identification although no conclusive proof is available. Cf. the detailed study of L. Radermacher, *ZNTW*, 25 (1926), pp. 287–299; cf. also Bigg, *op. cit.*, pp. 83ff.

[4] Cf. *The First Epistle of St. Peter*, Essay II, pp. 365–466. On the other hand, Beare (*op. cit.*, pp. 188ff.) has equally strongly criticized this hypothesis of a com-mon author behind Thessalonians and 1 Peter on the grounds of dissimilarity of style between the different writings and the existence of difference of tone. This view was shared by W. L. Knox in his criticism of Selwyn's position (*Theology*, XLIX, 1946, pp. 342–344). Cf. also B. Rigaux (*Les Epîtres aux Thessaloniciens*, EB, 1956, pp. 105–111), who appealed to parallels between Thessalonians and the 'Manual of Discipline' of the Dead Sea Community.

on the grounds of close connection of thought and language between
1 Peter, the Thessalonian Epistles and the Apostolic Decree in Acts xv,
of which Silas was one of the bearers. But similarities of thought are
capable of various explanations and the employment of expressions in
common use by different authors may be as reasonable an explanation
as common authorship (or co-authorship). Nevertheless, where a name
is known to have been associated with different groups of writings
similarity may be not insignificant. The Silvanus hypothesis cannot,
therefore, be ruled out, and forms a reasonable alternative for those
whose main objection to Petrine authorship is linguistic.

Certain criticisms of this amanuensis-hypothesis should not go
unnoticed. It is strongly rejected by F. W. Beare,[1] who calls it 'a device
of desperation'. To him the teaching of the Epistle, with its lack of
stress on the work of the Spirit, is proof enough against the theory of
early authorship.[2] But one's estimate of any hypothesis is partly
conditioned by presuppositions, and those for whom the other difficulties loom large will not be disposed to dispense with the linguistic
problem on such a basis as an amanuensis theory.[3] Another problem is
the absence of any salutation from Silvanus, which would be strange
indeed if he were the secretary or part-composer (cf. Rom. xvi. 22
where Tertius the scribe sends his own greetings). This suggests that
Silvanus played a far less important part than the amanuensis hypothesis
implies. Not only so, but v. 12 would stand as a rather obnoxious piece
of self-commendation, unless in fact Peter himself added this conclusion. It is further difficult to imagine that the direct appeal of v. 1ff.
could have been the indirect work of a secretary. The personal authority is so real that it would be necessary to maintain that for this part of
the letter the apostle had dictated. It is also significant that the statement
in v. 12 which mentions Silvanus may indicate either the bearer or the

---

[1] Op. cit., p. 183. In the appendix of his second edition, Beare gives a careful
criticism of Selwyn's arguments (op. cit., pp. 188ff.). Against Beare's comment,
cf. P. Carrington, 'St. Peter's Epistle', in The Joy of Study (ed. S. E. Johnson, 1951),
p. 58.

[2] Ibid., p. 28. Cf. A. F. Walls (op. cit., p. 29) for a sufficient answer to Beare's
contention.

[3] F. W. Beare regards the mention of Silvanus in v. 12 as no more than a part
of the machinery of pseudonymity (op. cit., p. 29). But pseudonymous writers
did not usually introduce such specific additions as this, which might be the means
of betraying their disguise, at least in epistolary impersonations. There is no
extant example of it in pseudepigraphical Christian literature.

secretary and some doubt exists therefore about the method of composition.[1]

Another criticism is based on the fact that Silvanus was a Jerusalem Christian and would not, therefore, be equipped with Greek as our author clearly was.[2] But there were certainly some Greek-speaking Jews in Jerusalem, and there is no basis for excluding Silvanus from their number. Indeed, he may have been chosen for this reason as a delegate to convey the letter of James to Greek-speaking churches of Antioch, Syria and Cilicia (Acts xv. 33ff.).

To sum up, the amanuensis theory has nothing to disprove it, but neither has it evidence enough to be conclusive about its correctness. If Peter had the help of Silvanus it would seem improbable, by reason of the whole tone of the letter, that the author allowed too much freedom to his secretary. At least the finished article was given out very definitely as Peter's personal message, invested with his own special authority.[3]

(ii) *Historical objections.* The question of the identification of the persecution reflected in this Epistle is crucial to this problem of authorship, as has already been pointed out. But a prior problem is scantiness of adequate data about early persecutions. Much of the weight of objection from an historical point of view has been based on the assumption of general provincial persecution directed against Christians in the reign of Domitian. But this assumption has met with recent suspicion, for there are very few data in support. It is known that Flavius Clemens and Domitilla his wife were persecuted in Rome with one or two others, but there is no more than a strong presumption that this limited persecution was on account of their Christian profession and no evidence at all for any widespread persecution affecting the prov-

---

[1] Cf. the detailed discussion of F. H. Chase (*HDB*, III, p. 790), who cites other instances where the Greek διά introduces the bearer and not the amanuensis of a letter. But P. Carrington (*op. cit.*, pp. 57, 58) argues (in opposition to Beare) that the expression signifies the producer of the Epistle on the analogy of the *Epistle of the Church at Smyrna* (relating Polycarp's death) as written 'through Marcianus' (διά) who must have been the composer since a separate amanuensis is mentioned.

[2] Cf. Beare, *op. cit.*, pp. 189f.

[3] G. Bornemann ('Der erste Petrusbrief—eine Taufrede des Sylvanus?' *ZNTW*, 19, 1919–20, pp. 157f.) accounted for Silvanus' connection with the Epistle by supposing that 1 Peter was really a baptismal address delivered by Silvanus (cf. also L. Radermacher, *op. cit.*, pp. 287–299). But this does not explain why it was then adapted into a letter in Peter's name.

inces named.[1] This makes it impossible to relate our Epistle with any
certainty to this period.

But assuming some official persecution was either active or imminent
in these provinces of Asia Minor, is it still possible that the situation
under Trajan may be reflected? The parallels are not as striking as has
often been claimed. The name 'Christian' may by that time, and in fact
for some time previously, have acquired a technical connotation, but
that does not immediately identify 1 Peter iv. 14 (being reproached for
the name of Christ) with this situation, for all Christian suffering from
the commencement of the Church was regarded as 'in the name'.
Indeed it was prepared for by our Lord Himself.[2] But it should further
be remembered that Pliny was requesting an imperial judgment which
involved a clarification of the whole position of Christians. Neither
Pliny's enquiries nor Trajan's reply suggest that procedure against
Christians was a new departure.[3] Moreover, there is no suggestion that
the kind of problem confronting Pliny was worldwide, and yet 1 Peter
v. 9 shows that the kind of suffering that the Christians were called
upon to endure was liable to befall Christians anywhere. Moreover,
there is a further difference between Pliny and 1 Peter, for in the former
a state of affairs is reflected which is a continuation of a past policy,
whereas in the latter a fiery trial seems to be regarded as a new experience (1 Pet. iv. 12). To sum up, there is little to commend this identification and it cannot be said to be demanded by the evidence.[4]

But does the Neronian persecution fare any better? It is true that no
evidence exists that provincial districts were affected, although Tertullian[5] makes a statement about an *institutum Neronianum* making
Christians outlaws, but no trace of this edict remains. Yet Christians
were certainly made scapegoats in Rome, and the savage nature of

[1] Cf. J. W. C. Wand's clear discussion of this point (*op. cit.*, p. 16). He cites
without disapproval E. T. Merrill's opinion that Domitian did not persecute
Christians at all (in his *Essays in Early Christian History*, 1924, pp. 148ff.). If the
Apocalypse is dated during Domitian's reign this would, of course, supply supporting evidence of hostile and general persecution in part, at least, of the provinces connected with the Epistle. See pp. 172f. for more detailed discussion of
the Domitianic persecutions.

[2] Cf. Mk. xiii. 13; Lk. xxi. 12.

[3] For a well-reasoned appraisal of the historic situation behind Pliny's correspondence, cf. J. W. C. Wand, *op. cit.*, pp. 15f.; A. F. Walls, *op. cit.*, pp. 54ff.

[4] A. M. Hunter (Introduction and Exegesis to *The First Epistle of Peter*, IB,
1957, p. 79) justifiably calls it 'very rash'.

[5] *Ad Nationes*, vii.

Nero's treatment of them must have been widely known throughout the provinces, where great apprehension must have arisen among the Christians. Peter may well have imagined an extension of the attack and wished to warn the Asian Christians of what was in store for them. There is nothing in the references to persecution in this Epistle which rules out this hypothesis.

One other question remains. Are the references to suffering in the Epistle sufficiently clear to show that official persecution was in mind? In the first part of the Epistle the sufferings are of a general kind (i. 6, 7, iii. 13–17), but in the latter part a fiercer opposition seems to be envisaged (iv. 12ff.). Yet there is much to be said for the view that the kind of sufferings are not martyrdoms but reproaches due to the fact that Christians were considered odious in the eyes of their neighbours. The *apologia* (iii. 15) which they must be prepared to give when necessary is equally well explained by the need for a general Christian testimony as by the need for legal defence. In fact there is little distinctive about the 'persecutions' in 1 Peter which would not apply to the opposition that Christians had to endure from the inception of the Church.[1] What Peter is concerned about is to prevent Christians from suffering for wrongdoing, but he implies that all other kinds of suffering were designed by God for their welfare. Suffering as a Christian is contrasted with suffering as a murderer, thief, evil-doer or busybody (1 Pet. iv. 15, 16), and although the parallelism would appear to demand legal penalties in both cases,[2] yet all that need be implied is some action on the part of magistrates, as for instance happened in the case of Paul's troubles with Silas at Philippi. The fiery trial (πύρωσις) of iv. 12 may indicate some form of persecution by incendiarism, in which case the Neronian persecutions would furnish a striking parallel, or it may be used metaphorically of any trial which has the refining effect of fire.

Although it may be impossible to reach any indisputable conclusion,

---

[1] C. F. D. Moule ('The Nature and Purpose of 1 Peter', *NTS*, 3, 1957, pp. 7ff.) maintains that there are parallels with other New Testament passages on the subject of persecution and concludes that this shows how much can be explained 'by postulating harrying by local opponents, sometimes leading to imprisonment by local authorities or even (as in the case of Stephen) death'. The same position was cogently maintained by E. G. Selwyn in his article 'The Persecutions in 1 Peter' in *Studiorum Novi Testamenti Societas Bulletin* (1950), pp. 39–50. Cf. also his article in *ET*, LIX (1948), pp. 256–259, in which he considered the persecution situation to be no different from that reflected in the Pauline Epistles and Acts.

[2] So Wand, *op. cit., ad loc.*

it may be maintained with confidence that nothing in these references to persecution excludes the possibility that the self-claims of the Epistle to be Petrine are genuine.

The problem of Peter writing to districts under Paul's supervision is not a serious one, for if Paul were now dead (as is most generally supposed) there would be no question of a clash of territories.[1] It would not be unnatural, in fact, for the surviving senior apostle to send a message of encouragement to Gentile churches if the apostle to the Gentiles was no longer alive. But it is certainly not established that this Epistle was, in fact, directed to Pauline churches. Of the provinces mentioned, Paul worked, as far as we know, only in Galatia and Asia, and even in the northern districts of these he had in all probability not worked.[2] No doubt these areas had been evangelized by converts of Paul, but had probably not known him personally. This may account for the absence of any reference to him, although there is no particular reason why such a reference should have been included in any case.[3] If the tradition of Peter's residence in Rome is correct,[4] too much emphasis must not be laid upon the present enlargement of Peter's commission as a minister to the circumcision, or the history of the period will be too unnaturally departmentalized.

That Peter would not describe himself as a fellow-elder and would not have claimed to be a witness of Christ's sufferings (v. 1) is by no means as self-evident as Streeter supposed. Quite apart from the fact that the term 'elder' seems to have been used as late as the time of Papias[5] as a description of apostles, and therefore could not have been regarded in the primitive Church as an inferior title, the context almost demands such a description for the exhortation of the elders to have its fullest effect. It is, as H. Windisch[6] pointed out, an expression of modesty on the writer's part. It is even more an evidence of his sympathy with his readers.[7] That Peter had not witnessed all of Christ's sufferings

---

[1] E. H. Plumptre (*The General Epistles of St. Peter and St. Jude*, 1879, pp. 60ff.) got over the difficulty here by supposing that the Epistle was addressed to Jews who came under Peter's jurisdiction.

[2] Cf. McNeile-Williams, *INT*, pp. 214, 215, for the probable route which the bearer traversed in his delivery of the letter. There is little doubt that the order of mention of the provinces indicates the sequence of visits.

[3] Cf. J. Moffatt, *ILNT*, pp. 339, 340.   [4] Cf. O. Cullmann, *op. cit.*, pp. 70–152.

[5] See the comments on Papias' statement on pp. 208ff.

[6] *Die katholischen Briefe*, ad loc.

[7] Cf. Selwyn, *The First Epistle of St. Peter*, ad loc.

would certainly not prevent him from calling himself a witness, and Streeter's objection on this score must be rejected as unworthy of further consideration.

(iii) *Doctrinal objections.* There has been such widespread assumption that Peter's Epistle is but an echo of Paulinism that it is refreshing to find an increasing tendency to mark the individual contribution of Peter in the field of New Testament theology. J. W. C. Wand[1] has pointed out both the absence of such Pauline doctrines as justification, law, the new Adam, and the flesh, and the presence of highly characteristic methods in Peter's own presentation, such as his copious use of Old Testament citations and moral codes, his church-consciousness, historic consciousness and Christ-consciousness. Peter's teaching cannot be systematized into a theological school of thought, but there is enough distinctiveness about it to differentiate it from Paul's approach. The most notable contribution is the doctrine of Christ's descent into Hades, which in its focus upon the resurrection of Christ stands in direct relationship to Peter's emphasis on the resurrection in the early Acts speeches. As an eyewitness of the risen Christ Peter would never forget the profound impression which that stupendous event made upon his mind, and the doctrine of the descent,[2] however obscure it is to modern minds, would surely be more natural as a part of primitive reflection upon the significance of the resurrection than as a later development, or as a peculiar fancy of a pseudonymous author.

At the same time, no serious student of Paul and Peter would deny that there is much common ground between them, which cannot wholly be explained by their common Christian background. Some Pauline influence on Peter's mind is generally supposed to be required by the content of the Epistle, but this would be damaging to Petrine authorship only if two presuppositions can be established. First, it must be shown that the New Testament presentation of Peter makes it

---

[1] *Op. cit.*, pp. 17ff. For a similar challenge to the theory of Paulinism, cf. Selwyn's article, *ET*, LIX (1948), pp. 256–259. He makes a strong point of the underlying common teaching of the Church.

[2] There have been several special discussions of this passage in recent years, particularly by Bo Reicke in his exhaustive monograph, *The Disobedient Spirits and Christian Baptism* (*Acta Seminarii Neotestamentica Upsaliensis*, ed. A. Fridrichsen, XII, 1946). Cf. C. E. B. Cranfield, *ET*, LXIX (1958), pp. 369–372; R. Bultmann, in *Coniectanea Neotestamentica, XI in honorem Antonii Fridrichsen* (1947), pp. 1–14; J. Jeremias, *ZNTW*, 42 (1949), pp. 194–201; and S. E. Johnson, *JBL*, LXXIX (1960), pp. 48–51.

psychologically inconceivable that he was susceptible to outside influence, particularly from so powerful a personality as Paul. But the data available do not depict Peter as a man of fertile ideas, but as a man of action. Paul's successful resistance to Peter's weak compromise at Antioch is sufficient indication of the direction in which mental influences were likely to flow. Indeed, traces of other New Testament literature such as James and Hebrews are further evidence of the receptive character of this author's mind, and such receptivity is not incompatible with the sympathetic character of Peter.[1] Secondly, it must be shown that Peter and Paul represent divergent tendencies which are unlikely to have permitted close liaison between them. But this is a view of history which is a legacy from the Tübingen school of criticism, with no basis in the New Testament. That both made their own contribution to Christian thought and that Paul's was the greater must be acknowledged, but there is such singular lack of any real divergence between their writings that it is fortuitous either to charge Peter with lack of originality or to regard the Epistle as an attempted reconciliation between opposing parties. The plain facts are that both represent vital aspects of early Christianity.[2]

c. Alternative theories

Before a full appraisal of the problem of authorship can be made, it is essential to examine the probabilities of the alternative views of authorship and these will now be listed and their difficulties noted.

(i) *A pseudonymous letter.* This is the most obvious alternative to Petrine authorship and the earliest critics of the traditional view automatically assumed it. Although the notion of the Tübingen school that the letter was a later celebration of the union between rival Pauline and Petrine parties, thus accounting for the Pauline elements under a Petrine pseudonym, has now been completely abandoned,[3] the idea of an intentional pseudonymous letter has been retained, harnessed to other less questionable motives. H. von Soden[4] suggested that Silvanus issued

---

[1] Cf. Zahn, *INT*, II, p. 176.

[2] Selwyn, in his article on the Eschatology of 1 Peter in *The Background of the New Testament and its Eschatology* (ed. Davies and Daube, 1956), pp. 394–401, shows the background to be essentially Jewish, a further reminder of a primitive origin.

[3] Cf. A. Harnack, *Die Chronologie der altchristlichen Literatur*, I, p. 456.

[4] *Die Briefe des Petrus, Jakobus, Judas* (1891), p. 117.

the letter in the name of Peter who was renowned as a martyr (1 Pet. v. 1 is understood in this sense), in order to encourage Christians who were suffering in the Domitianic persecutions. But this theory may at once be dismissed, for the sudden appearance of a letter from one so long dead would raise immediate suspicions.[1] Moreover, it would be unintelligible why Silvanus did not then publish the Epistle in his own name.[2] A. Jülicher[3] proposed as author an unknown Roman teacher, whose knowledge of Paul eminently fitted him for the task, but who chose Peter's name to invest his work with the authority of the apostle who had suffered beside Paul in Rome, but this is little more conceivable.

It has been more recently supposed that the main difficulties in this older conception of pseudonymity may be removed by the assumption that the pseudonym is not an intentional device to deceive, but merely an acknowledged literary practice. Thus F. W. Beare[4] argues that the readers would well recognize the pseudonym as a harmless device. They would even accept it as evidence that the author was more concerned about his message than about his own authority. Such a notion of pseudonymity as an accepted literary device has commended itself to many modern scholars because it appears to remove any moral stigma from the older hypothesis of wholehearted pseudonymity. For this reason the description of such a process as 'forgery' is ruled out as unfair and misleading. But to maintain this type of hypothesis at all it is clearly necessary to draw a definite distinction between ancient and modern literary practice, a distinction which in itself is open to criticism.

Basic to this suggestion is the assumption that the author had no intention to deceive. He may be represented, in fact, as a man who, through motives of modesty, uses the convention of pseudonymity to encourage much-harassed Christians in his own time. It would be further necessary to assume that the readers would readily recognize the device and presumably be prepared to overlook any incongruities such as those mentioned above. The readers would in that case even

[1] McNeile-Williams (*INT*, p. 219) rightly point out that to use Peter's name and yet refer to his martyrdom would be too great a blunder for any writer to commit. E. F. Scott (*op. cit.*, p. 221) rejected the idea of a deliberate forgery for much the same reason, although he disputed Petrine authorship.

[2] Cf. R. Knopf's criticisms, *op. cit.*, p. 18. F. W. Beare (*op. cit.*, p. 29) dismisses the theory with hardly a comment.

[3] *Einleitung*, pp. 199, 200.　　　　[4] *Op. cit.*, *loc. cit.*

applaud the author's selfless industry. But the crux of the theory is whether pseudonymity of this type was ever an accepted literary convention. Appeal to the mass of early Christian pseudepigrapha can only mislead unless there is careful differentiation of literary types. F. Torm[1] has demonstrated that early Christian epistolary pseudepigrapha were so rare that this cannot possibly be regarded as a conventional form, and, if it was not, the main basis of this type of theory collapses.

Thus when F. W. Beare[2] declares that there 'can be no possible doubt that Peter is a pseudonym', the grounds of his confidence may be challenged. In any case, his own attempt to explain the use of the pseudonym is most unsatisfactory, for he considers it to be a kind of dramatic re-creation of the personality of the pseudonym, comparable with the monologues of Browning. But are we to suppose that an author, under the stresses of an impending and serious persecution, composed a letter with such attention to a purely literary technique? The idea is surely incredible. It will not do to dismiss the whole problem, as Beare does,[3] by merely stating that the question of authorship was unimportant and that it was the teaching that mattered, for it is obvious that the teaching had to be authenticated by an authorized teacher. Clearly, to maintain a theory of literary pseudonymity as distinct from deceptive pseudonymity, it is necessary to provide more adequate parallels and more suitable motives than Beare has been able to do. The difficulty here is the general difficulty of all hypotheses of early Christian epistolary pseudonymity.

F. Torm[4] in his penetrating examination of pseudonymous methods and motives maintains that it is impossible to make out an intelligible case for the use of pseudonymity in 1 Peter. The fact that the author's purpose is encouragement means that personal relations between readers and writer would play a much more important part than apostolic authority. Why did not the author, if not Peter, publish his encouragements in his own name? There seems to be no satisfactory answer to this question. The Epistle deals with no heresy which might have required apostolic authority to refute it. Moreover, the mention of Silvanus and Mark cannot be regarded as part of the pseudepigraphical machinery, for a pseudo-Peter would surely avoid associating

---

[1] *Die Psychologie der Pseudonymität im Hinblick auf die Literatur des Urchristentums* (1932). Cf. the appendix on Epistolary Pseudepigraphy in the present writer's *New Testament Introduction: The Pauline Epistles*, pp. 282–294.

[2] *Op. cit.*, p. 25.   [3] *Op. cit.*, p. 29.   [4] *Op. cit.*, pp. 41–44.

so closely with Peter those who, according to the Acts and the Pauline Epistles, were associates of Paul. Nor would a pseudo-Peter make Peter echo the influence of Paul.

(ii) *An anonymous letter later attributed to Peter.* Conscious of the unsatisfactory character of theories of intentional pseudepigraphy which had been proposed, and yet persuaded that the Epistle possessed non-Petrine characteristics, Harnack[1] proposed a compromise. The opening and closing sentences (i. 1ff. and v. 12ff.) were, in his view, appended later, thus freeing the main body of the letter from any attachment to Peter's name and enabling him to propose that a Roman teacher familiar with Paul's letters felt free to address areas through which Paul had travelled in his mission work. A similar idea was maintained by B. H. Streeter,[2] who nevertheless divided the main material into (1) a bishop's homily to newly baptized converts (i. 3–iv. 11) and (2) a bishop's pastoral letter, addressed to neighbouring churches.[3] Neither Harnack nor Streeter could produce manuscript evidence in support of the spuriousness of the beginning and ending which entirely depends on subjective considerations. Streeter's suggestion that Aristion was the bishop and author of the main part does nothing to enhance his theory. A. C. McGiffert's[4] opinion that the attachment of Peter's name was no more than a scribal guess is no more probable.

Theories of anonymous circulation are generally proposed only as an offset to the difficulties of pseudonymous authorship.[5] But the problem is merely moved a stage farther to pseudonymous attribution. That an epistle circulated without the author's name presents no difficulty in view of the Epistle to the Hebrews,[6] but that it should later undergo scribal additions of the type conjectured raises serious problems.

In the absence of positive manuscript evidence any theories of inter-

---

[1] *Die Chronologie der altchristlichen Literatur*, I, pp. 457ff.

[2] *The Primitive Church*, pp. 123ff.; cf. W. Bornemann (*ZNTW*, 19, 1919–20, pp. 143–165) who regards i. 3–v. 11 as a baptismal address by Silvanus.

[3] See pp. 121ff. for discussion on partition theories.

[4] *A History of Christianity in the Apostolic Age* (1897), pp. 593ff. His own guess was that Barnabas was the author.

[5] Cf. K. and S. Lake, *INT* (1938), pp. 165ff.

[6] Harnack's citing of Ephesians, *Barnabas* and *II Clement* as not wholly dissimilar is inconsequential whatever view is taken of the author problem in these cases, since in none of them is an address and closing salutation 'added' to give precision to the author's name (cf. Chase's criticism, *HDB*, III, p. 787).

polation are highly suspicious, for two reasons. (1) It is difficult to conceive how an epistle originally circulating as anonymous could ever acquire an apostolic name, a specific address and concluding greetings without raising the least suspicion among any churches in the area purporting to be addressed. (2) Resort to interpolation theories is so thoroughly subjective that it is altogether too facile a means of removing difficulties. In the nature of the case theories which deal with the text as it stands are more credible than those which depend on speculative scribal additions for which no evidence exists.

Both the variety and dubious character of those alternative views are in themselves favourable to apostolic authorship, since disputants must not only produce good reasons for rejecting the traditional position, but must themselves produce an alternative explanation of all the facts which is more satisfactory than the rejected hypothesis. When so careful a critic as E. F. Scott[1] fairly acknowledged that the attribution of the Epistle to Peter must have been due to a misunderstanding no longer discoverable, this gives the measure of perplexity experienced by advocates of non-Petrine authorship.

d. Conclusion of the discussion on authorship

The result of this survey of various theories leaves us in no doubt that the traditional view which accepts the claims of the Epistle to be apostolic is more reasonable than any alternative hypothesis. We may see here a true reflection of the apostle's experience of Jesus Christ and his lasting contribution to the doctrine of the Christian Church. If there is not the depth of the mind of Paul, there is a warm affection which is unmistakable and a deep sympathy with those whom he seeks to help.

Indirect support for this view of the Epistle may be found in various echoes of Jesus' teaching,[2] some faint traces of events in which Peter played a part which are recorded in the Gospels (as e.g. the possible allusion in v. 5 to the girding incident in Jn. xiii. 4f., and the reference to shepherding the flock in 1 Pet. v. 2ff., and Jn. xxi. 15–17). There are also parallels with the Acts speeches[3] attributed to Peter which are not without significance.

[1] *Op. cit.*, p. 221.
[2] Cf. the list of references in Chase's article (*HDB*, III, pp. 787, 788).
[3] For details see the section on literary affinities on pp. 127ff. Cf. also Wand's discussion, *op. cit.*, pp. 26–28.

III. PURPOSE

Assuming that Peter is writing as he says he is to the 'dispersion scattered throughout Pontus, Galatia, Cappadocia, Asia and Bithynia' (I Pet. i. 1, RSV), we may ascertain the purpose of the Epistle with a fair degree of precision. It is clearly designed for a specific group of Christians although scattered over a wide area. The keynote of the letter is hope and Peter wishes to exhort these Christians to live in accordance with the hope they have received through Christ. He gives practical guidance to assist in their human relationships and particularly exhorts them to endure suffering in a joyful manner for Christ's sake. His main purpose is, therefore, hortatory, but not infrequently he introduces theological considerations which press home the ethical injunctions. In particular he presents the work of Christ as a stimulus for the Christian endurance of suffering, while at the same time drawing out more fundamental aspects of its meaning.[1] In this way he shows the indissoluble link between doctrine and practice.[2] This is possibly what he means when he states his own purpose in v. 12 as being to exhort and testify 'that this is the true grace of God'. Some difference of opinion exists over the precise meaning of the latter phrase, but it seems best to regard it as referring to the message of the gospel which the author is claiming to have written or, under the Silvanus hypothesis,[3] to have caused to be written.

Different explanations of the purpose are suggested by those who

[1] This emphasis on the work of Christ has led some scholars to see in this Epistle a homily designed for the Feast of Redemption (cf. Selwyn, *The First Epistle of St. Peter*, pp. 62ff.). Connected with this feast was the baptismal ceremony, and this would lend support to the hypothesis that this Epistle is based on a baptismal homily. Its applicability for such a Christian festival is undoubted, but this is very different from claiming that the author intended it for this purpose. The historic occasion appears to be too specific for that.

[2] That the author of I Peter in ii. 11, 12 is drawing out the close connection between Christian behaviour and preaching has been suggestively brought out by W. Brandt in his article in *Manet in Alternum, Eine Festschrift für O. Schmitz* (ed. W. Foerster, 1953), pp. 10–25. He concludes that Christian behaviour continues the challenge of the Word. Cf. also W. C. van Unnik's discussion on good works (*NTS*, 1, 1954–55, pp. 92–110; *NTS*, 2, 1956, pp. 198–202).

[3] J. W. C. Wand (*op. cit.*, pp. 29–30) conjectures that these words are added to authenticate Silvanus' teaching which Peter is claiming to be his own, and in view of the fact that some may have disputed it he also commends Silvanus himself as a faithful brother.

maintain a pseudonymous authorship and a later date. E. J. Goodspeed[1] holds that this epistle, like *1 Clement*, was called forth by the exhortation in Hebrews v. 12 that the readers (whom he identifies with the Roman Church) should become teachers. He also maintains that this Epistle aims to undo the harm done by the book of Revelation in its attitude towards the State.[2] But it is incredible that any who needed 'milk' (first principles) should be able so rapidly to reach the maturity and spiritual inspiration required to produce 1 Peter. Moreover, that Epistle is not primarily didactic but practical, while its brief and restrained advice on State relationships would be incredible as a counteraction to the Apocalypse. The whole idea may be dismissed as pure speculation without any basis in fact.[3]

Those who dispute the unity of 1 Peter naturally place a still different construction on the purpose. This will become clear when the various theories involving liturgical materials are examined below (see pp. 122f). But a typical hypothesis is that of F. W. Beare,[4] who regards the letter proper as confined to iv. 12–v. 11, in which the author sends an urgent message to those already in the throes of a fiery persecution and therefore in need of encouragement. To strengthen that message Beare believes that parts of a baptismal discourse were incorporated. Reasons will later be given for considering this hypothesis to be improbable.

IV. DESTINATION

Although this Epistle possesses the character of a circular letter, it differs from the other general Epistles of the New Testament in specifying the area in which the readers are confined. But there are certain problems attached even to this.

1. Are the districts which are mentioned to be taken politically or geographically? If the former, the area would be considerably greater than the latter, for the ethnic area of Galatia was but a part of the provincial district. Yet it seems most probable that only the northern part was intended, in which case the letter was directed to those parts north

---

[1] *INT*, pp. 267ff. It is far-fetched to see in 1 Pet. v. 12 (the word 'exhort') an echo of Heb. xiii. 22 (*ibid.*, p. 271).

[2] Other parallels which Goodspeed finds are the Asiatic address of both writings and the offsetting of Petrine authorship against Johannine (*ibid., loc. cit.*).

[3] It is quite unconvincing for Goodspeed (*op. cit.*, p. 280) to claim that such a theory fully explains both the pseudonymity and the address (i.e. churches other than Rome).

[4] *Op. cit.*, pp. 7, 8.

of the Taurus mountains. This conclusion is supported by the fact that Pontus and Bithynia, which formed one administrative Roman province, are yet not only mentioned separately, but one comes first and the other last.

2. Was any of this area within the sphere of Paul's influence? This has already been discussed (see p. 108) and the suggestion made that Paul did not in fact work in those areas, except Asia. The correctness of this depends on what view is taken of the North or South theory for the destination of Galatians. But the statement in Acts xvi. 6, 7 that Paul was forbidden by the Spirit to preach either in Asia or in Bithynia on his second journey would suggest that Luke is explaining the absence of any personal evangelistic activity by Paul in that district.

3. Why are the districts mentioned in the order in which they stand in i. 1? There have been four different explanations. First, those who regard the words as an interpolation see only an entire lack of order, for which the unintelligence of the scribe is held to be responsible.[1] Secondly, others who follow the pseudonymous interpretation and date the Epistle in the reign of Trajan connect the mention of Pontus first and Bithynia last with the governorship of Pliny over the joint province.[2] Thirdly, the hazardous guess that the order was dictated by rhythmical considerations is not likely to commend itself.[3] Fourthly, a more generally accepted explanation is that the order represents the itinerary of the bearer of the letter, who may well have landed at a port of Pontus, visited the churches in the districts named in that order and then returned to Bithynia.[4] Of these explanations there is no doubt that the last is the most reasonable, in spite of F. W. Beare's[5] objection that such a route could not be planned in an area of intense persecution. If the persecution has not yet reached the stage of intensity, this objection would be invalid.

Having established the destination, our next enquiry concerns the character of the readers, and this enquiry will be approached from two

[1] B. H. Streeter thought the address was added when Pliny began to persecute the Christians, but the occasion, even if correct, does not explain the strange nature of the addition, especially the splitting of Pliny's official province (cf. *The Primitive Church*, p. 126).
[2] Cf. Beare, *op. cit.*, pp. 23f.
[3] Cf. W. L. Knox, *Theology*, XLIX (1946), p. 344.
[4] Cf. F. J. A. Hort, *The First Epistle of Peter* (1898), p. 15; Moffatt, *ILNT*, p. 327.
[5] *Op. cit.*, pp. 22f.

angles, social and racial. The district was generally economically prosperous although there was a wide disparity between the landowners and merchants on the one hand and the working classes on the other.[1] The churches were mainly drawn from the latter group, if any significance may be attached to the fact that slaves but not masters are mentioned in the injunctions for social behaviour (ii. 18–25). Yet much is said about the duties of citizenship (ii. 11–17) which would apply mainly to free men (see especially verse 16), and our conclusion must be that these churches, like most in the primitive period, were mixed in respect of the social status of their members.[2]

As to their racial group there have been three proposals: Jewish, Gentile or Jewish-Gentile.

1. The theory that Jewish Christian readers are addressed is as old as Origen but has not gained much recent support.[3] B. Weiss,[4] made much of the wide use of the LXX in citations and the unintelligible character of the argument for those unfamiliar with its Old Testament background. Added to this is the strangely Jewish flavour of the address— 'elect strangers of the Diaspora', all three terms of which have Jewish connotations. But this line of argument proceeds on the assumption that what is true of the writer must be true of the readers. The Jewish background of the writer can hardly be denied, but this tells us nothing about the background of the readers.[5] At the same time caution must be exercised before concluding that Gentile readers would not have been sufficiently acquainted with the LXX. The use of 'diaspora' may be equally well interpreted as symbolical of the Christian Church conceived as the New Israel, a thought many times echoed in the New Testament. But the most damaging criticism of the theory of Jewish addressees is the manner in which the writer appeals to the readers' previously 'vain way of life' (i. 18), mentions their 'former lusts in ignorance' (i. 14), speaks of them having done what the Gentiles do (iv. 3, 4, then follows a list of Gentile vices), and reminds them that they were once a 'no-people' but were called out of darkness (ii. 9, 10). It is difficult to see

---

[1] Cf. Selwyn, op. cit., pp. 48, 49.

[2] Cf. Wand, op. cit., pp. 31, 32.

[3] Its most enthusiastic modern supporter has been D. Völter, Der I Petrusbrief— seine Entstehung und Stellung in der Geschichte des Urchristentums (1906). But his arguments gained little support. Yet cf. R. Leconte, Les épîtres catholiques (1953), p. 65.

[4] A Manual of Introduction to the New Testament (1887), II, pp. 137ff.

[5] Cf. Selwyn, op. cit., p. 43.

how these words could apply to any but Gentiles.[1] Moreover, there is no evidence of the existence of all-Jewish Christian churches in the provinces named in the address, and it would in any case be difficult to conceive in provinces such as Asia and Galatia which had, at least in part, come under Paul's influence.[2]

2. In the light of these considerations it would seem certain that Gentile Christians were mainly in mind, and this is supported by the fact that the areas addressed were predominantly Gentile. Yet in these same areas there were strong Jewish communities and the most probable solution is therefore the third.

3. That these churches were mixed[3] is highly probable from what we know of the primitive communities generally. Many of the Jews of the Dispersion were only loosely attached to Judaism, and would have formed, with the Gentile proselytes, a ready audience for the first evangelistic impact of the Christian missions. Of the origin of these churches nothing is known. As already pointed out, they lay mainly beyond the area evangelized by the apostle Paul, but two suggestions are, at least, probable. If Silvanus were known to them he may have been responsible for the establishing of at least some of these churches. The church at Ephesus, while Paul was ministering there, evangelized the province of Asia (Acts xix. 10), and the mission might well have continued beyond the borders of the province. It has been suggested that Peter had worked in this district, although the use of the third person in i. 12 would seem to exclude this suggestion. A more probable idea is that the nucleus of the churches in this district consisted of those who were converted on the day of Pentecost.[4]

V. DATE

In the course of the preceding discussions the problems of the persecution during which this letter was sent received careful attention and

---

[1] In reply to these criticisms, Leconte (*op. cit.*, pp. 65f.) maintains that i. 18 could refer to the futility of antiquated Jewish ritual, that similarly i. 14 could mean Jewish pre-Christian passions and that iv. 3, 4 refers only to Gentile behaviour as a pattern and does not necessarily identify the readers as Gentiles. Moreover, he thinks that iii. 20, 21, i. 17 and ii. 9 are all more applicable to Jewish Christians. While these arguments cannot be lightly dismissed the alternative interpretation of these references as addressed mainly to Gentile readers would seem more natural.

[2] R. Knopf (*op. cit.*, pp. 2ff.) made a strong point of this in criticizing Weiss.

[3] As Selwyn (*op. cit.*, p. 44) concluded.   [4] Cf. Moffatt, *ILNT*, p. 327 n.

since the answer to this problem determines the dating there is little more to be said. The three main proposals are: (1) in Trajan's reign (c. AD 111); (2) in Domitian's reign (AD 90–100); (3) in Nero's reign (c. AD 62–64). We have seen what little justification there is for preferring either of the first two and nothing prevents the third from being the most probable. Whether it was before or after the death of Paul is difficult to decide with certainty. There has in fact been some difference of opinion whether Peter was martyred before Paul, but the most generally accepted opinion is the reverse. Yet the dating of I Peter does not hinge upon any decision regarding this. There are a few internal considerations which favour the Neronian date mentioned above. Selwyn[1] pointed out that the doctrine and ecclesiastical organization are fairly early and would suit a date not much after AD 60. He also maintains, on a literal interpretation of the writer's own description of his readers as 'elect sojourners', that some crisis must recently have occurred to cause the scattering of the Christians. This he thinks was the martyrdom of James, the Lord's brother, at the hands of the Jews, thus making the breach between Christianity and Judaism public and decisive, with Christians unable to shelter under the legality of the Jewish faith. Selwyn even suggested that Paul's death may have been caused by James' martyrdom, since Nero's Jewishly-inclined mistress Poppaea may well have heard from Jewish sources of the way in which the Jerusalem Jews had treated the Christian leader, which would be tantamount to an official Jewish denunciation of Christianity.

Another indication of probable dating is the teaching of I Peter with regard to the State (I Pet. ii. 13–17). The approach is so conciliatory that it would better fit the period up to AD 64 than a later period. It seems difficult to imagine any writer urging submission to the infamous Nero after the commencement of his notorious blood-bath of AD 64. Yet it must be remembered that the civil administration of the provinces would not immediately be affected by the personal caprice of the emperor, and in any case it would have been folly for Christians to have shown any open evidence of sedition, since suspicion enough had already been stirred up against them by Nero's action. It is impossible to fix the date with any exactness, but the period immediately preceding or during the Neronian persecutions would appear to be the most probable.

[1] Op. cit., pp. 56ff.

VI. UNITY

Because of the doxology at iv. 11 and the different emphasis on the persecutions in the subsequent section, it has been proposed by various scholars that the Epistle as it now stands does not represent an original unity. The following are the various attempts to explain this break and the general method of composition.[1]

a. A combination of a baptismal sermon and a general address

This view was maintained by B. H. Streeter[2] who placed an interval of two or three years between the two parts to account for the greater severity of persecution and who suggested that an editor, at a considerably later time, joined the two parts to form an epistle, adding the opening address and closing salutations. Although the homiletical form of the Epistle is fairly plain, it is no more than might be expected from a man whose vocation was preaching and not writing. Such a man could hardly fail to dress up his thoughts in homiletical forms. Yet it is not impossible that the Epistle may embody an address, or even more than one address, given orally before being recorded. If there was need for exhortations and encouragements of this kind to be written, there was equal need for them to be spoken. But Streeter's partition theory is improbable on several grounds. (1) The second part (iv. 12–v. 7) does not strike the reader as a separate entity,[3] for its themes echo what is contained in the first part and follow quite naturally from it. (2) The appearance of a doxology in the body of the Epistle, which Streeter supposed marked the end of the first part, is not peculiar to 1 Peter.[4] In Paul's letters particularly there are doxologies that are included before the finale (e.g. Gal. i. 5; Rom. xi. 36; Eph. iii. 21; 1 Tim. i. 17). A readier explanation is the writer's natural outburst of praise when contemplating the purpose of all Christian service. It is certainly by no means evident that a doxology must mean the conclusion of the writer's train of thought. (3) The theory involves a clumsy process on the part of the compiler of the Epistle. The advantages of joining the two parts and turning them into a pseudonymous letter

[1] For a useful survey of the most recent theories, cf. the article by R. P. Martin on the composition of 1 Peter in *Vox Evangelica* (ed. R. P. Martin, 1962).

[2] *The Primitive Church*, pp. 123ff.　　　[3] Cf. J. W. C. Wand, *op. cit.*, p. 2.

[4] Cf. B. F. Westcott's note on the apostolic doxologies, *The Epistle to the Hebrews*[2] (1892), pp. 464, 465.

with closing greetings, which raise a number of difficulties, are altogether too obscure. Such procedure can claim no parallels and must be classified as an unsupported speculation.

b. An original liturgy adapted to a literary form

One presentation of this hypothesis is that of H. Preisker,[1] who considers that the first section is a liturgy for a baptismal service minus the rubrics (with the baptismal rite taking place between i. 21 and i. 22).[2] At iv. 12 the service is designed for the whole congregation, which explains why the present tense is used in connection with the persecutions, since these would affect established Christians but not novices. But if this were a true account of the origin of its contents, the liturgy must have been considerably adapted to make it suitable for an epistolary form. The many instances of 'now' in the Epistle need not be regarded as evidence of a liturgy in process (as Preisker assumes), but rather the realization on the part of the Christians of the importance of the present in their eschatological outlook.[3] The supposed references to baptism in this Epistle are certainly not strong (the only explicit reference is iii. 21) and the figurative expressions (such as are found in i. 23 and ii. 2) are more naturally explained of spiritual regeneration without reference to any external rite, particularly as the rebirth is specifically effected through the word[4] without reference to water.

Another form of this theory is the pascal hypothesis of F. L. Cross.[5] The key to this approach is the connection between the 'suffering' (πάσχω) so prominent in 1 Peter and the *pascha* (or Easter) festival.[6] Cross appeals to the similarity between the Pascal Baptismal Eucharist and the themes of this Epistle: baptism, Passover, passion, resurrection,

---

[1] In the third edition of H. Windisch's *Die katholischen Briefe* (1951), pp. 156ff.

[2] Preisker's idea of a baptismal act at this juncture was strongly criticized by F. Hauck in his review of Preisker's revision of Windisch's Commentary (*ThLZ*, I, 1952, pp. 34, 35) on the grounds that the perfect tense in verse 22 refers to sanctification attested in Christian living.

[3] Cf. E. G. Selwyn, in *The Background of the New Testament and its Eschatology* (ed. W. D. Davies and D. Daube, 1956), pp. 394f. This point is well criticized by C. F. D. Moule, *NTS*, 3 (1957), pp. 1ff.

[4] This λόγος cannot be the baptismal formula as Preisker would maintain (cf. Moule, *op. cit.*, p. 6; Beare, *op. cit.*, p. 86).

[5] *1 Peter: a Pascal Liturgy* (1954).

[6] This comparison between πάσχω and *pascha* is open to strong objection on lexical grounds. Cf. W. C. van Unnik's criticisms (*ET*, LXVIII, 1956, pp. 79–83).

moral duties. His main source is the *Apostolic Tradition* of Hippolytus, but not all scholars will agree on the inferences he draws from this source.[1] As A. F. Walls has pointed out, even if a correspondence is established, it should be possible to make sense of the Epistle without calling on such parallels. After all, the material is preserved for us in the form of an Epistle which is certainly not unintelligible apart from a liturgical explanation.[2] It is more likely, in fact, that the liturgy was moulded by the previously existing Epistle.[3]

c. A double letter which was later combined

A suggestion by C. F. D. Moule[4] that two letters (i. 1–iv. 1 plus conclusion, and i. 1–ii. 10, iv. 12–v. 14) were written by Peter at the same time and were united in the process of transmission, suffers the handicap of most partition theories in lacking all vestige of textual support, although it has in its favour the maintenance of the common authorship of the two parts.[5] Moreover, if, as Moule suggests, each letter was addressed to different parts where different conditions of persecution obtained, it is all the more difficult to imagine how they came to be united in the form in which we now have them. Such a combination by a copyist or editor would be rather unusual and requires some satisfactory explanation, not only of the compiler's purpose but also of his method. The whole theory has an artificial ring about it, which raises suspicions whether any ancient editor would ever have combined the two letters in this way. At the same time it cannot be pronounced impossible. Yet the crucial question is whether it is really necessary.

---

[1] Cf. A. F. Walls' criticism, *op. cit.*, pp. 61, 62.

[2] T. C. G. Thornton, in his article '1 Peter, a Paschal Liturgy?', *JTS*, New Series, XII, i (1961), pp. 14–26, complains that Cross uses the word 'liturgy' too vaguely and suggests that on the same basis liturgy could be found in most New Testament books.

[3] M. E. Boismard has carried the liturgical explanation which he favours for 1 Peter into other parts of the New Testament (e.g. Titus, 1 John, Colossians, James) in his attempt to demonstrate the influences of liturgies on Christian writings (cf. his articles in *RB*, LXIII, 1956, pp. 182–208; *RB*, LXIV, 1957, pp. 161–183; and his monograph *Quatre Hymnes Baptismales dans la Première Epître de Pierre*, 1961).

[4] *Op. cit.*, pp. 6ff.

[5] But W. Bieder (*Grund und Kraft der Mission nach dem ersten Petrusbrief*, *Theologische Studien*, 29, 1950), who similarly maintains two writings (i. 3–iv. 11, iv. 12–v. 11), regards both as post-apostolic.

d. A letter, with a postscript for a particular church

Somewhat akin to the foregoing is the view[1] that the concluding part may be regarded as a postscript designed for particular communities which were subjected to severe persecution and therefore needed special encouragement. This is a more likely explanation than the foregoing because it preserves the essential unity of the Epistle as it stands and is in harmony with the internal indication that it was sent to a specific group of churches. But it hardly seems to be demanded by the evidence. In v. 1 the author addresses 'the elders among you' and the advice given would be applicable to elders of any church. In fact, it is not easy to see what parts of iv. 12–v. 11 would not have been generally relevant.

e. A circular type of letter in its present form

None of the evidence set out by exponents of the preceding theories demands the surrender of the essential unity of the Epistle, and it remains, therefore, the most reasonable approach to assume that the whole was directed to all the churches in the areas mentioned, and that the writer may have intended to finish at iv. 11, but further developments prompted him to add the additional material before attaching the concluding salutations. Or else in the concluding part he may be giving a brief practical summary of points already mentioned theoretically.[2] A theory of this kind has the advantage of not requiring the postulating of any partition and assumes quite naturally that the double doxology merely indicates two stages in the process of composition. It is a safe principle that if the Epistle can be adequately interpreted as a unity, it should be.[3]

f. Interpolation theories

The subject of the unity of the Epistle cannot be left without mention of the attempts to find interpolations in the present text. Among earlier scholars who advocated such theories were A. Harnack,[4] whose theory

---

[1] Cf. J. H. A. Hart, *EGT*, v, pp. 29, 30.

[2] Cf. T. C. G. Thornton (*op. cit.*, p. 26), who considers that no theory is satisfactory which accounts for the first part without giving a satisfactory explanation of how and why the latter part was added.

[3] Many recent scholars have been anxious to maintain the unity; cf. F. V. Filson, *Interpretation*, IX (1955), pp. 400–412; W. Nauck, *ZNTW*, 46 (1955), pp. 68–80. C. E. B. Cranfield (*The First Epistle of Peter*, 1950, p. 18), although considering i. 3–iv. 11 as originally a sermon, still maintains the unity of the Epistle.

[4] *TU*, II, ii (1884), pp. 106–109.

of later additions in i. 1, 2 and v. 12–14 has already been mentioned; W. Soltau,[1] who made the discovery of a whole series of interpolations, which transformed an early tract into a Petrine Epistle; and in a similar vein, but differing considerably in detail, D. Völter.[2] These theories have commanded little support, for they appeal only to ultra-critical minds. A more recent tendency in the same direction is found in Bultmann's[3] treatment of the passage iii. 18–22, where he separates verses 19–21 for no other reason than that this section spoils his own interpretation of the passage as a hymn. Generally speaking there is far less inclination than formerly to resort to such drastic methods and little serious attention need therefore be given to such theories.

VII. PLACE OF WRITING

The author has given greetings from the church at 'Babylon' (v. 13) and it may reasonably be assumed that it is from 'Babylon' that he writes. But what does he mean by Babylon? Is it literal or is it a cryptogram? That Peter was in Mesopotamian Babylon[4] when he wrote this letter is most unlikely for several reasons. (1) Peter is nowhere else associated with this region; (2) the Eastern Church did not until a late period claim any association with Peter in its Church origins; (3) the area itself was very sparsely populated, especially in the period subsequent to the migration in AD 41[5] and the resultant massacre of large numbers of Jews at Seleucia; (4) early tradition centred the activities of Peter in the West

---

[1] *TSK*, 78 (1905), pp. 302–315; 79 (1906), pp. 456–460. W. Soltau considered that the original Epistle consisted only of i. 3–22a, i. 23–ii. 4, ii. 6–11, ii. 13–iii. 18, iv. 1–4, iv. 7–19, v. 6–11, which was later worked over by two different hands. C. Clemen (*TSK*, 1905, pp. 619–628) strongly criticized this theory, particularly because of the improbability of a final editor affixing so vague an address to a letter form, since this, according to Deissmann, was rare.

[2] *Op. cit.* Cf. also *idem*, *ZNTW*, 9 (1908), pp. 74–77. For details of all three of these theories, see Moffatt, *ILNT*, pp. 342–344.

[3] In his article 'Bekenntnis-und Liedfragmente im ersten Petrusbrief', in *Coniectanea Neotestamentica, XI in honorem Antonii Fridrichsen* (1947), pp. 1–14. This method of criticism is dismissed with little consideration by J. Jeremias, *ZNTW*, 42 (1949), pp. 194–201. Cf. also C. E. B. Cranfield, *ET*, LXIX (1958), pp. 369–372.

[4] This opinion was maintained by Calvin in an attempt to dissociate the name of Peter with Rome, in opposition to Roman Catholic claims. Cf. H. Alford, *Greek Testament*[4] (1871), IV, pp. 127, 128. H. C. Thiessen (*INT*[4], 1956, p. 285) is a recent upholder of this view.

[5] Cf. Josephus, *Antiquities*, xviii. 9. 8.

and not the East; (5) Mark almost certainly found a sphere of activity in the West, but nothing is known of him working in the East.

Another suggestion which may be dismissed with little consideration is that an Egyptian Babylon is meant.[1] But the Alexandrian church laid no claim to it and this Babylon was so small a district that it seems highly improbable that Peter made his headquarters there without such a fact leaving any trace in early tradition. Yet another idea is that the Epistle originated in the region of Antioch. Boismard[2] maintains this view on doctrinal grounds (the descent into hell idea, he thinks, was connected with that district) and historical grounds (the believers were first called Christians there).[3]

But the majority of scholars favour Rome as the place of writing taking 'Babylon' as symbolic, in the same sense as in the Apocalypse.[4] The Roman martyrdom of Peter is fairly well attested,[5] and if this is genuine tradition it seems highly improbable that in the immediate past Peter had been residing in Babylon.[6] But the problem arises why Peter resorted to symbolic expression. There is little indication in the context that any figurative meaning was intended, although the meta-

---

[1] Michaelis (*Einleitung*, p. 287) cites de Zwaan as a recent advocate of the view that a military colony named Babylon in the Nile delta is meant. Cf. also G. T. Manley, *EQ*, xvi (1944). This colony is mentioned by Strabo, xvii. 30 and Josephus, *Antiquities*, ii. 15. 1.

[2] *RB*, LXIV (1957), p. 181 n. 2. Beare (*op. cit.*, p. 204) disputes this because of the absence of trace in Ignatius and because of the links with *1 Clement*. Yet Beare noted that the *Apostolic Tradition*, with which 1 Peter shows some similarities (cf. F. L. Cross, *op. cit.*, pp. 12ff.), may point to a Syrian background (*op. cit.*, p. 204).

[3] Knopf (*op. cit.*, p. 25) having disputed Petrine authorship saw no more reason to regard the Babylon (= Rome) reference in v. 13 as authentic than the author's name in i. 1. As he maintained an Asiatic destination, he considered an Asiatic place of origin was therefore most probable. Beare (*op. cit.*, pp. 31, 202ff.) first favoured the same district as the addressees, but later changed to Rome.

[4] For a clear discussion of the whole matter, cf. O. Cullmann, *Peter: Disciple, Apostle, and Martyr* (1953), pp. 82–86. Cullmann thinks that Rome is most probable, but does not entirely exclude the possibility of an alternative.

[5] Cf. Cullmann's detailed discussion, *op. cit.*, pp. 89–152. He places most reliance on a statement of Gaius, a text of Tertullian against Callistus and the declaration of Porphyrius. For a briefer statement, cf. J. Lowe, *Saint Peter* (1956), pp. 23–45. Cf. also J. Munck (*Petrus und Paulus in der Offenbarung Johannis*, 1950, pp. 30ff.), who finds a reference to the martyrdom of both Peter and Paul at Rome in Rev. xi.

[6] E. Lohse (*ZNTW*, 45, 1954, pp. 83–85) maintains a Roman place of origin particularly on the grounds of affinities of language with *1 Clement*, which he sets out in detail. But it is not clear why this should demonstrate the place of despatch.

phorical use of 'diaspora' in i. 1 may give an indication of the author's bent of mind. It is probable that the cryptogram was used as a security measure.[1] At the time of writing, Rome was the centre of vicious action against Christianity and avoidance of any mention of the Roman church would be a wise move if the letter fell into official hands. The writer evidently assumed that the readers would have understood the symbolism.[2]

As a further proposition, some have seen in the reference to 'she in Babylon' a woman rather than a church, and linking this passage with 1 Corinthians ix. 5, have ventured on the conjecture that Peter's wife is intended.[3] But this is a strange description for his wife, and although it may be contended that an abstraction like 'the church in Babylon' is an unnatural partner for 'my son Mark' in the greetings of v. 13, yet the abstraction represents a specific group of people. There is nothing unnatural in this combination, and, in fact, 'the church and Mark' seems more probable than 'my wife and Mark'.[4]

VIII. LITERARY AFFINITIES

That there is behind this Epistle clear evidence of the author's Old Testament background will be disputed by few, in spite of Perdelwitz's[5] attempt to prove that the background is to be found in the mystery religions. Not only does 1 Peter cite the Old Testament several times, but the allusions are in many instances drawn from it (cf. for instance, the lamb (i. 19), the whole passage ii. 4–10, the parallels with Is. liii in ii. 21ff., Sarah (iii. 6) and Noah (iii. 20)).

Recently, in conjunction with liturgical theories for the Epistle, stress has been laid upon the use of the Exodus typology and of Psalm xxxiv. The former is used by Boismard[6] in support of his baptismal homily hypothesis and by Cross,[7] who finds several traces of it in 1

---

[1] Cf. Selwyn, *The First Epistle of St. Peter*, p. 243.

[2] C. F. D. Moule (*NTS*, 3, 1957, pp. 8, 9) disputes the security grounds because of the plain exhortation to loyalty in ii. 13–17. He regards the motive as homiletic, Babylon being used as symbolic of the Christian's exile in the world. It should be noted here that the metaphorical use of 'Babylon' is found in contemporary Jewish pseudepigraphical literature and in the Church Fathers (see Cullmann, *op. cit.*, p. 84, for details).

[3] Cf. C. Bigg, *op. cit.*, p. 197; and H. Alford, *op. cit.*, p. 387.

[4] Cf. Moffatt, *ILNT*, p. 328.

[5] *Die Mysterienreligionen und das Problem des ersten Petrusbriefes* (1911).

[6] Cf. *RB*, LXIII, pp. 182ff.   [7] *Op. cit.*, pp. 24f.

Peter i and ii, in support of his Paschal Vigil theory. But it is open to criticism on two grounds. (1) It is strange, if the Exodus motif was so dominant, that the flood allusion has been used rather than the wilderness allusion to illustrate baptism[1]; and (2) some allusions to Exodus are not surprising in an epistle which presents the Christian believers as the New Israel, and need not point to any liturgical use of the Old Testament.

The same may be said of Bornemann's theory[2] that the whole Epistle is a homily based on Psalm xxxiv, though here again a liturgical theorist such as Boismard[3] thinks that the Psalm formed part of the liturgical ceremony. It is better to regard this Psalm,[4] with its theme of God's protection of the loyal sufferer, as part of the author's own background, which would be clearly relevant to his present theme.

Several connections of thought have been found between this Epistle and other New Testament writings and the most important of these are Romans, Ephesians, Hebrews, James and the Acts. Sanday and Headlam[5] cite eight passages from Romans showing close affinities with this Epistle, although Wand[6] reduces their significance by accounting for the resemblances, either as showing common Old Testament influence or common lists of duties, or as evidence of the semi-liturgical character of the material. Yet some dependence of 1 Peter upon Romans is generally admitted. In the case of Ephesians C. L. Mitton[7] claims to have established sufficient parallels to conclude that the author of 1 Peter has used Ephesians. But because he regards Ephesians as non-Pauline he is obliged to regard 1 Peter as non-Petrine. The parallels may be admitted and the question of dependence granted, but if there are strong grounds for assuming the early dating of 1 Peter this should indicate an early and therefore Pauline origin for Ephesians.[8] On the other hand, literary

---

[1] Cf. Moule's criticisms, NTS, 3 (1957), pp. 4, 5.

[2] ZNTW, 19 (1919–20), pp. 143ff.

[3] Cf. RB, LXIV, pp. 180ff. Moule (op. cit., loc. cit.) disputes this on the ground that there is no evidence that Ps. xxxiv was ever connected with the Passover.

[4] Jeremias (ZNTW, 42, 1949, pp. 199, 200) finds evidence of the influence of Ps. xvi. 8–11 on the author's Descensus doctrine.

[5] The Epistle to the Romans (ICC, 1895), pp. lxxiv ff.   [6] Op. cit., p. 19.

[7] Cf. The Epistle to the Ephesians (1951), pp. 176–197; and his article 'The Relationship between 1 Peter and Ephesians', JTS, New Series, 1 (1950), pp. 67ff.

[8] C. L. Mitton (op. cit., p. 196) admits this result must follow if 1 Peter is ascribed to Peter. One of the reasons that Beare brings forward for the refusal of Petrine authorship to this Epistle is the Deutero-Pauline character of Ephesians, which he

dependence is not certain. In fact, it is impossible to *prove* such a theory in this case, for the similarities may be due to oral influences. If Peter had heard Paul discourse at Rome it may account for a similar sequence of ideas.[1] But since most scholars[2] incline towards literary dependence theories rather than oral influence theories, it remains to remark that it would not be altogether surprising if Peter at Rome had been acquainted with both Romans and Ephesians, since these bear the form of circulars and a copy of Ephesians might easily have been accessible at Rome.[3]

In the case of Hebrews there are certain similarities of phrases which have suggested to some that one author may have used the other's work, but the resemblances are not close enough to be certain of literary dependence and again a common milieu may be the reason for the similarities.[4] It is interesting to note, nevertheless, that both letters have a similar purpose of encouragement and both have a similar doctrinal emphasis in setting forth an objective and future hope, in connecting the sufferings of Christ with future glory and in their focus on the atoning work of Christ.[5]

There is little room to dispute the literary parallels between this Epistle and the Epistle of James.[6] Yet there is again difference of opinion

regards as established (*op. cit.*, 1958, pp. 195f.). But in this he underestimates the weight of opinion in favour of the Pauline authorship of Ephesians (see the discussion in the writer's *New Testament Introduction: The Pauline Epistles*, 1961, pp. 99ff.). It will be recognized that Ephesians and 1 Peter stand or fall together in this type of criticism.

[1] Selwyn (*op. cit.*, pp. 363–466) in a very thorough investigation traces most of the similarities to common material and if he is correct this would considerably lessen literary dependence. Cf. his article in *ET*, LIX (1948), pp. 256–259, in which he also challenges the theory of Paulinism. Others who take a similar line are E. Lohse, *ZNTW*, 45 (1954), pp. 73–83; and P. Carrington, 'Saint Peter's Epistle' in *The Joy of Study* (ed. S. E. Johnson) (1951), pp. 57–63.

[2] Among the most recent writers to do so are J. Coutts, *NTS*, 3 (1957), pp. 115–127, in comparing 1 Pet. i. 3–12 and Eph. i. 3–14, Mitton (see p. 128 n. 7) and Beare, *op. cit.*, pp. 193ff.

[3] Cf. Zahn, *INT*, II, p. 177.

[4] Cf. Moffatt's *ILNT*, p. 440, for a concise list of similar phrases and expressions.

[5] Cf. J. H. B. Masterman, *The First Epistle of Peter* (1912), pp. 36ff.; J. W. C. Wand, *op. cit.*, pp. 25, 26. Selwyn thought the author of Hebrews had either read 1 Peter or was in touch with someone who knew the author of 1 Peter (*op. cit.*, pp. 462, 463).

[6] Cf. the concise list in Wand, *op. cit.*, p. 25; Bigg, *op. cit.*, p. 23. Cf. also Boismard, *RB*, LXIII (1957), pp. 161–183.

as to the direction in which the dependence lies. It is more generally considered that Peter used James than the reverse,[1] and there is no intrinsic reason why he should not have echoed the language of his fellow 'pillar' apostle, in view of what has already been noted of his sympathetic and impressionable character.

More suggestive are the parallels between the Acts speeches of Peter and this Epistle. In the speech at Pentecost, compare Acts ii. 16ff. and I Peter i. 10 for the idea of fulfilment of Old Testament prophecy; Acts ii. 17 and I Peter i. 20 for the idea of Christ's manifestation in the last days; Acts ii. 23 and I Peter i. 20 for the fore-ordination by God of the death of Jesus; Acts ii. 24ff. and I Peter iii. 19 for the triumph over Hades; and Acts ii. 32–36 and I Peter i. 21 for the connection between the resurrection and exaltation of Christ. Similar comparisons may be made between the speeches in Solomon's porch (iii. 12–26) and in Cornelius' house (x. 34–43).[2] But what conclusions may fairly be drawn from these data? The answer will naturally depend upon the degree of veracity which is attached to the Acts speeches and to the *ipsissima verba* of the Epistle as authentically Petrine. Although these similarities may not be considered conclusive, yet they could be regarded as confirmatory, if at least the substance of the Acts speeches is traced to a Petrine source and there seems no strong reason for denying this.[3] These similarities are what we should expect in common material attributed to the apostle Peter. J. W. C. Wand[4] has, however, pointed out that in the Epistle there is a development of the ideas in the Acts speeches, but this development is of such a character that it is explicable as a maturing of thought in one mind.

IX. SOURCES

The question arises to what extent this Epistle is indebted to traditional Christian materials and it was one of Selwyn's[5] great contributions to the study of the Epistle to make a detailed investigation along these lines. He suggested three main sources: a liturgical source, a persecution

---

[1] Bigg, however, maintains that James used I Peter (*loc. cit.*).

[2] Cf. Wand's list, *op. cit.*, p. 27; A. F. Walls, *op. cit.*, pp. 35, 36.

[3] Cf. F. F. Bruce, *The Speeches in Acts* (1944), and *The Acts of the Apostles* (Greek text, 1951), pp. 18ff. Cf. also Selwyn (*op. cit.*, pp. 33–36), who regarded the connection as historical rather than literary, the mind of Peter being the common ground between them.

[4] *Op. cit.*, p. 28.   [5] *Op. cit.*, Essay II, pp. 365–466.

fragment and catechetical material. In his suggestions about the latter material he has been supported by P. Carrington's studies in the primitive Christian catechism.[1] It is not at all improbable that some of the ideas in this Epistle, especially in the sphere of moral exhortations, followed closely the patterns of early Christian instruction. The existence of Christian moral codes after the form of pagan equivalents and even influenced by their content, although with a Christian interpretation, may well be possible during the apostolic period. There must have been an interchange of language and ideas between the apostolic writings and the primitive catechesis which was so largely inspired by the apostolic oral teaching. But to what extent the catechesis can be disentangled from the writings and what precise value it would be if this could be achieved with any certainty is an open question. Selwyn's arguments, in fact, have not gone unchallenged, particularly by Beare,[2] who prefers to regard the Pauline Epistles as the main source of the material that Selwyn regarded as traditional. But since he uses this as an argument for the late dating of 1 Peter his estimate of the data on this issue is somewhat influenced by his presuppositions.[3]

Some reference must be made to theories that hymn fragments lie buried in 1 Peter, advocated mainly by Bultmann[4] and Boismard.[5] The former suggests three examples, iii. 18–20, i. 20 and ii. 21–24, but in each of these he claims that the fragments are mixed up with credal forms and need disentangling. But Bultmann's resort to textual emendations undermines confidence in his critical analysis. Boismard's presentation is rather less open to objection on these grounds. He finds four hymns—the first in 1 Peter i. 3–5, the second in i. 20, iii. 18, 22, iv. 6, the third in ii. 22–25, the fourth in v. 5–9. But he has to do some manip-

---

[1] *The Primitive Christian Catechism* (1940).   [2] *Op. cit.*, pp. 193ff.

[3] Two recent German writers have argued in the direction of Selwyn's position. E. Lohse (*ZNTW*, 45, 1954, pp. 68, 69) finds dependence on common paraenetic material rather than upon Paul's Epistles. He believes that moral instruction followed naturally from the kerygmatic (preaching) material, as 1 Pet. ii. 21–25 strikingly illustrates. W. Nauck (*ZNTW*, 46, 1955, pp. 68–80) finds similar patterns in 1 Peter on the theme of joy through suffering and compares this with the occurrence of the same theme in other New Testament books and even in the *Apocalypse of Baruch* and other Jewish apocrypha and pseudepigrapha. But see Beare's criticism that Nauck subordinates the data to an overriding theory (*op. cit.*, p. 194).

[4] *Op. cit.*, pp. 1–14.

[5] Particularly in his *Quatre Hymnes Baptismales dans la première Epître de Pierre* (1961).

ulating of his material to arrive at his rhythmic forms.[1] The theory cannot be examined here, but it may be noted as characteristic of an increasing tendency to discover hymn fragments within the New Testament writings.

One other source, although more of background than of literary dependence, has been proposed. Perdelwitz,[2] in maintaining that the form of the Epistle has been strongly influenced by the mystery religions, cited many pagan parallels to Christian baptism and the Christian mysteries. This type of theory has gained very little support. The evidences deduced are almost entirely questionable inferences, such as the idea that the allusion to the blood of Christ in i. 2ff. finds analogy in the bath of bull's blood, by which rebirth was attained in the cults of Cybele and Mithras. But the allusion is so plainly to the Old Testament sacrifices that to appeal to a revolting pagan ritual as its background is not only entirely unnecessary, but robs the words of 1 Peter of their deepest significance.[3] This whole hypothesis of the author's heathen background may be dismissed as unfounded.[4]

CONTENTS

I. GREETINGS (i. 1, 2)

Peter introduces himself as an apostle and addresses the believers in various provinces. He reminds them of their election, sanctification and redemption.

II. THE NATURE OF CHRISTIAN SALVATION (i. 3–ii. 10)

The apostle next draws attention both to the privileges and to the responsibilities of Christian salvation.

a. The blessings of the gospel (i. 3–9)

Believers are born into a new way of life and become heirs of a heavenly inheritance (verses 3, 4). But future hope is linked with present security

---

[1] For instance, in his fourth hymn, Boismard admits that what has been preserved is rather a paraphrase than the form of the hymn itself (*op. cit.*, p. 14).

[2] *Op. cit.*   [3] Cf. the criticisms of A. F. Walls, *op. cit.*, pp. 37–39.

[4] Beare (*op. cit.*, pp. 16ff., 27) is partially influenced by this theory.

in spite of trials and afflictions (5, 6). These have only a refining effect on true faith and they can, in fact, lead to inexpressible joy because faith has been fortified by love to Christ (7–9).

b. These blessings were foreseen (i. 10–12)

Christian salvation has a long history, for the prophets were granted insight through the Spirit into the sufferings and glories of Christ. The same Spirit has made it known to the readers, who have therefore become more privileged even than angels.

c. The heirs of these blessings must change their manner of life (i. 13–16)

The gospel involves transformation in thought and behaviour. The mind must be alert to make use of the grace provided (13) and the conduct must be conformed to God's holiness (14–16).

d. The basis of the believer's confidence must not be forgotten (i. 17–21)

The Christian, like the Israelite, must never forget the deliverance already obtained in the past and the cost of that redemptive act. Indeed his present faith has as its basis a divine purpose which reaches back to a period before the beginning of the world. In Christ the believer may have absolute confidence for present and future. The resurrection is the guarantee of this.

e. The heirs have present responsibilities (i. 22–ii. 3)

Purified souls have an obligation to love the brethren and this thought is supported by an appeal to the power of the Word of God in regeneration. Since the believers are regarded as new-born babes they have an ethical obligation to reject all that is opposed to love (see ii. 1) and to foster the development of a genuine spiritual appetite.

f. The heirs form a spiritual community (ii. 4–10)

The apostle thinks of the Christian Church as the new Israel and describes it in terms of the old. His mind goes to the temple and he thinks of Christians as living stones. And because this spiritual edifice consists of living people, he identifies them as a living priesthood (4, 5). But the thought of living stones leads his mind to dwell on Christ, the Chief Corner-stone. There have been two different reactions to Him: some have stumbled through disobedience, others have inherited wonderful privileges (6–10).

III. CHRISTIAN RELATIONSHIPS (ii. 11–iii. 12)

So far the apostle has dealt mainly with doctrine, but now he comes to practical issues affecting Christian life in the present world.

a. In the pagan world (ii. 11, 12)

Christians are aliens in a pagan environment, but their conduct may be the means of leading others to glorify God.

b. In the State (ii. 13–17)

Any government official, from the emperor downwards, who maintains just government, must be obeyed, for Christians are not intended to be anarchists. The problems of dishonest or illegal government are not discussed.

c. In the household (ii. 18–iii. 7)

Two different problems arose in domestic life and the apostle deals with both.

1. Slaves must respect masters, whatever their character might be (ii. 18). There should be no resentment even of wrong punishment, in view of the supreme example of Christ, whose punishment was not for His own sins but for ours (ii. 19–25).

2. Wives and husbands have specific Christian responsibilities (iii. 1–7). Wives with unbelieving husbands may win them by Christian example. Their approach to adornment should be modest and their relation to their husbands submissive. The husbands are more briefly exhorted, but are reminded to honour their wives as joint heirs.

d. In the Church (iii. 8–12)

The most pressing need is for Christian unity, which involves humility and a readiness to develop brotherly love. Retaliation must be excluded by blessing, a principle which is illustrated from Psalm xxxiv.

IV. CHRISTIAN SUFFERING AND SERVICE (iii. 13–iv. 19)

This is clearly a subject of great importance for the readers and the apostle discusses it in some detail.

a. The blessings of suffering wrongfully (iii. 13–17)

This at once constitutes a paradox, but several important principles are enunciated in support of it. 1. No-one can harm the righteous.

2. Fear of man must be replaced by reverence for Christ. 3. When defence is made before man it must be accompanied by a true Christian deportment. Whatever then happens will never destroy the believer's joy. 4. The Christian's conscience must be kept clear.

b. The powerful example of Christ (iii. 18–22)

Undeserved suffering is not alien to Christianity for Christ Himself suffered unjustly, but this has borne rich fruit in that He has been able to bring a people to God. The apostle then brings in a somewhat obscure reference to Christ's preaching to imprisoned spirits, which reminds him of God's patience in the time of the flood. This latter thought leads the apostle to think of baptism and to connect it with a Christian's cleanness of conscience. This forms somewhat of a digression but the apostle returns again to his theme of Christ's example.

c. Suffering in the flesh (iv. 1–6)

There is a marked contrast between suffering in the flesh and indulging in the flesh. Christ's example should lead to the ready acceptance of the former when God wills it and the firm rejection of the latter. Those who indulge in human passions must be prepared to render an account to the divine Judge.

d. The urgent need for holy living (iv. 7–11)

The thought of approaching judgment leads the apostle to urge certain practical principles of behaviour. Soberness, love, hospitality, liberality, the gift of speech, and service are all inculcated as means whereby God may be glorified.

e. Encouragements in special suffering (iv. 12–19)

A fiery ordeal is anticipated and the readers must be prepared. One encouragement is the thought of sharing Christ's glory as well as His sufferings. Another is the obvious contrast between a Christian and a common criminal in the reason for his suffering. If reproached for the name of Christ, the Christian must glorify God. The thought of judgment re-occurs, but this time relative to Christians (the household of God). The thing to do is to entrust one's soul to God.

v. CHRISTIAN DISCIPLINE (v. 1–11)

This is seen from two points of view, one in reference to corporate discipline and the other to personal discipline.

a. Corporate discipline (v. 1–6)

Elders have special responsibilities to tend the flock, but they must watch the spirit in which they do it. Younger men must submit to elders, and both groups must develop the grace of humility, which is the only befitting attitude before God.

b. Personal discipline (v. 7–11)

The believer must transfer his anxieties to God and develop a constant watchfulness particularly for the devices of his enemy the devil. This leads to another echo of the suffering-theme, but only for the purpose of reassuring the sufferers about the glories in store in the future. A doxology makes a fitting conclusion to this section.

VI. CONCLUSION (v. 12–14)

The apostle concludes with a reference to his helper Silvanus, to the church at 'Babylon' and to Mark, followed by a brief benediction.

CHAPTER FOUR

THE SECOND EPISTLE OF PETER

This is the most problematical of all the New Testament Epistles because of early doubts regarding its authenticity and because internal evidence is considered by many to substantiate those doubts. In short, the majority of scholars reject it as a genuine work of the apostle Peter, in spite of its own claims, and regard it as a later pseudepigraphon.[1] To obtain a true appraisal of all the evidence, the external attestation will first be considered in order to see the problem in its historical setting, then a review of the internal claims and internal difficulties will be considered, and finally a brief examination of alternative theories of authorship will be made.

I. THE EPISTLE IN THE ANCIENT CHURCH

There are various ways of approaching early evidence of canonicity or non-canonicity of New Testament writings.

1. We can take the earliest known quotation from a book and conclude that the book was not canonical until a period just prior to the date of citation.

2. We may give citations a relative value and enquire whether the authors whose works are extant and who wrote prior to the date of the first citation had any cause in their writing to cite the New Testament book in question, on the assumption that no Christian writer was obliged to cite all parts of the New Testament in his possession which he regarded as Scripture.

3. We can place most emphasis on evidence of rejection in part, at least, of the early Church.

Of all these approaches the first is clearly most likely to lead us astray in view of the paucity of evidence before the last quarter of the second century. This first approach needs balancing with the second and yet

---

[1] In many commentaries and works of introduction this is assumed without much discussion as if it has almost become an established fact. Cf. K. and S. Lake, *INT* (1938), pp. 167, 168; W. Michaelis, *Einleitung*, pp. 289, 290; H.Windisch-H. Preisker, *Die katholischen Briefe*, p. 83; C. E. B. Cranfield, *I and II Peter and Jude* (*TC*, 1960); J. Moffatt, *The General Epistles* (*MC*, 1928).

this is much more difficult to establish and is consequently generally neglected. The third approach, although seldom used, is not without considerable significance in determining the positive as opposed to the negative attitude of the contemporary Church. It has special point in the case of 2 Peter, where early doubts nowhere took the form of definite rejection. An attempt must, nevertheless, be made to ascertain the probable reason for the doubts.

It will be convenient to regard Origen as the pivotal Christian Father in this discussion, because reviews[1] of the evidence so often commence with the statement that the Epistle was not certainly known until his time and the authenticity becomes immediately suspect, especially as he also mentions doubts held by some about it. He uses the Epistle at least six times in citations and shows little hesitation in regarding it as canonical. Some uncertainty about the validity of this evidence has been expressed because the citations all occur in those works preserved only in Rufinus' Latin translation and it is not always certain that Rufinus can be relied upon.[2] At the same time there seems to be no reason why he should erroneously attribute to Origen citations from a New Testament Epistle such as 2 Peter. Some suggestion of doubt on Origen's part might be inferred from Eusebius' statement[3] that he held Peter to have left one acknowledged Epistle and 'perhaps also a second, for it is disputed'. But Origen mentions no explanation for the doubts which were apparently current among some Christians, neither does he give any indication of the extent or location of these doubts. It is a fair assumption, therefore, that Origen saw no reason to treat these doubts as serious, and this would seem to imply that in his time the Epistle was widely regarded as canonical.[4]

Before Origen's time, the evidence is somewhat inconclusive. His predecessor, Clement of Alexandria, is said by Eusebius[5] to have commented on all the Catholic Epistles in his *Hypotyposes*. If so, he must have regarded this Epistle as on the same footing as the others, as he probably did the *Epistle of Barnabas* and the *Apocalypse of Peter*. There are some

---

[1] Cf. J. W. C. Wand, *The General Epistles of St. Peter and St. Jude* (1934), pp. 140, 141.

[2] Cf. F. H. Chase, *HDB*, III, p. 803.   [3] *HE*, vi. 25.

[4] Origen (*Hom. in Josh.* vii. 1) speaks of Peter sounding aloud with the two trumpets of his Epistles, which M. R. James thinks is characteristic of his manner and, therefore, genuine (*The Second Epistle General of St. Peter and the General Epistle of St. Jude*, 1912, p. xix).

[5] *HE*, vi. 14.

similarities of language between 2 Peter and Clement's extant works, but these are not sufficiently clear to be regarded with certainty as citations.[1] The same may be said of Theophilus of Antioch, Aristides, Polycarp and Justin Martyr.[2]

There are one or two faint allusions in Irenaeus' writings, of which the most notable is the statement that the day of the Lord is as a thousand years,[3] but he does not attribute this to Peter. It is possible that Psalm xc. 4 was his source. But the widespread influence of Chiliasm, which held that the world would last six thousand years corresponding to the six days of creation, presupposes an origin of apostolic authority. There are one or two striking resemblances between our Epistle and the *Letter of the Churches of Lyons and Vienne*, which seem to demand the supposition that the author was acquainted with 2 Peter. Some have claimed to find traces of the Epistle in the writings of Ignatius, Hermas and Clement of Rome, but these again are too insubstantial to lead to any conclusion in favour of dependence.[4] One passage in the so-called *2 Clement* looks very much like an echo of 2 Peter, since both speak of the destruction of the earth by fire, but it is not a citation (cf. *2 Clement*, xvi. 3 and 2 Peter iii. 10).[5] Similar references to Noah in *1 Clement*, vii. 6 and 2 Peter ii. 5 may also be noted. Moreover, van Unnik has recently suggested that it may be referred to in the *Gospel of Truth*,[6] probably published in the early part of the second century.

An important consideration is the witness of the Muratorian Canon, which omits reference to the Epistle. If it could be concluded with certainty from this that the Epistle was unknown at that time in the West, it would be demonstrated that an early date for the Epistle is highly improbable. Yet, since the Muratorian Canon omits reference to 1 Peter and since its present text is almost certainly incomplete, no

---

[1] Cf. Bigg, *The Epistles of St. Peter and St. Jude* (*ICC*, 1901), pp. 202, 203 for details.

[2] Cf. *idem, op. cit.*, pp. 204, 205; Wand, *op. cit.*, pp. 141f. But James (*op. cit.*, p. xviii) considers the first two as probable.

[3] *Adv. Haer.*, v. 28. 3; cf. also v. 23. 2.

[4] Cf. Bigg, *op. cit.*, pp. 209, 210 for details. Much greater weight would be given to these allusions if on other grounds an early date proved probable. Cf. R. A. Falconer (*Exp.*, VI, vi, 1902, p. 225), who also includes a reference in the *Epistle of Barnabas*, xv.

[5] In the same passage, *2 Clement* refers to the imminence of the day of judgment, whereas 2 Peter mentions the day of the Lord.

[6] *The Jung Codex* (ed. F. L. Cross, 1955), p. 116. The allusions are to 2 Pet. i. 17, ii. 2.

such construction can be put on its omitting to mention 2 Peter.[1] T. Zahn[2] made an ingenious attempt to emend the text of the Canon to include a reference to both Epistles of Peter in place of the *Apocalypse of Peter*. But even if the emendation is possible it could hardly be used with any confidence in support of 2 Peter. Yet it should be noted that, unlike its reference to the Epistles to the Alexandrians and Laodiceans, the Canon does not pronounce either of the Petrine Epistles as spurious, and its evidence must, therefore, be regarded as purely negative. The argument from silence must, as always, be used with the greatest reserve.

So far no mention has been made of writers subsequent to Origen. The most important of these is Eusebius, who placed this Epistle among the *Antilegomena*. He makes it clear that the majority accepted the Epistle as authentic, together with James and Jude, but he himself had doubts about it. In fact he mentions two grounds for his doubts: first, writers whom he respected did not regard it as canonical, and secondly, it was not quoted by 'the ancient presbyters'. Under the latter objection Eusebius may have meant 'by name'.[3] In any case Eusebius' comments are important as giving the earliest record of the reasons for the doubts, but they would have more significance if Eusebius had said who the other writers were whose opinions he respected. As it is, we are obliged to conclude that Eusebius and certain others were doubtful about the Epistle, although the majority regarded it as canonical. Even Eusebius, however, did not class it within his 'spurious' classification, in which category he placed the *Apocalypse of Peter*.[4]

Although Cyprian does not himself cite 2 Peter, his contemporary Firmilian of Caesarea in correspondence with him[5] makes a clear reference to his Epistle and it is highly improbable that Cyprian would have been ignorant of the allusion. At a slightly earlier period Hippolytus several times makes use of the words of this Epistle, which means that in Origen's time it must have been known and used in the West as well as in the East. The evidence from Jerome is important because, although he unreservedly accepted the Epistle with the other Catholic Epistles,

[1] Bigg (*op. cit.*, p. 204) thinks that some words in the Canon attached to Acts may allude to 2 Pet. i. 14.

[2] See p. 96, n. 4.

[3] Cf. Bigg, *op. cit.*, pp. 200, 201. Eusebius (*HE* ,iii. 3. 1) says of 2 Peter that 'We have received it as not canonical' (οὐκ ἐνδιάθηκον).

[4] Cf. B. F. Westcott, *On the Canon of the New Testament*, p. 415.

[5] Cyprian, *Epp.*, lxxv. 6, cited by Bigg, *op. cit.*, p. 203.

he notes that doubts existed over its authenticity, based on the differences of style. He himself explains this supposed difficulty by suggesting that Peter used two different amanuenses for his two Epistles.[1] Subsequent to Jerome's time no further doubts were expressed (although the Syriac-speaking Church did not receive the Epistle until sometime later, i.e. between the Peshitta (AD 411) and the Philoxenian Version (AD 506)).

This external evidence has been given in some detail because of the important influence it has had on the entire problem of 2 Peter. As compared with other New Testament books, the early positive evidence in support of its authenticity is the most sparse, while the expression of doubts in the third and fourth centuries must be given full weight. Yet where the majority accept a given book, the minority opinion must be viewed with proportionate reserve. At the same time it must be admitted that the external evidence is not strongly favourable in the case of this Epistle. A mitigating factor, which has all too often been overlooked, is the influence of the pseudo-Petrine literature upon Church opinion. If Gnostic groups had used Peter's name to drive home their own particular tenets, this fact would cause the orthodox Church to take particular care not to use any spurious Petrine Epistles. Some of the more nervous probably regarded 2 Peter suspiciously for this reason, but the fact that it ultimately gained acceptance in spite of the pseudo-Petrine literature is an evidence more favourable to its authenticity than against it, unless the orthodox Church Fathers had by this time become wholly undiscerning, which is not, however, borne out by the firm rejection of other works attributed to Peter.

In the foregoing discussion no account has been taken of the evidence of either the *Apocalypse of Peter* or the Epistle of Jude. The latter Epistle is a clear case of literary borrowing, but the majority of scholars regard 2 Peter as the borrower. Some attention must later be given to this question, but for our present purpose it should be noted that certain, not inconsiderable, arguments have been advanced for the alternative theory. If this alternative could be substantiated Jude would become the earliest external witness to 2 Peter[2] and would considerably change the complexion of the external evidence as a whole.[3]

---

[1] Cf. *Epistle to Hedibia*, 120; *Onaest.* xi, cited by Bigg, *op. cit.*, p. 199.

[2] This was strongly maintained by R. A. Falconer in his essay dealing with the external attestation (*Exp.*, VI, vi, pp. 218ff.).

[3] See later discussion on this, pp. 243ff.

The relation of the Epistle to the *Apocalypse of Peter*[1] is of a different kind, although in this case also the direction of dependence has been variously understood. Some scholars have confidently affirmed that 2 Peter borrowed from the *Apocalypse* and others as confidently have maintained the reverse (see discussion on pp. 181ff.). Harnack[2] made much of the fact that earlier attestation existed for the *Apocalypse* than for 2 Peter. Certainly Clement of Alexandria had a high regard for the *Apocalypse*, commenting on it and perhaps even treating it as Scripture.[3] But the other evidence brought forward by Harnack is mostly later and of questionable value for the discussion. It is much more probable that the author of the *Apocalypse* takes his cue from 2 Peter and, if this is so, the former book will constitute valuable evidence for the circulation of the latter in the first half of the second century. Such evidence would not, of course, rule out the possibility that 2 Peter was a non-authentic work, but the nearer the attestation is traced back towards the first century, the greater is the presumption against this.[4]

It would seem a fair conclusion to this survey of external evidence to submit that there is no evidence from any part of the early Church that this Epistle was ever rejected as spurious, in spite of the hesitancy which existed over its reception. In view of this we may proceed to the considerations arising from the Epistle itself without prejudice, although we shall bear constantly in mind the doubts of the early Church,[5]

[1] For an English translation of this Apocalypse, see M. R. James, *The Apocryphal New Testament* (1924), pp. 505–521.

[2] Cf. his *Das Neue Testament um das Jahr 200* (1889), pp. 83f., in answer to Zahn's *Geschichte des neutestamentlichen Kanons*. Harnack cited Methodius, Porphyrius (who attacked it), an Asian bishop (who defended it) and the fifth-century Palestinian Christians, who read it during the Lenten season. He also thought that both the Clementine letters and Hippolytus show traces of the book (cf. *ThLZ*, 1884, p. xiv). It should be noted, however, that doubts are expressed about it in the Muratorian Canon.

[3] Although this was maintained by Harnack, it was disputed by Westcott, *op. cit.*, p. 352.

[4] If any credence could be given to F. W. Farrar's opinion that Josephus had read 2 Peter (*Exp.*, II, iii, 1882, pp. 401–423; III, viii, 1888, pp. 58–69), this would constitute very early attestation. But the idea seems rather improbable (see further discussion on p. 181).

[5] In view of the great emphasis often placed on the adverse external evidence for 2 Peter, it would be valuable to cite the conclusions of two scholars who did not accept authenticity, but nevertheless were cautious about the external attestation. F. H. Chase (*op. cit.*, p. 807), after his very full examination, admits that lack of early evidence does not *prove* its spuriousness, but nevertheless creates a presump-

of the Reformers[1] and of modern criticism regarding its authenticity.[2]

II. AUTHORSHIP

a. The Epistle's own claims

There can be no doubt that the author intends his readers to understand that he is the apostle Peter. He calls himself somewhat strikingly Symeon (or Simon) Peter, a servant and an apostle of Jesus Christ (i. 1). He states that the Lord showed him the approach of his own death (i. 14). He claims to have been an eyewitness of the transfiguration (i. 16–18) and records the heavenly voice which he had himself heard on the 'holy mount'. He mentions a previous Epistle which he had written to the same people (iii. 1) and refers to the apostle Paul in terms of intimacy as 'our beloved brother Paul' (iii. 15), although he admits with refreshing candour that Paul's letters contain many difficult statements.

Such evidence certainly leaves us with the impression that the author is the apostle Peter. But the veracity of all these statements has not only been called in question, but other internal evidence has been brought forward, which is alleged to make the self-claims of the Epistle untenable and these objections will need to be carefully considered. Before doing so it should be fully recognized, as E. F. Scott[3] has pointed out, that we have no choice but to regard 2 Peter as either genuine or

tion against its genuineness and throws the burden of proof on the internal evidence. J. B. Mayor (*The Epistle of St. Jude and the Second Epistle of St. Peter*, 1907, p. cxxiv) concludes by suggesting that 'if we had nothing else to go upon in deciding the question of the authenticity of 2 Peter except external evidence, we should be inclined to think that we had in these quotations ground for considering that Eusebius was justified in his statement that our Epistle πολλοῖς χρήσιμος φανεῖσα μετὰ τῶν ἄλλων ἐσπουδάσθη γραφῶν.'

[1] Erasmus regarded 2 Peter as either spurious or written by Silvanus on Peter's direction. Luther found reason for doubt in 2 Pet. ii. 9, 15, but still thought it credible that it may be an Epistle of the apostle. Calvin inclined to regard it as a letter written by a disciple at Peter's direction (see Zahn, *INT*, II, p. 283, for details).

[2] Modern critical doubts can be traced back to Grotius who dated the Epistle in Trajan's time, but it was not until J. S. Semler's (*Paraphrasis ep. Petri II et Judas*, 1784) time that the Epistle was characterized as a forgery. Later J. G. Eichhorn (*Historische-kritische Einleitung in das Neue Testament*, III, 1814, pp. 624–656) rejected it, chiefly because of its dependence on Jude, and his opinion dominated much later critical enquiry.

[3] *The Literature of the New Testament* (1932), p. 227.

as a later work deliberately composed in his name. In other words, if its genuineness is found to be untenable, the only alternative is to regard it as spurious, in the sense of being a forgery.[1]

b. The case against Petrine authorship

(i) *The personal allusions.* The claims of the Epistle itself are discounted by the majority of scholars on the grounds that these personal allusions are no more than a literary device to give the appearance of authenticity to a pseudonymous production. Support for this process is found in the mass of pseudepigraphic literature, Jewish and Christian, which flourished before and during the early period of Church history, in which some attempt was made to give verisimilitude to the pseudonym. In most of them the literary device is obvious enough and so it is assumed that the author of 2 Peter, in spite of his efforts to identify himself with the apostle Peter, has really betrayed his hand.

1. The addition of the Jewish name 'Simon' to the Greek name 'Peter' in the superscription (i. 1) looks like a conscious attempt to identify the Peter of the Epistle with the Peter of the Gospels and Acts, where alone the double name is found.[2] But in all the Gospels, 'Peter' is more common than the compound.[3] The usage in 2 Peter is, therefore, unexpected, especially in view of the absence of 'Simon' from the salutation of 1 Peter. If the alternative reading 'Symeon' is accepted, the form of the name might be claimed as a further indication of the author's interest in archaic forms.[4]

2. The reference to the Lord's prediction of Peter's death as imminent in i. 14 is generally supposed to be an allusion to John xxi. 18f.[5] If this is a case of literary dependence, it clearly rules out the apostolic author-

---

[1] Not all scholars, however, agree that these are the only alternatives. J. W. C. Wand regards the Epistle as pseudepigraphic, but declines to call it 'a deliberate and unabashed forgery' (*op. cit.*, p. 144) and many modern scholars would share his reluctance. See further comments on p. 168.

[2] 'Simon Peter', apart from the few instances where 'Simon surnamed Peter' occurs, is found only in Mt. xvi. 16; Lk. v. 8, and in many of the references to Peter in John's Gospel (16 times).

[3] Cf. the note on this combination in C. Bigg, *op. cit.*, p. 89.

[4] Cf. J. W. C. Wand (*op. cit.*, p. 146), 'Simeon is used of Peter only in Acts xv. 14 and its use here may be an intentional archaism.' But Wand is not too sure about this.

[5] Cf. Feine-Behm, *op. cit.*, p. 254; T. Henshaw, *op. cit.*, p. 394; F. H. Chase, *op. cit.*, p. 809. J. Moffatt (*ILNT*, p. 366) definitely claims that this is a method used by the author to add *vraisemblance* to his writing.

ship of 2 Peter, because of the late dating of John. Moreover, how did the apostle know that his end was to be so soon? This is considered to be an attempt to indicate that the letter was written just before the apostle's death.[1]

3. The statement in i. 15 looks like a promise of the publication of literary work after Peter's departure. This is often supposed to refer to the production of Mark's Gospel,[2] and it is, therefore, a self-conscious attempt on the author's part to identify his work by means of the apostolic 'source' of that Gospel.

4. The references to the transfiguration narrative (i. 16ff.) are considered to be forced. Undoubtedly one of the greatest privileges which Peter enjoyed was to witness the transfiguration of Christ, but it is maintained that the incident is introduced into 2 Peter merely to add verisimilitude to the narrative,[3] as much as to say that this Peter is the Peter who witnessed Christ's glory and heard the heavenly voice. Moreover, the description of the mount as 'holy' is generally thought to indicate a time when sacred places were revered, which is most unlikely in apostolic times.

(ii) *Historical problems.* There are many problems of an historical kind which are cited as adverse to apostolic authorship. The main problems may be grouped as follows:

1. The reference to Paul and his letters (iii. 15). Several indications are claimed to be found here of a period subsequent to the apostles. A corpus of Pauline Epistles is known. Indeed, 'all his letters' may well suggest a time when the complete corpus is known.[4] Further, these letters are placed on an equality with 'the other scriptures', which would seem to indicate a time well after the apostolic age. Quite apart

---

[1] Cf. E. Käsemann's idea that 2 Peter was intended to be a last testament of Peter, *ZTK*, 49 (1952), p. 280 (reproduced in his *Exegetische Versuche und Besinnungen*, 1960, p. 142).

[2] Cf. J. B. Mayor's discussion, *op. cit.*, pp. cxlii ff.

[3] Cf. Chase, *HDB*, III, pp. 809, 810. Chase did not consider that in themselves the references to Peter's approaching death and to the transfiguration are unnatural, but that when considered against the background of the omission of the passion, resurrection and ascension, they become a serious ground for questioning the authenticity.

[4] Cf. Wand, *op. cit.*, p. 143. This fact weighs heavily with A. E. Barnett, *The Second Epistle of Peter* (IB), 1957, p. 164. Cf. also Moffatt (*ILNT*, pp. 363, 364) who calls this 'an anachronism which forms an indubitable water-mark of the second century'.

from this, a difficulty is felt over Peter's admission of his inability to understand Paul's writings.

2. Another problem is the reference to the 'second letter' in iii. 1. If 2 Peter is pseudepigraphic, it is highly probable that this reference has been included to claim a definite connection with 1 Peter,[1] a process not unknown among pseudepigraphists. That there are difficulties in this assumption will be demonstrated later, but it should be noted for the present that the datum does not necessarily require this interpretation.

3. It is also thought that the occasion reflected in the Epistle is too late for Peter's time. It is often confidently affirmed that the situation envisaged in the Epistle belongs to the second century, particularly to the period of intense Gnostic activity.[2] If this affirmation is correct, there can be no question of apostolic authorship and the Epistle must be firmly dated in the sub-apostolic period. But rather less confidence is now being put in the identification of early Gnostic movements and the evidence, as will be seen later,[3] is not sufficient to declare that 2 Peter's false teachers were, in fact, second-century Gnostics. Nevertheless, if other evidence pointed to a later origin, the connections with Gnostic thought might be corroborative evidence.[4] A further consideration is the mixture of past and future tenses, which is thought to suggest an author who first assumes a prophetic rôle and then lapses into a description of his own contemporary scene.[5]

4. The statement in iii. 4 suggests that the first generation of Christians is now past. 'Since the fathers fell asleep' would seem to suggest a second or third generation dating, which would put the Epistle well outside the apostolic period.[6] This, of course, assumes that the 'fathers' are the first generation of Christians, including the apostles, but this interpretation is by no means certain and too much weight should not

---

[1] Cf. Moffatt, op. cit., p. 365.

[2] Cf. Wand, op. cit., p. 144: 'It probably belongs to the Egypt of the first quarter of the second century, and was written to circumvent the Christian Gnosticism that was soon developed into a specific system by Basilides.'

[3] Cf. R. M. Wilson, The Gnostic Problem (1958). Cf. the present writer's discussion of the Colossian heresy in New Testament Introduction: The Pauline Epistles (1961), pp. 162ff.

[4] Cf. Feine-Behm, op. cit., p. 256.   [5] Cf. F. H. Chase, op. cit., p. 811.

[6] So writers of such widely differing viewpoints as Barnett, op. cit., loc. cit.; Michaelis, op. cit., p. 290; Cantinat, op. cit., p. 597. Indeed, most disputants of non-Petrine authorship make much of this.

be placed upon it. At the same time, it is undoubtedly possible to interpret the evidence as supporting a late date.

5. The reference to 'your apostles' in iii. 2 (rsv) is considered strange for an apostolic author. This statement is thought to be too cold and general coming from the apostle Peter. Moreover, the combination of prophets and apostles is characteristic of second-century writers when referring to Scripture (e.g. Muratorian Canon and Irenaeus).[1]

(iii) *Literary problems.* The remarkably close parallels between this Epistle and that of Jude cannot be left out of the authorship problem of this Epistle. If, as is generally supposed, 2 Peter is the borrower from Jude, the date of 2 Peter would then be directly governed by the date of Jude. The latter date is not usually fixed as early as Peter's lifetime and, therefore, it follows that 2 Peter cannot be by Peter.[2] The difficulty here is the appeal to two factors over which there has been, and still is, some difference of opinion. It is not absolutely conclusive, in spite of an overwhelming majority verdict in favour, that 2 Peter actually borrowed from Jude,[3] neither is it certain that Jude must be dated later than Peter's lifetime. But those who are convinced that these can be asserted without fear of contradiction are quite entitled to point out the difficulty. At the same time the bare use of Jude does not in itself exclude Petrine authorship, as some scholars who have maintained authenticity together with Jude's priority have recognized.[4]

Not only is there literary connection between these two Epistles, but also between 2 Peter and the Pauline Epistles and 2 Peter and 1 Peter. Unlike 1 Peter, which seems to show definite links with some of Paul's Epistles (see pp. 128f.), this Epistle is far less clearly influenced by Paul's thought. Nevertheless, the author is clearly acquainted with a

---

[1] For details, cf. Chase, *op. cit.*, p. 811. He regarded this reference as an elaboration of the simple phrase in Jude 17 by a post-apostolic author using phraseology current in his own days.

[2] Cf. J. W. C. Wand, *op. cit.*, p. 142; F. H. Chase, *op. cit.*, p. 814, who did not support the priority of 2 Peter to Jude, but nevertheless did not consider it impossible that Peter should cite Jude. The latter Epistle, he thought, may not be later than Peter's lifetime.

[3] See the discussion of this on pp. 240–248. Spitta, Zahn and Bigg were staunch supporters of the priority of 2 Peter.

[4] Cf. most recently E. M. B. Green, *2 Peter Reconsidered* (1961), pp. 10, 11. But cf. H. F. D. Sparks (*The Formation of the New Testament*, 1952, p. 136) who considers that 2 Peter's use of Jude is decisive against Petrine authorship. The same view was expressed by Knopf, *Die Briefe Petri und Judä* (1912), p. 253.

number of Pauline Epistles, including one sent to the same readers as his own Epistle (iii. 15). There have been many suggestions regarding the identity of this letter,[1] but it is impossible to come to any conclusion. It was probably an epistle now lost. The main difficulty is in the apparent overlap of apostolic provinces. If Paul had previously written to them, why does Peter now address them? It could be that Paul was dead and Peter is, therefore, taking a pastoral interest in some of the former's churches. This difficulty has already cropped up in connection with I Peter (see p. 108), where it was seen that very little weight can be attached to it.

The relationship between I and 2 Peter is variously interpreted according to whether the former is regarded as authentic or not. If not, then the decision regarding 2 Peter must follow suit.[2] But if I Peter is by Peter, this supplies a standard of comparison, which is of vital importance. In other words, the question must be posed whether the author of I Peter could have written 2 Peter, and the verdict given by the majority is in the negative.[3] Those who regard the author of 2 Peter as definitely borrowing ideas from I Peter, but putting them in a different way, consider this a strong argument against the authenticity of 2 Peter. The linguistic and doctrinal problems arising from a comparison between the two Epistles will be considered under the next two heads. Moreover, the literary question of their different use of the Old Testament needs noting. The first Epistle is certainly more full of obvious citations and allusions, whereas the second has no formal quotations and fewer allusions. It is felt, therefore, that we are here dealing with different minds. Chase,[4] for instance, refers to the

[1] Of the various suggestions which have been made, the most notable is the Epistle to the Romans (cf. Mayor, *op. cit.*, pp. cxxxvii, 164, 165). Mayor cites the following other suggestions which have been proposed—Ephesians (sometimes with Galatians and Colossians), I Corinthians, Hebrews, Thessalonians. Zahn considered that the Epistle is now lost (*INT*, II, p. 199).

[2] This follows from the fact that no scholar unconvinced of the authenticity of I Peter would ever be convinced of any arguments for 2 Peter. Moreover, if 2 Pet. iii. I refers to I Peter, it must clearly come later (cf. R. Knopf, *op. cit.*, p. 250).

[3] Wand's statement of the case may be cited as representative. Referring to the author he says, 'But if he is St. Peter, it is certainly not the Peter that we know: it is not the bluff fisherman of Galilee, nor the Spirit-possessed preacher of Acts, nor the courageous theologian of the first Epistle. The two Epistles indeed show a contrast at nearly every point' (*op. cit.*, p. 143).

[4] *Op. cit.*, p. 813.

writer of 1 Peter as 'instinctively and apparently unconsciously' falling into Old Testament language, but this is less obvious in 2 Peter.

(iv) *Stylistic problems.* It has been seen that as early as the time of Jerome the stylistic differences between 1 and 2 Peter were noted and an attempt was made to explain them by referring both Epistles to different amanuenses. Those modern scholars who regard 1 Peter as having been written by Silvanus make any stylistic comparisons with 2 Peter irrelevant. But the Greek of 2 Peter is more stilted than that of 1 Peter. Chase[1] characterized the vocabulary of the writer as 'ambitious' and yet considered its extraordinary list of repetitions as stamping it as 'poor and inadequate'. The style shows a great dearth of connecting particles and an aptitude for cumbrous sentences. Nevertheless, after carefully setting out this evidence, Chase admitted that there is nothing which absolutely disproves Petrine authorship, although he thought it was hard to reconcile such authorship with the literary character of the Epistle.[2] On the other hand, if the view that the Greek of 2 Peter is an artificial literary language learnt from books is correct, and if it is as far removed from everyday language as is often supposed,[3] the difficulty in attributing it to Peter would clearly be considerable.

(v) *Doctrinal problems.* Much emphasis has been placed on the irreconcilability of the doctrine of 1 and 2 Peter. It is pointed out that many of the major themes in 1 Peter do not occur at all in 2 Peter (e.g. the cross, resurrection, ascension, baptism, prayer).[4] The great emphasis in 2 Peter is rather on the *parousia*. Käsemann[5] goes so far as to discover an inferior view of Christ (who is no longer regarded as a redeemer);

---

[1] *Ibid.*, p. 809. R. H. Strachan (*The Second Epistle General of Peter, EGT*, 1910, pp. 110–112) criticized Chase's statements as too sweeping, although he agreed with him in rejecting Petrine authorship.

[2] Mayor is equally cautious in pressing the linguistic argument, *op. cit.*, pp. lxviii ff.

[3] Cf. J. H. Moulton and W. F. Howard's confident assertion to this effect (*A Grammar of New Testament Greek*, II, 1929, pp. 5, 6).

[4] Chase (*op. cit.*, p. 812) considered that the omission of the resurrection was the crucial point.

[5] *ZTK*, 49 (1952), pp. 272–296. In Käsemann's view, three passages presuppose a post-apostolic situation (iii. 2, ii. 21, and i. 12) and hence he thinks an apostolic mask had to be worn to show the connection between the author's own message and apostolic times. W. Michaelis (*op. cit.*, p. 290) disputes Käsemann's opinion that the eschatology is the central theme of the Epistle, but he is impressed by the argument that the eschatology is far removed from apostolic times.

an eschatology not orientated to Christ; and an inadequate ethical outlook in which the major evil is imprisonment in a material existence.
Although not everyone who disputes the authenticity of the Epistle
would go all the way with Käsemann, most would agree that the two
Epistles differ in outlook. Indeed, many would consider that the
change in approach to the *parousia* presupposes a considerable delay
after the publication of 1 Peter.[1] It will be necessary to examine this
kind of argument more carefully when putting the case for Petrine
authorship, but in order to appreciate its true weight, it should be noted
that much of the evidence brought forward in support is due to
subjective assessments which naturally appeal differently to different
minds.

Another factor which may be mentioned here is the Hellenistic
background. Certain expressions seem to suggest acquaintance with
Greek modes of thought and this is considered highly improbable for a
Galilaean fisherman. The idea of ἀρετή (moral excellence) applied to
God, of virtue combined with faith, of knowledge, of sharing the
divine nature and the term 'eyewitnesses' (ἐπόπται), which was used in
the mystery religions, are the major examples of such Greek expressions.[2] If the use of these terms is indicative of the impact of Hellenistic
ideas on the author's mind, it may certainly be difficult to maintain
Petrine authorship, especially because in 1 Peter they are not so frequent.

When all these considerations are taken together they build up so
great an impression of non-authenticity that many scholars do not even
discuss the possibility that the tradition of apostolic authorship might
after all be correct. But the impartial critic must also examine carefully
the foundations for the non-authenticity theory and present in the best
possible light the evidence which many able scholars have produced in

---

[1] Cf. J. Cantinat, in Robert-Feuillet's *Introduction à la Bible*, II, p. 597.

[2] Cf. Feine-Behm, *op. cit.*, pp. 255, 256. Cf. also H. Windisch's note for further
examples, *op. cit.*, p. 85. Of ἐπόπται, Chase remarked that 'it is not one which we
should have expected St. Peter to use'. Indeed he called it 'artificial'. But the corresponding verb ἐποπτεύω is used twice in 1 Peter (ii. 12, iii. 2) and nowhere else
in the New Testament. A. Deissmann (*Bible Studies*, 1901, pp. 360ff.) has drawn
attention to many verbal parallels between 2 Peter and an inscription containing
a decree of the inhabitants of Stratonicea in Caria in honour of Zeus Panhemerios
and Hekate, the most striking of which is the parallel use of the expression τῆς
θείας δυνάμεως. Deissmann suggested that the similarities show that the author of
2 Peter has 'simply availed himself of the familiar forms and formulae of religious
emotion' (p. 362). There is, of course, no reason why Peter himself might not have
done this.

support of Petrine authorship. It will, therefore, be our next task to examine the arguments stated above and then to produce any positive arguments for apostolic authorship.

c. The case for Petrine authorship

(i) *The personal allusions.* In spite of the widespread custom of appealing to contemporary pseudepigraphic practice in support of the view that the personal allusions are merely literary devices, considerable caution is necessary before this kind of argument can be allowed any weight. It must at once be recognized that there are no close parallels to 2 Peter, if this Epistle is pseudepigraphic. The normal procedure was to adopt a fairly consistent first person style, particularly in narrative sections. This style was not specially adapted for Epistles, and this is probably the reason for the paucity of examples of pseudepigrapha in this form. It is much easier to account for the development of pseudonymous Acts and Apocalypses (as those attributed to Peter), although even these appear to be later developments than 2 Peter (see pp. 181ff. on the relationship of 2 Peter to the *Apocalypse*). Comparative study of pseudepigraphy cannot, of course, lead to a conclusive rejection of a pseudepigraphic origin for 2 Peter, because 2 Peter may be in a class of its own, but it does lead to the demand that evidences for pseudepigraphic origin should be conclusive. It is against this background that the following examination will be conducted.

1. It must at once seem strange that the author uses the double name Simon Peter, when the name Simon does not appear in 1 Peter, which was presumably used as a model, if 2 Peter is pseudepigraphic. The difficulty is even greater if the form 'Symeon' is the correct reading, for neither in the Apostolic Fathers nor in the Christian pseudepigraphic literature is it used. Indeed, it occurs elsewhere only in Acts xv. 14 and is obviously a primitive form. M. R. James,[1] who disputed the authenticity of 2 Peter, admitted that this was one of the few features which made for the genuineness of the Epistle. We should certainly expect that an imitator of 1 Peter would have kept closer to his model in the salutation, since in iii. 1 he is going to imply that his present letter is in the same sequence as the first. It is not possible in this case to treat the variation as an unconscious lapse on the part of the author, for he would hardly have begun his work with a lapse and, in any case, would not have lapsed into a primitive Hebrew form no longer in use in his own

[1] *The Second Epistle of St. Peter and the General Epistle of St. Jude* (1912), p. 9.

day. The only alternative is to assume that the use of the name Simeon was a deliberate device to give a greater impression of authenticity. In that case it would be necessary to suppose that the author had been studying the book of Acts or else that the form had independently survived orally in the author's own circles. On the whole, the author's name presents much greater difficulty for the pseudepigraphic writer than for Peter himself, who, in any case, would enjoy greater liberty in varying the form. If Zahn is right in holding that the recipients were Jewish Christians, it might be possible to explain the Hebrew form of the name on the grounds that for such readers this would be more appropriate. But Zahn's hypothesis is generally disputed (see discussion below).

2. There is undoubtedly a connection between 2 Peter i. 14 and the saying in John xxi. 18f., but there is no need to explain this by literary dependence. If Peter himself wrote 2 Peter and heard with his own ears the Lord's prediction, there would be nothing extraordinary in the connection. The main problem is how Peter would have known that the event was so imminent. The situation would be modified if the word ταχινή meant not 'soon', as it is generally rendered, but 'swift', which is the meaning it must sustain in ii. 1 of this Epistle. There is a strong presumption that it means the same in both places. The emphasis would not then be on the imminence, but on the manner of Peter's death. But in any case, if a pseudepigraphist was making an indirect allusion to John xxi. 18,[1] where Peter is told that some violent death awaited him when he was old, there would be less point in the ταχινή to indicate imminence. It did not require much foresight for an old man to suggest that his end was not far away. Moreover, a pseudepigraphist writing this would not appear to add anything to the information contained in the canonical sources, in spite of writing after the event. This may, of course, be a tribute to the pseudepigraphist's skill, but it could equally well be a witness to the veracity of Peter's own statement.

3. The meaning of 2 Peter i. 15 is problematic. The statement reads, 'And I will see to it that after my departure you may be able at any time to recall these things' (RSV). But to suppose that this refers to Mark's

[1] It is just possible that it is not Jn. xxi. 18 which is in mind but some other special revelation from the Lord, similar to those which Paul seems to have had (cf. Acts xx. 23, 25, 38, xxi. 11). H. Windisch cites other similar cases from extra-canonical sources, *op. cit.*, p. 88. F. Spitta (*Der zweite Brief des Petrus und der Brief das Judas*, 1885, pp. 88f.) denies any connection with Jn. xxi.

Gospel is precarious for there is no evidence to support it. 'These things' are presumably things already mentioned in verse 12, which points back to the doctrinal statements of the preceding verses.[1] Evidently the anticipated document was to be doctrinal in character and it is difficult to see how this was fulfilled in Mark's Gospel. It is better to suppose that this projected letter was either never written or has since been lost. It can hardly be regarded as an evidence of a pseudepigraphist's hand, in spite of Käsemann's suggestion that this allusion was included to give 2 Peter the character of a testament of Peter.[2] Yet there is a great difference between this Epistle and Jewish apocalyptic books in testamentary form, which all share the pattern of a discourse addressed to the immediate descendants, but which is really destined for future generations. This latter type of literature proceeded from a review of the past to a prophecy of the future. While both these elements may be found in 2 Peter, the Epistle can be clearly understood without recourse to the testamentary hypothesis, which could certainly not be said of the farewell discourses of Jewish apocalyptic.

4. But are the references to the transfiguration narrative natural for the apostle Peter? There is no denying that the pseudepigraphists were in the habit of making passing allusions to known events in the lives of their assumed authors, in order to create the historical setting necessary for their literary productions. But there is no parallel to Peter's allusion to the transfiguration, for the prophetic section does not require such a setting to make it intelligible. Indeed, it is difficult to see why a pseudepigraphist would have chosen this particular incident, especially as it does not, like the death and resurrection of Jesus, play a prominent part in early Christian preaching.[3] The only justification for the choice would be the possibility of using it as an introduction to an esoteric revelation in the same way as the book of Enoch uses Enoch's journey through the heavens. But the author of 2 Peter does not claim to be making any new revelation on the basis of his hero's experiences on the mount of transfiguration. He appeals to it almost incidentally as a verification of the

---

[1] Cf. Zahn, *INT*, II, p. 201.

[2] J. Munck compares 2 Peter with other farewell discourses, especially in Jewish apocalyptic, in his article on 'Discours d'adieu dans le Nouveau Testament et dans la littérature biblique', in *Aux Sources de la Tradition Chrétienne* (1950), pp. 155–170.

[3] The same difficulty does not arise if Peter himself were author, because his choice of the incident may have been influenced by the desire to cite the occasion when the greatest glory was seen.

prophetic word he intends to impart. But this is a perfectly natural procedure and does not in itself demand a pseudepigraphic author. Peter himself could just as naturally have referred to his own remarkable experience, as he does in 1 Peter v. 1.

Moreover, the form of this transfiguration account differs from the Synoptic accounts in certain details, and this demands an explanation. Is this easier to account for on the authenticity hypothesis than the pseudepigraphic? It would, at first sight, seem strange that any writer, introducing an allusion to an historical incident, would have varied the account. There is no mention of Moses and Elijah; the Synoptic 'hear him' is omitted; an emphatic ἐγώ is added; the order of words is changed; and the words ὃν εὐδόκησα are only partially paralleled in Matthew and not at all in Mark and Luke. Such variations suggest an independent tradition,[1] and as far as they go favour a Petrine authorship rather than the alternative. It is, of course, possible to suppose that 2 Peter is reproducing an account from oral tradition, but it is much more natural to assume that this account is a genuine eyewitness account. It is significant that there is a complete absence of embellishments, such as are often found in the apocryphal books, and in fact can be illustrated in relation to the transfiguration from the fragment attached to the *Apocalypse of Peter*.

The idea of the 'holy mount' (τὸ ὄρος τὸ ἅγιον) need not be as late a development as some scholars suppose,[2] for the central feature is not the veneration of a locality, but the appreciation of the sanctity of an impressive occasion in which the writer himself shared. The real issue is whether a pseudepigraphist would have singled out this particular mountain for special veneration. There does not appear to be any compelling reason why he should have done so. If he merely sensed that Peter would have regarded the mount as holy because of the theophany, the description might just as well reflect the real reactions of the apostle. As a genuine eyewitness account, it is highly credible; as a pseudepigraphic touch, it would have been a device of rare insight, which for that very reason makes it less probable.

It will be seen from these considerations so far that there is little tangible evidence for non-authenticity from the personal allusions.

---

[1] Cf. E. M. B. Green, *op. cit.*, p. 27.

[2] The same description of the mount as holy is found in the *Apocalypse of Peter*, but since the author of this work has clearly used 2 Peter (see discussion on pp. 181ff.) this cannot be cited as independent evidence in support.

There is, in fact, nothing here which requires us to treat the Epistle as pseudepigraphic.

(ii) *Historical problems.* 1. Many scholars who might be prepared to admit that the preceding evidences are not conclusive but corroborative, consider that the allusion to Paul tips the scales against Petrine authorship. But here again caution is needed. It must at once be noted that Peter's words need not imply the existence of an authorized corpus of Paul's letters. The 'all' in iii. 16 need mean no more than all those known to Peter at the time of writing.[1] There is no suggestion that even these were known to the readers. Indeed, the writer is informing them of the difficulties in understanding these letters and it can hardly be supposed that they would have been unaware of this had they been acquainted with them. On the other hand, the Epistles in question have had sufficient circulation for the false teachers to twist them from their true interpretation.

Of much greater difficulty for the authenticity of the Epistle is the apparent classification of Paul's Epistles with the 'other scriptures'. Now this again is a matter of interpretation. It is possible to contend that γραφαί does not mean 'scriptures' but writings in general.[2] The meaning would then be that these false teachers show no sort of respect for any religious writings and that this attitude was extended to Paul's writings. Such an interpretation is supported by the fact that in i. 21 Old Testament prophecy is clearly regarded as bearing the mark of divine inspiration, whereas the reference to Paul lacks such a distinctive claim. He writes 'according to wisdom', but it is nonetheless a wisdom given to him (iii. 15). Moreover the writer appears to be classing his own writing on the same level as Paul's, which would point to a time before the accepted veneration of Paul's writings (unless, of course,

---

[1] If *all* of Paul's Epistles were now collected it is extraordinary that an author who indicates his respect for them shows such comparatively little reflection of their thought in his Epistle. Indeed there is much greater evidence of their influence in 1 Peter, a fact which may be explained by the greater amount of similar material common to those Epistles and 1 Peter. The major theme of 2 Peter does not provide such close parallels. This seems a better solution than that of R. A. Falconer (*Exp.*, VI, vi, 1902, pp. 468, 469), who maintained that 2 Peter was published earlier than 1 Peter, at a time when Paul's letters were less well known.

[2] This was Zahn's view, *INT*, II, p. 277. Cf. also Spitta (*op. cit.*, p. 294), who interpreted it of other writings of Paul's associates. Falconer (*op. cit.*, p. 469) took the same view.

a pseudepigraphist is doing this to secure authority for his own writing —but see the discussion below, pp. 169f.).

But the usual New Testament interpretation of γραφαί is 'Scriptures' (i.e. Old Testament) and it must be considered as more likely that that is its meaning here. Is it possible to conceive of Paul's writings being placed so early on a par with the Old Testament? It is not easy to answer this question with any certainty. Many scholars[1] would answer categorically in the negative on the grounds that allowances must be made for a considerable delay before such veneration of Paul's writings was reached. Indeed, some[2] would maintain that a period of neglect followed Paul's death and that interest was revived only after the publication of Acts, but this hypothesis is open to serious criticism.[3] When all has been said there is practically no evidence at all to show precisely when Paul's letters first began to be used alongside the Old Testament.

There is no denying that Paul himself considered his own writings to be invested with a special authority and, moreover, that he expected his readers generally to recognize this fact (cf. 2 Thes. iii. 14; 1 Cor. ii. 16, vii. 17, xiv. 37–39). We may either interpret this as the overbearing attitude of an autocrat or else as evidence of the apostle's consciousness of writing under the direct inspiration of God. But if the latter alternative is correct and if it were recognized by the churches generally, there would be less surprise that during the apostolic age writings of apostolic men were treated with equal respect to that accorded to the Old Testament. There can be no doubt that in both 1 and 2 Peter the prophetical and apostolic teaching is placed on a level (cf. 1 Pet. iv. 11, i. 10, 11).[4] That this was characteristic of the primitive period seems to be borne out by the readiness with which the sub-apostolic age treated the apostolic writings with such respect. Admittedly, the Apostolic Fathers do not as explicitly place Paul on the same level of inspiration as the Old Testament, but it may be claimed that this is implicit in their approach. If by AD 140 Marcion could be sufficiently daring to exalt his *Apostolicon* to the complete detriment of the Old Testament, at

---

[1] To cite one of the most recent among these, A. E. Barnett, *The Second Epistle of Peter* (IB, 1957), p. 204. Cf. also Chase, *op. cit.*, p. 810.

[2] Cf. E. J. Goodspeed, *New Chapters in New Testament Study* (1937), pp. 22–49; *The Key to Ephesians* (1956), pp. v ff.

[3] For a full discussion of this hypothesis, see pp. 255ff. of the writer's *New Testament Introduction: The Pauline Epistles*.

[4] Cf. E. M. B. Green's discussion of this, *op. cit.*, pp. 30ff.

some time previously the orthodox Christian Church must virtually have treated them as equal. Marcion was not introducing a *volte-face*, but pushing the natural development to an extreme limit in the interests of dogmatic considerations. Similar developments are found in the growth of second-century pseudepigraphic apostolic literature, which must presuppose an existing body of *authoritative* apostolic literature. To place 2 Peter in the vanguard of this movement may at first seem a reasonable hypothesis, but it does not explain why this writer is so much in advance of his contemporaries in his regard for Paul's writings. Is it not more reasonable to suggest that in the apostolic period Peter may have recognized the value of Paul's Epistles even more fully than the later sub-apostolic Fathers? These latter do not speak of Paul as 'our beloved brother', but in more exalted ways as, 'the blessed and glorious Paul' (Polycarp, *Ad Phil.* iii); 'the blessed Paul' (*1 Clement*, xlvii. 1; Polycarp, *Ad Phil.* xi); 'the sanctified Paul . . . right blessed' (Ignatius, *Ad Eph.* xii. 2). The description in 2 Peter would be almost over-familiar for a pseudepigraphist, although it would be wholly in character with what we should expect of the warm-hearted apostle portrayed in the Synoptic Gospels.[1] This is either a genuine appreciation on the part of Peter himself or skilful representation by his imitator. The former alternative is rather easier to conceive than the latter.

Another consideration arises here. Would a pseudepigraphist have adopted the view that Peter did not understand Paul's writings? It is strange, at least, that he has such an idea of Peter's ability in view of the fact that he considers it worthwhile to attribute the whole Epistle to Peter. The history of Jewish and early Christian pseudepigraphy shows a marked tendency towards the enhancement of heroes and there is no parallel case in which the putative author is made to detract from his own reputation. Rather than pointing to a later origin, this self-candour of Peter's is a factor in favour of authenticity. It is surely not very surprising that Peter, or any of the other original apostles for that matter, found Paul difficult. Has anyone ever found him easy?

2. In evaluating the reference to the 'second letter' in 2 Peter iii. 1, the first problem to settle is whether or not this is a reference to 1

---

[1] Mayor (*op. cit.*, p. 166) candidly admits, 'There are many difficulties in the way of accepting the genuineness of this Epistle; but the manner in which St. Paul is spoken of seems to me just what we should have expected from his brother apostle.'

Peter. It is generally taken for granted and probability seems strongly
to support this contention. Since there is a clear reference to an earlier
letter and since 1 Peter already is known to us, it is a natural assumption that the two letters are to be identified. Both Spitta[1] and Zahn[2]
rejected this assumption because they held that, whereas 1 Peter was
addressed to Gentiles, 2 Peter was addressed to Jewish Christians. Few,
however, have followed them in this (see further comments on readers
below, pp. 171f.). In addition they both maintained that in 1 Peter the
author does not seem to have preached personally to these people,
whereas in 2 Peter he has (cf. 1 Pet. i. 12; 2 Pet. i. 16). This distinction
may be right, but is not absolutely demanded by the evidence. Bigg[3]
maintained that 'nothing more need be meant than that the recipients
knew perfectly well what the teaching of the apostles was'. A much
more weighty consideration is that 1 Peter does not fit the context of
2 Peter iii. 1, which clearly implies that the former Epistle is like the
present in being a reminder about predictions of coming false teachers.[4]
There is much to be said for the view that the former Epistle of 2 Peter
iii. 1 is not 1 Peter, but a lost epistle.[5] On this assumption the reference
could not be regarded as a literary device, for it would have no point
unless the previous letter were well known. On the other hand, 2
Peter iii. 1 does not absolutely demand that both Epistles should say
the same thing and it may be possible to make 1 Peter fill the bill by
appealing to the frequent allusions to prophetic words within that
Epistle. Since there is room for difference of opinion on the matter,
it can hardly be claimed that here is a clear indication of pseudonymity,
although it might be corroborative evidence if pseudonymity were
otherwise established. There is, in any case, nothing unnatural about
the reference if both Epistles are Petrine.

3. The next problem to discuss is the occasion reflected in the
Epistle. It is a legacy from the criticism of F. C. Baur and his school
that a tendency exists for all references to false teachers in the New
Testament in some ways to be connected up with second-century
Gnosticism. In spite of greater modern reluctance to make this un-
qualified assumption, the idea dies hard that no heresy showing the

---

[1] *Op. cit.*, pp. 486ff.   [2] *INT*, ii, p. 208.
[3] *Op. cit.*, p. 289.   [4] Cf. Zahn, *op. cit.*, ii, pp. 195ff.
[5] This may be maintained quite apart from the theory that 1 and 2 Peter were
addressed to different racial groups. R. A. Falconer (*op. cit.*, pp. 47f., 117f., 218f.)
suggested that 2 Peter was a circular to the church throughout Samaria.

slightest parallels with Gnosticism could possibly have appeared before the end of the first century. The facts are that all the data that can be collected from 2 Peter (and Jude) are insufficient to identify the movement with any known second-century system. Rather do they suggest a general mental and moral atmosphere which would have been conducive for the development of systematic Gnosticism. Indeed, it may with good reason be claimed that a second-century pseudepigraphist, writing during the period of developed Gnosticism, would have given more specific evidence of the period to which he belonged and the sect that he was combating.[1] This was done, for instance, by the author of the spurious *3 Corinthians* and might be expected here. The fact that the author gives no such allusions is a point in favour of a first-century date and is rather more in support of authenticity than the reverse. (But see the further discussion on these false teachers, pp. 176ff.)

4. The objection based on iii. 4, regarded as a reference to a former generation, is rather more weighty, although it is subject to different interpretations. Everything depends on the meaning in this context of οἱ πατέρες (the fathers). Most commentators assume that these are first generation Christians who have now died. The meaning of the verse would then be that questions have arisen over the veracity of the *parousia*, because ever since the first generation of Christians died everything has continued in the created order, just as they always have done previously. This interpretation would make good sense, but would clearly imply some interval since the first generation and this would at once exclude Petrine authorship. But is it correct? Nowhere else in the New Testament nor in the Apostolic Fathers is πατέρες used of Christian 'patriarchs' and the more natural interpretation would be to take it as denoting the Jewish patriarchs,[2] in which case the statement

[1] Cf. E. M. B. Green's comments on this, *op. cit.*, p. 26.

[2] Mayor (*op. cit.*, pp. 148f.) discusses this view but rejects it, first because the word πατέρες is sometimes used of the pre-Mosaic patriarchs, sometimes of Moses and his contemporaries, sometimes of the prophets; and secondly because no-one, in view of the rise of the Christian Church, could say that all things continue as they were. But the predominant New Testament use of the word, used absolutely, is of the ancient patriarchs and there is nothing against that interpretation in 2 Peter. With reference to Mayor's second point, the context clearly shows that the scoffers would go back not merely to apostolic times but to creation itself and their thought would relate to the winding up of the created order. For this reason Peter points out that the same God whose word brought it into being will finally bring it to consummation. This is surely what is meant by 'the day of the Lord' (2 Pet. iii. 10).

would amount to a rather exaggerated declaration of the changeless-ness of things. This would certainly give a reasonable connection with the allusion to the creation account and later to the flood.

Either interpretation is possible, but if this is the report of a second-century pseudepigraphist it needs to be explained how he could have thought that Peter would be able to look back on the first generation of Christians from some even earlier age.[1] We should need to assume that he gave himself away through a foolish slip in historical detail, a not uncommon failing among pseudepigraphists. But the explanation is not very substantial since the statement in 2 Peter iii. 4 is put into the mouths of the scoffers and would on this hypothesis presumably reflect current opinions. But questions regarding the *parousia* would be much more natural in the apostolic age than later. The Apostolic Fathers do not betray such concern over the delay in the *parousia*.[2]

5. Zahn's[3] interpretation of the reference to 'your apostles' was to restrict it to those who had actually worked among the readers and he saw no difficulty in the writer including himself. The point of the ὑμῶν is that of contrast with the false teachers who in no sense belong to the readers. The combination of prophets and apostles is, of course, found in Ephesians ii. 20, and is no certain evidence of a second-century provenance.[4]

(iii) *Literary problems.* Assuming for our present purpose that Jude is prior to 2 Peter (but see the discussion on this on pp. 240ff.), the problem arises whether the apostle Peter could or would have cited the lesser-known Jude. It has been suggested that no apostle would ever have

---

[1] If the reference is to Christian 'fathers', it is, of course, possible that some of these would certainly have died before Peter (so Spitta and Zahn maintained). In this case the reference would constitute no difficulty for Petrine authorship, although it would be difficult in a pseudepigraphic writing, for the writer would hardly have worked out such a subtle possibility. On the other hand the article would not naturally denote a few.

[2] A very similar statement about the continuity of things in relation to the Lord's coming is, it is true, found both in 1 *Clement*, xxiii. 3f. and 2 *Clement*, xi. 2f., but the latter looks like a borrowing from the former since the same vine illustration is used (unless both borrowed from a lost apocalypse of Eldad and Modad; cf. K. Lake, *The Apostolic Fathers*, 1912, I, p. 51). 1 *Clement* cites it as γραφή and 2 *Clement* as a 'prophetic word', and both are, therefore, referring to questionings which must have arisen much earlier.

[3] *INT*, II, pp. 204, 205. Cf. the same kind of thing in 1 Pet. i. 12.

[4] On this, cf. the present writer's discussion, *New Testament Introduction: The Pauline Epistles*, pp. 124, 125.

made such extensive use of a non-apostolic source,[1] but this supposition is fallacious, for it has already been seen from 1 Peter that Peter was the kind of man who was influenced by other writings. But the position in 2 Peter is admittedly of a different character in that it seems to involve the author in an expansion of an existing tract without acknowledgment. If Jude is prior to 2 Peter, therefore, it must be regarded as unexpected that such use is made of it and this would weigh the evidence rather against than for authenticity. At the same time it is equally, if not more, unexpected for a pseudepigraphist to adopt such a borrowing procedure. Indeed, it is quite unparalleled among the Jewish and early Christian pseudepigrapha. The question arises why so much of Jude needed to be incorporated. About the only reasonable suggestion on the late-date theory is to suppose that Jude's tract had failed because of its lack of an impressive name and so the same truths with considerable additions were attributed to Peter.[2] But did no-one have any suspicions about this process? It would have been less open to question had the author made his borrowing from Jude less obvious.

Yet perhaps not too much emphasis should in any case be placed on this feature since there is no mention of difficulty over borrowing in any of the comments of Church Fathers concerning the retarded reception of this Epistle. If 2 Peter is prior, the difficulty would vanish altogether as far as that Epistle is concerned and it would then be necessary only to explain why Jude published an extract of a major part of 2 Peter under his own name. In that case, it would seem that Jude is writing when the situation predicted in 2 Peter has already been fulfilled and his Epistle would then be intended to remind the readers of this fact (cf. Jude 17).

Nothing need be added to what has already been said on the literary connections between this Epistle and Paul's Epistles, but the relation-

[1] E. H. Plumptre (*The General Epistles of St. Peter and St. Jude*, 1879, p. 80) made the suggestion that Peter was sent Jude's letter, realized the seriousness of the dangers mentioned and wrote a letter about it to the recipients of 1 Peter, for whom his name would carry more weight than Jude's.

[2] M. Dibelius (*A Fresh Approach to the New Testament and Early Christian Literature*, p. 209) makes an ingenious attempt to explain 2 Peter's wide use of Jude. Because he believes that Jude 17, 18 prompted the production of 2 Peter, he supposes that the author of 2 Peter desired to make clear that his Epistle was the source of Jude and, therefore, incorporated nearly the whole of it. But this extraordinary procedure finds no parallel and looks too much like an artificial expedient to support a theory.

ship between 1 and 2 Peter is more significant. Several similarities between the Epistles exist, but not all scholars are agreed as to the reason for these. If Peter were author of both, there would be a ready explanation. If he were author of 1 Peter but not 2 Peter, direct imitation would need to be postulated, although this is difficult in view of the differences. If both were pseudepigraphic, it would be the first Christian instance of the development of a group of writings attributed to a famous name.

The difference in the use of the Old Testament in the two Epistles should not be exaggerated. While the variation in formal quotation must be admitted, it is a remarkable fact that where 2 Peter approaches the nearest to direct quotations, these are made from Psalms, Proverbs and Isaiah, all of which are formally cited in 1 Peter. Indeed Proverbs and Isaiah are particular favourites of both authors.[1] This kind of subtle agreement suggests the subconscious approaches of one mind rather than a deliberate imitation. It is difficult to regard it as purely accidental. Two other factors may be mentioned by way of corroboration. The similar appeal to the history of Noah is suggestive, although this could conceivably have been due to imitation. The estimate of the Old Testament in both authors is remarkably similar, for the statement in 2 Peter i. 20, 21 regarding the inspiration of Scripture prophecy through the agency of the Spirit of God is fully consonant with the obviously high regard for the prophetic Scriptures in the first Epistle (cf. 1 Pet. i. 10–12).

(iv) *Stylistic problems.* It is notoriously difficult to devise any certain criteria for the examination of style and this is particularly true where comparison is made between two short Epistles. The area of comparison is so restricted that the results may well be misleading. Moreover, subjective impressions are likely to receive greater stress than is justified. At the same time, no-one can deny that the stylistic differences between the Epistles are real enough. Mayor[2] pointed out that the vocabulary common to the two Epistles numbers 100 words, whereas the differences total 599. Variations of subject-matter would naturally account for many of the differences and it is not easy to decide what significance is to be attached to the rest. Both Epistles have a number of words found nowhere else in the New Testament (59 in 1 Peter, 56 in 2 Peter)[3] and among these there are in both certain words of particular

---

[1] Cf. R. A. Falconer, *Exp.*, VI, vi (1902), p. 51.   [2] *Op. cit.*, p. lxxiv.

[3] Cited from Mayor's totals, *op. cit.*, pp. lxxii, lxxiv.

picturesqueness. On the whole these word totals have little importance in view of the small quantities of literature from which they are taken. But the grammatical words are rather a different matter. The fewer particles in 2 Peter than 1 Peter point to a different style, which may indicate a different hand. It may be possible to account for some of this variation by reference to the different mood of each writing. 1 Peter is more calmly deliberative than 2 Peter, which seems to have been produced in a state of strong feeling.

The aptness for repetitions found in 2 Peter has been noted and it is certainly marked.[1] But, although it is rather more noticeable in 2 Peter than in 1 Peter, there are many instances of it in the latter.[2] At times the author of 2 Peter falls into metrical cadences and this has been found a difficulty, but prose writers at times use poetic forms and this need occasion no great surprise.[3]

If the linguistic characteristics are considered too divergent to postulate common authorship between 1 and 2 Peter, the difficulties would, of course, be considerably lessened, if not obviated, by the amanuensis hypothesis for one Epistle. If Peter, for instance, were author of 1 Peter, with the assistance of Silvanus as amanuensis, and author and scribe of 2 Peter, it would be possible to account for these stylistic differences and similarities.[4] Or, if Jerome's hypothesis is preferred, both Epistles might be attributed to different amanuenses. This may be regarded by some as a desperate expedient to avoid a difficulty, but so widespread was the use of amanuenses in the ancient world that it ought not to be dismissed from consideration, at least as a possibility. There is now no means of telling what liberty of expression would be granted by Peter to any amanuensis whom he may have employed. It is in the realm of conjecture to declare that an apostle would or would not have done this or that.[5]

---

[1] Cf. Bigg, *op. cit.*, pp. 225, 226.   [2] Bigg, *op. cit.*, pp. 226, 227, gives a list.
[3] Cf. *Ibid.*, pp. 227, 228.

[4] This is Zahn's solution, but was criticized by Chase (*op. cit.*, p. 813) on the grounds that it involves giving up the real Petrine authorship of 1 Peter in order to defend the authenticity of 2 Peter.

[5] It has been suggested that Peter may have written the letter in Aramaic, which was later translated into Greek (cf. G. Wohlenberg, *Der erste und der zweite Petrusbriefe und der Judasbrief*, Zahn xv,[3] 1923, p. xxxvi). But Moulton and Howard (*A Grammar of New Testament Greek*, II, 1929, pp. 27, 28) can find very few traces of any Semitisms in the language. Yet cf. J. Chaine (*Les Epîtres catholiques*, 1939, p. 18) for a list of Hebraisms in both Epistles. E. G. Selwyn (*The

(v) *Doctrinal problems*. Much New Testament criticism is dominated by an over-analytical approach and this is particularly true in doctrinal comparisons. It is a fallacious assumption that any author of two works must give equal attention in both to the same themes, or must always approach any one theme in a similar way. The fact that 2 Peter deals more fully with the *parousia* theme than 1 Peter constitutes no difficulty for those who consider this difference to be due to difference of purpose. But is this sufficient to explain the important omissions of Petrine themes from 2 Peter? Could the author of 1 Peter have written an Epistle without mentioning the cross or resurrection of Christ? This is an important question which cannot be lightly dismissed. Whereas in 1 Peter there are specific references to the atoning work of Christ (e.g. i. 18, ii. 21ff.), there are less specific allusions in 2 Peter. Frequently Christ is called Saviour (σωτήρ).[1] Through Him men are purged from sin (i. 9). It is the Master who has 'bought' believers (ii. 1), and this cannot refer to anything other than a redemptive act in Christ. Apart from the implicit background of the cross, these allusions in 2 Peter would be unintelligible.

The resurrection and ascension of Christ appear to be replaced by the transfiguration, and this is certainly unexpected. But the author's purpose is to authenticate his own personal knowledge of the glory of Christ, which appears to have been more illuminated on the mount of transfiguration than during the resurrection appearances.[2] In the latter

Christian Prophets and the Prophetic Apocalypse, 1900, p. 157) argued with some plausibility that Luke may have been instructed by Peter to write this Epistle. He based his suggestion on parallels with Luke-Acts.

[1] It is not enough explanation for Käsemann to refer to this title and to that of Lord (κύριος) as stereotyped predicates of Christ (*op. cit.*, p. 285). To call a thing stereotyped at once labels it as secondary, but the use of the titles, whether separately or combined, in this Epistle need not be so explained. The combination is not found precisely in this form elsewhere in the New Testament, but the combination of the two ideas is certainly primitive. It should be noted that 'our Lord Jesus Christ', which is used six times in 2 Peter, is found several times in Paul's letters and cannot be designated 'stereotyped'. Indeed, a sure witness to the fact that the language here does not belong to the period of formal titles is the absence of such forms from the earlier Apostolic Fathers. 'Our Lord Jesus Christ' occurs six times in 1 *Clement*, once in Ignatius and five times in Polycarp, but not once in combination with 'Saviour'. 'Jesus Christ our Saviour' occurs only in the greeting in Polycarp's letter.

[2] The writer is not here dealing with a denial of the resurrection as far as we know from the context. It was a question of the fullest possible authentication of his witness to Christ's glorious nature. (Cf. R. A. Falconer, *op. cit.*, pp. 463, 464.)

the full majesty was veiled. But does the emphasis in 2 Peter betray a degenerate Christology? A fair assessment of the evidence would not support such a contention. The titles applied to Christ are 'Saviour', 'Lord' and 'Master'. He is central in the whole thinking of the believer (cf. ii. 20, i. 2, 8). To Him is ascribed eternal glory (iii. 18). Käsemann is dominated by the thought of non-Christian religious notions in the text, but these do not proceed naturally from the Epistle itself. It should be noted that the great emphasis on the Lordship of Christ in this Epistle presupposes the resurrection and ascension, since without these the doctrine could not have developed.[1]

Turning to the eschatology of the Epistle, we must enquire whether Käsemann is justified in regarding this as sub-Christian. The hope of the *parousia* with its practical outcome in providing a motive for holy living is fully in accord with the eschatology of the rest of the New Testament (2 Pet. iii. 1ff.; cf. 1 Jn. ii. 28, iii. 3).[2] If anything, the eschatology is more primitive than in some parts of the New Testament and this is a point in its favour.[3] The description of the ἔσχατον ('end'), although dramatic with its accompanying destruction of the heavens and earth by fire,[4] is seen to be extraordinarily restrained when compared, for instance, with the *Apocalypse of Peter*. An important factor for the dating of the Epistle is the absence of the second-century Chiliastic interpretation of Psalm xc. 4, in spite of the fact that this

---

[1] H. Alford (*The Greek Testament*,[4] IV, 1871, p. 155) maintained that the Lordship of Christ is most prominent here because of the purpose to warn and caution against rebellion.

[2] This is acknowledged even by some who deny the authenticity of the Epistle. H. F. D. Sparks, for instance, sees in the answer of 2 Peter to the eschatological problem 'fundamentally no more than a second-century reaffirmation of the central hope of the primitive gospel' (*op. cit.*, p. 137).

[3] This is well brought out by E. M. B. Green (*op. cit.*, pp. 18f.). He finds in 2 Peter the paradoxical tension betweeen realized and unrealized eschatology, which was so typical in the apostolic period.

[4] This idea of the destruction of the world by fire (ἐκπύρωσις) had its origins perhaps in Persian thought, but occurs nowhere else in the Bible. In Stoic thought it was linked with ἀποκατάστασις and it may be significant that this latter word occurs in a Petrine speech in Acts iii. 21. It is found in the Dead Sea Scrolls and in the fourth Sibylline Oracles (lines 172–177). It was nevertheless regarded with suspicion by Irenaeus (*Adv. Haer.* i. 7. 1) and Origen (*Contra Celsum*, iv. 11. 79), a fact which no doubt contributed to the hesitations over 2 Peter. But the Christian belief must have been founded on an authoritative document, i.e. in all probability 2 Peter.

passage is quoted in 2 Peter iii. 8.[1] A second-century pseudepigraphist would have done well to avoid this possible pitfall.

The different terms used in 1 Peter and 2 Peter to describe the Lord's coming have often been noted (ἀποκάλυψις and its cognate verb in 1 Peter and παρουσία, ἡμέρα κυρίου, ἡμέρα κρίσεως in 2 Peter), but little weight may be put upon this. Paul in 1 Corinthians and 2 Thessalonians uses both ἀποκάλυψις and παρουσία, and there is no reason why Peter should not have used both words on different occasions.

As to the ethics of 2 Peter, there are exhortations in the Epistle which show the ethical appeal to be based on doctrine (cf. i. 8f., where fruitfulness is particularly stressed; iii. 11ff., where Christian behaviour is geared to the eschatological hope). There is emphasis on stability, restraint of passion, righteousness, purity. A variety of moral virtues is enumerated (i. 5ff.). But is the impetus mainly self-effort? Käsemann[2] and many others believe that it is. Moreover, the work of the Holy Spirit is mentioned only once (i. 21) and then in relation to the inspiration of Scripture. The reason for this may lie in the particular tendencies of the readers. It is evident that the false teachers, at least, do not put much self-effort into their 'Christian' behaviour, and the writer is clearly fearful lest their lax approach should infect the Christian believers to whom he is writing. This would explain the stronger emphasis on individual zeal than is found in 1 Peter. The absence of any close connection between ethics and the doctrine of the Spirit does not mean that the writer did not recognize such a connection, but rather that he saw no need to emphasize it (cf. Paul's approach in Colossians where the Spirit is mentioned once only, Col. i. 8).

On the whole it cannot be said that there are any substantial differences in doctrine when this Epistle is compared with other New Testament books. Although there are omissions, there are no contradictions. There are no features which are of such a character that they could not belong to the apostolic age. The doctrinal considerations are, in fact, rather more favourable to a primitive than to a later origin for the Epistle.

[1] J. Moffatt (*ILNT*, p. 362 n.) objected that Chiliasm was not universal in the second century, neither was Ps. xc. 4 its starting-point, as Rev. xx. 4f. shows. But the latter reference cannot be cited as evidence for second-century Chiliasm, while Chiliastic tendencies are found in as widely differing writers as Barnabas (xv. 4), Justin (*Dial.* 81) and Irenaeus (*Adv. Haer.* v. 28. 3, 23. 2).

[2] For a concise and clear discussion of the position of Käsemann, cf. E. M. B. Green, *op. cit.*, pp. 19, 20.

Little comment is needed on the Hellenistic terms used in this Epistle, for it is impossible to say what degree of impact on an author's mind environment might be expected to have. It will obviously differ with different minds. The main problem over 2 Peter is whether the apostle Peter, with his Jewish fisherman's background, could reasonably be expected to be acquainted with these expressions. None of the terms is of a type which could not have formed part of the vocabulary of a bilingual Galilaean. The difficulty arises only when it is assumed that in 2 Peter they are used in a developed sense as in Greek philosophy or the mystery cults. In that case a fisherman would have to be ruled out. But the bandying about of some such terms as 'knowledge' (γνῶσις) or 'virtue' (ἀρετή) need not suppose acquaintance with current philosophical discussions, any more than it does today. This is the kind of evidence which is most convincing to those who have already concluded on other grounds that 2 Peter cannot have been produced in the first century AD.

So far the approach to Petrine authorship has been mainly negative in the course of examining the arguments brought against it. But there are a few considerations of a more positive character.

(vi) *Additional considerations.* 1. Similarities with the Petrine speeches in Acts will first be considered. No great weight can be attached to these similarities since they are merely verbal and their significance will naturally depend on the degree of credibility assigned to the Acts speeches. At most they can be corroborative. For instance, the words 'obtained' (i. 1; cf. Acts i. 17), 'godliness' (i. 6; cf. Acts iii. 12), 'day of the Lord' (iii. 10; cf. Acts ii. 20) and 'punished' (ii. 9; cf. Acts iv. 21) all occur in both books. The incidental character of these parallels could be a point in their favour, since a pseudepigraphist might be expected either to have included more obvious parallels or else to have ignored the Acts source altogether. They might be regarded as echoes of one man's vocabulary, but the argument obviously cannot be pressed.

2. There are certain indirect personal reminiscences, which might support Petrine authorship. Words are used (σκηνή, 'tabernacle' and ἔξοδος, 'departure') which are found together in Luke's transfiguration narrative. They are used in a different context in 2 Peter, but this in itself would support the suggestion that they had made a deep impression on Peter's mind and are subconsciously brought into play as Peter muses about the transfiguration (i. 17f.). It may be a subtle psychologi-

cal support that these two words are used *before* the transfiguration account is included, but at a point in the Epistle where the writer's mind is moving rapidly towards its inclusion.

3. The superiority of 2 Peter over the Petrine spurious books is another point in its favour. A comparison of its spiritual quality with the spiritual tone of the *Gospel of Peter*, the *Preaching of Peter*, the *Acts of Peter* and the *Apocalypse of Peter* cannot fail to impress even the most casual reader with the immeasurable superiority of the canonical book. This is in itself no conclusive evidence of the authenticity of 2 Peter, for if this Epistle is pseudepigraphic it could conceivably follow that this pseudepigraphist excelled himself, while the others did not. But the problem goes deeper than this, for spiritual quality is not a matter of skill, but of inspiration. In spite of all the doubts regarding the Epistle, the discernment of the Christian Church decided in its favour because the quality of its message suggested its authenticity. It was the same discernment which confidently rejected the spurious Petrine literature.

d. Conclusion

The summing up of the case for and against authenticity is not easy, because there are strong arguments on both sides. The external evidence, at least, indicates a certain lack of confidence in the book, although the cause is not specifically stated. At the same time the internal evidence poses many problems, not all of which can be answered with equal certainty, but none of which can be said categorically to exclude Petrine authorship. The dilemma is intensified by the difficulties confronting alternative views of authorship. If, in deference to the repeated demands of many modern scholars, the word 'forgery' is omitted from the discussion,[1] we are left as our only alternative to suppose that a well-intentioned author ascribed it to the apostle Peter, presumably in order to claim his authority for what was said, but nevertheless supposing that no-one would have been deceived by it. The latter supposition is difficult to substantiate, but even if it be taken as possible, the writer must have paid minute attention to the process of introducing allusions to give an air of authenticity. If the whole process was a contemporary literary convention, it is difficult to see

[1] There was less hesitancy about this at the beginning of this century as is evident from E. A. Abbott's monograph, *Contrast; or a prophet and a forger* (1903), in which he calls the author of 2 Peter not only a forger, but a pilferer, a false prophet, vulgar and dishonest.

why the personal authentication marks were used at all. The fact is that
the general tendency among pseudepigraphists was to avoid rather
than include supporting allusions to their main heroes. It was enough
to allow them to introduce themselves by means of some ancient name.

In addition to this there are difficulties in finding a suitable occasion
which might have prompted such a pseudonymous Epistle. It is a fair
principle to suppose that pseudonymity would be resorted to only
if genuine authorship would fail to achieve its purpose. In this case
it would require a situation in which only apostolic authority would
suffice. In most of the acknowledged Christian pseudepigrapha,
a sufficient motive is found in the desire to propagate views which
would not otherwise be acceptable. Thus the device was used widely
among heretical sects. But in orthodox circles the need would be less
pressing, for the whole basis of their tradition was apostolic and any
literary works whose doctrine was wholly in harmony with that
tradition would not need to be ascribed rather artificially to an apostolic author. The writer of 2 Peter says nothing which the apostolic
writers of the other books of the New Testament would not have
endorsed. There is no hint of esoteric doctrine or practice. What was
the point, then, of ascribing it to Peter? Since the false teachers were
showing no respect for Paul (2 Pet. ii. 16), would they have shown any
more for Peter? If it be maintained that these teachers were using
Peter's name against Paul and that this obliged the orthodox Church
to answer them in Peter's name, would they not be using the very
method they would condemn in their opponents? The fact is that
no advocate of a pseudonymous origin for 2 Peter has been able
to give a wholly satisfactory account of the motive behind it,[1] and

[1] Examples of recent attempts to do this may be cited. A. E. Barnett (op. cit., p.
165) is content to call 2 Peter, 'a plea for loyalty to the tenets of primitive Christianity', and to claim that the pseudonym would symbolize original and authoritative
Christianity. P. Carrington ('Saint Peter's Epistle', in The Joy of Study, ed. S. E.
Johnson, 1951, p. 61) says, 'In 2 Peter the stage is carefully set so as to re-create in
the imagination of the reader a bygone age; for a work of fiction is obliged to
produce a complete illusion'. The Catholic writer Cantinat in Robert-Feuillet's
Introduction à la Bible, II, p. 599, accounts for the pseudonym as being the means
used to cover with the authority of his chief the teaching of one of Peter's disciples
who was endeavouring to reproduce the essential message of the apostle. K. H.
Schelkle (Die Petrusbriefe, der Judasbrief, 1961, p. 181) adopts a similar view.
Dibelius (op. cit., p. 208) finds the fundamental motive for writing in the author's
desire to provide the literary reference for the prophecy referred to in Jude 17, 18.
Thus Jude would ostensibly appear to be citing 2 Pet. iii. 3. But it is difficult to

this must be taken into consideration in reaching a verdict on the matter.

The choice seems to lie between two fairly well defined alternatives. Either the Epistle is genuinely Petrine (with or without the use of an amanuensis), in which case the main problem is the delay in its reception. Or it is pseudepigraphic, in which case the main difficulties are lack of an adequate motive and the problem of its ultimate acceptance.[1]

Both obviously present some difficulties, but of the two the former is easier to explain. If 2 Peter was sent to a restricted destination (see discussion below) it is not difficult to imagine that many churches may not have received it in the earlier history of the Canon.[2] When it did begin to circulate it may well have been received with some suspicion, particularly if by this time some spurious Petrine books were beginning to circulate. That it ultimately became accepted universally must have been due to the recognition not merely of its claim to apostolic authorship, but also of its apostolic content.[3] Under the latter hypothesis it would be necessary to assume that its lack of early attestation and the existence of suspicions were because its pseudepigraphic

believe that Jude 17, 18 would lead anyone to compose an epistle in the name of Peter. If 2 Peter were not in our possession, it would be more natural to take Jude's ἔλεγον as indicating oral teaching. Käsemann (*op. cit.*, pp. 279, 280) sees the need for the pseudonym in the author's intention to authenticate the orthodox teaching in face of the Gnostic challenge. For this purpose, he thinks, an apostolic name was necessary. A. Schlatter (*Die Briefe des Petrus, Judas, Jakobus, der Brief an die Hebräer*, 1950, p. 89) suggests vaguely that Peter was chosen as he was chief apostle.

[1] A third alternative has often been advocated and has recently been maintained by the Catholic writers J. Chaine (*op. cit.*, p. 31) and R. Leconte (*Les Epîtres catholiques*, 1953, p. 96) who, while denying Petrine authorship, yet consider that the author was a disciple of Peter. But this still strictly comes under the category of pseudepigraphy; indeed Chaine admits this.

[2] The poor state of the text may provide some indication of limited early circulation, especially if A. Vansittart is right that for some time it existed in a single copy only (*Journal of Philology*, III, 1871, pp. 357ff.).

[3] Something of the perplexity arising from the apostolic content is seen in the opinion of E. G. Homrighausen (Exposition, *The Second Epistle of Peter*, IB, XII, 1957, p. 166) who, while maintaining its pseudonymous origin, nevertheless admitted that it 'breathes Christ and awaits his consummation' and, furthermore, he asserted that 'what we have is Petrine in character and spirit'. One wonders if the early Christians were as cautious and yet conflicting in their assessment as this modern writer.

origin was known, and that its later acceptance was due to the fact that this origin was forgotten and the Epistle mistakenly supposed to be genuine. While there is nothing intrinsically impossible about this reconstruction, it requires greater credibility than the authenticity hypothesis. The dilemma for pseudepigraphic hypotheses is caused by the fact that attestation for the book would be expected very soon after its origin on the assumption that some would at once assume from its ascription that it was genuine. This evidently happened in the case of the *Apocalypse of Peter* which is attested in the Muratorian Fragment, but never commanded any further acceptance except in Egypt. But in spite of Harnack's arguments for placing 2 Peter in the late second century, few modern advocates of pseudepigraphic origin place it so late. At a period when the orthodox were on the alert to test the validity of all literary productions, it is difficult to see how an earlier pseudepigraphic production would have gained currency after a considerable interval of time, especially against marked suspicions.

III. THE READERS

The Epistle is vaguely addressed 'to those who have obtained a faith of equal standing with ours in the righteousness of our God and Saviour Jesus Christ' (RSV). This very general destination contrasts strikingly with the specific provinces mentioned in 1 Peter. But does this mean that the author has no particular community in view, but is addressing a kind of circular to Christians everywhere? At first sight, his opening words would certainly give that impression, but this must be tested by the contents of the subsequent subject-matter and by the various historical allusions.

The first necessity is to determine whether 1 and 2 Peter were sent to the same readers. Those who interpret 2 Peter iii. 1 as a reference to 1 Peter have an immediate answer. The second Epistle is meant to be addressed primarily to the readers of the first, who may, therefore, be specifically localized. But under this interpretation it would be necessary to suppose that the more general address was used because of the more general applicability of the message to Christians of all areas. Yet there are difficulties in this view, for the author appears to be thinking of particular people known to him personally. In i. 16 he refers to the time 'when we made known to you the power and coming of our Lord Jesus Christ' (RSV), which clearly presupposes a period of previous mission work among the readers. He also sees the particular threat from false teachers who evidently are already active (cf. ii. 1of.) and will gain admittance to the church secretly (ii. 1). He may, of course, be speaking generally here,[1] but his words become more intelligible if he has definite people in mind.

On the basis of i. 16, Zahn[2] considered that the author had been associated with the other eyewitnesses of the transfiguration in mission work among the readers and these would, therefore, be particularly described as 'your apostles' (iii. 2). But the plural in i. 16 need not absolutely refer to more than one and may be here no more than a stylistic avoidance of the singular. Nevertheless, since in the immediately preceding verses the singular is used, the change to the plural probably has some significance in including other eyewitnesses beside the writer. This helps us in ascertaining the readers only if we assume with Zahn[3] that the people concerned must be Jewish Christians, largely on the grounds of a distinction between 'your apostles' and other apostles, and of the absence of specific reference to Gentile readers. Zahn suggested the destination as Palestine and the adjoining regions, but few others have been convinced that the readers are more Jewish than Gentile. The reverse seems rather to be true since the author is clearly apprehensive lest his readers will be affected by the practices of the false teachers, which are much more closely allied to Gentile vices than Jewish. The truth probably lies between the two extremes, and the people in mind may well have been a Jewish-Gentile community or communities. In this connection it should be recalled that nowhere in 2 Peter is the Old Testament certainly cited, although there are many allusions to its examples and echoes of its language. Evidently Peter assumes his readers' acquaintance with it, even more so than in 1 Peter, where it is several times cited, but where there are fewer passing allusions. This might perhaps support Zahn's contention, but the absence of specific appeal to scriptural authority is difficult to conceive if the readers were Jewish Christians.

In the absence of sufficient data there is no option but to leave the location of the readers as an open question, but in this case it makes no vital difference to the interpretation of the Epistle.

---

[1] Moffatt (*ILNT*, p. 368) even regards i. 12f. and iii. 1f. as 'literary drapery', and thus argues that 'there is an entire absence of any personal relation between the writer and the church or churches'.

[2] *INT*, II, pp. 204f.   [3] *Ibid.*, pp. 206ff.

IV. OCCASION AND DATE

Some reference has already been made to both occasion and date when discussing authenticity, and it will be necessary, therefore, only to gather together the different suggestions which have been made.

a. On the assumption that 2 Peter is genuine

As indicated in the discussion on the readers, Peter has apparently worked among these people and is now addressing exhortations to them which he would have delivered orally had he been present among them. He clearly realizes his own work is nearly finished for he alludes to his own passing and this no doubt provides the impetus for the present letter. Yet this Epistle has about it such an air of urgency that it must be supposed that some definite threat of an infiltration of false teachers had suddenly arisen which necessitated its despatch. But since the future tense is mainly used, it must further be supposed that this Epistle is intended to have a preventative effect. The author wishes to strengthen these Christians in faith and practice so that they will be in a position to resist the ungodliness of these threatening false teachers. In this respect the occasion of 2 Peter differs from that of Jude, where the author is obliged to deal with a situation which has already arisen.

The date of the Epistle under this assumption would be towards the end of Peter's life, i.e. before AD 68. It seems most probable that 2 Peter was written not long after 1 Peter, i.e. at a time when Peter was old enough to realize that his passing could not be far away.[1]

b. On the assumption that 2 Peter is pseudepigraphic

Once get away from the apostolic period and both occasion and date become very difficult to specify. In fact, a variety of dates from late first century to late second century have been proposed. There are few fixed points, since no Gnostic sect can be identified with the false teachers. But a *terminus ad quem* is certainly fixed at AD 150 in view of the use made of the Epistle by the author of the *Apocalypse of Peter*,

[1] Two other features which support a date just before AD 70 are the absence of references to the fall of Jerusalem and the fact that Paul seems to be dead, since Peter writes to people to whom Paul had previously written (so Kühl, cited by Chase, *HDB*, III, p. 798). The second argument is stronger than the first. F. W. Lewis (*Exp.*, V, x, 1899, pp. 319, 320) argued that it was inconceivable that Mark or Silas left Paul during his lifetime to join Peter.

which must have been issued shortly after this date. Those who date 2 Peter later are obliged to regard that Epistle as the borrower, but the evidence is strongly against this.[1]

The most generally proposed occasion is the rise of Gnosticism and the consequent need to combat it in the name of the leading apostle Peter. Because no definite Gnostic movement is in mind, there is a greater readiness to date the Epistle during the first quarter of the second century before the more organized Gnostic movements developed. But the false teaching reflected in the Epistle is of such a character that a first-century date would suit equally well and there is no strong reason for postulating a second-century date, even if pseudepigraphy is admitted. In the end the predominating factor has been the external attestation. The later the Epistle can be placed the less difficulty is thought to be found in the neglect of it until the third century. Some advocates[2] of non-apostolic authorship date the Epistle about AD 80 on the assumption that it cannot be too far distant from that period if it was written by a personal disciple of the apostle.

V. THE INTEGRITY OF THE EPISTLE

This Epistle has not escaped the attentions of source-critical advocates and various partition theories have been proposed. These may briefly be summarized as follows:

1. Some theories are based on the view that interpolations have been made from Jude. It was first proposed by L. Bertholdt[3] that 2 Peter ii was a later interpolation based on Jude. A similar view was expressed by E. Kühl,[4] who added iii. 1, 2 as well, while W. F. Gess[5] extended the interpolation to encompass i. 20b to iii. 3a, and J. V. Bartlet[6] modified it to ii. 1–iii. 7.

---

[1] See discussion on pp. 181ff. Among those who affix a late date may be cited A. Harnack, *Das Neue Testament um das Jahr 200* (1899), pp. 81ff.; M. Dibelius, *op. cit.*, p. 209; R. Knopf, *op. cit.*, p. 257; and E. J. Goodspeed, *INT*, p. 349; *A History of Christian Literature* (1942), pp. 52–54. The latter's dating of the *Apocalypse* is AD 125–150 and of 2 Peter AD 140–160. J. Moffatt, *ILNT*, pp. 367, 368, is more cautious.

[2] So Leconte, *op. cit.*, p. 96, and J. Chaine, *op. cit.*, pp. 33, 34.

[3] In his *Historischkritische Einleitung in sämmtliche kanonische und apokryphische Schriften des alten und neuen Testaments* (1812–19), pp. 3157ff.

[4] *Die Briefe Petri und Judä*[6] (1897), supported by W. Weiffenbach, *ThLZ*, 23 (1898), cols. 364ff.

[5] *Das apostolische Zeugniss von Christi Person II*, II (1879), pp. 412ff.

[6] *The Apostolic Age* (1907), pp. 518–521.

2. Other theories are based on combinations of different sources. As early as H. Grotius,[1] questioning arose over the integrity of the Epistle, for that Dutch scholar regarded 2 Peter iii as originally a letter distinct from chapters i and ii. There is some superficial support for this in the form of the opening of chapter iii, provided the first letter is regarded as a reference to the earlier part of our present Epistle (i.e. chapters i and ii). A similar theory has quite recently been proposed by M. McNamara,[2] who restricts the former letter to chapter i and thinks chapter ii is probably another independent letter. This writer interprets i. 15 to mean that the author intends to write further letters and this interpretation has prompted him to find these in parts of 2 Peter. An even more complicated theory was proposed by E. I. Robson,[3] who claimed to discover the following: a moral fragment (i. 5b–11); a personal statement and narrative (i. 12–18); a prophetic discourse (i. 20b–ii. 19); and an apocalyptic fragment (iii. 3b–13). These, he thought, were of apostolic origin or bore an apostolic imprimatur.[4]

Now all these theories are vitiated by the continuity of style through-out all parts of the Epistle.[5] The same peculiarities, such as frequent repetitions, are constant throughout. Admittedly the peculiar words are more concentrated in chapter ii than in the rest of the letter, but this is mainly due to the special subject-matter and can certainly not be regarded as evidence of an interpolation. In fact, there are no evidences of any sutures which would naturally suggest the patching together of different sources. There is, moreover, no textual evidence in support of such theories. The false teachers in both chapters ii and iii appear to be the same people. The doctrinal approach in the separate parts is uniform.[6] In short, the Epistle wears the appearance of a unity and may be quite intelligibly interpreted under this supposition. There is, therefore, no compelling reason to consider interpolation theories as at all necessary, and since the various hypotheses differ widely in detail, it is reasonable

[1] *Adnotationes in Actus Apostolorum et in Epistolas Catholicas* (1641).
[2] 'The Unity of Second Peter: A Reconsideration', *Scripture*, XII, 17 (1960), pp. 13–19.
[3] *Studies in the Second Epistle of Peter* (1915).
[4] In this way he endeavoured to save something of the authenticity of the Epistle.
[5] McNamara (*loc. cit.*) recognized this difficulty and was forced to suppose that his three letters were either the work of the same author or had the same redactor.
[6] Cf. Feine-Behm, *op. cit.*, p. 255.

to suppose that they proceed more from the imagination of their originators than from the demands of the facts.

No more convincing are any theories of scribal displacements, such as that proposed by P. Ladeuze,[1] who rearranged the Epistle so that iii. 1–16 stood after ii. 3a. The idea was to smooth out the awkwardness of the sequence of tenses in chapter ii and the apparent digression in the same chapter. But Moffatt[2] has well criticized this type of theory on the grounds that the process required by such a copyist's error seems too elaborate and is anyway unnecessary as an explanation of the interchange of present and future tenses. If it happened at all, it must have happened to the archetype of all extant manuscripts, leaving no trace of the 'original' behind. This kind of theory must be dismissed as highly improbable.

VI. THE FALSE TEACHERS

Unlike the parallel Epistle of Jude, 2 Peter does not at once plunge into a discussion of the false teachers. It introduces the subject gradually, and although the main data occur in chapter ii there are some indications in chapter i which are significant. For instance, the writer contrasts the authentic truth with 'cleverly devised myths' (i. 16), which suggests the speculative and even imaginative character of the teaching. He then maintains that Scripture prophecy is not by private interpretation, which further suggests that he had in mind people who were interpreting the Scriptures in this way (i. 20, 21). This same thought is still uppermost in his mind in iii. 16 and was evidently a particular characteristic of these teachers. It is noteworthy in this respect that the author does not merely denounce their tendency to twist the Scriptures, but prepares for this in a positive way by asserting his own view of inspiration.

There is no break between i. 21 and ii. 1, for Peter now contrasts the outlook and actions of the false teachers with the true interpretations of which he has just spoken. Their teachings are 'destructive heresies', of which the worst example is their denial of the Master who bought them. It is noteworthy that the last phrase (τὸν ἀγοράσαντα αὐτοὺς) does not occur in the parallel passage in Jude, and it is possible that these particular false teachers made a special point of denying the redemptive work of Christ. It would also appear that their doctrine of God was defective for they 'deliberately ignore this fact, that by the word of God heavens existed long ago' (iii. 5, RSV). What their doctrine of

[1] RB, x (1905), pp. 543–552.   [2] ILNT, pp. 370, 371.

creation was is not stated, but they apparently did not ascribe to God His rightful power.

The details in chapter ii are almost wholly concerned with practical errors and most of the points mentioned are those which also occur in Jude (for a fuller description of these characteristics, see pp. 233ff). Licentiousness and exploitation are the first two details mentioned (ii. 2, 3), and these are followed by descriptions of ancient judgments on similar excesses, particular stress being laid on Lot's reactions to his licentious environment, presumably as a special example for the believers in the face of their approaching threat. There is a promise of deliverance for the godly at the same time as certain judgment for those who indulge their passions (ii. 9, 10). The description of the behaviour of these people is vivid: revelling in dissipation, carousing, adulterous, slaves of corruption. Moral looseness could hardly be more clearly delineated and this must be reckoned as a major factor in the way of life which these people were threatening to introduce. Indeed, their behaviour is not only condemned in itself, but its enticing effects are also strongly denounced (ii. 18f.). These immoral practices were, moreover, not done in the dark as if the doers were ashamed, but openly in broad daylight (ii. 13). Another characteristic is insubordination to authority (ii. 10ff.), which could only lead to anarchy.

A special feature of 2 Peter's false teachers, as distinct from Jude's, is a denial of the *parousia* and a consequent mockery of those who looked forward to it (iii. 3ff.). 2 Peter iii is largely devoted to maintaining, not only the reality of the *parousia*, but the consummation of the present world order and the establishment of the new. The teachers were clearly advocating an approach strongly opposed to primitive eschatology and we may detect a large element of rationalism.

Bearing in mind these characteristics, to what extent do they approximate to any of the Gnostic movements? Certainly most of the features are found in Gnosticism, but care must be taken to ensure that tendencies are not confused with fully developed systems. The Gnostics' approach to Scripture would be well described by 2 Peter iii. 16, for they objected to proofs from Scripture on the grounds that the living voice was more authoritative.[1] By the living voice they meant their own secret traditions, which led them to deny the validity of the orthodox apostolic writings and to substitute their own. But the 'twisting'

---

[1] Irenaeus frequently charges the Gnostics with dishonesty in the treatment of Scripture (cf. *Adv. Haer.* i. 3. 6, 8. 1, 9. 1).

of apostolic writings and in particular those of Paul did not need to wait until developed Gnosticism.[1] Rather was it a cause than an effect. The derogation of existing apostolic sources was a necessary prelude to the substitution of pseudo-apostolic writings to bolster up contrary opinions. The state in 2 Peter appears very primitive. Teaching which challenged their licentious behaviour (which Paul's Epistles constantly do) was a ready target for mishandling and this must have occurred during the genesis of these movements.

The emphasis on γνῶσις in this Epistle may at once suggest a counter-balance to the claim to superior knowledge in all Gnostic systems, but in 2 Peter γνῶσις is only one of a number of virtues and in the list given in i. 5, 6, it is not stressed out of proportion to the rest, as we should expect if the writer were controverting any Gnostic system. The mere occurrence of the idea is not sufficient to provide any certain connecting link.[2]

As to the remaining data, there is little to assist in any identification. Extreme licentiousness was not unknown in second-century Gnosticism, particularly among the Carpocratians (see comment on Jude, p. 235). But licentious behaviour was so general in the pagan world that it is precarious to use this as a point of contact with Carpocratianism. This is the kind of threat that one would expect to occur as soon as Christianity challenged its pagan environment. Indeed it was found in the Corinthian church in Paul's day and in the Asiatic churches reflected in Revelation ii, iii. There are in fact many points of contact between the false teachers in 2 Peter, the libertines of Corinth and the Nicolaitans of Asia.[3]

---

[1] Chase (op. cit., p. 811) objected that there is no trace in apostolic times of false teachers supporting their views by a dishonest interpretation of Scripture. True, but our total knowledge of them is slight, and such practice is certainly not impossible.

[2] Some support may possibly be found in that the earliest sects who claimed the name 'Gnostic' were noted for their active advocacy of immoral living (Iren., Adv. Haer., i. 25. 6; Hippolytus, Haer. v. 6). This would, of course, fit in well with the description in 2 Peter of the active propagandists for immorality. But it is impossible to affix a commencing date to this tendency. E. Käsemann (ZTK, 49, 1952, p. 272) strongly maintains a Gnostic situation, but he comes to the subject already convinced that 2 Peter is a second-century document.

[3] E. M. B. Green (op. cit., p. 26) gives the following suggestive parallels with the Corinthian situation:

2 Pet. ii. 19; 1 Cor. vi. 12, 13.	2 Pet. ii. 1; 1 Cor. xi. 18ff.
2 Pet. ii. 1; 1 Cor. vi. 18–20.	2 Pet. iii. 4; 1 Cor. xv. 12.
2 Pet. ii. 10; 1 Cor. viii.	2 Pet. iii. 3; 1 Cor. xv. 32.
2 Pet. ii. 13; 1 Cor. xi. 21.	

Some of these similarities are closer than others, but there is sufficient proximity

The approach to the *parousia* does not fit any known system of Gnosticism. Too great an interval had passed for interest to be maintained in an imminent coming, but the form of the scoffers' question (iii. 4) suggests a time when belief in the near return was still very much alive. This feature certainly fits a first-century date better than a second.

In concluding this discussion it should be noted that these threatened trouble-makers are called 'false prophets' (ψευδοπροφῆται) and 'false teachers' (ψευδοδιδάσκαλοι), both of which terms would seem to emphasize false doctrine rather than behaviour and yet the Epistle is mainly about the latter. The total details given are not sufficient to allow any more precision than to speak of a general antinomian tendency.

VII. RELATION TO I PETER

It is important to bear in mind the precise literary relationship between these letters and this can be done quite independently of any particular decision regarding authorship, although it clearly has some bearing upon that subject. The similarities between them go far beyond the common ascription to Peter. Both contain a group of remarkable and vivid words which occur only in their respective Epistles in the New Testament. There are, moreover, a few striking words and ideas common to both, e.g. the word ἀρετή in both is ascribed to God (2 Pet. i. 3; 1 Pet. ii. 9), ἐπιχορηγήσατε in 2 Peter i. 5 compares with χορηγεῖ in 1 Peter iv. 11, and there are many other verbal comparisons of the same kind.[1] On stylistic points of comparison, the most notable is a similar use of the article. Both use nouns frequently without articles and both use phrases introduced by articles.[2] The dissimilarities of language and

to claim that the tendencies seen at Corinth would very rapidly develop into the errors found in the 2 Peter teachers. (Cf. also W. M. Ramsay's comparison of 2 Pet. ii. 1ff. with 1 Cor. x.; *Exp.*, VI, iii, 1901, pp. 106ff.)

[1] Cf. the following:

The salutations (2 Pet. i. 2; 1 Pet. i. 2).
Brotherly affection (2 Pet. i. 7; 1 Pet. i. 22, iii. 8).
The testimony of the prophets (2 Pet. i. 19, 20; 1 Pet. i. 10–12).
The reference to Noah (2 Pet. ii. 5, iii. 6; 1 Pet. iii. 20).
'Without spot or blemish' (2 Pet. iii. 14; 1 Pet. i. 19).
The reference to the consummation of all things (2 Pet. iii. 10; 1 Pet. iv. 7).
The reference to freedom (2 Pet. ii. 19; 1 Pet. ii. 16).
For a detailed discussion of similarities and differences, cf. Mayor, *op. cit.*, pp. lxviii–cxiv.

[2] Cf. Mayor, *op. cit.*, pp. lxxix–lxxx, for details.

style have already been mentioned in discussing authorship (see pp. 148f). Mayor's[1] conclusion is worth quoting, 'There can be no doubt, I think, that the style of 1 Peter is on the whole clearer and simpler than that of 2 Peter, but there is not that chasm between them which some would try to make out.' In addition to these differences in vocabulary and style, Chase[2] brings four other differences—the use of the Old Testament; the reminiscences of the Lord's teaching; the use of Paul's Epistles; and doctrinal differences. All of these have already been considered and reasons have been given for them.

The whole question of the relation between these Epistles has been brought into sharp relief by G. H. Boobyer's attempt to show how the author of 2 Peter has used 1 Peter.[3] He suggests that 2 Peter iii. 1 was written with 1 Peter i. 10–12 in mind and, on the strength of this, suspects further allusions to the first Epistle. He then compares 2 Peter i with 1 Peter i, and having concluded for the dependence of the former on the latter, he thinks dependence must have continued beyond the salutation. Although he admits differences, he thinks 2 Peter i. 3–11 was written under the influence of 1 Peter i. 3–9. Similarly he compares 1 Peter i. 10–12 with 2 Peter i. 12–21 and claims to find an allusion to 1 Peter v. 1 in the introduction to the transfiguration account. 2 Peter i. 14 is particularly examined from this point of view and Boobyer thinks that a combination of the 1 Peter allusion and a knowledge of the Synoptic narrative of the transfiguration (probably Matthew or Mark) accounts for it.

Now Boobyer has examined this evidence from the point of view that the author of 2 Peter has made a *literary* use of 1 Peter, for he does not regard the former as Petrine. His justification for maintaining a literary dependence is based on his acceptance of 2 Peter's literary use of Jude. But his evidence here would equally well support the contention that the same author wrote both 1 and 2 Peter, for in that case we should expect the kind of parallels to which he refers. It may not be possible to dispute *literary* dependence, but neither is it possible, on the kind of evidence cited by Boobyer, to *exclude* common authorship. When, for instance, in considering 2 Peter i. 12–13, Boobyer says,

---

[1] *Op. cit.*, p. civ. This caution is in marked contrast to Moffatt's approach (*ILNT*, p. 364).

[2] *Op. cit.*, pp. 812, 813.

[3] 'The Indebtedness of 2 Peter to 1 Peter' in *New Testament Essays: Studies in Memory of T. W. Manson* (ed. A. J. B. Higgins, 1959), pp. 34–53.

'Much in this section, in fact, could be an outflow from 1 Peter i. 10–12',
this could equally well have happened in the mind of one man through
association of ideas, as in two minds with one drawing from another.
There is no critical principle which can enable an indisputable choice to
be made between these two alternatives, but it is a fair conclusion that
the kind of relationship which is found between the two Epistles does
not prohibit the tradition of Petrine authorship from being maintained.

VIII. OTHER LITERARY CONNECTIONS

In 1882, Ezra Abbott[1] maintained that both 2 Peter and Jude were dependent on Josephus, particularly on two passages of his *Antiquities*.[2]
This was based on a number of parallel words in both groups of writings,
the assumption being that one was dependent on the other and, since
Josephus shows no acquaintance elsewhere with the New Testament,
the only solution is to suppose that the writers of 2 Peter and Jude were
acquainted with Josephus' works. But the argument is fallacious on
several grounds. Most of the words cited were in common use and are
found in other writers (e.g. in Philo).[3] Moreover, the contexts bear no
relationship to each other and it is impossible to establish literary dependence unless they do.[4] Further, if a pseudepigraphic writer, wishing
to produce a Petrine Epistle, consulted Josephus, his method of ensuring
verisimilitude is puzzling in the extreme. Farrar[5] argued that Josephus
was dependent on 2 Peter, but this seems highly unlikely. If the writer
of 2 Peter was a Jew, as he was if the Epistle is authentic, some similarities between him and Josephus might not be so surprising. The evidence
in any case is quite insufficient to establish any literary connection.

As this line of argument has now fallen into disuse, so is there less
readiness than formerly to maintain the dependence of 2 Peter on the
Apocalypse of Peter. Both contain references to the transfiguration[6] and

[1] *Exp.*, II, iii (1882), pp. 49–63.
[2] Paragraph 4 of the Preface and iv. 8. 2. The relevant passages are quoted in full
in Mayor (*op. cit.*, pp. cxxviii f.), who admits marked resemblances of language.
[3] Cf. Zahn, *INT*, II, p. 291 n. 14. Salmon cites from Dr. Gwynn similar evidence
for 1 Peter (*INT*, p. 506).
[4] Cf. G. Salmon (*op. cit.*, p. 499) whose criticisms of both Abbott and Farrar are
very lucid.
[5] *Exp.*, III, viii (1888), pp. 58–69.
[6] In *The Apocryphal New Testament* (1924), p. 507, M. R. James regards this
incident as part of the *Gospel of Peter* and not the *Apocalypse*, and if this is correct,
the above statement would need modification.

both describe certain eschatological features, but apart from the additional fact that both are ascribed to Peter, there is not a great deal to be said. Verbal coincidences are slight. In the list cited by M. R. James,[1] only two extend to more than one word, although common ideas are stronger. There is a reference to false prophets who shall teach perverse doctrines (cf. 2 Pet. ii. 1), although the *Apocalypse* does not emphasize, as 2 Peter does, any particular Christological error.

In the *Apocalypse* the main attention is upon the continuous torments of the lost, which is most naturally understood as an imaginative reconstruction from 2 Peter's hint of the condemnation and destruction of the false teachers (note especially the reference to the continuity of these in 2 Pet. ii. 3). Other incidental verbal parallels are all more easily explained on the assumption of the priority of 2 Peter than vice versa, and this conclusion must have an important bearing on the date and authenticity of 2 Peter. The two works, while touching superficially on similar themes, differ widely in the spiritual grasp of their respective authors and there are few who would regard the *Apocalypse* as in anywhere near the same spiritual class as 2 Peter. From this point of view alone, it is hardly conceivable that the superior work was prompted by the inferior, for imitations have a greater tendency to deteriorate than to improve.[2] Bigg's[3] opinion that 2 Peter i. 15 prompted the whole prolific family of pseudo-Petrine literature is highly probable.

The main problem about 2 Peter and the *Apocalypse of Peter*, if this conclusion is correct, is the apparently later reception of the former as compared with the latter. Perhaps the greater obscurity of 2 Peter during the second century may be because the nature of its subject-matter did not have the same popular appeal as the *Apocalypse*, which promised retribution (or rather retaliation) to those under whom the Christians

[1] *The Second Epistle general of St. Peter, and the general Epistle of St. Jude* (1912), p. xxvii. Cf. also Chase's clear comparison of parallel texts, *op. cit.*, pp. 814, 815.

[2] For those maintaining that 2 Peter was basic to the *Apocalypse*, cf. F. Spitta, 'Die Petrusapokalypse und der zweite Petrusbrief', *ZNTW*, 12 (1911), pp. 237–242; Bigg, *op. cit.*, pp. 207–209; J. Chaine, *op. cit.*, pp. 3, 4; Mayor, *op. cit.*, p. cxxxiii; Zahn, *INT*, II, p. 273. This is a formidable list, yet in spite of it many have maintained the contrary opinion (N.B. especially A. Harnack, *op. cit.*, pp. 81ff.; F. C. Porter, *The Message of the Apocalyptic Writers*, 1905, p. 355; and Moffatt, *ILNT*, p. 367). For the alternative view that both books proceeded from the same circle of thought, cf. F. H. Chase, *HDB*, III, p. 816; M. R. James, *op. cit.*, p. xxviii; McNeile-Williams, *INT*, p. 247. W. Sanday (*Inspiration*, 1893, p. 347) posited the same author for both books.

[3] *Op. cit.*, p. 215. Cf. also Wand, *op. cit.*, p. 140.

were suffering. Its period of appeal was, however, short and in this it contrasts strikingly with 2 Peter.

IX. THE MODERN MESSAGE

It is relevant to enquire into the contemporary usefulness of this Epistle in view of the widespread denial of its authenticity. It has largely been neglected, in common with the companion Epistle of Jude. But, although it deals with a local situation, it is not without a positive contribution for any age. Some scholars would restrict its value to its historical contribution to our knowledge of Antinomianism and early Christian eschatology.[1] But while this must be acknowledged, its primary value is religious. It contains passages of spiritual illumination which have been, and will undoubtedly continue to be, a means of strength and challenge to Christians in all ages.[2] The first chapter is particularly notable in this respect. But even the description of false teachers is not without salutary warning for an age in which moral standards are declining, while the sombre description of the approaching consummation of the age is lightened by the assurance of the Lord's forbearance. In spite of its apocalyptic ring, the dissolution of the elements by fire sounds strikingly relevant in an age of multi-megaton atomic bombs. The consequent exhortation to self-examination in 2 Peter iii. 11 could not be more relevant than for today, and we may be grateful indeed that this precious letter has been preserved for us in spite of all the questionings regarding it.

CONTENTS

I. GREETING (i. 1, 2)

The writer introduces himself in this Epistle as Simon Peter and addresses those who share the same faith as he possesses.

II. TRUE KNOWLEDGE (i. 3–21)

a. The quest for a higher nature (i. 3, 4)

Every Christian has access to a divine power which enables him to live

[1] Cf. T. Henshaw, *op. cit.*, p. 396.
[2] E. F. Scott (*op. cit.*, p. 229), who rejects its authenticity, admits the real religious value of some impressive passages which it contains.

a godly life. His attitude towards the present world must be to escape from its corruption through receiving a share of the divine nature. This is real knowledge.

b. The progressive character of Christian virtues (i. 5-11)

This Christian knowledge is many-sided and contains aspects far removed from mere intellectual apprehension although it includes this. The apostle gives a list of virtues which should be striven for, reaching a climax in love (verses 5-7). This is the way to become fruitful in the knowledge of Christ, and those who are diligent in this direction will have an abundant entrance into God's kingdom.

c. The apostolic attestation of Christian knowledge (i. 12-21)

1. The author expresses his intentions to remind the readers of these things, not only while he still lives, but also after he has died, through his writings (verses 12-15).

2. The content of the Christian message is contrasted with mythology, for the author has had first-hand acquaintance with a real event, the transfiguration, which testified to the glory of Christ (verses 16-18).

3. On the basis of this an exhortation is addressed to the readers to pay attention to the prophetic word to which the apostle and his fellow eyewitnesses bear testimony. A warning is added about the private interpretation of prophetic Scriptures, because these are inspired by the Spirit of God (verses 19-21).

III. FALSE KNOWLEDGE (ii. 1-22)

By way of contrast attention is now focused upon advocates of false knowledge who will trouble the Church.

a. What may be expected from the false prophets (ii. 1-3)

Their coming will be secretive. They will deny the Master. They will lead others into immoral practices. They will exploit others in their greed by deceptive methods. But their destruction is certain.

b. What they may expect from God (ii. 4-10)

Examples of God's judgment are quoted from earlier history to illustrate the fate of these enemies of the truth. The fate of the fallen angels, the ante-diluvian world, and Sodom and Gomorrah shows the certainty of judgment against sin, but also the assurance of divine mercy towards the godly by the examples of Noah and Lot.

c. A description of ungodly people (ii. 11–22)

The apostle now describes people he has already observed and draws attention to their arrogance, their irrational outlook, their immoral conduct, their bad effect on others, their greed and their deceptive promises. Some of these people have already known something of Christ, but their return to their former ways is deplored in strong terms. It would have been better for them not to have known the truth at all.

IV. THE PRESENT CHALLENGE (iii. 1–18)

In this closing portion of the Epistle, the apostle turns to present problems and exhortations.

a. A reminder (iii. 1, 2)

The present letter, like the former one which the readers have received, has for its purpose to remind them of the apostolic prediction about scoffers to come. Since it is witnessed by the prophetic word and the Lord's own teaching, the rise of these scoffers should not take them unawares.

b. An explanation (iii. 3–10)

There are some who are turning the delay in the Lord's return into an occasion for scoffing. But they ignore that creation itself is the work of God, who in His own time will bring it to consummation. As God acted in judgment by water in the time of the flood, so He will act in judgment by fire at the day of judgment. The delay in the coming should therefore be interpreted as an act of mercy, and not as an evidence of God's indifference to His promises. In any case, the timing of the final act is unknown, but will surely come.

c. An exhortation (iii. 11–18)

In view of approaching judgment what sort of persons ought the Christians to be? The apostle mentions three things: holiness, godliness, expectancy. The life must conform to the hope of a new creation where righteousness dwells. There must be a zeal for purity, and tranquillity. Paul's letters mention the Lord's forbearance and this should be an encouragement, although some have twisted his meaning. The Epistle ends with a warning to the readers against being carried away by error, and an earnest plea to them to grow in the grace and knowledge of Christ.

CHAPTER FIVE

THE JOHANNINE EPISTLES

THE FIRST EPISTLE

This Epistle has always been loved and meditated upon in the Christian Church and with good reason. It combines profound thoughts with simplicity of expression. It is both practical and reflective. It gives insight into early Christian conditions in such a manner as to provide principles of thought and action which are applicable in any age. Yet nevertheless the Epistle poses many critical problems and attempts must be made to settle these if a full appreciation of its message is to be attained.

I. AUTHORSHIP

In one sense the authorship is not the most important issue, for the exegesis of the letter is not greatly affected by our conclusions regarding authorship. Yet it becomes more personal if an individual name can with any confidence be attached to it. And this is particularly so when tradition has anything to contribute on this question.

a. External evidence

The earliest clear allusion to the content of this Epistle is to be found in Polycarp.[1] Probably Papias may also be cited in support.[2] Some have found coincidences of language in Justin, Barnabas, Hermas and even Clement of Rome, but since these might possibly be explained as the common milieu of Christian thought, it is better to appeal to the more certain evidence. Irenaeus cited the Epistle as by the Lord's disciple John, the writer of the Fourth Gospel.[3] Both Clement of Alexandria[4] and Tertullian[5] similarly cite it as John's. The Muratorian Fragment is somewhat confused on the Johannine Epistles, although it cites 1 John

[1] Ad Phil. vii, cf. 1 Jn. iv. 2. A. E. Brooke, The Johannine Epistles (ICC, 1912), p. liii, adds 1 Jn. iii. 8, ii. 18, ii. 22 and 2 Jn. 7, as partial parallels.

[2] Cf. Eusebius, HE, iii. 39. 3, 17 (a reference here to John's former Epistle—ἀπὸ τῆς Ἰωαννοῦ προτέρας ἐπιστολῆς).

[3] De Haer. iii. 16. 5, 8.

[4] Strom. ii. 15. 66, iii. 4. 32, iii. 5. 42, 44, iv. 16. 100.

[5] Adv. Marc. v. 16; Adv. Prax. xxviii; Adv. Gnost. xii.

evidently as authoritative.[1] Origen frequently cites the Epistle and refers to it as by John. Dionysius, Origen's pupil, regarded the Epistle as written by the author of the Gospel, but distinguished its style from that of the Apocalypse, which he consequently attributed to a different author.

This evidence[2] is sufficient to show that from very early times the Epistle was not only treated as Scripture but was assumed to be Johannine, in spite of the fact that no specific claim to this effect is made by the writer himself. This strong tradition cannot easily be set aside, especially as no alternative theory of authorship was suggested in the early Church, as it was, for instance, in respect of the Apocalypse. It is against this strong traditional background of Johannine authorship that the internal evidence must now be examined to ascertain whether or not the ancient Church was uncritical in its assumptions.

b. Internal evidence

(i) *The writer's own claims.* This Epistle and the Epistle to the Hebrews are the only New Testament Epistles in which no author's name is given, but in 1 John, unlike Hebrews, the introduction is clearly intended to tell us something about the author. He is writing about what he (or rather 'we') had heard, seen, looked upon and touched (1 Jn. i. 1). In no more vivid way could the writer indicate that he was an eyewitness.[3] When he says further that 'the life was manifested, and we saw it', he draws attention at once to the times when he companied with Christ. Yet not all scholars would so interpret the first person plural. If this is no more than an epistolary device by which the author is associating his message with that of the original eyewitnesses,[4] or is using the first person plural generally of all believers (as in iv. 7–19), it would

[1] See further discussion of this evidence in reference to 2 John (p. 207).

[2] For a fuller statement and examination of it, cf. A. E. Brooke, *op. cit.*, pp. lii–lxii.

[3] Cf. Feine-Behm (*op. cit.*, p. 261), who appeal to the same phenomenon in Jn. i. 14.

[4] C. H. Dodd (*The Johannine Epistles*, 1946, pp. 2, 3) suggests that the neuter pronouns must refer to the contents of the announcement and not to Christ. To him the 'we' is generalizing for all believers (cf. p. 12). H. Conzelmann, in his article 'Was von Anfang war', in *Neutestamentliche Studien für Rudolf Bultmann* (ed. W. Eltester, 1954), pp. 194–201, maintains that the author of the Epistle has imitated the Gospel in 1 Jn. i. 1–4 and has feigned (*fingiert*) the rôle of the Evangelist. But see Michaelis' criticisms of this view, *Einleitung*, Ergänzungsheft zur 3, Auflage, p. 38.

no longer be evidence for the author's own claims. But is such an interpretation defensible? When the author says in iv. 13, 'By this we know that we abide in him' (rsv), the plural clearly stands for general Christian experience, but the actions described in i. 1–5 do not appear to be of this general character. 'What we have seen with our own eyes' loses its point unless it is specific. What the writer is concerned to claim at the outset is that his proclamation is based on his own personal experience and the experience of those closely associated with him. Admittedly the 'we' soon broadens out, and the statement in iv. 14 in which the words 'we have seen' (τεθεάμεθα) also occur could be understood generally, but it is much more natural to understand the words as referring to actual eyewitnesses.[1] It would bring no authentication of his message if the author were referring only to the fact of the incarnation which all Christians generally had 'seen'. This is, in fact, an unwarranted weakening of the author's language, and we can confidently proceed on the assumption that he intended his readers to understand that he was one of the original eyewitnesses of the life of Jesus.

This is important in dealing with authorship, for obviously if this indication is taken at its face value and is not regarded as a literary device to create the impression of authenticity, it narrows the field of possible authors. It is clearly in complete harmony with the traditional ascription to John, the apostle.

(ii) *The general impression of the Epistle*. Quite apart from this specific eyewitness claim, the Epistle contains an unmistakable air of authority. The much repeated address to 'little children' (τεκνία) could have been written only by someone of considerable authority to those who would at once acknowledge his right to address them in this manner—a veritable father in God. He clearly expects not only to be heard, but to be obeyed (cf. iv. 6, as well as the whole impression of the Epistle). He writes in categorical, almost dogmatic, terms. There is no disputing the truth of what he says. He condemns error in no uncertain terms (cf. ii. 18ff., iv. 1ff.), and leaves no opportunity for compromise. His letter at once creates the impression that here is a man who knows beyond question where he stands and expects all other Christians to conform to the same standard, because he knows it to be true. The author, in short, stands out as a man of considerable spiritual stature.

His use of τεκνία to describe his readers would also seem to suggest

[1] As A. E. Brooke, *op. cit.*, p. 121, does.

an elderly man who could use more familiar terms without fear of being misunderstood, and this again is in full agreement with the traditional picture of the venerable apostle John during his later years of ministry in Ephesus. There is, moreover, a style of language, with its somewhat restricted powers of expression, its limited vocabulary and its lack of literary polish, which is not surprising in an ageing man to whom maturity of thought was much more important than elegance of expression.

(iii) *The relationship to Johannine thought.* The connection of this Epistle with the Fourth Gospel deserves a section of its own and is dealt with below, but some comments upon it are necessary here since the problem of authorship cannot be discussed apart from it. It will be shown that similarities of thought and even expression are so striking that it is a fair assumption, disputed by only a minority of critics, that the author of this Epistle was the author of the Fourth Gospel. This at once raises many problems which cannot here be fully discussed. It is the prevailing opinion that John the apostle did not write the Gospel and those who have come to that conclusion must naturally exclude him from the authorship of the Epistle. But there is a danger here of arguing in a circle. It is better to examine the relationship of Gospel and Epistle in the light of what has already been discussed from external and internal evidence. If the tradition is correct which attributed the Epistle to the apostle John, is there anything in its relationship with the Gospel which is out of keeping with this?

Since the same traditions which ascribed the Epistle to John ascribed also the Gospel, it is not surprising to find such strong marks of similarity between the two works, in thought, style, expression, ideas and imagery. There are undoubtedly some differences, mainly in emphasis and subject-matter, but these are explicable by the difference in purpose, occasion and form of the two works.

It may, therefore, be said that what is known as 'Johannine thought' pervades the Epistle, as would be expected if John the apostle were the author. But this does not demonstrate his authorship *per se*, since the same would be true if some other writer wrote both Gospel and Epistle. Some of the alternative theories of authorship must next be considered.

(iv) *Various proposals regarding authorship.* 1. The apostle John has the support, as has been shown, of tradition, and is in harmony with the self-claims of the Epistle. Many able scholars[1] have sided with the tradition in the absence of any conclusive arguments to the contrary and this seems the most reasonable approach. But many others, probably the majority, reject this view. There is no doubt that this is largely due to the trends of criticism on the Fourth Gospel, but there are signs that conclusions on the authorship of the latter book may not be as final against apostolic authorship as many have supposed.[2]

2. The most popular alternative theory, that a second John, known as John the Elder, was the author of this Epistle, gains strong support from the fact that 2 and 3 John, which may reasonably be regarded as being written by the same author (see discussion on p. 217), both introduce their author as 'the elder'. The theory has also claimed support from Papias' reference to John the Elder,[3] a much discussed passage which does not, however, leave it indisputable that John the Elder was ever a personality distinct from the apostle John.[4] This theory really involves attributing the writings to an unknown in all but the vaguest name, and while there is nothing intrinsically impossible about this (as the anonymous Epistle to the Hebrews shows), it is extremely difficult on this hypothesis to account for the unchallenged tradition of the Church in favour of apostolic authorship. It is admitted by most students of the New Testament Canon that this Epistle gained acceptance on the ground of its supposed apostolic origin, but were the Church Fathers likely to become confused about two Johns? And if John the Elder were author of 1 John, why did he not introduce himself more clearly (even the Elder of 2 and 3 John is nameless)? An anonymous epistle from him is more difficult to conceive than from John the apostle, since all would admit the authority of the latter without further description and 1 John clearly implies that the readers will recognize the writer's personal authority. Yet it has been argued in the

---

[1] Cf. W. Michaelis, *Einleitung*, pp. 293, 294. Cf. also B. F. Westcott, *The Epistles of John* (1892), pp. xxx, xxxi; G. Findlay, *Fellowship in the Life Eternal* (1909), pp. 47ff.

[2] Cf. J. A. T. Robinson's article in *The Gospels Reconsidered* (1960), pp. 154–166. The whole question will be fully discussed in the volume on the Gospels and Acts in this *New Testament Introduction*.

[3] D. Smith (*The Epistle of John, EGT*, v, 1910, pp. 161, 162) suggested that since Papias echoed 3 Jn. 12, which shows that he was acquainted with John's self-description as Elder, he may have used the same title for this reason.

[4] A. E. Brooke (*op. cit.*, p. lxii), who attributes the Epistles to John the Elder, admits that no satisfactory solution exists regarding his personality.

reverse direction that an apostle writing to combat false teaching (see below) would surely weight his exhortations by appeal to his apostolic office. But the fact remains that the early Church recognized his apostolic claims.

On the whole the Elder theory, although it appears to have many plausible aspects, raises more difficulties than the traditional view.

3. A third theory is that the author was a disciple of the Evangelist. Those who deny identity of authorship with the Gospel are obliged to hold this even more remote theory if they regard John the Elder as the author of the Gospel. Thus C. H. Dodd agrees with the commonly held view regarding the Gospel, and speaks simply of the Presbyter in connection with the Epistle. He is content to leave him without a name, although he thinks the author has left 'a recognizable self-portrait in his three epistles'.[1]

Much the same kind of theory is maintained by M. Dibelius who also distinguishes between the writer of the Gospel and the writer of 1 John. The former he calls 'the unknown evangelist', while the latter is 'a less original person and essentially of a type common in the Church'.[2] But this reduces the Epistle itself to the commonplace in a manner contrary to the testimony of most Christians of both ancient and modern times. If the author of this Epistle was a 'common type' the early Church must have been well supplied with spiritual geniuses whose literary productions were, oddly enough, not sufficiently appreciated to have been preserved. Such an approach to the author problem is too far-fetched to command general consent and provides no solution to the question why this particular letter should ever have been preserved.[3]

In spite of all assertions to the contrary, it must be admitted that these alternative theories do not provide as adequate an explanation of the high regard in which this Epistle was held as the traditional testimony.

II. OCCASION AND BACKGROUND

It is impossible to grasp the purpose of this Epistle until something has been said about the background of thought to which it belonged.

[1] Op. cit., p. lxxi.

[2] A Fresh Approach to the New Testament and Early Christian Literature (1937), p. 211.

[3] J. Moffatt (ILNT, pp. 592, 593), although disinclined to hold to identity of authorship for Gospel and Epistle, is nevertheless very cautious in suggesting an alternative. The best he can do is to maintain that the two authors belonged to the same circle, the writer of 1 John having 'an individuality and purpose of his own'. Cf. also H. Windisch-H. Preisker, Die katholischen Briefe[3] (1951), p. 110.

Although the data from the Epistle itself are very slight, there are just enough indications of false teaching being combated to enable a general comparison to be made with the earliest of the Gnostic tendencies, particularly with Docetism. This evidence is as follows: ii. 22, 'who is the liar but he who denies that Jesus is the Christ? This is the antichrist, he who denies the Father and the Son' (RSV); and iv. 3, 'and every spirit which does not confess Jesus is not of God. This is the spirit of antichrist, of which you heard that it was coming, and now it is in the world already' (RSV).

The main feature in the form of heresy being contested was, therefore, a denial of the incarnation. This was true of all Gnostics (using the term in its broadest sense of those who sought salvation by illumination). The idea of an incarnate deity was unintelligible and, therefore, rejected. Docetism evolved a means of getting over the intellectual difficulty by making a distinction between the human Jesus and the heavenly Christ, the latter only appearing to take a human form.[1] The incarnation was not, therefore, a reality. This solution, which made a wide appeal, had the added advantage, so it was thought, of avoiding the anomaly of Christ sharing in such an inherently evil thing as matter. As these Gnostics believed that all matter was evil there was nothing for it but to deny that Christ had contact with flesh. The dangerous character of this heresy is at once apparent, for it was an attempt to preserve Christ's deity at the expense of His humanity, and all in the interests of a higher intellectualism. But the question arises whether developed Docetism is really in view in this Epistle. That similar tendencies are in mind seems highly probable, but John gives no indication of any apparent or phantasmal body, and this suggests that the form of heresy being forged out was no more than an adumbration of the type attested by Ignatius.[2]

It is, at least, certain that these false teachers came within the general category of Gnosticism,[3] although that term needs further definition in

---

[1] Cf. G. G. Findlay's discussion of this, op. cit., pp. 218ff. Jülicher-Fascher, Einleitung, pp. 227f., maintained that John was combating Docetism.

[2] Ad Trall. x; Ad Smyrna, ii, iii; Ad Ephes. vii. J. Cantinat, in Robert-Feuillet's Introduction à la Bible, II, p. 699, rightly points out that the heretics in this Epistle, unlike the Docetists, did not regard Jesus as either Messiah or Son of God. Yet there is clearly some connection of thought between the two outlooks, if not identity.

[3] We may at once reject the view that Judaizers or Jews are in view (cf. G. Bardy, RB, xxx, 1921, p. 349), for these false teachers had themselves withdrawn from the Christian community, and it is highly improbable that they would then

view of the wider understanding of it obtained from the recent discovery of the Nag Hammadi library. If we restrict the term Gnosticism to those developed second-century systems of thought which absorbed within their pagan background certain Christian ideas, and by this means threatened the orthodox Church, our Epistle would seem to belong to a stage somewhat before these developed Christian Gnostic systems, although there were many straws to indicate the direction of the mental winds which were surrounding the Church.

One of the movements which may lie behind this Epistle was that of Cerinthus. Whatever truth there may be in Polycarp's story of the apostle John's encounter with Cerinthus at the baths of Ephesus, from which the apostle is said to have fled when Cerinthus entered lest judgment should fall upon him, it is not improbable that Cerinthus was spreading his doctrines when John resided in Ephesus. His doctrine of the unknown Father could perhaps be combated in ii. 23f.; and v. 6, the linking of water and blood in reference to Christ's coming, could reflect Cerinthus' denial of the necessity of the cross in the messianic work of salvation and his emphasis on Christ's baptism.[1] The teaching of this heretic had a decidedly Jewish flavour about it, but there is nothing to lead us to suppose that the readers generally were Jewish Christians. The concluding verse (v. 21), which warns against idolatry, would seem to rule this out. But there may well have been Jewish Christian Gnostics who were troubling the Church.[2]

In addition to wrong doctrine, the false teachers were also guilty of wrong practice. They had an inadequate sense of sin (i.e. an antinomian approach) which John shows to be fallacious. The constant emphasis on mutual love was no doubt to offset the pride engendered in the initiates of Gnostic-like systems.[3]

According to iv. 1, it would appear that the false prophets had

attempt to influence the Christians from outside if their purpose was a Judaizing of Christianity. For a full study of these false teachers, cf. A. Wurm, *Die Irrlehrer im ersten Johannesbrief* (1933).

[1] For a full discussion, see A. E. Brooke (*op. cit.*, p. xlv), who concludes that although other forms of false teaching are alluded to in 1 John, the main teaching attacked is that of Cerinthus. Feine-Behm (*op. cit.*, pp. 260, 261) are much more uncertain about such an identification, although they point out the similar features.

[2] H. Windisch (*op. cit.*, p. 127) points out that the language of the Epistle suggests a group of antichrists not simply a single individual.

[3] Cf. J. Moffatt, *ILNT*, p. 586. H. Windisch (*loc. cit.*) is sceptical about this because it is nowhere in the Epistle applied to Gnostic haughtiness.

belonged to the Christian community, but had now gone out into the world (κόσμος seems to be used of the non-Christian sphere). In this case the probability is that they are still harassing the believers from an outside position, possibly by appealing to the intellectual attractions of their systems. Such a state of affairs was regarded as serious by the apostle and provides the immediate occasion for the Epistle. Christians generally must be informed of this insidious error.

III. PURPOSE

In an atmosphere of rising interest in a merging of Christianity with the higher forms of paganism to the detriment of the former, there was, therefore, a pressing need for the presentation of adequate Christian antidotes to combat the danger. It was a critical period for the Church, and the apostle recognizes this. He will write a letter, somewhat in the form of a tract (see section below on literary form), to warn and instruct the believers in his own district about the seriousness of the peril. But his approach is to be wholly positive. He will present a wholesome picture of true Christian life, and only incidentally denounce the error. He believes that truth is the best answer to false teaching, although he makes perfectly plain what his own estimate of that teaching is. He refers to these prophets as antichrists (ii. 18) because they possess the spirit of *the* Antichrist (ii. 18, 22, iv. 3).

Fortunately the author has stated his own purpose in such terms as to leave in no doubt his immediate intention. In i. 3f., he writes, 'That which we have seen and heard declare we unto you also, that ye also may have fellowship with us . . . and these things we write, that our joy may be fulfilled (i.e. completed)' (RV). In v. 13 he is even more specific, 'These things have I written unto you, that ye may know that ye have eternal life, even unto you that believe on the name of the Son of God' (RV). A comparison of this latter statement with John xx. 31 shows a close connection in the purpose for which both writings were written, that is, to instruct in true knowledge those who already believe. And the knowledge to be imparted is a fellowship and a possession ('eternal life').

Quite apart from the false teachers, therefore, the author has an edificatory purpose.[1] Christians need to be challenged about the dis-

---

[1] A. E. Brooke (*op. cit.*, p. xxx) wisely remarks of the writer, 'He is a pastor first, an orthodox theologian only afterwards.' Several scholars have stressed the writer's purpose of presenting a true Christian Gnosis in opposition to the Gnosis of the false teachers; cf. R. Rothe, *Der erste Johannis Brief praktisch erklärt* (1878), p. 4.

tinctive features of their faith, especially the necessity for the exercise of love. Nowhere else in the New Testament is the combination of faith and love so clearly brought out, and it seems probable that this is emphasized because the behaviour of the readers leaves much to be desired. The writer needs to exhort them not to love the world (ii. 15ff.) in terms which suggest a condition of worldliness among them, while the warning against idolatry in v. 21 gives an illuminating insight into their spiritual condition.

According to C. H. Dodd,[1] the writer has in mind people who are unworthily using such phrases as: 'we are born of God', 'we are in the light', 'we have no sin', 'we dwell in God', 'we know God'. He uses the same phrases himself, but puts them into their true Christian context, a procedure which can be illustrated from Paul's occasional use of the language of current Greek philosophy or pagan mysticism (e.g. 'wisdom', 'knowledge', 'fullness'). In other words, this Epistle expresses the true Christian method of conveying the message by the sublimated use of current catchwords. There is something to be said for this interpretation, although it must be borne in mind that some, at least, of the catchwords had originated from Christian sources. Such ideas as sin, light, rebirth and knowledge may have a wrong connotation in Gnostic circles, but for the Christian they belong to the essence of the message he has to proclaim.[2]

IV. FORM AND DESTINATION

This Epistle does not conform to the general characteristics of contemporary letters. It has no introductory material, no author's greeting, no thanksgiving and no concluding salutations. It mentions no-one's name throughout. It reads more like a homily than an epistle. It is not difficult to imagine a Christian congregation listening to its delivery with its frequent personal exhortations.[3] It is only occasionally that words occur which remind us that this is not an address but a letter (e.g. ii. 1, 26).

[1] *Op. cit.*, p. xix.
[2] There is no support for the view of D. W. Riddle (*JR*, 13, 1933, p. 65) that the unique feature of these Epistles is that belief is now mediated by an institutional ecclesiasticism. Only a strained exegesis can make 1 Jn. i. 1, 2 refer to sacramental ordinances.
[3] Among those who regard the Epistle as a homily are E. Lohmeyer, *ZNTW*, 27 (1928), pp. 256–261; C. H. Dodd, *op. cit.*, p. 21; and J. Moffatt, *ILNT*, pp. 583, 584, who calls it a 'tract or manifesto which is thrown into a vague epistolary form' and further identifies it as a catholic homily.

Several scholars have classed this Epistle as a general tractate or a diatribe in letter form.[1] But there are difficulties in this view because a definite historical situation lies behind the letter. When the false teachers are mentioned, the readers themselves are referred to by way of contrast in a manner which suggests the writer's acquaintance with them personally (cf. ii. 21, iv. 4). The reader-circle is, therefore, fairly limited, and is confined to those with Christian experience (i. 3, ii. 1, 20, 27). The addressees are many times called 'children' and many times addressed as 'beloved', which indicates a personal relationship between readers and writer which would be lacking in a general tractate.[2]

The suggestion has been made by R. Bultmann[3] that the original Epistle ended at v. 13 and that verses 14–21 were added later by an ecclesiastical editor. But this idea is not likely to commend itself, not only because far less confidence is now being placed in editorial theories, but also because the style and characteristic ideas of the concluding portion do not differ from the former part.[4]

The most satisfactory explanation is that 1 John was written to a group of people, possibly in more than one Asiatic community, with whom the author was personally acquainted and who were threatened with the same infiltration of false teaching. The supposition of Augus-

---

[1] Cf. M. Dibelius, *op. cit.*, pp. 209ff.; A. Deissmann, *Light from the Ancient East*[2] (1927), p. 244; H. Windisch, *op. cit.*, p. 136. M. Meinertz (*Einleitung*, p. 277), who regards this Epistle as a covering letter for the Gospel, considers that the absence of a literary beginning and conclusion can be explained only on the assumption that the readers knew the author to be an outstanding apostolic personality. On the contrary Moffatt considered that this type of hypothesis was 'suggested by the early juxtaposition of the two writings in the canon rather than by any internal evidence' (*op. cit.*, p. 594).

[2] Cf. Feine-Behm, *op. cit.*, p. 259.

[3] 'Die kirchliche Redaktion des 1 Joh.', in *In memoriam Ernst Lohmeyer* (ed. W. Schmauch, 1951), pp. 189–201.

[4] R. Bultmann bases his argument on a comparison of verses 14–21 with the appendix to John's Gospel (chapter xxi), which he also regards as a later addition. Thus he considers 1 Jn. v. 13 to be a conclusion like Jn. xx. 31. Moreover, he maintains that this passage does not fit the rhythm of the preceding sections, where ethical paraenesis alternates with Christological instruction, nor does he consider the content of the passage to be in keeping with the preceding point of view.

W. Nauck (*Die Tradition und der Charakter des ersten Johannesbriefes*, 1957, pp. 133f.) criticizes Bultmann's position. He cannot conceive how a later editor could be so skilful as to compose an appendix showing the same literary characteristics as the earlier part (Nauck cites similar rhythm patterns).

tine that the churches of Parthia are in mind has no foundation and probably arose from a corruption of the text.[1]

A further question affecting the unity of the Epistle is the use or non-use by the author of a previously existing document, which has been worked over and in the process has been modified. Again it is Bultmann[2] who has been the most zealous exponent of this theory. His main contention is that i. 5b–10 is stylistically different from ii. 1f., and that the latter passage is the author's own commentary upon and modification of the former. There is, therefore, a distinction between the authors of the two parts. Moreover, Bultmann considers the earlier part to belong to a particular type of literary production (a Revelation-discourse). Various other German scholars[3] have produced modifications of Bultmann's theory, but this type of hypothesis which rests on source-differentiation has very slender support and can certainly not point to difference of authorship. W. Nauck[4] has recognized this, for although admitting the author's use of an earlier document, he maintains that the author had himself prepared it for an earlier occasion (perhaps a previous letter, ii. 12–14). 1 John is so obviously a unity as it now stands that all attempts to disentangle possible sources must inevitably be highly speculative and can hardly hope to achieve any general agreement. At the same time the group of scholars who have worked on this Epistle have done well to draw attention to its literary characteristics, particularly its rhythmic qualities. This may well be partly due to the

[1] Cf. Michaelis, *op. cit.*, pp. 291, 292; Westcott, *op. cit.*, p. xxxii.

[2] 'Analyse des ersten Johannesbriefe', *Festgabe für A. Jülicher* (1927), pp. 138–158; and more recently in his article (see note 3 above). But it was E. von Dobschütz (*ZNTW*, 8, 1907, pp. 1ff.) who really started this line of enquiry by making an examination of iii. 1–10. Cf. E. Haenchen's comprehensive survey of recent literature on the Johannine Epistles, *TR*, n.f., 26 (1960), pp. 1–43, especially pp. 30ff.

[3] H. W. Beyer, *ThLZ*, 54 (1929), pp. 606–617; H. Windisch-H. Preisker, *op. cit.*, pp. 168–171; H. Braun, *ZTK*, 48 (1951), pp. 262–292. Windisch, in his edition, had adopted a modified editor-hypothesis, in which he envisaged that 1 John had been issued in two editions, thus accounting for the apparent contradictions between the various parts (*op. cit.*, p. 136). But Preisker, in his appendix to Windisch's Commentary (*op. cit.*, pp. 168–171), advances a theory of two earlier documents which the final author (or editor) used. This hypothesis is based on supposed differences of eschatology within the Epistle itself. For one of these documents, Preisker follows the theory of E. von Dobschütz, Windisch and Bultmann and for the other proposes the following passages: ii. 28, iii. 2, 13, 14, 19, 20, 21, iv. 17, v. 18, 19 (pp. 170, 171).

[4] *Op. cit.*, especially pp. 122–127. Cf. also O. A. Piper, *JBL*, LXVI (1947), p. 450.

catechetical method employed in teaching important Christian truth after the pattern of Jewish teaching.[1] This would certainly help to explain such phenomena as the constant repetitions and the antithetical parallels.[2] These and similar devices would ensure the retention of the teaching and we may well suppose that our author, particularly if he were the apostle John, would, after long years of this method of teaching, have developed such a style in letter writing.[3]

V. RELATION TO THE FOURTH GOSPEL

Because of the particular importance of this subject for both authorship and date, some brief indication will be given of the nature of the two views which are held: (1) that the points of contact are so strong as to be accounted for only on the theory of common authorship; or (2) that the differences are so great that common authorship must be excluded. Were it not that the latter has such an able advocate as C. H. Dodd,[4] it would almost have been unnecessary to discuss the matter, since the majority of scholars have not favoured it. Only the briefest summary can be given here of either view, but the following comments will enable some assessment of the position to be made.

[1] Cf. the discussion of F. Büchsel (*ZNTW*, 28, 1929, pp. 235–241), who found various forms of antithesis in the Epistle and by comparison with similar cases in the Mishnah concluded this style to be of Hebraic origin. He is critical of Bultmann's contention of an opposition between i. 5b–10 and ii. 1f. Piper (*op. cit.*, pp. 437ff.) finds various expressions which point to a common faith, expressed in credal statements, axioms, prophecies, commandments and eschatological rules. Some of Piper's details may be challenged, but there can be no doubt that the author's background reflects early catechetical usage.

[2] W. Nauck (*op. cit.*, pp. 15ff.) cites many examples of this phenomenon from various parts of the Epistle.

[3] E. Lohmeyer (*op. cit.*, pp. 225–263) attempted to find in this Epistle a sevenfold structural form. But there is an artificial ring about all such theories. The Epistle does not strike the reader as an elaborately worked out homiletical exercise. At the same time it is just possible that the author may have had such a predisposition for the number seven that this number coloured his literary arrangement. Lohmeyer maintained that the same phenomenon is found in John's Gospel and in the Apocalypse. He also suggested that it may have been a current form, since it occurs in the Apocalypses of Ezra and Baruch (*op. cit.*, pp. 261–263). As contrasted with Bultmann, Lohmeyer traced the different styles within the structure to the personality of the author and to his religious outlook (*op. cit.*, p. 260).

[4] *Op. cit.*, idem, *BJRL*, xxi (1939), pp. 129–156. Another advocate of note was H. J. Holtzmann, 'Das Problem des 1 Johannesbrief in seinem Verhältniss zum Evangel', *JPTh*, 7 (1881), pp. 690–712, 8 (1882), pp. 316–343.

a. Similarities

Certain similarities are at once apparent even on a casual reading of
the two books. The same use in both of such abstract ideas as 'light',
'life', and 'love', the same occurrence of 'eternal life' as the believer's
possession, and the same description of Christ as Logos, at once come to
mind.[1] But this first impression is strongly reinforced when detailed
comparisons of language are made. As in the Gospel, so in the Epistle
there are frequent repetitions almost to the point of monotony, while
both works are noted for the simplicity of constructions used; both
contain Hebraistic antithetical parallelisms and both contain characteristic phrases such as 'to have sin', 'to do the truth', 'to abide', 'to overcome the world', 'the spirit of truth'. Similar antitheses occur, such as
light and darkness, truth and error, God and the world, love and hate,
the children of God and the children of the devil. Some of the more
notable extended parallels in language are found in the following comparisons.[2]

1 John i. 2, 3; John iii. 11	1 John iii. 16; John x. 15
1 John i. 4; John xvi. 24	1 John iii. 22; John viii. 29
1 John ii. 11; John xii. 35	1 John iii. 23; John xiii. 34
1 John ii. 14; John v. 38	1 John iv. 6; John viii. 47
1 John iii. 5; John viii. 46	1 John iv. 16; John vi. 69
1 John iii. 8; John viii. 14	1 John v. 9; John v. 32
1 John iii. 13; John xv. 18	1 John v. 20; John xvii. 3.
1 John iii. 14; John v. 24	

These parallels are enough to show either that one author produced
both works or else that the author of one was intimately acquainted
with the other work and has echoed its language in his own. Both
books belong to the same background of thought, with their emphasis
on the importance of the incarnation, on the new birth as the method of
entering upon the spiritual benefits of Christ's work, and on the overthrow of the devil, who is conceived as exercising a powerful influence
on the present world order. The traditional view that both works
proceeded from one mind would appear to be well based, and yet cer-

[1] As early a critic as Dionysius of Alexandria pointed out these and other ideas
in which the Gospel and Epistle agree together (see Eusebius, *HE*, vii. 25. 18–21).
[2] Cf. B. F. Westcott (*op. cit.*, pp. xli–xliii) for these parallels set out conveniently
in the Greek text, or more fully in Holtzmann, *JPTh*, 7 (1881), pp. 691–699.

tain differences have been pointed out which require careful consideration.

b. Differences

It will be useful, as a basis for discussion, to give a brief summary of the grounds on which C. H. Dodd[1] has disputed this traditional opinion.

(i) *Stylistic differences.* The language of the Epistle is not reckoned to be of the same intensity as that of the Gospel, although Dodd admits this kind of impression is apt to be subjective. He therefore demonstrates the impression by means of linguistic data, such as the fewer number of compound verbs in the Epistle and the greater absence of particles and conjunctions. Moreover, the language of the Epistle is said to approximate more to that of Hellenistic philosophy and to have no examples of Semitisms in contrast to the Gospel. Certain expressions (about forty in number) occur in the Epistle and not in the Gospel and the same is true in the reverse direction, many of them being characteristic of the Gospel.[2]

(ii) *Religious background.* Whereas the Old Testament background is indisputable in the case of the Gospel, where many direct citations are made and where the author shows close acquaintance with Jewish ideas, in the Epistle there is only one definite reference to the Old Testament (iii. 12). On the contrary, according to Dodd, the Hellenistic element is more dominant (e.g. 'God is Light', seed and unction conferring supernatural knowledge, 'God is love'). He concludes, 'the Epistle is not only less Hebraic and Jewish; it is also more free in its adoption of Hellenistic modes of thought and expression'.[3]

(iii) *Theological differences.* C. H. Dodd[4] notes three theological differences which he considers to be of particular significance. (1) The eschatology is more primitive than in the Gospel, i.e. there is an absence of that reinterpretation which has come to be known as realized eschatology; (2) the interpretation of the death of Christ is claimed to be more primitive, which is particularly seen in the author's use of 'ex-

---

[1] *The Johannine Epistles*, p. xlviii.

[2] Holtzmann had earlier cited a list of fifty peculiarities in the Epistle. These are conveniently listed in A. E. Brooke, *op. cit.*, pp. xiii ff.

[3] *Op. cit.*, p. liii.

[4] *Ibid.*, pp. liii, liv. Dodd drops the earlier argument against the Epistle based on confusion between the action of God and of Christ. Brooke has effectively dealt with this (*op. cit.*, pp. xvi and xvii).

piation' (ii. 2, iv. 10); and (3) the doctrine of the Spirit is confined to popular belief and is not as elevated as in the Gospel (hence the new birth can be spoken of without mentioning the Spirit's activity in the process as in Jn. iii. 5–8). Differences on such important themes of Christian theology as these, according to Dodd's view, point to a widely different outlook from that shown by the writer of the Fourth Gospel.

It should be noted that in spite of his emphasis on these differences Dodd maintains a close connection between the two authors, i.e. that the writer of the Epistle was a disciple of the Evangelist. But are his objections to unity of authorship really valid?

The linguistic objections have been well answered by W. G. Wilson,[1] who has produced statistical evidence to show that more variations of 'grammatical' words occur in the acknowledged Pauline letters than Dodd has claimed to exist between 1 John and the Gospel. He also questions some of the Aramaisms, which Dodd finds in the Gospel but not in 1 John. Arguments from vocabulary are precarious, for as Wilson again shows, similar and even greater variations occur within the Pauline letters. It is impossible by this method to pronounce with any confidence that the two works could not proceed from one author, particularly in view of the disparity in length and variation in purpose.

As for the difference in religious background, this must not be overstressed without due regard to the different purpose of the two writings. The Epistle has always in mind the background of Gnostic ideas and it is to be expected that the writing would be more flavoured by Hellenistic than by Hebraic modes of expression. Old Testament citations may have had little interest for the readers of the Epistle, who were evidently influenced by current Hellenistic ideas, and the absence of them may well tell us more about these readers than about the author unless we are to suppose that the early Christian writers were indifferent to the type of language which would most achieve their purpose. We may perhaps assume that authors would make some adjustment in different writings to suit the background of the readers. Nevertheless, in the case of these two works it may not be quite as easy to explain if both were designed, as is often supposed, for the same audience (see below). Yet it should not be overlooked that of the direct Old Testa-

---

[1] 'An examination of the Linguistic Evidence adduced against the Unity of Authorship of the First Epistle of John and the Fourth Gospel', *JTS*, XLIX (1948), pp. 147ff. Cf. also the criticisms of W. F. Howard, *JTS*, XLVIII (1947), pp. 12–25.

ment citations in the Gospel, all but a few are attributed to various speakers in the course of the narrative. Only a few appear to be introduced by the writer himself for apologetic purposes (cf. ii. 17, xii. 38, 40, xix. 24, 36). It is not so striking, therefore, that in the Epistle, with its completely different motive, the apologetic or even didactic use of the Old Testament is lacking. There may, of course, be greater approximation in the Epistle to Hellenistic thought, but not all would agree with Dodd over his derivations, as when, for instance, he makes 'God is light' and 'God is love' to be of Hellenistic origin. It is equally possible to construe them as Christian developments from a Hebrew background, due to our Lord's teaching that He is the Light of the world and the supreme example of love. To appeal to the Hermetic literature to explain this usage, as Dodd does,[1] is to appeal to later notions to account for earlier, for there is no certain evidence that the Hermetic literature reflects the thought-background of Hellenistic mysticism at this period. We may treat with some reserve, therefore, the claims to an exclusively Hellenistic background to this Epistle.

The theological differences are equally inconclusive as the following considerations show.

1. The force of the argument from eschatology depends almost entirely on acceptance of Dodd's own interpretation of the eschatology of the Fourth Gospel, but there are strong grounds for rejecting his contention that the primitive eschatology is lacking (cf., e.g., Jn. v. 25–29).[2] Admittedly, the word Antichrist does not appear in the Gospel and occurs three times in the Epistle (1 Jn. ii. 18, 22, iv. 3), but this indicates not difference of eschatology but difference in the expression of it (cf. the Johannine expression, 'prince of this world', Jn. xii. 31, xiv. 30, xvi. 11, which serves a similar purpose).[3]

2. Is there any fundamental difference in the interpretation of the

---

[1] Op. cit., pp. 108–110.

[2] The idea of the ἔσχατον in Jn. vi. 39, 40, xii. 48 is not so very different from its use in 1 Jn. ii. 18. It is difficult to maintain difference of authorship on such grounds.

[3] A. E. Brooke (op. cit., p. xviii) points out that the Epistle presents what he calls 'the spiritualizing of the conception of Antichrist as fulfilled in many forms of anti-Christian teaching'.

O. A. Piper, in his article, '1 John and the Didache of the Primitive Church', JBL, LXVI (1947), pp. 444, 445, draws a distinction between ἀντίχριστος and ψευδόχριστος (Mk. xiii. 22; Mt. xxiv. 24) and considers the former to be a development from the latter, yet the change is terminological and not theological.

death of Christ? That there are some different ideas is undeniable,[1] but this tremendous event was too great to be confined within narrow limits and it is a tortuous kind of argument to relegate the 'expiatory' (or more accurately the 'propitiatory') explanation to the primitive apostolic preaching and then to maintain that the Fourth Gospel approach is more developed. Dodd gives far too little attention to the sacrificial language of the Gospel, and, therefore, gives a one-sided picture of the work of Christ in terms of exaltation and triumph.[2]

c. The problem of priority

Another problem which is of importance for the dating of this Epistle is the question of its priority or otherwise to the Fourth Gospel. Such questions are difficult to establish on literary grounds, for so much depends on subjective impressions, but the main arguments for the priority of each book will be tabulated, if only to give some indication of the highly inconclusive character of the evidence. The following details are taken mainly from Brooke, who has a full discussion on this question.

The arguments for the priority of the Epistle are:

1. The introductory passage (i. 1–4) is said to present a less developed Logos doctrine than that of the Johannine prologue.

2. The reference to Christ as Paraclete (ii. 1) has been claimed to prepare for the use of the same term for the Holy Spirit in the Gospel.

3. The eschatology of the Epistle is supposed to be more primitive (see discussion above).

4. The conception of the work of Christ in the Epistle in reference to propitiation approximates nearer to Paul's ideas and is, therefore, supposed to be earlier than the Gospel.

5. The passage John xix. 34f. is thought by some to be a misunderstanding of 1 John v. 6.

6. It is supposed that the Greek of the Gospel is better than that of the Epistle—a highly subjective judgment.[3]

[1] Although the word ἱλασμός does not occur in the Gospel, the idea lying behind it is not absent (cf. i. 29, xi. 51ff., xii. 24, xv. 39).

[2] B. F. Westcott (op. cit., p. xlv) considered the propitiation doctrine in the Epistle to be a development from the discourse of Jn. vi. 51, 56f.

[3] A glance at these will suffice to show that they almost all depend on a particular interpretation of the relevant passages, but, as Brooke (op. cit., pp. xix ff.) has shown, these are capable of entirely satisfactory alternatives which make them quite inconclusive as evidence for priority. For instance, the description of 'the

7. Attestation for the Epistle is claimed to be earlier than that for the Gospel.

Not more conclusive are the arguments for the priority of the Gospel, which consist of the following considerations.

1. Several passages in the Epistle, which are parallel in thought to statements in the Gospel, are said to be more intelligible if the Gospel was already known to the readers.[1] While it may readily be agreed that the Gospel throws light upon the language of the Epistle, this concession need not be proof of the priority in publication of the former, since the readers may well have been acquainted with its content orally long before this time.

2. Some indications have been found within the Epistle of direct references to the Gospel. Thus i. 3, 5, which mentions a proclamation that God is light is accordingly thought to refer to the Gospel, where this theme is prominent. Similarly ii. 14 (the aorist ἔγραψα ὑμῖν three times repeated) is supposed by some to refer to an earlier writing, which is then rather precariously identified as the Gospel.[2] But neither of these references is at all conclusive, for the former could well be understood and appreciated by the readers apart from the Gospel, whereas in the latter case, the thrice repeated ἔγραψα is immediately preceded by a thrice repeated γράφω, and the context in each case gives no justification for supposing that the three aorists were any more retrospective than the presents, quite apart from the fact that what the writer says he has written bears no relation to the contents of the Gospel.

Logos of life' would appear more intelligible if the readers knew the content of Jn. i, even if not the written record of it. Christ as Paraclete is alluded to in John by the reference to 'another' Paraclete. The eschatology has already been dealt with, as also the conception of Christ's death. Argument 5 is ruled out if the incident related in Jn. xix. 34 (the 'water and blood' passage) was an actual occurrence, while argument 6 need not be taken seriously. The concluding argument is based on a fact not altogether surprising, since the briefer and simpler Epistle may have been more popular and therefore more cited.

T. Henshaw (op. cit., pp. 379, 380) maintains that both books may have been written by a bi-lingual person whose native language was Aramaic, but who habitually spoke Greek. He then claims that the Gospel is written in more idiomatic Greek than the Epistle. But if this were so, we should expect more Aramaic flavouring in the Epistle than in the Gospel, which is not, however, supported by the facts.

[1] For a detailed comparison of these in the Greek text, cf. Brooke, op. cit., p. xxiii. Holtzmann, JPTh, 7 (1881), pp. 691–699, made the same point.

[2] Cf. Meinertz, Einleitung, p. 275.

In view of these considerations it is difficult to be certain about the question of priority, although the balance seems rather more in favour of the priority of the Gospel.[1] The theory that 1 John was a kind of covering letter for the Gospel[2] is improbable, for there appears to be no adequate *raison d'être* for such a letter. The introduction makes it clear that the readers of the Epistle are not unacquainted with the Christian message and its purpose cannot, therefore, be evangelistic. Its dealing with a specific situation would seem to account better for its origin (see under Purpose above).

VI. RELATION TO THE TEACHING OF PAUL

This problem assumed greater proportions at an earlier age than it does today, for an antithesis between Paul and the original apostles, which was assumed as the basis of Baur's reconstruction of early Christian history, is no longer reckoned to be valid by the majority of scholars.[3] That there is no essential antithesis, although many differences of emphasis, between Pauline and Johannine teaching has been amply demonstrated and the whole movement of modern biblical theology is away from divisive theories. For a careful summary of coincidences of doctrine between this Epistle and the Pauline Epistles, reference may be made to A. Plummer's chapter on this subject.[4]

VII. DATE

There is little specific material to which to appeal in affixing a date. The letter belongs to a period when Gnosticism is certainly on the horizon, although not as yet fully developed. A date towards the end of the first century would well suit this circumstance. Again, the close connection with the Fourth Gospel, whatever decision is reached regarding priority, requires a date during the same period as the publication of the Gospel and, as this is generally dated about AD 90–95, it is usual to suppose that the Epistle followed it at a slightly later date.[5]

---

[1] W. Michaelis (*op. cit.*, p. 294) favours the reverse conclusion, supposing that 1 John was issued before the appearance of chapters i–xx of John's Gospel.

[2] Cf. Meinertz, *op. cit.*, p. 277. This view was earlier maintained by J. H. A. Ebrard, *Biblical Commentary on the Epistles of St. John* (1860), pp. 14–34.

[3] It still finds some echoes in such writers as S. F. D. Brandon, *The Fall of Jerusalem and the Christian Church*[2] (1957).

[4] *The Epistles of St. John* (1886), pp. lxii–lxvi.

[5] E. F. Scott (*The Literature of New Testament*, pp. 260, 261) dates both books rather later, at the beginning of the second century. Some writers, such as T.

This dating rests on the assumption of common authorship for the Gospel and Epistle, but if this is denied, other grounds for dating must necessarily be brought into play. Thus Dodd[1] tentatively dates all three Johannine Epistles between AD 96 and 110, but his reasoning is far from conclusive. The upper limit is fixed by Ignatius' letters, which Dodd admits represent a rather later situation. The earlier date he fixes by the cessation of the Domitian persecutions (i.e. on the accession of Nerva in AD 96), since the Epistles reflect tension but not persecution. But this state could equally well have obtained before Domitian's persecutions commenced.[2]

THE SECOND EPISTLE

This letter, like 3 John, is so brief that it could have been contained on a single papyrus sheet. Yet both letters have been preserved for their importance for the Christian Church. No-one would suppose that their influence on Christian thought has been great, but they nevertheless make a contribution to our knowledge of contemporary affairs, even if it is no more than a glimpse that is given. In spite of their brevity they both raise problems for criticism, some of which are not easy to answer with any confidence.

I. AUTHORSHIP

Although these two Epistles are known as Epistles of John, they do not in their text give their author's name and it is consequently necessary to investigate the history of their attribution to John. It is in the light of this that the internal evidence must be viewed.

a. External evidence

That the attestation for 2 John is not as strong as for 1 John must at once be admitted. Yet the brevity of the letter and the lesser likelihood

Henshaw (*op. cit.*, pp. 378f.), place some interval between the two books in order to account for the differences. Henshaw, in fact, suggests a date about AD 80 for the Epistles and AD 100 for the Gospel, if both are by one author.

[1] *Op. cit.*, pp. lxviii, lxix. H. J. Holtzmann (*JPTh*, 8, 1882, pp. 316–342), who maintained dissimilar authorship, suggested that a fairly developed form of Gnosticism was in view, which therefore required a later date.

[2] Always assuming that the Domitian persecutions were as widespread as is generally supposed (see pp. 272f.).

of its being quoted by Christian authors must be given full weight in assessing the evidence (the same applies to 3 John).[1] It is possible that Polycarp[2] contains an allusion to 2 John 7, but since 1 John iv. 2, 3 furnishes a better parallel, no weight can be placed on this. The evidence from Irenaeus[3] is more certain, for it is clear that he not only knew 2 John, but assumed it to be by the apostle John.

The Muratorian Fragment is ambiguous in its witness to the Johannine Epistles, since it specifies only two, while in the earlier part of the list dealing with John's Gospel a quotation is made from 1 John i. 1f. The evidence has been variously interpreted, but all agree that if two Epistles only were known, they must have been 1 and 2 John (but see discussion under 3 John).[4]

Clement of Alexandria knew of more than one Johannine Epistle,[5] and in a Latin fragment of one of his works[6] refers to the second Epistle, although in this fragment it is erroneously said to be written to virgins, a mistake which may possibly have originated with the translator. Origen cites neither 2 nor 3 John, although he knew of their existence. He mentions that all do not admit their genuineness.[7] Another Alexandrian, Dionysius,[8] mentions the second and third Epistles as circulating as works of John, and the implication is that he accepted them as such, in spite of the fact that the title 'Elder' is used. Eusebius placed this Epistle (with 3 John) among the disputed books,[9] while even in the time of Jerome some were ascribing 2 and 3 John to a different author (John the Elder) from 1 John.[10] But after his time, the Epistles were both received without question, except in the Syriac Church, where the earliest evidence for their canonical authority is at

[1] C. H. Dodd (*The Johannine Epistles*, 1946, p. xvi) writes of 2 and 3 John, 'It should however be borne in mind that both are extremely short and contain very little material for quotation.'
[2] *Ad. Phil.* vii. 1.   [3] *Adv. Haer.* iii. 16. 3, 8.
[4] P. Katz (*JTS*, New Series, VIII, 1957, pp. 273, 274) considers it improbable that 2 and 3 John would be separated and suggests an emendation to this Canon to make it mean 'two in addition to the Catholic (epistle, i.e. 1 John)'. Cf. the view of E. C. Selwyn (*The Christian Prophets and the Prophetic Apocalypse*, 1900, pp. 140–142) that at that time 2 and 3 John formed one Epistle. This avoids any emendation.
[5] *Strom.* ii. 15. 66.
[6] Latin *adumbrationes*: cf. also Eusebius, *HE*, vi. 14. 1, for a statement suggesting that Clement commented on all the Catholic Epistles.
[7] *In Joann.* v. 3 (Eusebius, *HE*, vi. 25).
[8] Eusebius, *HE*, vii. 25.   [9] *Ibid.*, iii. 25. 3.   [10] *De Vir. Ill.* xi. 18.

the beginning of the sixth century, although they had no doubt been used as Scripture for some time before this.[1]

It has already been pointed out that absence of citation may be accounted for by the character of the letters, but does this equally account for the doubts which were expressed regarding them among later writers? It is significant that the earlier writers appear to have less hesitation about apostolic authorship than the later,[2] which is the reverse of what would be expected if the doubts were based on accurate tradition. It is just possible that the ascription to John the Elder caused more confusion at a later date because of the belief in some circles in a John the Elder distinct from John the apostle. Once these Epistles were attributed to a non-apostolic presbyter, their canonical status would have been more difficult to establish.[3] But the evidence for John the Elder is very restricted and of dubious value and this explanation must be received with reserve. On the whole, there are no conclusive external reasons for denying the authenticity of these Epistles.

b. *Internal evidence*

(i) *The Epistle's own claims.* The author describes himself as 'the Elder' (2 Jn. 1) and it is clearly necessary to discuss the significance of this title. The Greek word πρεσβύτερος primarily indicates seniority. It may mean no more than 'the old man' and be an affectionate title used of and by the venerable author. This interpretation need not suppose it to be a rather familiar nickname, as sometimes happens in modern usage,[4] but merely a descriptive title indicative of both the age and authority of the author. Evidence is not wanting that supports this idea of seniority, particularly in relation to apostolic authority, for

[1] Since they are not in the Peshitta, it must be assumed that they were added to the Syriac Canon later than AD 411.

[2] A. Plummer (*op. cit.*, p. lxx) pointed out that the nearer the witnesses are to the apostle John, the more favourable they are to his authorship. In fact, they express no alternative view.

[3] The interesting form of the Cheltenham (or Mommsenian) Canon (*c.* AD 360), which gives an African Canon of about the same date as Athanasius' list (*c.* AD 367) in which all three Johannine Epistles were included in the Canon, witnesses to lingering doubts. Although this African Canon includes '*Epistulae Iohannis* III', the words '*una sola*' appearing on the next line indicate a preference for the first Epistle only.

[4] C. H. Dodd (*op. cit.*, p. 155) seems to assume this and therefore rules out this explanation of the term.

Papias' well-known reference to John the Elder includes within it   b.
references to a number of the apostles apparently under the same title.[1]
Quite apart from the dispute whether Papias intended to make a
distinction between John the apostle and John the Elder, it would seem
that he saw no incongruity in calling apostles 'elders' and it would,
therefore, be wrong to conclude *ipso facto* that the Elder of 2 and 3
John could not be John the apostle.[2] At the same time, the question
must be faced why the author, if he were John the apostle, calls himself simply 'the Elder', particularly as in 2 John there is a matter over
which some authority must be exercised. Yet it is surely intelligible
that the aged apostle, in writing more intimate letters, would prefer
the more affectionate and less formal title than the more official one,
particularly as by this time he was no doubt the last surviving of the
original apostles.[3]

Although there is no strong reason to question the possibility that
'the Elder' means the apostle John, as it has generally been interpreted
in the tradition of the Church, some serious consideration must be
given to the alternative view that another writer known as John the   c.
Elder was the real author and that he was later confused with the
apostle. This view is certainly possible, but it stands on shaky foundations unless it can be demonstrated with reasonable certainty that such
a person as John the Elder really existed. But Papias is the real key
to this problem and he has expressed himself in a manner which falls
short of lucidity. Since Eusebius tells us that Papias was 'a man of very
mean intellectual power', it is not surprising that his powers of expression were limited. At all events it is highly probable that Papias

---

[1] 'And again, if any one came who had been a follower of the Elders, I used to
enquire about the sayings of the Elders—what was said by Andrew, or by Peter,
or by Philip, or by Thomas or James, or by John or Matthew, or any other of the
Lord's disciples, and what Aristion and the Elder John, the disciples of the Lord,
say. For I did not think that I could get so much profit from the contents of books
as from the utterances of a living and abiding voice' (Eusebius, *HE*, iii. 39. 4).

[2] Many scholars do not agree that Papias calls the apostles 'elders', but claim
that he distinguishes between them (cf. C. K. Barrett, *The Gospel according to St.
John*, 1956, pp. 89ff.).

[3] R. H. Charles (*Commentary on the Revelation of St. John*, 1920, I, p. xliii n. 1)
rejected this view because in 3 John 'he would naturally have availed himself of his
power as an apostle to suppress Diotrephes and others who disowned his jurisdiction and authority, which they could not have done had he been an apostle.' But
Charles seems to overlook that 3 John was addressed to an individual well known
to John, who certainly did not need to be impressed by apostolic authority.

never meant to distinguish between John the apostle and a John the Elder, for both appear to be called Elders and both are described as disciples of the Lord.[1] This method of differentiating between two men who shared the same name is quite unintelligible. Moreover, Aristion is mentioned with the elder John, but is given no title and the only fair inference is that John was marked out from Aristion. If the title of Elder was meant to indicate the apostle, this is fully intelligible, but if not it must be supposed that Aristion was not even of sufficient importance to hold any office, although described as a disciple of the Lord.[2]

A few later writers assumed that Papias meant to indicate two Johns, and this fact has often been supposed to show that this is the correct interpretation. The most important of these is Eusebius, who appealed to Papias' Elder John as an alternative to an apostolic author for the Apocalypse. Jerome assigned 2 and 3 John to the Elder John and 1 John to the apostle. The evidence of Dionysius is inconclusive, for although he mentions two tombs of John in Ephesus, he does not suggest John the Elder as the probable writer of the Apocalypse, although he denied it to the apostle John. This evidence is not strong and is further considerably weakened by reference to Irenaeus, who knew Papias' work well and also knew much about Ephesus, but makes no mention of John the Elder. He refers to a presbyter, but not by name, describing him rather as 'a disciple of the Apostles', which at once distinguishes him from Papias' Elder John. This presbyter, in fact, was Irenaeus' own teacher and was not improbably Polycarp. Such evidence suggests that 'Elder' was much used during the sub-apostolic age, but it is not evidence for the existence of an Elder John.

d.   Is there then a possibility that 2 and 3 John were written by an un-

[1] Moffatt's opinion (*ILNT*, p. 600) that Papias' statement contains an implicit distinction between οἱ πρεσβύτεροι and οἱ τοῦ Κυρίου μαθηταί is not borne out by the more obvious interpretation of the Greek. Cf. C. K. Barrett's discussion along the same lines (*op. cit.*, pp. 88–92). T. Zahn (*INT*, ii, p. 452), who strongly maintained that Papias referred to only one John, pointed out that Eusebius' interpretation of Papias' evidence was self-contradictory. He rejected the view of Haussleiter (*Theologisches Literaturblatt*, 1896, cols. 465–468) that ἢ τί 'Ιωάννης was an interpolation of Papias' text. Moffatt comments quite characteristically on both Zahn's and Haussleiter's opinions, 'John the presbyter is not to be emended out of existence in the interests of John the apostle' (*op. cit.*, p. 601).

[2] It should be noted that Papias' statement refers to ὁ πρεσβύτερος 'Ιωάννης not 'Ιωάννης ὁ πρεσβύτερος which would be more natural if intended to distinguish him from 'Ιωάννης ὁ ἀπόστολος.

named Elder, who later became confused with the apostle John? There are difficulties with this view. It is difficult, for instance, to see how or why such an attribution would be made unless the close similarity of these Epistles with 1 John and the Gospel should be appealed to. But if so it must be supposed that the unknown Elder had either consciously imitated John's style to give the impression of Johannine authorship, which is highly improbable since in that case he would have chosen a different title from 'the Elder',[1] or, if the similarities with the other Johannine writings were accidental, he must have been so close a student of John that subsequent Church Fathers were unable to distinguish his own writings from the master's and this can hardly have happened accidentally. The case for considering the Elder as a simple description of the aged apostle seems much more intelligible than either of these alternatives.

(ii) *Relationship to other Johannine writings*. In the last paragraph reference was made to the similarity of 2 John to 1 John and the Fourth Gospel and this requires further comment. A. E. Brooke[2] has set out the evidence very fully in his commentary and it is necessary here to give only a general indication of the position. There are many phrases in both 2 and 3 John which are either identical with phrases in 1 John or appear to be reminiscent of these.[3] Moreover, the two smaller Epistles become more intelligible on a number of points if a knowledge of the First Epistle is presupposed.[4] Brooke's own conclusion is as follows: 'We are compelled to choose between common authorship and conscious imitation. And the freedom with which the same and similar tools are handled points clearly to the former as the more probable alternative.'[5]

What bearing has this conclusion on the question of authorship? If common authorship with 1 John is assumed it will be seen that the solution of this question is inseparably bound up with the origin of the Fourth Gospel, since all these writings share so many common characteristics (see discussion of authorship of 1 John on pp. 186ff.). The

---

[1] C. H. Dodd (*op. cit.*, p. lxv) regards deliberate imitation as less likely than unconscious habits of speech as an explanation of the similarities.

[2] *Op. cit.*, pp. lxxivff.

[3] C. H. Dodd (*op. cit.*, p. lxiv) even goes so far as to assert that a large part of 2 John is a sort of résumé of 1 John.

[4] A. E. Brooke (*op. cit.*, p. lxxv) mentions especially 2 Jn. 9 and 3 Jn. 11 (cf. respectively 1 Jn. ii. 23 and 1 Jn. iv. 20, iii. 6). [5] *Ibid.*, *loc. cit.*

fact is that common authorship with 1 John and the Gospel is the assumption which best explains all the similarities, although there are unquestionably certain differences. These latter can be explained generally by the changed circumstances and purposes of the second and third letters as compared with the other writings.[1]

(iii) *Summary of views on authorship.* To sum up, the following comments may be made:

1. Authorship by the apostle John, which has such strong external support, is seen to be a quite reasonable deduction from the internal evidence.

2. Authorship by the Elder John, proposed by most of those disputing apostolic authorship either of the Epistles or the Gospel, has far less ancient attestation but far more modern opinion behind it. It would have greater weight if the Elder John (i.e. as distinct from the apostle) were known with certainty to have existed.

3. Authorship by an unknown Elder has even less ancient testimony and cannot be considered as probable.

The conclusion reached is that John, the Son of Zebedee, was the author of all three Epistles.

II. DESTINATION

The writer of 2 John addresses his letter to the Elect Lady, but little did he realize the problems he was creating for later critics in using so enigmatic an address. The fact is that his words (ἐκλεκτῇ κυρίᾳ) have been construed in five different ways: 'the Elect Lady', 'an Elect Lady', 'Electa the Lady', 'the elect Kyria', 'Electa Kyria'. Of these, however, the last three can almost certainly be eliminated, for there is no parallel use of Electa[2] as a lady's name, while Kyria is used only very rarely in this sense. The combination of two such rare uses would be incredible,

---

[1] Earlier writers who have emphasized differences are Pfleiderer, Jülicher, Schwartz. Cf. A. E. Brooke (*loc. cit.*, pp. lxxv f.) for a criticism of their main positions. Some scholars, such as W. Bousset (*Die Offenbarung*, 1906, pp. 43f.) and J. Moffatt (*ILNT*, pp. 480ff.) differentiated 1 John from 2 and 3 John and then identified the author of the latter with the John of the Apocalypse (John the Elder). Cf. also E. C. Selwyn, *op. cit.*, pp. 133ff.; and J. H. A. Ebrard, *op. cit.*, pp. 359ff. But this position is contested by R. H. Charles, *op. cit.*, I, pp. xli ff., and H. Windisch, *op. cit.*, pp. 143, 144.

[2] Verse 13, where the same word is used to describe the lady's sister, is sufficient to dismiss this possibility, for it would be incredible for two sisters both to bear the same name and a name which was nowhere else attested.

while even if either could be used separately the accompanying description (i.e. 'elect' or 'lady') would normally require the article (as in Γαΐῳ τῷ ἀγαπητῷ in 3 Jn. 1). 'The elect Kyria' is just possible on the analogy of Rufus, the elect, in Romans xvi. 13, although even here the article is used. Of the other two possibilities, that which inserts the article is probably to be preferred since the address is evidently intended to be specific.

But who was the Elect Lady? To this two quite different answers have been given. Either she was an individual acquaintance of the writer, or else she was a community under his general supervision. There have been advocates for both alternatives although the majority of scholars prefer the latter. In favour of the former it may be said that: *An Individual*

1. This is the most obvious understanding of the words, and it is a fair canon of criticism that if the literal meaning makes sense recourse should not be made to a metaphorical treatment.

2. The reference to the lady's children is quite intelligible if these were by now grown-up.

3. The greeting from the lady's nephews in verse 13 is also quite possible if taken literally.[1] According to this interpretation, the writer is addressing a lady of some standing, warning her of certain dangers and preparing the way for his coming visit.

Yet there are strong arguments for the alternative view. *A Church*

1. The lady is not only beloved by the writer but by all who know the truth, which could mean that 'she' was known universally by Christians.[2] This would be more intelligible if used of a community than of an individual.

2. Neither she herself nor any of her children or nephews is mentioned by name, which detracts from the personal character of the letter (this is in strong contrast to 3 John).

3. The subject-matter is probably more suitable for a community

---

[1] J. Rendle Harris (*Exp.*, VI, iii, 1901, pp. 194–203) suggested that Κυρία should be understood as an affectionate and not a formal term (i.e. as equivalent to 'my dear lady'). It therefore supports an individual destination. But his evidence has been criticized by G. G. Findlay, *op. cit.*, pp. 24ff., and A. E. Brooke, *op. cit.*, pp. lxxx, lxxxi. W. M. Ramsay (*Exp.*, VI, iii, 1901, pp. 354–356) pointed out that Κύριος and Κυρία were colourless terms.

[2] The 'all' need not here be understood in a general sense as Dom J. Chapman supposed in concluding that some important church such as Antioch or Rome must be in mind (*JTS*, v, 1904, pp. 357ff., 517ff.). It can quite naturally be understood of all the Christians within the author's own district.

than an individual, with its warnings against false teachers, although this might have been equally necessary for a prominent private person in the habit of entertaining visitors freely.

4. The predominance of the second person plural rather than the singular suggests a composite understanding of the addressee (cf. verses 8, 10, 12).

5. 'The new commandment' of the Lord, referred to in verse 5, has more point if applied to a community rather than to the narrower limits of a family circle.

6. The personification of the Church in a feminine form is in harmony with other New Testament usage, for not only does Paul develop the idea of the Church as the Bride of Christ (Eph. v. 29f.; 2 Cor. xi. 2ff.), but Peter uses a feminine expression to describe the Church 'in Babylon' (1 Pet. v. 13—although the usage here may be occasioned only by the feminine form of ἐκκλησία, which is omitted but inferred).

7. The greeting in verse 13 is more natural if sent from one church to another than from a group of people to their aunt by means of a third party.

When these arguments for the collective interpretation are considered carefully, it cannot be said that they are conclusive, and they do not specifically exclude the possibility of the alternative view. For instance, a Christian who was particularly generous in hospitality may well have been known throughout a wide circle of churches and the 'all' of verse 1 need not be regarded too rigidly of every single Christian. What the writer seems to mean is that all true Christians who knew the lady loved and respected her as he himself did. The anonymous character of the personal allusions are as perplexing for either view, while the sub-ject-matter is not irrelevant for an individual household, neither is the collective plural of verses 8, 10, 12 if the exhortations are directed both to the lady and her children. The salutation from nephews and nieces to their aunt via the writer may be regarded as perfectly natural, in view of what often happens in correspondence, when relatives may say, 'Give them our greetings when you write'.

It is difficult to decide, and sympathy must be felt for Bishop Westcott's[1] conclusion that the problem of the address is insoluble. This would undoubtedly be the safest course to adopt, but if some preference is desired, it would seem rather better to adopt the more literal meaning

[1] *Op. cit.*, p. 224.

because this would help to account for the reluctance of some of the early Christians to use the Epistle. A private letter written to a lady would not seem of sufficient importance to receive canonical status. On the other hand some ancient commentators not only regarded the Epistle as addressed to a church, but to the universal Church,[1] a notion untenable in view of the mention of the sister in verse 13. Attempts to identify a particular church have not been highly successful. Findlay[2] suggested Pergamum on the grounds that the church there was troubled by false teachers, probably of the same type as mentioned in this Epistle. Chapman,[3] far less probably, suggested Rome. The fact is that nobody knows, although somewhere in Asia is highly probable.

III. OCCASION AND PURPOSE

Certain data may be culled from the Epistle to indicate the setting. There can be no doubt that the false teachers mentioned in verse 7 are the same as those referred to in 1 John (see discussion on pp. 191 ff.). This means that they were Docetists whose doctrine was seriously threatening the church. The false teachers were itinerating among the churches and were taking advantage of the hospitality of Christian people. There was need for these people to be put on their guard against these dangerous teachers. The advice to have nothing to do with these men may at first sight appear harsh and ungracious, but it must be remembered that the teaching which was denying the true humanity of Christ was, in fact, undermining the foundations of the Christian faith and strong action was necessary. Hospitality was an indispensable requisite for the spread of propaganda and the refusal of it would be an effective deterrent, whether the content of the propaganda were true or false. The New Testament makes it clear that it was the Church's responsibility to offer hospitality to the messengers of truth, which meant that it was an equal responsibility to use discernment in refusing hospitality to the opponents of truth (cf. also the *Didache*, xi). To do otherwise was actively to participate in the spreading of error.

It would seem, therefore, that John is desiring to forewarn his readers against the infiltration of this error and his primary purpose in writing

---

[1] E.g. Clement (cited by A. E. Brooke, *op. cit.*, p. 169).

[2] *Op. cit.*, pp. 30ff.

[3] *Op. cit.*, *loc. cit.*, based on a comparison with 1 Pet. v. 13. But cf. J. V. Bartlet (*JTS*, VI, 1905, pp. 204ff.), who disagreed with Chapman and tentatively suggested Thyatira.

is to put them on their guard and to stress in no uncertain tones the serious character of the false teaching. He makes quite clear that the doctrine is not the doctrine of Christ and that these people are not of God (verse 9). They are, in fact, opposed to Christ (symbolized in one expression, ὁ ἀντίχριστος). The readers are challenged to self-examination, lest they should lose what they have gained.

Many scholars have linked the occasion of 2 John with that of 3 John. Findlay,[1] for example, considered that 2 John was the letter referred to in 3 John 9 and that both are complementary in respect of hospitality, since 3 John deals with the refusal of Diotrephes to do what he should have done, i.e. offer hospitality to the emissaries of the truth. This interpretation necessitates treating κυρία as a reference to the same church of which Gaius (3 Jn. 1) was a member, the idea being that Gaius was incurring the displeasure of Diotrephes by keeping an open house for John's representatives, whom Diotrephes had banned. This interpretation is certainly possible, but in the absence of any allusion in 3 John to the false teaching of 2 John, it is better to keep them apart. The more recent and somewhat revolutionary view of Käsemann on these Epistles will be discussed when dealing with 3 John, although his interpretation of 3 John affects the purpose of 2 John. (See pp. 219 f.)

IV. DATE

If internal evidence alone be relied on as an indication of date, there is little data available. Since the false teaching links this Epistle so closely to 1 John, it must be supposed that it was issued about the same time, probably soon afterwards.[2] If any credence can be given to the view[3] that the ἔγραψα of 1 John ii. 26 refers to our 2 John, the reverse order would obtain, but the identification is doubtful since ἔγραψα can be understood to refer to 1 John, in conformity with frequent literary custom.

THE THIRD EPISTLE

So close is the connection between this Epistle and the last that much of what has already been said sheds light on the problem of this Epistle. The problem of authorship will practically resolve itself into a discussion of the relationship between the two letters.

[1] Op. cit., p. 8. C. H. Dodd (op. cit., p. 161) describes this suggestion as 'not very probable'.

[2] See discussion on the date of 1 John, pp. 205 f.

[3] Cf. H. H. Wendt, ZNTW, 21 (1922), pp. 144–146.

I. AUTHORSHIP

As in 2 John the writer introduces himself as 'the Elder', and so the decision reached with respect to 2 John should apply here. Little further discussion is needed except to elucidate one or two particular features of 3 John which differ from 2 John. First, the external attestation is not quite so strong for this Epistle. It is not certain that any evidence for it can be cited before the third century, if the Muratorian Canon is thought to refer to two Johannine Epistles only. But the absence of early attestation is not very surprising in view of the character of its contents.[1]

Next to be noted are its similarities to 2 John and also its differences. In both Epistles much stress is laid on the 'truth', although in 3 John it is not so clearly opposed to error. A similar context of erroneous teaching may nevertheless be assumed. Both speak of hospitality, although in 2 John it is forbidden for the false teachers and in 3 John it is commended for the true. In both the writer rejoices over others who walk in the truth: the elect lady's children (2 Jn. 4) and Gaius (3 Jn. 3). In both the author intimates, in almost identical words, his intention to visit the recipients (cf. 2 Jn. 12 and 3 Jn. 14), and in both he intimates that he had much to write but would rather not write (cf. 'paper and ink' in 2 Jn. 12 with 'pen and ink' in 3 Jn. 13). The conclusion seems inescapable that the same writer is at work in both letters. This is further confirmed by the differences. The more specific occasion of 3 John accounts naturally for the diversity in subject-matter and for the closer conformity of this Epistle to the form of a genuine private letter. There would, in fact, be less grounds for disputing 3 John than 2 John on the basis of literary form.[2]

II. DESTINATION

3 John has one advantage over 2 John in that the recipient is named. Who the 'beloved Gaius' was, however, is anyone's guess. It is highly unlikely, with so common a name, that he is to be identified with any other Gaius mentioned in the New Testament. He is clearly well known to the author, who warmly commends him not only for his consistent Christian life, but also for generous hospitality. Whether he held any office in any church is not known, nor is it certain that he belonged to

---

[1] C. H. Dodd (op. cit., pp. lxiii, lxiv) points out that it is so unimportant that it is difficult to suggest why anyone should have fabricated it.

[2] C. H. Dodd (op. cit., p. lxv) discusses the possibility that 3 John is genuine and 2 John is an imitation based on 1 and 3 John, but considers that such a theory is not completely plausible.

the same church as Diotrephes,[1] whose high-handed behaviour forms the main subject of the letter.

It is not possible to be any more specific than this,[2] but as it has already been shown that this Epistle is closely related both to 1 John and 2 John, and as these Epistles are fairly reasonably assigned to an Asian destination, it may be supposed that Gaius' church was one of the circuit of Asiatic churches under the general supervision of the apostle John.

III. OCCASION AND PURPOSE

It is possible to be rather more certain here. John has apparently sent out some itinerant representatives, who have returned and reported to him their experiences (verse 3). They speak highly of Gaius who entertained the strangers (verses 3, 5), who were probably acting for the apostle because, due to old age, he was no longer able to move among his churches. But one man, Diotrephes, has not been prepared to receive these brethren and has even banned the members of his church who were prepared to do so. In addition Diotrephes had been making none too complimentary remarks about the apostle himself ('prating against me with evil words', verse 10, RSV). From the manner in which Diotrephes has exerted authority, it is reasonable to suppose that he occupied the position of leader of this church, although he may even have assumed this position himself. At least, he did not acknowledge John's authority (verse 9), and there appears to exist something of a personal feud between them.

Thus the apostle writes to Gaius to acquaint him with the present position. There are two possibilities here. If Gaius belongs to the same church, it would seem that the apostle wrote two letters: one to the church, which he feels certain will not be received because of Diotrephes' personal antipathy towards him and the other to the only faithful member of the same church whose loyalty he could trust.[3] But it is

---

[1] J. V. Bartlet (*op. cit.*, p. 213) assumes that both were elders, but disputes that Diotrephes held any authoritative office above his fellow presbyters.

[2] G. G. Findlay (*op. cit.*, pp. 36f.) makes the conjecture that Gaius belonged to the church of Pergamum on the grounds of his identification of the elect lady of 2 John with this church and some rather precarious evidence from the Apostolic Constitutions to the effect that the apostle John appointed Gaius of Derbe as bishop of Pergamum (although Findlay does not regard the bishop as Paul's companion of Acts xx. 4).

[3] This is G. G. Findlay's theory, *op. cit.*, p. 38. Cf. also A. E. Brooke, *op. cit.*, pp. lxxxi ff.

possible that Gaius belonged to a neighbouring church and was being forewarned about the high-handed activity of Diotrephes. The former alternative appears to be slightly more probable.

If we assume the correctness of this interpretation of the occasion, the writer must be commending Gaius for his stand against Diotrephes and assuring him that he will deal with him as soon as he visits the church. But the position of Demetrius must also be taken into account. John holds him in great regard (verse 12) and appears to be commending him to Gaius. The Epistle, therefore, partakes of the character of a letter of commendation for Demetrius. Some have supposed him to have been a member, if not even the leader, of the band of itinerant missionaries. But this seems ruled out because Gaius has already received these and so would not need the apostle's commendation—unless, of course, even Gaius had not sufficiently respected him, which seems quite out of character with what we know of him from the opening portion of the Epistle. The most natural assumption is that Demetrius has no connection with John's representatives whom Diotrephes has already rejected, but that because of his commission from John it is anticipated that Diotrephes will treat him similarly. John therefore commends him to Gaius' private hospitality rather than to the church. He was in all probability the bearer of the letter.

Some reference must be made to the somewhat revolutionary interpretation of the evidence given by Käsemann.[1] He is not the only scholar who has seen in Diotrephes an early example of monarchical episcopacy, mainly on the ground of his power to excommunicate (as Käsemann understands verse 10). But he has gone further and deduced that the Elder has acted against the authority of the monarchical Diotrephes (understanding 'elder' in its second-century official sense). The assumption is that it is the Elder who is undisciplined and who has organized his own Gentile mission contrary to the authority of Diotrephes. The Elder writes, therefore, to justify his actions and to re-establish himself before the church from which he has been excommunicated (so Käsemann infers from verse 10).

This theory, which defends the reputation of Diotrephes and defames the writer of the letter into 'a simple presbyter of the third Christian

---

[1] E. Käsemann, ZTK, 48 (1951), pp. 292–311 (reproduced in his *Exegetische Versuche und Besinnungen*, 1960, pp. 168–187). But cf. G. Bornkamm's examination of and disagreement with this theory, in his article 'πρεσβύτερος', Kittel's *Theologisches Wörterbuch*, VI, p. 671.

Ag. Käsemann's view

generation',[1] must be rejected on several grounds. The tone of authority within the letter and also the specific mention of authority is sufficient to show that the Elder is more than a simple late presbyter. Moreover, verse 10 is not naturally to be understood of excommunication, but of refusal to grant hospitality.[2] The writer does not write as a pleading excommunicant, for verse 10 does not suggest that he expects any difficulty in gaining a hearing when he comes to the church. Indeed, the terms in which he refers to his approaching visit suggest an authoritative visit (cf. 1 Cor. iv. 19). An even more serious difficulty for Käsemann's view is the Johannine colouring of the letter, which he explains as a working in of traces of Johannine theology. But the skill required to do this vitiates the whole theory, for it is highly improbable that a simple presbyter would have been capable of giving such a presentation of Johannine flavouring that the original purpose of the letter became entirely forgotten. As Michaelis rightly points out, this theory does nothing to lead to a better understanding of the Johannine literature as a whole.[3]

Nothing has so far been said about the doctrinal views of Diotrephes, because the Epistle supplies no data on this matter. Yet W. Bauer[4] considered him to be a heretical leader ('Ketzer-haupt'). There might be something to be said for identifying this man with the same heresy which is condemned in 2 John, but if so it is strange that nothing is said about Diotrephes' heretical views. Gnostic tendencies might well have fostered such an exhibition of pride as is seen in his love of the pre-eminence (verse 9), but Gnostics were not the only ones addicted to arrogance and it is not necessary to appeal to heretical views to account for a failing which is all too often the accompaniment of orthodoxy.

IV. DATE

There is nothing further to add to the comments on 2 John, for this Epistle must have been written about the same time as that. Those who maintain that the two Epistles are complementary suggest that they were written and sent on the same occasion; but, even if this supposi-

---

[1] *Op. cit.*, p. 311.

[2] Cf. W. Michaelis' careful criticism of Käsemann on this point (*op. cit.*, p. 299).

[3] *Op. cit.*, p. 300. E. Haenchen (*TR*, n.f., 26, 1960, pp. 267–291) gives a useful summary of different explanations of the occasion of 2 and 3 John, and includes a careful criticism of Käsemann's views.

[4] *Rechtgläubigkeit und Ketzerei im ältesten Christentum* (1934), p. 97. Käsemann (*op. cit.*, p. 298) rejects this view, and most other scholars would agree with him.

tion is rejected, it is quite clear that no great time interval separated them. Naturally if 2 John is the earlier letter referred to in 3 John 9[1] the sequence of publication would be established, but since this is unlikely, there is no clear indication whether 3 John preceded or followed 2 John. In all probability this Epistle and 2 John were the latest Johannine writings and the latest of all the New Testament literature, but some would concede this position to the Fourth Gospel.[2]

CONTENTS OF 1 JOHN

I. THE MESSAGE AUTHENTICATED (i. 1–4)

In place of the usual salutation and specific address, the writer claims first-hand knowledge of the living message which he intends to impart. He gives some indication of the content of that message; that is, the fellowship which Christians enjoy both among themselves and with God. The writing is intended to deepen that fellowship.

II. THE PRINCIPLES OF FELLOWSHIP EXPLAINED (i. 5–ii. 29)

a. The necessity for purity (i. 5–ii. 2)

Against the background of God as light, it is impossible to have fellowship with Him unless we are equally pure and this can be achieved only by the sacrificial act of Jesus Christ, who has thus become the believer's constant Advocate. There is, however, a demand for the believer to walk continually in the light.

b. The manifestations of the life of fellowship (ii. 3–17)

1. There must be obedience to God's commandments. It is not sufficient to claim to do so by words, without supporting it by

---

[1] A view maintained by T. Zahn, *INT*, III, p. 378; G. G. Findlay, *op. cit.*, p. 8. M. Dibelius (*op. cit.*, p. 212) thought that it may have been 2 John. On the other hand B. F. Westcott (*op. cit.*, p. 240) emphatically regarded the letter as lost and most scholars have inclined to this view. It is very improbable that 1 John is meant because 3 John is obviously intended for a much smaller reader circle, and the letter in 3 Jn. 9 would seem to have been concerned with a specific situation (cf. W. Michaelis, *op. cit.*, p. 301).

[2] So W. Michaelis, *op. cit.*, pp. 294, 301.

deeds. The believer's walk is a sure test of his fellowship with God (ii. 3–6).

2. A new commandment requires the exercise of love. Light and love go together as do darkness and hate. Only those who show love are truly walking in the light (ii. 7–11).

3. The life of fellowship is applicable for all age-groups. Children, young men, and fathers are all in turn addressed and the possibility of victory over evil is assumed, on the basis of their knowledge of God (ii. 12–14).

4. The fellowship means a rejection of worldliness. The apostle thinks of the world in the sense of a harmful environment which must never be the object of the believer's affection (ii. 15–17).

c. Threats to those in the fellowship (ii. 18–29)

Already many antichrists have come and the apostle foresees a time when all opposition will be focused upon one impersonation of evil. Those who have dissociated themselves from the believers clearly do not belong to them. Antichrists are first contrasted with God's anointed ones and then defined as those who deny both God and Christ (ii. 18–22). But believers are in a very different position as heirs of eternal life, for they have the inner anointing of God and need no other teacher (ii. 23–27). Believers are, therefore, exhorted to abide in Christ so as to be unashamed at His coming. Their righteous deeds are evidence of their regeneration (ii. 28, 29).

III. THE CHILDREN OF GOD (iii. 1–24)

1. First the privileges of believers are set forth and the chief of these is the assurance that they will bear Christ's likeness (iii. 1–3).

2. Next, sin is regarded as lawlessness. But again believers have nothing to fear if they abide in Him. Their lives will be without sin, in the sense of an habitual attitude of mind. They are God's children in contrast to the devil's and as such they must act rightly and love the brethren (iii. 4–10).

3. Love to one another is illustrated by its antithesis. The case of Cain is cited in contrast to Abel. In contrast to hate, which is likened to murder, love is essentially sacrificial. Christ's own self-offering is in fact cited as a pattern for ours. Again the fallacy of profession without deeds is emphasized (iii. 11–18).

4. The believer should enjoy confidence before God. This he may

do if his own heart does not condemn him. Where self-condemnation exists God will deal with it, but the believers' responsibility is again defined as love to one another (iii. 19–24).

IV. THE SPIRIT OF TRUTH (iv. 1–6)

Because of the prevalence of error, there need to be sure tests of truth. One of the tests is the attitude towards Christ. A real grasp of the fact of the incarnation is essential. Any who deny this are regarded as being possessed by the spirit of Antichrist who dominates the world, but the Christian believers are assured that they will overcome error.

V. MORE ON THE THEME OF LOVE (iv. 7–21)

a. The powerful effect of God's love (iv. 7–12)

Since God is love, the believer's love to God must reflect the same love. Its supreme example is seen in the sending of Christ to be a propitiation for our sins. But this high concept of love is the pattern for Christians' love for one another.

b. The perfecting of God's love in us (iv. 13–21)

We have received (1) the Spirit and (2) the testimony that God sent His Son to be our Saviour. Our duty is to confess Christ and in this way we shall experience more of God's love until it becomes perfected. When it is perfected it will cast out fear and give confidence for the judgment day. Again mere profession is strongly condemned and brotherly love is made a test for the reality of our love to God.

VI. SECRETS OF A VICTORIOUS FAITH (v. 1–5)

The first requirement mentioned is obedience to God's commandments, which has already been mentioned before. But now the character of Christian commandments is explained as not burdensome. Obedience to God is not, therefore, onerous. Moreover, duty when linked with faith leads to victory. The world is a defeated foe for the believer in Christ.

VII. GOD'S WITNESS TO THE GOSPEL (v. 6–12)

As the Epistle began with the authentication of the message, so it closes with the same theme. A threefold witness to Christ is mentioned, the Spirit, the water and the blood, the latter two probably referring to the baptism and sacrificial death of Christ. This testimony is greater than human testimony, and anyone who does not believe it makes God a liar.

VIII. SPIRITUAL CONFIDENCE (v. 13–20)

There are a number of affirmations in this concluding passage which reflect a strong confidence in God.

1. The writer's purpose is that his readers should know that they have eternal life (v. 13).

2. We know that God hears and answers our prayers and we should pray for those who are not already past hope (v. 14–17).

3. We know the regenerate soul does not make a habit of sinning for God preserves him (v. 18).

4. We know we belong to God (v. 19).

5. We know the purpose of the incarnation (v. 20).

IX. WARNING AGAINST IDOLS (V. 21)

CONTENTS OF 2 JOHN

I. GREETING (verses 1–3)

It is noticeable that the word 'truth' occurs three times in this greeting and this may be said to be the keynote of the Epistle. The triple benediction is grounded in truth and love.

II. WALKING IN THE TRUTH (verses 4–6)

The combination of truth and love is again found in this section, and the latter is mentioned as in the first Epistle as a new commandment.

III. ERRONEOUS TEACHERS (verses 7–11)

1. The nature of their error is stated as a denial of the incarnation.

2. The rise of this error should lead to self-examination.

3. The exponents of the error should not be offered hospitality.

IV. CONCLUSION (verses 12, 13)

The writer mentions future plans and sends greetings.

CONTENTS OF 3 JOHN

I. GREETING (verse I)

Gaius is named as the recipient.

II. COMMENDATION OF GAIUS (verses 2–8)

The writer not only loves the man, but prays for him and rejoices over him, for he is a follower of the truth. He gives him instructions about giving hospitality to the brethren and even to strangers.

III. CRITICISM OF DIOTREPHES (verses 9, 10)

This man is ambitious and arrogant and has acted in a high-handed manner which does not meet with the writer's approval.

IV. COMMENDATION OF DEMETRIUS (verses 11, 12)

He is highly spoken of both by the visiting brethren and by the writer himself.

V. CONCLUSION (verses 13–15)

Reference to future plans and the formal greetings bring the letter to a close.

CHAPTER SIX

THE EPISTLE OF JUDE

I. CANONICITY

Not only in early times, but also increasingly in our own day doubt has been expressed regarding the authenticity of this Epistle. It is therefore necessary to give careful attention to the external evidence. There are traces of Jude in the letter of Clement of Rome, the *Shepherd of Hermas,* Polycarp, *Barnabas,*[1] and perhaps the *Didache,*[2] although it is impossible to say whether the slight allusions found in these writings are due to literary acquaintance. Polycarp's allusions are perhaps the most certain, while at a later time Athenagoras definitely knew the Epistle.[3] The Muratorian Canon mentions the Epistle of Jude together with two Epistles of John as being received, but the form of the statement may suggest that some had doubted their authenticity.[4] They are mentioned rather strangely after the spurious Marcionite works as in definite contrast to these.[5] Tertullian knew Jude and mentioned his use of Enoch.[6] Clement of Alexandria commented upon it in his *Hypotyposes,*[7] while Origen did not appear to question the authenticity himself, although he mentioned the doubts of others.[8] Later, at Alexandria, Didymus[9] found it necessary to defend Jude against its disputants (on the ground of its citing apocryphal books). Eusebius, at Caesarea, was less certain about its authenticity and classed it among the disputed books.[10] As in the case of other disputed books, Jude was not received into the Syriac Canon until a late date due, no doubt, to the extremely cautious approach of the Eastern Church.

[1] For the evidence, cf. C. Bigg, *St. Peter and St. Jude* (*ICC*, 1901), pp. 307, 308.
[2] Cf. *Didache*, ii. 7 and Jude 22f.; *Didache*, iii. 6 and Jude 8–10.
[3] Bigg (*op. cit.*, p. 307) considers that there is a 'clear reference to Jude'.
[4] Cf. Bigg, *op. cit.*, p. 14.
[5] After commenting on these 'fel enim cum melle misceri non congruit', the Fragment proceeds, 'Epistula sane Iudae et superscripti Johannis duas in Catholica habentur'.
[6] *De cultu fem.* i. 3.　　　　　　　　　　[7] Cf. Eusebius, *HE*, vi. 14.
[8] Cf. Bigg, *op. cit.*, p. 306, for the evidence.　　[9] Cf. Bigg, *op. cit.*, p. 305.
[10] *HE*, iii. 25. 3. But in ii. 23. 25 he seems to imply that Jude with James should be classed as *notha* (spurious) because of lack of citation by name among the ancients.

Enough has been said to show that the Epistle had considerable use at an early period, and the later doubts which occurred must not be allowed to obscure this fact. The attestation for it is particularly strong and questionings appear to have arisen mainly because of the author's use of apocryphal books.

II. AUTHORSHIP

The writer introduces himself as 'Jude, the servant of Jesus Christ and brother of James' (verse 1). The first question that arises is the identification of this Jude. It was a common name and there would have been no need to identify him with any other Jude mentioned in the New Testament, were it not for the special phrase which shows his relationship to James. There can be no doubt that the author intended his readers to think of this James as James of Jerusalem, the Lord's brother.[1] This would have been a very natural assumption since James of Jerusalem was well known. It is also natural to suppose that the lesser-known Jude wished to commend himself on the strength of his brother's wide rreputation. As seen in the discussion on James (p. 73) the other description ('a servant of Jesus Christ'), which prefers the idea of service to any claim of flesh-relationship to the Lord, need occasion no surprise. If we assume this identification is correct, we may suppose that Jude, as some of the other brothers of the Lord, engaged in itinerant preaching (1 Cor. ix. 5). It may well be, therefore, that the people whom Jude has in mind in this letter are those among whom he has been itinerating. So far the evidence for authorship seems fairly definite, but some objections have been raised to this identification.

1. The letter is supposed by some to be too late to make it possible that Jude, the Lord's brother, was author. The evidence of Hegesippus, recorded by Eusebius,[2] of Jude's grandsons being brought before Domitian is sometimes used to support a second-century origin for the Epistle.[3] It is cited as conclusive evidence that Jude could not have survived long enough to write this Epistle. But this line of argument is faulty. As J. B. Mayor[4] shows, it is at least probable that Jude, if still alive, was in his seventies at the commencement of Domitian's reign

---

[1] Cf. Mk. vi. 3 where a Jude is mentioned among the brethren of the Lord.
[2] *HE*, iii. 19.
[3] Cf. J. Moffatt, *ILNT*, p. 356.
[4] *The Epistle of St. Jude and the Second Epistle of St. Peter* (1907), p. cxlviii.

(i.e. AD 81),[1] and there is no ground, therefore, for disputing that this Jude could have been author, provided the Epistle was not written later than the ninth decade of the first century. But many scholars believe that it was.

2. The effect of dating on authorship can be considered only against a full discussion of the occasion of the Epistle (see discussion on pp. 230 ff.). But, anticipating the result of that discussion, we may dispute all the grounds on which a late dating is based. At most, the arguments cited (the description of the heretics and their connection with Gnosticism, the references to apostles as of an earlier generation and the fact that the faith is now well established) are capable of an interpretation which dates them well before the turn of the century and it is precarious, therefore, to pre-judge the question of authorship on this basis alone.[2]

3. Some have disputed the reading of verse 1, claiming that ἀδελφός is an interpolation and regarding the author as an unknown Jude who was *son* of an unknown James.[3] But this solution is not only unsupported by any textual evidence, but is altogether improbable.[4] For it would never have gained any general circulation unless it had been assumed that the James was the well-known Jerusalem leader of that name.[5] If that had been intended it would come under intentional pseudonymity, which seems highly unlikely when so obscure a name as Jude has been used. Moreover, this would be quite out of character in a pseudepigraphon, since in such writings one of the major factors was attribution to an already well-known name.[6]

---

[1] Bigg (*op. cit.*, p. 318) regards Jude as older than our Lord and thinks he could not have written much after AD 65. R. Knopf, *Die Briefe Petri und Judä* (1912), p. 207, similarly argues that by AD 70 Jude must have been an old man.

[2] As do E. F. Scott (*The Literature of the New Testament*, p. 226) and J. Moffatt (*op. cit.*, pp. 355, 356).

[3] So E. F. Scott, *op. cit.*, p. 225; T. Henshaw, *op. cit.*, p. 389. A. Harnack, *Die Chronologie der altchristlichen Literatur bis Eusebius* (1897), pp. 465ff., supposed the interpolation to extend to the whole phrase ἀδελφός δὲ Ἰακώβου, added later to increase the authority of the writing.

[4] Cf. W. Michaelis, *Einleitung*, p. 303.

[5] It was Hegesippus who first referred to Jude as the brother of the Lord, as far as records go (cf. Bigg, *op. cit.*, p. 317).

[6] A pseudonymity theory for Jude is particularly difficult. Jülicher–Fascher (*Einleitung*, p. 216) are hard pushed to explain the choice of name and can do no better than suggest that the writer belonged to a group where James was revered, but was satisfied with a lesser member of the family for his pseudonym. R. Knopf (*op. cit.*, p. 207) makes no attempt to explain, but recognizing the difficulty of the omission of the title of honour (the Lord's brother) weakly suggests that for the author Christ, the heavenly Lord, had no brothers.

4. Another idea which has been circulated is that the Jude was Jude the apostle, called Judas of James in Luke vi. 16; Acts i. 13.[1] It is supposed that 'Ιούδας 'Ιακώβου means Jude the brother of James rather than the son of James, but the latter rendering is the most probable. Moreover, our author not only does not claim to be an apostle, but seems to regard the apostles as apart from himself (verses 17, 18), although this statement does not conclusively exclude an apostolic author.[2]

5. Yet another hypothesis is that of Grotius[3] who identified this Jude with a second-century bishop of Jerusalem, who bore that name. This necessitated treating the words, 'brother of James', as equivalent to an episcopal title at Jerusalem. But there are no parallels to support this view.

There seems, therefore, no reason to suppose that this Jude was other than the Lord's brother.[4] In fact, although kinship with Christ was not stressed as a qualification of importance in the New Testament era,[5] Christians would undoubtedly treat the Lord's brethren with respect, and this would account, not only for the authority with which Jude writes, but also for the wide regard which the Epistle gained in the Christian Church.

III. DATE

The fact that the suggestions of scholars regarding the date of writing vary between AD 60 and 140 is a sufficient reminder that much of the so-called evidence on this subject amounts to little more than guesses.

---

[1] Bigg (op. cit., p. 319) cites Keil as holding this view.

[2] There is even less to be said for E. C. Selwyn's idea that the Jude intended was the Judas Barsabbas who accompanied Silas as a messenger carrying the letter from the Jerusalem church (Acts xv. 22) (The Christian Prophets and the Prophete Apocalypse, p. 148).

[3] Cf. Moffatt, ILNT, p. 357 n. Streeter, The Primitive Church (1929), pp. 178–180, considered Jude to be third bishop of Jerusalem on the slender evidence of a passage in the Apostolic Constitutions.

[4] Some, as in the case of James, have professed to find a difficulty in the character of the Greek, which is claimed to be too good for a Galilaean. But see the remarks on James, pp. 71 ff. Cantinat, in Robert-Feuillet's Introduction, II, p. 607, suggests that some Jewish Hellenist assisted in the writing of the Greek.

[5] Clement of Alexandria thought that Christians may have been in the habit of calling Jude 'the Lord's brother' and that Jude purposely called himself 'servant of Jesus Christ and brother of James' to correct this usage (see Bigg's discussion of this, op. cit., p. 318).

As it would not be profitable to discuss all the propositions, three main periods will be considered—the apostolic age, the latter part of the first century and the first part of the second century.

a. Evidence for an early date

This dating depends very largely on the decision reached regarding authorship. If Jude, the Lord's brother, was the author, the dating must naturally be confined to the reasonable limits of his life. Unfortunately we cannot be sure whether Jude was younger or older than our Lord, although the former is more probable. If the latter, he would be a son of a former marriage, but there is no evidence which clearly suggests the correctness of this view.[1] Assuming then that Jude was born in the early part of the Christian era, it would seem necessary to suppose that the Epistle could not have been later than about AD 70. But such an early dating has been rejected by many scholars for the reasons given below.[2]

b. Evidence against an early date

It is claimed that verse 3 relates to a time when Christianity was established sufficiently to have an orthodox body of doctrine ('our common salvation').[3] On the basis of this assumption it is supposed that the author could not have belonged to the first generation of Christians.[4] But this deduction is fallacious, for the expression 'common salvation' does not belong any more clearly to a late date than to an earlier. From the first there was a 'common' basis of belief among all Christians, although no doubt the contents of this common salvation became clearer as time went on. The exhortation to contend for the faith once for all delivered to the saints (verse 3) is equally indefinite regarding its timing. It may imply such development that 'faith' is now equivalent to a fixed body of doctrine, and orthodoxy is to be gauged by this standard. But the evidence does not demand a long time interval. If the apostle Paul could speak of a specific standard of teaching to which the Roman Christians had already been committed before

---

[1] This view is maintained by Bigg, op. cit., p. 318.

[2] F. H. Chase (art., 'Jude, Epistle of', HDB, II, p. 804) suggested a date late in the apostolic age, particularly because he found echoes of the language of Colossians and Ephesians.

[3] Cf. E. F. Scott, op. cit., p. 226.

[4] Cf. T. Henshaw, op. cit., p. 389; J. Moffatt, ILNT, p. 357.

he wrote to them (Rom. vi. 17), there is no need to relate this allusion in Jude to a much later period.[1] Our knowledge of the development of early Christian doctrine is after all far too limited to conclude with any confidence the precise date when Christians had a formal basis of faith. It would be strange indeed if the apostles themselves had never conceived the need for defining the common faith.[2]

The next consideration is the reference to the apostles in verse 17 ('But you must remember, beloved, the predictions of the apostles of our Lord Jesus Christ'—RSV). Does this mean that the apostolic age is past? This would certainly be a very natural interpretation and would imply some interval during which there has been a tendency to forget the apostolic teaching.[3] But it should be remembered that Jude is referring to apostolic predictions of scoffers who would arise in the Church, and the fulfilment of such predictions does not necessarily require a long period. It would seem, of course, that the readers were in possession of the apostolic writings to which this statement refers and this would require one of two alternatives: either the apostolic writings have by now been widely distributed, which would require an interval of time, or else some specific prediction is intended, which would suggest that an earlier epistle was sent by an apostle to the same people.[4] Zahn, who maintained that 2 Peter preceded Jude, strongly contended that Jude is here referring to that Epistle. This raises the whole question of the relation between the two Epistles (see discussion below, pp. 240 ff.), but few scholars have followed Zahn's opinion in this. 2 Peter iii. 3 would certainly furnish a very suitable antecedent to this reference. But the apostles are referred to in the plural and it is therefore somewhat difficult to confine the reference to one particular writing.

Leaving aside for the moment Zahn's interpretation, it is, of course,

[1] Cf. J. B. Mayor (*op. cit.*, pp. 61f.) for a full discussion of Paul's approach in its bearing on the present passage.

[2] The word 'common' (κοινή) has been understood somewhat differently as pointing to a time when the opposition between Jewish and Gentile Christianity had passed (cf. Feine-Behm, *op. cit.*, p. 253). This is possible, but is probably too restricted an interpretation. If true, however, it could not require a date later than Ephesians, where the middle wall of partition is already demolished.

[3] Cf. E. F. Scott, *op. cit.*, p. 226.

[4] A third possibility would be to suppose that the readers had actually heard the apostles speak (cf. J. W. C. Wand, *op. cit.*, p. 190). But some literary reference seems more probable.

true that more than one of the apostles forecast the rise of scoffers and
trouble-makers and it seems, therefore, to have been a general expectation in the Church. At the same time Jude appears to be making a
specific quotation and evidently has in mind one particular statement
which he regarded as fully representative of the whole group. To cite
Peter in this way would be most natural and so far supports Zahn's
view. It is difficult, at least, to make any late dating depend on an
interpretation of this verse.[1]

Another problem is the identification of the false teachers who have
crept in unawares (verses 4f.). Many scholars have confidently pronounced these to be Gnostics and have, therefore, relegated the Epistle
to the second century.[2] The connection of these teachers with Gnosticism is more fully discussed below (p. 235), but in view of the
caution with which many scholars are now pronouncing on the limits
of Gnosticism, and in view of the need for a clearer distinction between
developed Gnosticism and incipient Gnosticism, it is unsafe to base
calculations of date on such evidence.

It is further maintained that the description of the false teachers
bears a close resemblance to passages in the Pastoral Epistles. If these
latter are dated late, this line of argument would require a still later
date for Jude.[3] But since there are good reasons for assigning an early
date to the Pastorals,[4] these descriptions in Jude constitute no difficulty.
Once again evidence of this kind is so governed by other considerations
that different minds form different estimates of it. Clearly it can form
no certain basis for dating.

To conclude, it is not possible to be very precise on the matter of
dating. The most specific evidence is drawn from the probable life-

[1] J. W. C. Wand (*op. cit.*, p. 188) rightly points out that there is no need to
suppose that all the apostles were now dead.

[2] So E. F. Scott (*loc. cit.*) confidently asserts, 'The type of Gnosticism attacked in
the Epistle is one which came into existence considerably after Apostolic times.'
But no evidence is produced in support. Moffatt (*ILNT*, pp. 353ff.), after surveying
the evidence, is more cautious and agrees with Harnack in describing the teaching
as 'the incipient phases of some local, possibly syncretistic, development of liberti-
nism upon Gnostic lines'. But such a tendency is almost impossible to date with
any certainty.

[3] J. Moffatt (*op. cit.*, p. 355) suggested that Jude 17 referred to 2 Tim. iii. 1f. and
1 Tim. iv. 1ff. T. Henshaw (*op. cit.*) finds similarities not only with the Pastorals
but also with Ignatius' writings.

[4] Cf. the present writer's *The Pastoral Epistles* (*TNT*, 1957), pp. 16ff., and *New
Testament Introduction: The Pauline Epistles* (1961), pp. 198ff.

span of Jude, if he were the Lord's brother. Bigg[1] thought this fixed a limit of about AD 65, because he accepted the theory that Jude was older than our Lord. But others,[2] who regard him as younger, find it possible to extend the period to AD 80. It is difficult to be more precise than to suppose a date somewhere between AD 65 and 80. Advocates of the theory that Jude combats developed Gnosticism naturally date the Epistle well into the second century,[3] but many who do not identify Jude as the Lord's brother are more cautious and date the Epistle at the turn of the century.[4] Once accept an unknown author and anyone's guess becomes as valid as another's.

IV. THE FALSE TEACHERS

This short Epistle contains a number of details regarding the troublemakers, which enable a picture to be drawn of them, but which are insufficient to ensure a close alignment with other known heresies. These facts will first be set out under the two categories of doctrine and practice, and then the implications will be discussed.

Under the heading of doctrine there is not a great deal of evidence, but what there is is highly significant. In verse 4, Jude says that these teachers are denying the one Master and Lord, Jesus Christ, and in this they are in line with such heresies as were influencing the Colossian church. Since the majority of heresies introduce errors regarding the person of Christ, this feature alone offers little assistance in tracing the origin or connections of these false teachers. It could even be that Jude means that their licentiousness is in fact denying Christ, without thinking of any doctrinal error, but the two things usually go together.

Lying behind their immoral practices was a fundamental misconception of the Christian doctrine of grace. They were essentially libertines who disregarded the restraints of God's grace (verse 4) and considered that immoral indulgence was perfectly legitimate. Another

---

[1] Cf. *op. cit.*, p. 315. R. Leconte (*Les épîtres catholiques*, 1953, p. 49) dates the Epistle rather less specifically as during the last years of the apostolic age.

[2] E.g. J. B. Mayor, *op. cit.*, p. cxlv. T. Zahn (*INT*, II, p. 255) prefers *c.* AD 75.

[3] J. Moffatt (*op. cit.*, p. 357) cites many older scholars who maintained this view (i.e. dates ranging from AD 130 to 160), but the external evidence for attestation makes such a theory impossible. E. J. Goodspeed (*INT*, p. 347) dates it about AD 125.

[4] So H. Windisch-H. Preisker, *Der katholischen Briefe*, p. 48; W. Michaelis, *op. cit.*, p. 303.

feature which touches upon doctrinal error is their preference for their own dreamings (verse 8) rather than for God's revelation. These dreamings may be ecstasies during which they claimed to receive messages from God, but the whole method was fundamentally opposed to God's method of making Himself known, for it involved some definite defiling of the flesh (verse 8). From verse 19 it would be a fair inference that their doctrine of the Holy Spirit was sadly wrong, in fact entirely absent. It has been suggested that these people were making themselves out to be spiritual in conformity with the well-known Gnostic description of higher initiates, and in all probability Jude is making it clear that, from a Christian point of view, they are devoid of the Spirit. One concluding feature is their doctrine of angels, to which there appears to be a reference in verse 8, where Jude mentions their insolence towards the glorious ones (δόξαι). But all that can be inferred from this is that they were critical of the orthodox doctrine of angels.

Their moral culpability is much more plainly illustrated. Indeed, it seems to have been of such a character that Jude is deeply shocked by it. The people are acting worse than irrational animals (verse 10, RSV). They are licentiously indulging in unnatural lust (verses 4, 7, 16, 18). Their passions apparently rule them. They have consequently become defiled (verses 8, 23). Not only so, they are also discontented, arrogant, avaricious (verse 16). In some way, they were using their very errors to further their own financial gains.

So much for their characteristics.[1] It remains to enquire what the historical circumstances of these people were. From verse 4 it would seem that these teachers were, at least outwardly, members of the church. They were affecting it from within in spite of the fact that their whole approach was opposed to true Christianity. Had they been allowed to continue they would have destroyed the church, which no doubt accounts for Jude's severity. The next question is whether these teachers were Jews or Gentiles, but this is easily answered since none of their characteristics is prominent, if found at all, in Jewish Christianity. Because the author cites Jewish pseudepigrapha it cannot at once be inferred that all his readers are Jewish, although it may well suggest that he himself is. A further matter that should be noted is the

---

[1] T. Zahn (INT, II, pp. 242ff.) has a very full discussion on these false teachers, including some valuable comments on exegetical details. Cf. also H. Werdermann, *Die Irrlehrer des Judas-und 2 Petrusbriefes* (1913).

fact that Jude represents these men as being a direct fulfilment of an earlier prophecy (verses 17, 18) and as having been already designated for condemnation (verse 4). Whatever these statements may specifically refer to, it is quite certain that Jude feels that the Christians should not have been taken unawares. Moreover, it should also be noted that the mention of Cain and Balaam may give some indication of the connection of these teachers with other heretical movements, especially as the latter is mentioned in Revelation ii. 14 in connection with both false teaching and immorality in the church of Pergamum. Balaam appears to have been an all-inclusive symbol of heretical doctrine and practice.[1]

Some have seen in these allusions definite connections with certain second-century Gnostic sects. Pfleiderer[2] argued that Jude was combating the Carpocratians, a mid-second-century sect noted for their immoral practices, particularly their advocacy of promiscuous sexual indulgence. Clement of Alexandria[3] noted the close connection between Jude's false teachers and this sect, but regarded Jude's references as prophetic. Undoubtedly the description in Jude would fit any heresy in which immoral practices played a major part, but this similarity alone is not sufficient to identify Jude's references with any particular sect. The same goes for attempts to connect them up with the Ophites, of which a branch was called 'Cainites'. These people appear to have reversed good and evil and it is not surprising that their behaviour conformed to immoral patterns. But these sects, as far as our knowledge of them goes, belong to a date too late for our Epistle and we are obliged, therefore, to suppose that in the first century there were adumbrations of the moral degeneracy which was to reach its climax in these later sects.

As with the other heretical movements or tendencies which are reflected in the New Testament, so with Jude's false teachers, we must regard them as embryonic forms of later developments. They appear to present us with a kind of cross-section of movements which were inevitable as soon as Christianity had made a deep enough impact on the world of pagan thought and behaviour out of which it grew. As far as Jude is concerned, he saw at once that this subversive move-

---

[1] Cf. J. B. Mayor, op. cit., p. clxxvi.

[2] Mentioned by J. W. C. Wand, op. cit., p. 211, from his Urchristentum, pp. 835ff.

[3] Strom. iii. 2. 6–10. Cf. also Irenaeus (Adv. Haer. i. 25. 1), who mentions that the adherents of Simon Magus and the Carpocratians scoffed at angels.

ment was highly dangerous and that the only possible treatment for it was downright condemnation.

It will be noted that many of the characteristics of the movement in Jude are found equally strongly in 2 Peter, but a few striking differences may be seen. The author of 2 Peter is less drastic in his approach towards those whom he combats and it may well be that the error has less of a grip.[1] In 2 Peter the special targets for attack are the newly converted (2 Pet. ii. 18, 19), but this is less clear in Jude. Moreover, Jude says nothing about these teachers' wrong handling of the Scriptures, which is prominent in 2 Peter iii. 15, 16, nor does he mention erroneous teaching about the *parousia* (cf. 2 Pet. iii. 1ff.). Both writers, however, in dealing with the heretics make much of the judgments of God, especially illustrating their theme from the Old Testament, although Jude omits to mention the flood, which receives special attention in 2 Peter iii. Whereas the two Epistles deal with very closely related situations, the differences should put us on our guard against too readily identifying them.

V. PURPOSE

When Jude began to write, his purpose was to produce a treatise on the 'common salvation' for the edification of his readers (verse 3). Since he speaks of his eagerness (σπουδή) to do this, it is abundantly clear that a far more pressing need arose before which the original purpose had to be dropped. This former purpose must not, however, be entirely lost sight of in considering the circumstances of the readers. Jude evidently recognized their need of some constructive teaching about the Christian faith before he was faced with the problem of the insidious false teachers.

The nature of the error, described in the last section, presented an immediate challenge to Jude who devoted almost the entire Epistle to an all-out denunciation of the false teachers. At the close (verses 17ff.) he suddenly seems to realize the need for being positive in his approach to his readers, and gives a series of exhortations which were clearly intended to offset the evil effects of the false teachers. Indeed, even these exhortations finish with a direct challenge to them to rescue any who are not yet in the grip of the evil, like brands snatched from the fire

---

[1] J. W. C. Wand (*op. cit.*, p. 209) interprets the change differently, maintaining that by the time of 2 Peter the error has gained such a grip that Jude's forthright approach would be less effective.

(verse 23). There is little theological content in the letter, for the purpose was essentially practical. Jude does not give any reasoned refutation of the tenets held by the false teachers, as Paul did when dealing with the Colossian heresy. Their moral lapses were too blatantly obvious to need such refutation. They deserved only unconditional denunciation. Yet it should be pointed out that Jude regarded his own Epistle as an exhortation (verse 3, παρακαλῶν) exactly as did the writers of Hebrews and I Peter (Heb. xiii. 22; I Pet. v. 12). His main purpose was to warn rather than to condemn.

VI. DESTINATION

The address is so vaguely expressed that it gives no indication whatever of the locality of the readers. Those who are 'called', 'beloved' and 'kept' (verse 2, RSV) might be Christians anywhere and the question immediately arises whether Jude intended his letter to be a general circular.[1] This seems to be excluded by his apparent acquaintance with certain specific people whom he knows to have crept into the church by guile and whose behaviour is so vividly portrayed that it suggests first-hand acquaintance with the false teachers too. It can hardly be doubted that Jude has in mind a concrete situation, however much he may have supposed that the Church generally needed the same message.

Because of the use of Jewish Apocrypha, it has been maintained by some that the destination must be placed in a Jewish setting.[2] But this evidence points more to the author than to the readers and any attempt to fix the region (as, for instance, in Syria) must be regarded as purely speculative. Nevertheless, certain data point to a district within the region of Palestine. The probability is that verses 17, 18 mean that these readers had heard at least some of the apostles and that they had some acquaintance with Paul. On the strength of these considerations Wand[3] suggests Antioch and this seems as good a suggestion as any. Some scholars[4] have maintained a Gentile destination because of the improbability of a Greek epistle being sent to Jewish readers, but this would only apply to Palestine. The syncretistic heresy combated might suggest Gentile rather than Jewish Christian readers, but there is insufficient information about this period to decide. If Wand's suggestion is

[1] T. Henshaw (op. cit., p. 390) understands it in this way.
[2] Cf. M. Meinertz, Einleitung⁵ (1950), p. 258.
[3] Op. cit., p. 194.   [4] Cf. R. Knopf, op. cit., p. 203.

valid both Jews and Gentiles would, of course, be involved and this theory is probably correct.

VII. USE OF APOCRYPHAL BOOKS

This brief Epistle is alone among the New Testament books in citing a Jewish apocryphal work, the book of Enoch. It also appears to make references to another pseudepigraphon, the *Assumption of Moses*,[1] although no text has been preserved which contains the account of the dispute between the archangel Michael and the devil over the body of Moses (verse 9).

When in verse 14 Jude refers to Enoch, the seventh from Adam, as prophesying and then cites words which are preserved in 1 Enoch i. 9 almost *verbatim*, there can be very little doubt that he was making a direct citation from the apocryphal book, which he assumes his readers will be not only familiar with, but will also highly respect. Some have supposed that Jude regards Enoch as Scripture, but the word προφήτευω is used on only one occasion in the New Testament for a citation from the Old Testament.[2] Nevertheless, if it cannot be demonstrated that Jude regards Enoch as Scripture, he clearly holds it in high esteem and considers it legitimate to cite it in support of his argument. This has been regarded by many, ancients as well as moderns, as a difficulty. How can a writer who cites an apocryphal book be inspired? Tertullian[3] gets over the difficulty by maintaining the authenticity of Enoch, but in this he is unsupported by any others. Jerome[4] gives expression to a quite different point of view when he mentions that the doubts which had arisen about the Epistle were due to its using an apocryphal book in an authoritative way. This latter approach was much more widespread. Some modern exegetes, wishing to preserve the integrity of Jude, but imagining that this would be impaired if the Enoch citation were admitted, deny the latter and claim that oral tradition had preserved a true saying of Enoch and that Jude is citing the tradition, not the book.[5] But under this theory the book must have included the oral

[1] This book is named in several canonical lists. It is quoted by Clement of Alexandria and Origen and was mentioned by Didymus. (Cf. R. H. Charles, *The Assumption of Moses*, 1897, pp. 107–110, for the Greek fragments.)

[2] Cf. Mt. xv. 7 (Mk. vii. 6) which uses it to introduce a citation from Is. xxix. 13. The cognate noun, προφήτης, could even be used for a heathen poet (Tit. i. 12).

[3] *Idol.* xv; *Apol.* xxii.   [4] *De Vir. Ill.* iv.

[5] Cf. the view of J. Stafford Wright, *EQ*, xix (1947), p. 102. Most of the older conservative commentators took the same view (cf. H. Alford, *The Greek Testament*,[4] 1871, IV, p. 198, who mentions this as possible).

tradition in a form almost directly in agreement with that cited by Jude. Yet since the book of Enoch, at least in its major parts, was written long before the Epistle of Jude, this theory is highly improbable. It could hardly have arisen apart from a desire to shield Jude from doing what was considered impossible for an inspired writer.

But is it possible to maintain Jude's dependence on Enoch and still leave in no question his inspiration, or his right to a place in the Canon? The difficulties are not insuperable if Jude is not citing Enoch as Scripture, and there is no conclusive evidence that he is. He seems rather to be recognizing that what Enoch had said has turned out to be a true prophecy in view of the ungodly conduct of these false teachers. On the other hand, when Jude specifically calls Enoch 'the seventh from Adam', this would appear to indicate that he regarded the book as a true work of the ancient Enoch, in which case he would certainly have regarded the book as a part of Scripture. But against this it must be noted that in the book of Enoch itself Enoch is twice mentioned as being in the seventh generation from Adam, a description obviously added for identification purposes.[1] Whatever the answer to this problem, it is clear that Jude regards the words he cites as invested with some authority, although this need give no indication of what he thought of the rest of the book. This may be indicated by the claim that he echoes its language in other parts of his Epistle. F. H. Chase,[2] for instance, sets out parallels with words and phrases from fourteen other verses in Jude, and if these can be maintained it would be evidence enough of the dominating influence of the book of Enoch on the author's mind. But many of the parallels are very slight and have weight only on the prior assumption that Jude definitely used the book as a basis.

The use of the *Assumption of Moses* is of interest as adding further evidence of Jude's regard for non-canonical accounts. It is unfortunate that in this case the original text has been lost and there is no means of verifying the extent of Jude's indebtedness. But since Clement, Origen and Didymus all assume that Jude used such a book, it is quite possible that he quoted it. He may, on the other hand, be citing a traditional story, which was the basis of the apocryphal book. The evidence is

[1] In Enoch lx. 8 (from the Book of Noah), xxxvii. 1ff.; cf. also the symbolic significance of the number seven in xciii ('I was born the seventh in the first week').

[2] *HDB*, III, pp. 801, 802.

insufficient to be certain. But in any case the allusion tells us nothing about Jude's view of Jewish pseudepigrapha generally, but only of his acceptance of the validity of the particular incident to which he alludes.

To conclude this comment, it should be noted that the mere citation of non-canonical books cannot be construed as a point unfavourable to the canonicity of the Epistle. Paul refers to a rabbinical midrash in 1 Corinthians x. 4, a heathen poet in his speech at Athens (Acts xvii. 28), and names the magicians who withstood Pharoah as Jannes and Jambres (2 Tim. iii. 8), evidently drawn from some non-canonical source, but his Epistles are not for that reason regarded as of inferior value as inspired literature.

VIII. RELATION TO 2 PETER

In order to deal adequately with the relationship between Jude and 2 Peter, it would be necessary to set out in detail the parallel texts and to indicate the verbal agreements. Such an examination would not only fall outside the scope of our present purpose, but would be unnecessary since it has already been thoroughly carried out.[1] All that is possible here is to give some indication of the nature of the relationship and of the various theories that have been proposed to account for it.

a. Its nature

That the relationship is very close is clear from the most casual comparison of the Epistles. Most of 2 Peter ii is paralleled in Jude. There are also parallels in the other two chapters.[2] The common material deals almost wholly with the false teachers and only incidentally touches on other subject-matter. 2 Peter contains more positive Christian teaching, while Jude concentrates on denunciations. That the two groups of false teachers were closely allied is undeniable, but it has already been shown (see pp. 233–236 above) that they were not absolutely identical. The problem at once arises, therefore, how it came about that both Epistles use such similar descriptions of these people[3] and the natural conclusion is that one has used the other. This has given rise to two different theories of dependence, of which the view that Jude is the basis of 2 Peter is much more widely held than the reverse. But there is

---

[1] This is most clearly done in Mayor's Commentary where the parallel Greek texts are set out side by side.

[2] The main parallels are between Jude 4–18 and 2 Pet. ii. 1–18 and iii. 1–3.

[3] The similarities often stretch to the parallel use of unusual words, striking metaphors and similar Old Testament illustrations.

a third possibility—that both have used the same source, incorporating the materials into their Epistles in different ways. These three possibilities will be considered in turn.

b. *The hypothesis that Jude is prior*

1. Since Jude is briefer than 2 Peter, it is considered more probable that this was the source rather than the borrower. There would be an obvious point in an enlargement of an earlier work where the additions would enable the author to append his own special features. But the opposite is less easy to imagine, especially when the briefer Epistle appears merely to extract a portion of the longer and append little more than a salutation and a doxology. There seems to be no adequate reason for the publication of the shorter Epistle at all if 2 Peter already exists, and still less so under so obscure a name as Jude. This argument is undoubtedly a strong one for the priority of Jude.

2. A comparison between the manner in which both approach the problem of the false teachers would also seem to confirm the priority of Jude. His treatment gives the appearance of greater spontaneity. He goes right into the subject without the long introduction that 2 Peter thinks necessary. Moreover, he refers to the trouble-makers as if he has already had first-hand acquaintance with them, whereas in 2 Peter the tenses of the verbs vary between the future and the present.[1] This argument is not as strong as the first, but deserves consideration.

3. Jude is harsher than 2 Peter, which suggests that the latter recognized the need to tone down the model. However, while it may seem easier to explain the change in this way, the reverse relationship is not absolutely excluded. It is at least conceivable that Jude considered that 2 Peter's rather softer approach needed more strength in it when applied to his own particular reader-constituency. There is no certain criterion for deciding whether harshness must always be prior. Common experience knows only too well that both harshness and softness can at times claim priority.

4. Supposing Jude to be prior, it is possible to suggest in some cases of minor changes the reason for the modification in 2 Peter. One example will suffice. In 2 Peter ii. 17 and Jude 12, 13 occur the combination of waterless 'clouds' carried by winds and the reference to outer darkness. In 2 Peter the darkness is reserved for those likened to clouds and mists but in Jude it is reserved for those likened to

[1] See further comment on these tenses on pp. 244 f.

wandering stars. Whereas the former, according to most commentators, is inappropriate, the latter exactly fits. It may well be explained as 2 Peter's telescoping of Jude's metaphors, causing the reference to the meteors to be omitted, but if Jude is using 2 Peter it would have to be supposed that he noticed the inappropriate metaphor and adjusted it in his own production, a less likely (though nevertheless not impossible) procedure.[1] Such occurrences could be multiplied.

5. A far less probable line of argument is that which sees in some of 2 Peter's allusions indirect echoes of hints contained in Jude. Thus the number seven is mentioned in both Jude 14 and 2 Peter ii. 5 (see RSV),[2] but the totally different contexts make any argument based on this seem fanciful (cf. also the 'building up' metaphor found in 2 Peter i. 5–7 and Jude 20, but again the connection is extremely slight).

6. Jude's use of apocryphal books and the absence of any direct citation from them in 2 Peter is thought to be an almost conclusive argument that Jude is prior and that 2 Peter has intentionally excised these references because of their unorthodox character. The example which is generally cited in support is 2 Peter ii. 11 and its parallel in Jude 9. Jude refers to the archangel Michael, but 2 Peter only vaguely to 'angels' and, according to Wand,[3] 'blurs the point of the railing at dignities'. Similarly 2 Peter's reference to 'great swelling words' (ii. 18) is thought to be an 'unnecessary expansion' (Wand) of Jude 16, culled probably from the same apocryphal book. But this method of argument is not conclusive, for Jude might have cited some specific example known to him to illustrate 2 Peter's reference to angels. Nevertheless, there is something to be said for the argument that apart from Jude the reference in 2 Peter ii. 11 is barely intelligible. It is significant that 2 Peter contains no reference to the book of Enoch,[4] which Jude

---

[1] R. A. Falconer (*Exp.*, VI, vi, pp. 220, 221) argues with some force that Peter would hardly have emptied Jude's powerful metaphor of its picturesqueness had he been echoing it.

[2] J. B. Mayor (*op. cit.*, p. 192) finds a symbolic contrast between Noah as the eighth (in 2 Peter) and Enoch as the seventh (in Jude), but such a method of exegesis is by no means obvious or convincing.

[3] *Op. cit.*, p. 133.

[4] In spite of the efforts of some scholars to emend the text of 1 Pet. iii. 19 to include a reference to Enoch. Cf. J. Rendle Harris, *Exp.*, VI, v (1902), pp. 317–320; but against, cf. C. Clemen, *Exp.*, VI, vi, pp. 318ff. More recently, E. J. Goodspeed, *JBL*, LXXIII (1954), pp. 91, 92, maintains the emendation, against B. Metzger, *Theology To-day* (1946), p. 562.

formally cites. It may be possible to consider this as prudent on his part since Enoch was not regarded as Scripture, but it could equally well be explained by the author's ignorance of the book, or at least lack of interest in it.

7. A comparison of the theology of both Epistles led Mayor[1] to conclude for the priority of Jude. In references to God, for instance, certain periphrases which have a Hellenistic flavour are found in 2 Peter but not in Jude (cf. 2 Pet. i. 3, 4). While differences of emphasis may be noted in relation to the teaching on grace, apostasy, punishment, the possibility of repentance, and eschatology, yet it is difficult to use such data as indications of the priority of one Epistle.

8. Linguistically the Greek of Jude is less awkward than the Greek of 2 Peter.[2] Chase[3] argues that the use of parallel words and phrases in Jude is more natural than in 2 Peter, and this is considered an argument in support of Jude's priority. In other words it is considered more likely that the more polished language has been obscured by a writer less at home in Greek than that a more obscure style has been polished up by another writer. But this contention is open to challenge. Indeed, the opposite is generally assumed to be an argument for the priority of Mark over Matthew in examinations of the Synoptic problem. It is difficult, therefore, to attach much weight to such evidence.

c. The hypothesis that 2 Peter is prior

The three main advocates of this view are Spitta, Zahn and Bigg, but in more recent times their opinion has been very largely discounted. All three, contrary to most of the adherents of the view discussed above, maintained the Petrine authorship of 2 Peter and were, therefore, rather more disposed to consider it prior to Jude. The main reasons for this view are as follows:

1. It is first of all maintained that Jude makes reference to 2 Peter. This is based on a particular interpretation of Jude 4 and 17. The former verse mentions condemnation which had already been designated (οἱ πάλαι προγεγραμμένοι). This is understood to refer to an earlier

---

[1] *Op. cit.*, pp. xvi ff.
[2] Moulton and Howard, *A Grammar of New Testament Greek*, II (1929), pp. 27f., contrast Jude, who was quite at home in Hellenistic idiom (citing the opinion of Mayor), and the author of 2 Peter, whose Greek is an artificial dialect learnt from books.
[3] *HDB*, II, p. 803.

writing,[1] which may then be identified with 2 Peter, since that Epistle does in fact refer to condemnation on precisely the kind of people mentioned in Jude. Moreover, in Jude 17 the readers are exhorted to remember the apostles' predictions, and words are there cited which occur almost *verbatim* in 2 Peter iii. 3. Zahn maintained that in view of this evidence 'by the ordinary canons of criticism we should conclude that Jude knew and prized 2 Peter as an apostolic writing and made it the basis of parts of his letter'.[2] But this view has been criticized on the grounds first that πάλαι in Jude 4 means 'of old' and not 'lately', in which case the reference is to the book of Enoch (as in verses 14, 15) and not to 2 Peter[3]; and secondly that if a genuine 2 Peter were being referred to in Jude 17, why was not Peter mentioned by name? And why is the statement attributed to the apostles as a group?[4] And further, why is it introduced with the word ἔλεγον, which suggests habitual oral teaching? None of these objections is strong enough to overthrow the *possibility* that Jude refers to 2 Peter, although whether he is actually doing so is a different matter. The interpretation of πάλαι is impossible to decide with confidence, while Jude might conceivably have had a reason for grouping the apostles together. The context of verse 17 shows the statement against the background of 'loud-mouthed boasters' and the apostolic witness is evidently intended to be a conclusive contrast to this kind of thing. This type of plural is so frequently used in the New Testament that it seems to have been employed here quite generally, almost with an adjectival significance. It is obvious that *all* the apostles had not given expression to this precise statement, but all had endorsed it. In fact in 2 Peter iii. 3 the readers are exhorted to recall the predictions of the prophets and the commandment of the Lord through the apostles. Jude 17 looks like a combination of both statements.

2. The use of the future tense in 2 Peter and the present tense in Jude with reference to the false teachers is also thought to point to the priority of 2 Peter. What 2 Peter foresaw, Jude has now experienced. This would be a strong argument if 2 Peter had consistently used the

---

[1] So T. Zahn, *INT*, II, pp. 250f., 265.

[2] Cf. Zahn, *loc. cit.* The same contention was made by Spitta, *Der Zweite Brief des Petrus und der Brief des Judas* (1885), pp. 145, 146.

[3] Cf. Wand, *op. cit.*, p. 198; Mayor, *op. cit.*, pp. 24, 25. The latter stresses the fourfold occurrence of ἀσεβεῖς and its cognates in Jude 14, 15.

[4] Cf. F. H. Chase, *op. cit.*, p. 802.

future in preference to the present (but cf. ii. 10, 17, 18, iii. 5 where the present is used). The generally held interpretation of the usage in 2 Peter is that the author assumes a prophetic rôle to add verisimilitude to his message, but he could not sustain it.[1] But a better explanation of the mixture of tenses is the supposition that the beginnings of the movement are already visible, but that further developments are anticipated in the future. In that case the tenses of Jude would be more intelligible if subsequent to 2 Peter.[2]

3. It is claimed to be inexplicable why an 'apostolic' writer (i.e. Peter, or an admirer of Peter, if 2 Peter is not genuine) should take over so much of the writing of an obscure man like Jude, whereas it is highly intelligible why the lesser man should be influenced by the greater.[3] This is another kind of argument whose value is difficult to assess, for there is no reason why Peter himself should not have borrowed from others (indeed he appears to have been influenced by Paul, see pp. 109f). Nevertheless, if both Epistles are genuine, it may be said that we should expect the writing of Peter to be basic to Jude rather than vice versa. But the argument should not be allowed too much weight especially on the strength of Jude's obscurity, for as a brother of the Lord he may have been well known to a fairly wide circle of Christians.[4]

4. None of the above arguments is conclusive for the priority of 2 Peter, although each could support it. In the final analysis, priority can be decided only on minute comparisons of style, but even here the criteria are almost wholly subjective. To take the reference to railing at dignitaries as an example (Jude 8; cf. 2 Pet. ii. 10), whereas Wand[5] considers 2 Peter blurs Jude's point (as mentioned above), Bigg[6] considers Jude has 'altered and spoiled St. Peter's point and quite destroyed the parallel'. Obviously both approach the data having already made up their minds in which direction the dependence lies and both have reasonable arguments in support. A full-scale stylistic comparison between the two Epistles would not lead to any more certain criteria. Does this then mean that the examination of the whole question must

[1] Cf. Wand, *op. cit.*, p. 132.

[2] Another possibility is to suppose that Peter knew of the activity of the false teachers through Jude's Epistle and writes to warn a different reader-circle of the approaching threat, an intelligible suggestion in favour of Jude's priority.

[3] Mayor (*op. cit.*, p. xxiii), who admits that probability would favour this latter alternative, is not prepared to press it because of such well-known borrowers as Milton and Handel, who drew from the works of lesser men.

[4] Cf. Wand, *op. cit.*, p. 132.   [5] *Ibid.*, p. 133.   [6] *Op. cit.*, p. 217.

end in deadlock? Some have proposed a *via media*, which must next be considered.

d. The hypothesis that both used a common source

It is a tempting solution of the difficulty to suggest that both writers are drawing from an existing tract and that this accounts for their similarities. Such a solution has not found many advocates because it is assumed that the similarities are too close to be accounted for in this way and because the situation in both Epistles seems too concrete. Zahn[1] further objected to this idea because it would involve Jude in making references to a lost epistle (i.e. in Jude 17), which was also used by 2 Peter, and this seemed to him a less acceptable solution than to regard the earlier epistle as 2 Peter itself.

The whole idea was worked out particularly by E. I. Robson,[2] who considered that several independent tracts of this nature were circulating (see discussion on the unity of 2 Peter, pp. 174ff.) and that both writers have incorporated one of these in their writings, with editorial adaptations. It is certainly possible that some general writing, dealing with moral perverters and their condemnation, may well have been circulating, and there is nothing intrinsically unlikely in the idea that both Peter and Jude may have drawn from it. But Jude is more difficult in this respect than 2 Peter, since he seems to refer back to earlier *apostolic* teaching, and if the tract postulated were an apostolic tract, it seems incredible that it needed to be incorporated into two other writings to ensure its preservation. Moreover, did Jude take it over as it stood, adding only salutation and doxology? If so, what was the point of it? There seems no satisfactory answer.

e. Conclusion

The problem, like so many other purely literary problems of New Testament criticism, must be left unresolved. It does not affect the authenticity problem of either letter.[3] But before assuming that no definite solution can be found, there are one or two considerations which ought to be given more weight than they are generally ascribed.

---

[1] *INT*, II, p. 266.   [2] *Studies in the Second Epistle of St. Peter* (1915).
[3] Some scholars have maintained the authenticity of 2 Peter, while at the same time admitting the priority of Jude (cf. E. M. B. Green, *2 Peter Reconsidered*, 1961, p. 11). Zahn (*op. cit.*, p. 285) cites Hug, Wiesinger, Weiss and Maier among earlier scholars who adopted this position.

The first is to decide which hypothesis furnishes the more reasonable occasion for the production of both letters. If Peter wrote 2 Peter for a certain constituency and shares the contents of his letter with Jude, suggesting that the latter use the passages about the false teachers in a letter to be sent to his own constituency, where the trouble-makers were not only threatening but were actively operative, all the phenomena would be accounted for. This is Bigg's[1] solution and appears to be, at least, a reasonable probability. The other alternative, if both are genuine, is to suppose that Jude took the initiative and sent his production in a similar way to Peter. But if one or both of these letters were pseudonymous, the wholesale borrowing is less easy to explain. It was not the normal practice of pseudepigraphists to incorporate other material in this way, however indebted the authors were to earlier works, and no very satisfactory reason has yet been given for such a procedure in this case. An admirer of Peter, who published a letter in his master's name, but incorporated into it almost the whole of Jude, looks more like a figment of imagination than a real person, for it is difficult to conceive why he kept closer to Jude than to 1 Peter. If, on the other hand, a pseudo-Jude extracted portions of a pseudo-Petrine Epistle in order to publish the extract under the name of a less auspicious pseudonym, his mysterious purpose becomes all the more obscure.

One concluding comment is necessary. The unity of 2 Peter (see pp. 174 ff.) means that if Peter used Jude he adapted it to fit in with his own style, so that no grammatical seam joining his 'source' to his own additions is now visible.[2] He has, therefore, incorporated his source into his own mind. And this phenomenon would obviously be easier to conceive in the reverse direction, where less 'seaming' was necessary. The vocabulary too tells rather more in favour of 2 Peter's priority, for Jude uses many words not used by Peter and this is readily intelligible if a new mind is brought to bear on Peter's material.[3] Yet the

[1] *Op. cit.*, p. 316. If, as Bigg suggests, Peter sent his letter to Jude because he was alarmed at the spread of the errors, this may account for Jude's change of purpose (verse 3).

[2] Cf. Bigg's careful study of the grammar (*op. cit.*, pp. 224, 310).

[3] It is often overlooked that although the parallels between these Epistles stretch to a wide range of subject-matter, yet verbal agreements are not impressive. If statistics are any guide, the following data may supply some indication. Out of the parallel passages comprising 2 Peter i. 2, 12, ii. 1-4, 6, 10-12, 15-18, iii. 2, 3 and Jude 2, 4-13, 17, 18, the former contain 297 words and the latter 256 words, but they share only 78 in common. This means that if 2 Peter is the borrower he has

Epistles are too short to lead to certainty. The verdict must remain open.

Jude's language is influenced by his familiarity with the Old Testament. Chase[1] even suggested that the writer was steeped in the LXX, but Bigg[2] disagreed with this judgment. Certainly Jude's mind is full of Old Testament allusions although he does not directly cite from it. It is a fair assumption that he was well acquainted with its text, since it served as the Scriptures of the early Church. His style has a vividness and vigour which well expresses his intense abhorrence of the immorality he has observed. At times it has a poetical ring (cf. verses 12, 13). Yet the Epistle is not the work of a literary artist, but of a passionate Christian prophet. Chase[3] has pointed out that the Greek lacks the ruggedness of broken sentences (as in Paul), the power of epigram (as in James) and oratorical persuasiveness (as in Hebrews). The writer's vocabulary is stronger than his power to connect up his separate statements. Chase concludes that 'the writer's Greek is a strong and weighty weapon over which, however, he has not a ready command'. A special feature is the love of threes,[4] which, with the carefully constructed doxology, points to an orderly mind.[5] In the way he ends his Epistle with a doxology Jude shows kinship with Paul in his Roman letter. These two letters are, in fact, the only two with this form of elaborate ending in the New Testament.

changed 70% of Jude's language and added more of his own. Whereas if Jude borrowed from 2 Peter, the percentage of alteration is slightly higher, combined with a reduction in quantity. Clearly there can be no question of direct copying or of editorial adaptation. It is also significant that out of twelve parallel sections, Jude's text is verbally longer than 2 Peter's on five occasions, showing that neither author can be considered more concise than the other. The passages showing the greatest verbal agreement are 2 Pet. iii. 2, 3 and Jude 17, 18 (16 words), the very passages which Zahn maintained prove that Jude was citing 2 Peter. Perhaps at this point the author relied on his 'copy' rather than his memory. The only other passages where extended verbal agreement is found are 2 Pet. ii. 12 and Jude 10, 12a (14 words), the only passages incidentally where the order of the two Epistles slightly diverges (Jude 11 corresponds to 2 Pet. ii. 15, 16).

[1] HDB, II, p. 800.   [2] Op. cit., p. 311.   [3] Ibid., p. 801.
[4] Cf. Moffatt's discussion (ILNT, p. 347) and Mayor's much fuller treatment (op. cit., p. lvi).
[5] Chase (loc. cit.) suggests that Jude may be echoing words which had been repeated so often for liturgical purposes that they had acquired a set form, a not impossible idea.

CH

THE BOOF

I. THE BOOK II

Among many Christians this l
due to its apparent obscurities
thought and expression.¹ Bu
earliest history of the book. N
to be included in the Canon, ;
not belong to the earliest peri
valued the book.²

In many ways this early rec
fact that it was originally ad
Asiatic churches, which would
siderable area. Moreover, its 1
cation that it would readily spi
of Asia.

In all probability it was kno
Fathers, although not all schol;
ing parallels are proof of acqua
Hermas several times refers to
5, 7, iii. 6) which in all probabil:
while i. 1, 3 may be compar
carrying the prophet into a w
parallels there are many comm
most naturally explained if Her
the representation of the Churc
description of fiery locusts pro
idea of the apostles being part of

¹ There has been no neglect of the
special bibliography will show. E
pp. 269–314; TR, n.f., 7 (1935), p
articles between 1920 and 1934, an
diminished.
² For a thorough examination of
The Apocalypse in the Ancient Church

It is not certain that the author was acquainted with Paul's writings, although some scholars[1] have confidently asserted this. Literary dependence is difficult to establish on the basis of isolated phrases, which after all might be no more than language common among Christians. At any rate no certain conclusion can be reached over this.

X. THE VALUE OF THE EPISTLE

Perhaps more than any other New Testament book, the Epistle of Jude is assumed to have little or no permanent value and is, therefore, virtually excluded from the practical, as distinct from the formal, canon of the many sections of the Church. E. F. Scott[2] can find little permanent religious value except in the concluding doxology. Henshaw[3] takes up a similar position, but attaches to it a value for historical purposes. But to deny a permanent spiritual value to the letter is to miss its main message, which is relevant to any period of history. Indeed, Jude illustrates his theme of divine judgment on evil practices by quoting examples from the past. If the examples Jude cites for his own day (Israelites, Sodom and Gomorrah, Cain, Balaam, Korah) had relevance then, his whole Epistle must have relevance now, unless the nature of divine justice and the character of human lasciviousness and kindred evils has changed. As long as men need stern rebukes for their practices, the Epistle of Jude will remain relevant. Its neglect reflects more the superficiality of the generation that neglects it than the irrelevance of its burning message.

CONTENTS

I. GREETING (verses 1, 2)

Jude addresses those who are called, beloved and kept.

II. THE REASON FOR WRITING (verses 3, 4)

He intended to write a doctrinal treatise, but changed his mind because

¹ Chase (op. cit., p. 802) finds verbal parallels in 1 Thes. i. 4, 2 Thes. ii. 13, Rom. i. 7, 1 Cor. i. 2 with the salutation; Col. ii. 7 with verse 20; and Rom. xvi. 25ff., Eph. i. 4, iii. 20, Col. i. 22, 1 Thes. v. 23, 2 Thes. iii. 3, 1 Cor. i. 8 with the doxology. Wand (op. cit., p. 192), who relates the doxology to a stereotyped liturgical form, concludes that the parallels 'are worthless as proofs of literary dependence'.
² Op. cit., p. 226.   ³ Op. cit., pp. 391f.

the faith of the beli
who were immoral

III. REN

Three examples of
certainty of retribut
the fallen angels; ar

IV. TH

1. Their insubordin
the archangel Mich;
They act in fact like
2. Their greed fo
and Korah (verse 11
3. Their unseeml
striking metaphors
4. Their activitie
character of their u
speech. They are at
with their own inte
5. Their rise wa
character should at

V. EXHORT

Jude has said enough
positive instruction.
(2) to pray in the S
mercy; (5) to help w
merciful; and (8) to
much exhortation is

The Epistle conclud
people and who will
presence.

---

of the faithful in white garments with crowns on their heads.[1] Yet it is just possible that both books are drawing from the same milieu of thought and that dependence of one upon the other is not the only explanation.[2] It is perhaps surprising that a work so largely eschatological as the *Shepherd* should not contain more definite parallels, but no strong argument can be made to depend on absence of such reminiscence.

The parallels from *Barnabas* and Ignatius are less convincing. *Barnabas* vii. 9, xxi. 3 may be compared with Revelation i. 7, 13, xxii. 10f. respectively, but the parallels are not sufficient to establish dependence. In Ignatius the most notable parallels are *Ad Eph*. xv. 3 (cf. Rev. xxi. 3), *Ad Philad*. vi. 1 (cf. Rev. iii. 12), but these are not only very slight, but appear to have nothing to do with each other, apart from incidental verbal parallels. Clearly this kind of evidence cannot be pressed.

In the period subsequent to the Apostolic Fathers[3] the position was very different, for there is clear attestation of circulation over a wide area. Justin[4] knew the book and attributed it to the apostle John and considerable weight must be attached to this witness.[5] Melito, who was bishop of Sardis (one of the seven churches addressed), apparently wrote a treatise on the Apocalypse of John (according to Eusebius, *HE*, iv. 26). In the Syrian church it was equally well known and respected, for Theophilus of Antioch cites it.[6] When Irenaeus wrote his book against heresies, he explicitly cited the Apocalypse generally as by 'John, a disciple of the Lord', whom he clearly meant to identify with the apostle [7].

[1] *Vis*. ii. 4, Rev. xii. 1ff.; *Vis*. ix. 6–10, Rev. xiii; *Vis*. iv. 1, 6, Rev. ix. 3; *Vis*. iii. 5, 1, Rev. xxi. 14; *Vis*. viii. 2. 1, 3, Rev. vi. 11. Cf. also ii. 10, iii. 11.

[2] Cf. I. T. Beckwith, *The Apocalypse of John* (1919), p. 337. H. B. Swete (*The Apocalypse of St. John*, 1907, pp. cvi, cvii) does not even mention these parallels with *Hermas*, but R. H. Charles, *A Critical and Exegetical Commentary on the Revelation of St. John* (1920), I, p. xcvii n. 2, considers they may rightly be appealed to.

[3] Whether Papias knew the book or not is uncertain. According to Andreas, Papias not only knew it, but witnessed to its credibility (cf. Charles, *op. cit.*, I, p. xcviii for details), but Eusebius gives no supporting evidence for this (*HE*, iii. 39).

[4] *Dial*. 81. *Cf*. also *Apol*. i. 28 for a clear allusion to Rev. xii. 9, xx. 2.

[5] As this is mentioned by Eusebius (*HE*, iv. 18), who did not himself accept apostolic authorship, its reliability cannot be questioned. It is particularly important, as Justin for a time lived in Ephesus.

[6] Cf. Eusebius, *HE*, iv. 24.

[7] Cf. *Adv. Haer*. iv. 14. 2, 17. 6, 18. 6, 21. 3; v. 28. 2, 34. 2, where he cites as 'John in the Apocalypse', and iv. 20. 11, v. 26. 1 as 'John the disciple of the Lord'. In iii. 1. 1 he uses this description and then adds by way of further identification that he leaned on Jesus' breast, and published the Gospel while residing in Ephesus.

Since he also mentioned ancient copies of the book, it is clear that he knew of its circulation at a much earlier time.[1] It is further significant that the *Letter of the Churches of Vienne and Lyons* cites the Apocalypse in one place as Scripture.[2] The Muratorian Canon shows that no doubts existed over the Apocalypse in the Roman church towards the end of the second century.[3]

Tertullian cited the book frequently and regarded it as by the apostle John.[4] Similarly Clement of Alexandria accepted the apostolic authorship and cited the book as Scripture.[5] The same goes for Origen.[6] There is no need to cite further evidence in support, for there are few books in the New Testament with stronger early attestation. But mention must be made of the beginnings of doubts regarding the book.

Marcion rejected it, but this occasions no surprise in view of his exclusive Pauline preferences. A vigorous attack was made on the book by the Alogi, a group of people so nicknamed by Epiphanius[7] because they rejected John's Logos doctrine. These people not only rejected both Gospel and Apocalypse, but attributed the latter to Cerinthus,[8] as did Gaius of Rome.[9] But this attack was not treated seriously by other Western Christians, for subsequent to this no other Western writer seems to have doubted the book, except Jerome, but even he showed vacillation about his own position.[10]

It was in the East that more sustained criticism was brought to bear upon the book, particularly in the comments of Dionysius, although he still regarded the book as inspired.[11] His main attack was against apostolic authorship, which he questioned on the basis of a comparison with the

[1] Cf. Eusebius, *HE*, v. 8.

[2] Cf. Eusebius, *HE*, v. 1. 58, where the formula ἵνα ἡ γραφή πληρωθῇ is used.

[3] 'Johannes enim in apocalypsi, licet septem ecclesii scribat, tamen omnibus dicit.' Some consider that the *Apocalypse of Peter* was accorded similar status, but the most natural interpretation of the text does not support this, since the further words occur, 'Apoealypsin etiam Johannis et Petri tantum recipimus, quam quidam ex nostris legi in ecclesia nolunt'. At the same time it is evident that some treated them as of equal standing, at least for reading purposes in the church.

[4] *Adv. Marcion.* iii. 14.   [5] *Paed.* ii. 119; *Quis dives*, 42; *Strom.* vi. 106, 107.

[6] *In Johann.* v. 3; cf. Eusebius, *HE*, vi. 25. 9.   [7] *Haer.* li. 3.   [8] *Ibid.*, li. 33.

[9] According to Eusebius, *HE*, iii. 28. 1, 2. Westcott (*On the Canon of the New Testament*, p. 275, n. 2) disputes that Gaius meant the Apocalypse, but rather books written in imitation of it.

[10] Cf. Charles, *op. cit.*, p. cii, for details.

[11] Cf. Eusebius, *HE*, vii. 25. He mentioned that some before his time disputed that the work was John's or that it was a revelation.

Gospel of John, and concluded that both could not have been written by the same author. Most of his arguments have been taken up and developed by modern scholars and will be considered when we deal with the problem of authorship. Eusebius,[1] who records this criticism of Dionysius, is himself inclined to follow it, although it is worth noting that he appears to be uncertain whether to place it among the undisputed books (ὁμολογούμενα) or the spurious books (νόθα). There was doubt about the book at the Council of Laodicea (c. AD 360), for it was not included among the canonical books, while in the Eastern Church it was at first omitted, for the Peshitta Version (early fifth century) does not include it, although the later Philoxenian Version (early sixth century) does. Even so, doubts lingered on in the Syrian church.[2]

It is against this background of early Christian testimony that the internal problems connected with authorship must now be considered.

II. AUTHORSHIP

Although the author calls himself only 'John', it was traditionally assumed that this John was the apostle and consequently it will be most convenient to set out first the various considerations for this opinion, next to consider arguments against it and finally to survey the various alternative suggestions.

a. The case for apostolic authorship

(i) *External testimony.* Much of this evidence has already been given in the previous survey, but it will be as well to summarize here those witnesses who testified not only to the use of the book, but also to its authorship. In the second and early third centuries, the following writers clearly witness to their belief in apostolic authorship: Justin,[3] Irenaeus, Clement, Origen, Tertullian and Hippolytus. Indeed they

---

[1] *HE*, iii. 24. 18, 25. 4.

[2] Junilius mentioned doubts about it (c. AD 551). Much later Bar Hebraeus (died AD 1208) regarded it as by Cerinthus or some other John. In the Armenian church it was not until the twelfth century that the book was regarded as canonical. See Charles, *op. cit.*, I, p. cii, for details.

[3] Some have questioned the reliability of this evidence for *apostolic* authorship because Justin only twice out of forty-seven occurrences of the name John calls him 'the apostle', while on sixteen occasions he is described as 'disciple'. Cf. J. E. Carpenter, *The Johannine Writings* (1927), p. 41. But the descriptions are not mutually exclusive.

assume it without discussion. So strong is this evidence that it is difficult to believe that they all made a mistake in confusing the John of the Apocalypse with John the apostle. The usual treatment of this evidence by those who deny apostolic authorship is to suppose that these early Fathers were unaware of the true origin of the book and, therefore, guessed that the John must have been the well-known son of Zebedee. This has frequently been based on the theory of two Ephesian Johns, who could quite easily be mixed up, or else on the theory that the only John of Ephesus was the Elder who was later mistaken for the apostle. If all this evidence is due to a mistake it would be an extraordinarily widespread case of mistaken identity. It must be conceded that taken as a whole it points very strongly to the probability that the John of the Apocalypse was, in fact, John the apostle.

But the advocates of apostolic authorship must take account of the later questionings, particularly on the part of Dionysius, whose views had so great an influence on Eastern opinion. Since this Alexandrian, with his critical turn of mind, rejected apostolic authorship, his testimony must certainly be set against the earlier witnesses already mentioned. Now Dionysius came to his conclusion on the basis of a comparison with the Gospel of John in which he considered, first the character of the writer, then his thought and style, and finally the linguistic differences between the two writings.

Under the first point, he particularly emphasized the fact that the writer of the Apocalypse mentions his own name, whereas the writer of the Gospel does not. It was while commenting on this that Dionysius mentioned other possible identifications of John—John Mark or a second John in Asia, the latter on the basis of hearsay about two tombs said to be John's at Ephesus. Under the second point, Dionysius, while admitting marks of agreement, nevertheless claimed that the Apocalypse presents a different range of thought from the Gospel, omitting as it does such frequent mention of 'life', 'light', 'truth', 'grace' and 'love'. The concluding objection was based on the claim that the Gospel and Epistle are in correct Greek, whereas the Greek of the Apocalypse is inaccurate. Such a careful and scholarly weighing of the evidence cannot be lightly dismissed, especially as all the grounds to which Dionysius appealed are still the mainstays of the opponents of apostolic authorship. The criticisms will be dealt with later, but it is necessary here to assess their historical weight. Are they to be regarded as more important than the unquestioning pronouncements of earlier Christian writers, in view of the fact that they proceed from an obviously serious and able critic?

Three comments may be made about Dionysius' criticisms.

1. They are not based on ancient testimony, but on subjective judgment. They, therefore, derive no value from the fact that a third-century Christian made them, having, indeed, no more value than a twentieth-century critic's assessment of the differences.

2. Dionysius' statements about the Greek tend to be misleading, for he seems to have overlooked the Semitic flavouring behind the Greek of the Gospel, and his opinion on the inaccuracies of the Apocalypse does not stand up to modern critical judgment, which generally admits that the grammatical deviations are not due to ignorance (see discussion below).

3. Dionysius' alternative suggestion does not inspire confidence, for his 'second John' has remarkably flimsy testimony to his existence. It is strange that such a scholar as Dionysius should give credence to a traveller's tale about the two tombs of John in Ephesus without entertaining the possibility that the rival tomb may be due to some local opportunist, after the pattern of the extraordinary multiplication of relics in subsequent history. In any case, Dionysius' inference that there may have been two Johns is an interpretation of the tale which seems to have been drawn out by his critical dilemma. If John the apostle was not the writer there must have been two Johns at Ephesus and the tale could, therefore, be made to do service in support. In this Dionysius foreshadowed, as a man born before his due time, those modern schools of criticism which have peopled early Christian history with a whole army of unknown writers, whose works attained as great a prominence as their authors obtained obscurity.

(ii) *Evidence from the book itself.* Although the book does not claim to be written by John the apostle and gives no incidental allusions in support of this claim (for these factors as a basis of criticism, see below pp. 262f.) yet there are internal considerations which are difficult to explain unless the author were the apostle John. The first is that he is clearly known by the name John to the seven Asiatic churches and is fully acquainted with the history of each church. He is, moreover, a man of considerable authority, who can expect the churches to receive what he has written as a revelation from God. But this leads to another consideration. His book, although belonging to the genre of apocalypse, nevertheless differs from the Jewish patterns in that it is not ascribed to an honoured ancient name (such as Enoch, Ezra or Baruch). This apocalyptist prophesies in his own name, a departure from tradition which could have arisen only through the conviction that the spirit of prophecy had once again become active and that there was no need for pseudonymous devices.[1] But such a bold departure from precedent demands an author of such stature that all would naturally acknowledge his leadership. This kind of departure is favourable to apostolic authorship, although this argument is not conclusive. The *Apocalypse of Peter* might be cited as an early example of a pseudonymous apocalypse, but there are vital differences between the two situations, as well as a glaring disparity between their contents. The *Apocalypse of Peter* is a poor imitation of the canonical book and seems to have arisen in competition with it. It will not do, therefore, to cite this book in support of the contention that the Apocalypse of John is pseudepigraphic.

The strong impression given in John's Apocalypse of the author's own personality, although perfectly in harmony with apostolic authorship, may, of course, be equally applicable to some such unknown John as John the Elder or John the Prophet (see discussion below). But one feature which seems more in accord with apostolic authorship is the writer's own consciousness of inspiration.[2] In Revelation xxii. 9 the writer is included by the angel among 'your brethren the prophets'. In x. 10 he symbolically eats a scroll received from the hand of an angel and is then commanded to prophesy. In i. 1, 11, 19 he claims to be writing down a divine revelation as he has seen it. In xxii. 6–8 an angel assures him that what he has heard is trustworthy and that the God of the spirits of the prophets has sent His angel to make known what is soon to take place, thus suggesting that the writer was in a direct line of succession with the older prophets. The conclusion of the book, xxii. 18ff., is itself sufficient to show the writer's own awareness of the importance of his own writing. Grim penalties are promised for those who add to or detract from the words of the book. Whereas something

---

[1] Cf. F. C. Burkitt, *Jewish and Christian Apocalypses* (1914), p. 6. 'The Christian Apocalypse of John . . . breathes a new Spirit' (i.e. as compared with the Jewish apocalypses).

[2] C. C. Torrey (*The Apocalypse of John*, 1958, pp. 79f.) goes as far as to say that in calling his book a 'prophecy', the writer was, in fact, making a specific claim for his work to be included in the Jewish Scriptures. This theory rests on Torrey's assumption that at the time of its production no differentiation was made between Jews and Jewish Christians, and that the writer conceives of the Church as made up exclusively of Jews (cf. Rev. vii. 3–8, xxi. 12).

of this kind of thing can be illustrated from pseudepigraphic writings, in which similar statements are made in order to increase the validity of the book, yet in this case there is no attempt to bolster the writer's own authority—the authority is that of Christ Himself.

A fair conclusion from the book's own claims would be to maintain that the evidence is quite inconclusive, but that there does not appear to be anything which makes apostolic authorship impossible[1] (some minor objections and difficulties will be considered below).

(iii) *Comparisons with the Synoptic description of John.* If the apostle John were the author it would be a relevant enquiry to ascertain whether the representation of him which the Apocalypse gives accords with the Synoptic picture. There are, in fact, some remarkable parallels. John and James are called 'Boanerges', 'sons of thunder', and the Apocalypse certainly contains its share of stormy descriptions. These were the two who wanted the Lord to call down fire from heaven upon Samaritan villages, indicative of their own fiery temperament and their aptitude to give vent to righteous anger. Something of this temperament appears in the apocalyptic writer, as is seen in his description of the hostile Jews (ii. 9, iii. 9), of the Beast and all whom he represents, of Rome in the image of the harlot, of the plagues and judgments which will be the expression of the righteous wrath of God. The picture of John, found in the Fourth Gospel, is noticeably presented in a softer light and this will be considered under our next heading. But this concurrence with the Synoptic tradition, as Swete[2] pointed out, 'may well lead us to hesitate before we definitely reject the attribution of the Apocalypse to the Apostle John'.

(iv) *Relationship with other Johannine books.* It is possible here to give only a brief indication of the similarities of thought which have led most scholars to admit a close connection between our book, the Gospel of John and 1, 2 and 3 John, and have convinced many of common authorship. The whole subject is complicated by the problems surrounding the authorship of the other Johannine books, particularly the Gospel. Since the latter problem cannot be discussed here and since the present argument naturally depends on whether apostolic authorship can be maintained for the Gospel, the evidence will have to be presented

---

[1] E. Stauffer (*Theology of the New Testament*, 1955, pp. 40, 41) strongly maintains that this book, together with the Gospel and Epistles, is the work of the apostle John.

[2] *Op. cit.*, p. clxxxii.

for the moment on the assumption that the traditional ascription is correct. If common authorship can be established, it will at least mean that the problem of the authorship of this book cannot be settled apart from the other literature, although, of course, the arguments adduced may suggest different things to different minds.

The similarities are mainly seen in common ideas and common theology, but they also reach to terminology. Both books use the word 'Logos' of Christ, an expression used nowhere in the New Testament apart from the Johannine literature (Jn. i. 1; Rev. xix. 13). Here, as also in the other writings, Christ is described as a Lamb, although a different Greek word is used (ἀρνίον in Revelation, ἀμνός in the Gospel). In both Gospel and Apocalypse, figures of speech involving waters, springs, etc., are used (cf. Jn. iv. 10f., 14, vii. 38; Rev. vii. 17, xxi. 6, xxii. 17). In both the figure of the Shepherd is used of Christ (Jn. x. 1ff., cf. xxi. 16f.; Rev. vii. 17). Both contain the suggestion that a temple is no longer needed for the worship of God (Jn. iv. 21; Rev. xxi. 22) and both contain a symbolical allusion to manna (Jn. vi. 31f.; Rev. ii. 17). A notable similarity is the common variation in the citation from the Old Testament found in John xix. 37 and Revelation i. 7, where Zechariah xii. 10 is cited in a form differing from the LXX.

There is a noticeable love of antithesis in both books. The contrasts between light and darkness, truth and falsehood, the power of God and the power of this world, which are so frequently reiterated in the Gospel, lie behind the whole conception of the Apocalypse. Moreover, several technical terms which are characteristic of the Gospel recur in the Apocalypse, such as ἀληθινός, μαρτυρία, νικᾶν and such a phrase as τηρεῖν τὰς ἐντολάς.

These similarities are, at least, sufficiently striking to point to a common milieu of thought if not to common authorship.[1] They will need, of course, to be set over against the various differences which will be considered later, but our present purpose is to demonstrate what internal support might be found for the remarkably strong early tradition. Before proceeding with this, there is one more line of argument of a rather more subtle kind. It is brought out by Austin Farrer, in his contention that behind all the Johannine literature there is an

---

[1] In his recent book on *Zeit und Geschichte in der Offenbarung des Johannes* (1952), p. 56, M. Rissi asserts that the style and thought peculiarities of the Apocalypse in reference to the end time are very strongly reminiscent of John's Gospel and the Johannine Epistles and this opinion would seem to be justified.

underlying identity of rhythm.[1] Comparing the Gospel and Apocalypse, he finds the same kinds of pattern and thinks this is not the sort of thing that can be invented.[2] This kind of argument is very difficult to assess and its value will clearly depend on the validity of the images which Austin Farrer extracts, but one factor which is undeniably common between the two writings is the symbolical use of the number seven. The Apocalypse is constructed on this pattern and so is the Fourth Gospel (cf. for instance its seven 'signs', its seven-day opening of the Lord's ministry, its seven-day account of the passion story). This characteristic would not be so significant were it not confined in the New Testament to the Johannine writings.[3] While it is not conclusive for common authorship, since it might represent a literary device of a certain school of thought, yet it would certainly seem to point in that direction.

b. The case against apostolic authorship

In spite of the strong tradition and the internal support just considered, many scholars reject apostolic authorship either with or without a rejection of common authorship with the Gospel. The grounds of both positions will be considered together.

(i) *Linguistic differences.* As already mentioned,[4] as early as Dionysius (third century AD) the strange Greek of this book constituted a difficulty. The irregularities are undeniable. The writer seems on the surface to be unacquainted with the elementary laws of concord. He places nominatives in opposition to other cases, irregularly uses participles, constructs broken sentences, adds unnecessary pronouns, mixes up genders, numbers and cases and introduces several unusual constructions.[5] That the grammatical usages of this book differ from those of the Gospel would seem to be demonstrated beyond doubt. But the real problem is whether one mind could adopt these different usages. Many scholars

---

[1] *A Rebirth of Images* (1949), pp. 25ff. Farrer considers that the author was not an apostle but an apostolic man (p. 23).

[2] *Ibid.*, p. 25.

[3] Cf. Lohmeyer's elaborate sevenfold theory for 1 John. See p. 198, note 3 for details.

[4] See p. 255.

[5] For exhaustive examples, cf. R. H. Charles' section on The Grammar of the Apocalypse, *op. cit.*, I, pp. cxvii–clix. Swete (*op. cit.*, pp. cxxii f.) gives more concise examples. ἀπὸ ὁ ὤν (i. 4) obviously transcends normal grammatical accord.

are strongly biased towards dissimilar authorship on this ground alone.[1]
But various explanations of the difference have been offered.

1. Westcott[2] maintained an early date for the Apocalypse and supposed that an interval of some twenty years would suffice for John to
improve his Greek sufficiently to write the better Greek of the Gospel.
But this solution is inadequate, for quite apart from the doubtfulness of
the early dating (see discussion on pp. 278ff), the Greek of the Apocalypse is not simply an inaccurate form of Greek such as a learner
writes before he has mastered the laws of the language, but a mixture
of correct and incorrect forms which appear to be due to choice,[3] not
to accident, carelessness or ignorance. It would probably be going too
far to speak of 'the grammar of ungrammar' as Archbishop Benson[4]
did, although there is no doubt that the author had his own very
definite reasons for using unusual grammatical constructions. Thus
the theory of an improvement period would appear to break
down.

2. Zahn[5] had a different explanation. The apocalyptic language was
influenced profoundly by Old Testament models, especially as the
book claims to be a prophecy. This at once distinguishes it from the
Gospel. The same author, writing now in a prophetic and now in a
didactic style, would naturally use different language. Moreover,
Zahn suggested that since prophecy was given in an ecstatic state, the
form as well as the content was received and the writer, therefore, had
less freedom in polishing up the finished product. There may be truth
in this suggestion, but its force will depend upon the degree to which
the author is assumed to have had a genuine ecstatic experience.[6]

[1] E.g. R. H. Charles, loc. cit.

[2] The Gospel according to St. John (1887), p. lxxxvi.

[3] Thus Charles (op. cit., p. clii) concludes that most of the abnormalities 'are
not instances of mere licence nor yet mere blunders, as they have been most
wrongly described, but are constructions deliberately chosen by our author'.
Charles thought that a good number of them were due to reproduction of Hebrew
idioms.

[4] E. W. Benson, The Apocalypse (1900), pp. 131ff.

[5] INT, III, pp. 432f. W. Hendriksen, More than Conquerors (Tyndale Press
edition, 1962), pp. 12f., and J. B. Phillips, The Book of Revelation (1957), p. xiii,
make similar suggestions.

[6] Some writers, who take the view that the apocalyptist selected and arranged
his material in order to produce a drama of visions, suggest that the style might
unconsciously have been adopted to fit in with a supposed prophetic or ecstatic
experience (cf. Beckwith, op. cit., p. 355).

3. Yet another possibility is the use of amanuenses. There is no certain information about this in the case of either the Gospel or the Apocalypse and the explanation must be regarded as purely suppositional. But it could perhaps have happened that someone better acquainted with Greek was responsible for the final form of the Gospel, while the Apocalypse is the author's own work.[1] This would seem more reasonable than vice versa,[2] and might indeed account for the greater preponderance of Hebraisms in the Apocalypse as compared with the Gospel (see further discussion below). Such an hypothesis would account for both the similarities and the differences, since one dominant personality would be behind the two writings. It should be noted, incidentally, that in spite of linguistic and grammatical differences the Apocalypse has a closer affinity to the Greek of the other Johannine books than to any other New Testament books.

(ii) *Internal indications of non-apostolic authorship.* 1. The most obvious objection which has been brought is the absence of any apostolic claims. Thus Charles[3] was suspicious of apostolic authorship on the grounds that John claims to be a prophet and not an apostle. This objection is based on the assumption that no apostle could write without claiming his apostolic authority. But this is a misconception. Certainly Paul had to assert his apostleship in most of his letters, but that was because he was not one of the twelve and there were people who never allowed him to forget this. But the case would be different with John. He would not need to claim his office among those who never disputed it.[4] It was not on the strength of his apostolic commission, but on the strength of his prophetic inspiration that he gave out his revelation.

2. This non-apostolic claim is further thought to be buttressed by the absence of any allusions to incidents in the Gospels in which John had a part, and by the fact that he does not claim to have known Christ

[1] Beckwith (*op. cit.*, p. 356), who regards this suggestion as plausible, cites the cases of Josephus and Paul. If the Apocalypse was written on Patmos, the use of an amanuensis would be improbable for that book.

[2] W. Michaelis (*op. cit.*, p. 307) strongly criticizes the view of P. Gaechter, who advocated in several studies in the Roman Catholic *Theological Studies*, VIII (1947), IX (1948), X (1949), that an amanuensis was used for the Apocalypse. If the theory were correct the secretary must have been extremely incompetent.

[3] *Op. cit.*, p. xliii.

[4] Cf. F. J. A. Hort, *The Apocalypse of John, I–III* (1908), pp. xxxvi f. It is true that Peter makes clear his apostolic identity in 1 Pet. i. 1, but this is the sole example transmitted to us.

in the flesh.[1] But this kind of argument must be discounted, for it cuts both ways. Had the author brought in numerous personal reminiscences, as the author of the *Apocalypse of Peter* does, he would just as certainly have been charged with overdoing his identification, as this author is now charged with underdoing it. Clearly such a method of argument is too subjective. In any case there are few appropriate places in a book dealing with the glorified Christ for the inclusion of references to His human life.[2]

3. More objective but no more conclusive is the argument based on the references to apostles in Revelation xviii. 20, xxi. 14, which are regarded as retrospective to a period now past.[3] Dealing first with xviii. 20, it should be noted that this argument would exclude the author from the prophets also, but he expressly claims to be among their number (see p. 262 above), and in view of this little weight can be attached to it. In xxi. 14, where the twelve apostolic names are inscribed on the foundation stones of the New Jerusalem, it is supposed that this number could not include the writer. A similar argument is made for the non-apostolic authorship of Ephesians on the basis of Ephesians ii. 20, iii. 5.[4] In any case, if an apostolic author has a message to impart which mentions the apostolate, is he to emend the message out of motives of modesty or append a note indicating his own inclusion in the number?[5] Such a statement could surely be made by an apostolic author without any trace of presumption.

(iii) *Non-Johannine elements.* Many scholars, in spite of admitting that strong similarities exist between the Apocalypse and the other Johannine literature, yet maintain that the differences far outweigh the similarities. The linguistic problem has already been discussed. It remains, however, to consider the theological and other differences.

1. The doctrine of God is said to be mainly concerned with His creatorship and majesty, whereas in the Gospel and First Epistle the

---

[1] So Charles, *op. cit.*, p. xliii. T. S. Kepler (*The Book of Revelation*, 1957, p. 17) argues from this that the author was not an eyewitness.

[2] Cf. Beckwith, *op. cit.*, p. 351.   [3] Cf. Charles, *loc. cit.*

[4] See the present writer's *New Testament Introduction: The Pauline Epistles* (1961), pp. 124ff.

[5] Zahn (*INT*, III, p. 430) cites as a parallel the statement in Lk. xxii. 30 (= Mt. xix. 28) in which our Lord speaks of the apostles occupying twelve thrones, but which could have been reported only by the apostolic hearers themselves. Cf. also F. J. A. Hort, *The Apocalypse of St. John, I–III* (1908), p. xxxvi.

emphasis is on God's love.[1] This is true but the two are not mutually exclusive. The justice of God which is so powerfully stressed in the Apocalypse is but the complement of the love of God so strongly presented in the Gospel. The wrath of God is seen in opposition not so much to individuals as to the principles of evil behind them. God is doing battle with the personification of wickedness. He can do no other than hate that wickedness and pour forth His judgment upon it. If it were not so vividly expressed in the Apocalypse it would have to be deduced from His character as holy love. But in any case it is not absent from other parts of the New Testament where the love of God is also stressed (cf. Rom. ii. 4–9; Mt. xxii. 7, 12f., xxiv. 28, 30, xxv. 12; Jn. iii. 36, ix. 39; 1 Pet. iv. 17f.).

2. The Christology of the Apocalypse and the Gospel may at first seem to be different, since Christ is portrayed in the Apocalypse as the all-conquering Messiah who rules nations with a rod of iron, whereas in the Gospel He is the Revealer and Renewer. But again there is no contradiction, for in a book whose theme is mainly judgment, this is just the kind of picture one would expect. At the same time, the Christ of the Apocalypse is Redeemer of His people as Lamb of God (i. 5, v. 9, vii. 14, xii. 11, xiv. 4) and as the Fount of Life for those who thirst (xxi. 6, xxii. 17). It has already been pointed out that the Logos conception occurs in both books, but some scholars find a difference of usage.[2] It is true that in the Gospel the idea is absolute whereas in the Apocalypse the descriptive τοῦ θεοῦ is added, but no serious objection can be based on such a difference.

3. The doctrine of the Spirit similarly shows no essential difference in spite of the fact that in Revelation i. 4 mention is made of the seven spirits. Admittedly this does not occur in the Gospel, but it is not alien to the Paraclete concept, if the symbolism is understood as depicting perfection.[3] The spirit addresses the messages to the churches (ii, iii), speaks from heaven (xiv. 13) and issues the concluding invitation (xxii.

---

[1] Cf. Moffatt, ILNT, p. 502.

[2] So Lohmeyer, Die Offenbarung des Johannes[2] (1953), pp. 202, 203. Cf. also Moffatt, loc. cit.

[3] R. H. Charles (op. cit., I, p. cxiv) considered the conception to be 'grotesque' and therefore assigned it to an editor. But his reason for doing so is purely arbitrary. When the same phrase occurs in iii. 1 it becomes a 'redactional addition' instead of a 'manifest interpolation' (p. 78). Cf. the same phrase in iv. 5, v. 6. It may have arisen, as Swete suggests (op. cit., p. 6), because the Spirit is described as operating in seven churches.

17). It cannot be maintained that the writer of the Gospel could not have expressed the Spirit's activity in this form, although it is perhaps surprising that no mention is made of His regenerating activity. But again the different emphasis in the book might explain this.

4. Eschatology is another doctrine on which differences have been noted, since the Gospel is more interested in the present age than the future. Much of this difficulty has been occasioned by the assumption that the author of the Gospel has a wholly spiritual view of the *parousia* contrasted with the Synoptic view, which is more in harmony with the Apocalypse. The modern notion of realized eschatology for the Gospel[1] tends to obscure the traditional eschatology which also occurs in the Gospel (e.g. v. 25ff. and the references to the 'last hour'), although without the traditional imagery found in the Synoptists. Since the Apocalypse has an eschatological theme it is not surprising that a different emphasis is found, but only a one-sided interpretation of the Johannine eschatology could definitely exclude the possibility that Gospel and Apocalypse were both written by the same author.

(iv) *Historical difficulties.* In recent years much discussion has surrounded the problem of the date of the apostle's death. There is evidence for two conflicting traditions. The strongest tradition maintained that John lived to a ripe old age at Ephesus, while a challenging tradition considered that he was martyred at the same time as James. Support for an early death, however, is none too reliable. Nevertheless, since many scholars prefer this tradition to the other, which is disposed of as a mistake on the part of Irenaeus, it naturally cannot be left out of any discussion on the authorship of the Apocalypse. If the apostle died at the same time as James, he is at once ruled out as author of either Gospel or Apocalypse, no matter how strong other evidence against this might be. If, on the other hand, as even the alternative tradition allows, he died as a martyr, although not at the same time as James, the apostolic authorship is not at once excluded since no time limit is set. Yet it may be said that the tradition of an early death is by no means so certain as to override the strong tradition to the contrary.[2]

The whole matter is, of course, bound up with the further problem of the two Johns at Ephesus (see p. 255f.), for if it be decided that

[1] Cf. C. H. Dodd, *The Apostolic Preaching and its Developments*[2] (1944), pp. 65ff.
[2] W. Bousset (*Die Offenbarung Johannis*,[2] 1906, pp. 35, 36) considered that the evidence for John's early death was so strong that he did not discuss apostolic authorship, but concluded for John the Elder.

there was only one and that he was not the apostle, the exile on Patmos must *ipso facto* be some other John. On the other hand, if there were two Johns at Ephesus, the tradition of the apostle's early death must clearly be wrong.

A further difficulty has been raised against apostolic authorship on the grounds that if the apostle were still alive towards the close of the first century he would have been too old to produce such literature and especially the Apocalypse with its virile imaginativeness.[1] Advocates of an early date for the Apocalypse naturally find less difficulty here.[2] But the difficulty would remain for the Gospel if written by the same author. The criticism is not without point, but requires considerable caution since we cannot be certain of John's age when he was first called to be an apostle, neither do we know at what age his mental capacities would be incapable of producing literature. If an 'uninspired' George Bernard Shaw could continue writing until well into his nineties, who can restrict the capabilities of an 'inspired' apostle?

To sum up the discussion on apostolic authorship, it is not easy, indeed not possible, to come to any definite conclusion. Whether we are biased one way or the other will depend very largely on the weight given to the early tradition, and the convincing character of any alternative. The various other suggestions will, therefore, next be listed in order to set the whole evidence in its true light. Suffice it to say that no evidence makes the traditional apostolic ascription impossible.

c. Alternative theories

(i) *John the Elder*. Papias' statement regarding the 'two' Johns has been discussed elsewhere (p. 209, n. 1) and the opinion expressed that it is far from conclusive that a John the Elder ever lived. But since many scholars are inclined to put faith in his existence, it is well to consider what implications this has for the identification of the author of the Apocalypse. Advocates of the theory that John the Elder wrote the Apocalypse appeal at once to Dionysius' statement about a second John at Ephesus. It is to be observed that Dionysius does not cite Papias for this, but a traveller's report (φασίν), and his suggestion about a second John is no more than tentative ("Ἄλλον δέ τινα οἶμαι τῶν 'Ασία γενομένων). Nevertheless supposing his conjecture was correct, does this solve the problem? Presumably Dionysius ascribed the Gospel to one John and the Apocalypse to the other. But modern scholars ascribe the Gospel and

---

[1] Cf. Hort, *op. cit.*, p. xl.   [2] Cf. A. Farrer, *op. cit.*, p. 23.

Epistles to the Elder, in which case the only possibilities are to ascribe the Apocalypse to the apostle, if identity of authorship is denied, or to the Elder, if identity is accepted or to a third John if apostolic as well as identical authorship is rejected.[1]

Leaving aside the problem of the Gospel, which cannot be discussed here, we must decide whether it is conceivable that John the Elder could have been author of this book. At first sight there seems nothing against it, but, since our knowledge of the shadowy Elder is nil, this is not surprising. The main problem it raises concerns the consciousness of the author. If he used his own name 'John' he must have assumed that all his readers would at once have known who he was. But he must also have known that, if the apostle was also resident at Ephesus, many would confuse the two and the writer would then be culpable for not making his own identity clearer. It is difficult to see how confusion of the two could have become so widespread, and indeed unchallenged, so soon after its publication. The Elder theory seems tenable only on the supposition that John the apostle had never lived at Ephesus, and that from the early second century the whole Church mistakenly assumed that he had.

(ii) *John the prophet*. Charles[2] was obliged to invent this third John because he had attributed the other Johannine books to the Elder. Since we know no more, if as much, about John the Prophet than we do about John the Elder it is difficult to assess this proposition. It really says no more than what the book itself claims, i.e. that the author was called John and that he prophesied. This is really a confession of defeat. And yet does any closer identification really matter? Different minds will have different answers, but this is not quite in the same category as an anonymous book like the Epistle to the Hebrews. The undefined 'John' would naturally be mistaken for the apostle, but would the churches of Asia really be able to distinguish between John the Prophet and John the Elder? Was the Asiatic church overrun with brilliant Christians by the name of John, who would only need to announce their name for the Christians to know which was meant? The position must have been very complicated and seems hardly credible.

In similar vein, with similar difficulties, is the postulation of an 'uni-

---

[1] Bousset (*op. cit.*, p. 49) regarded the Elder as being the author of the Apocalypse and 2 and 3 John and the witness behind the Fourth Gospel.

[2] *Op. cit.*, p. xliii.

dentified John',[1] or an inspired apostolic man,[2] for in either case he must have intended to gain acceptance under an apostolic name (even if he shared the same name) or else have achieved this end without intending it.

(iii) *An intentional pseudonym.* The improbability of this view has already been mentioned, and it is included here only for the sake of completeness.[3] A writer could never have palmed off his work as apostolic after the assumed writer was known to be dead without some attempt to explain why the book had not appeared before, a device common among pseudepigraphists. This procedure certainly happened at a later date, but was always detected and was never granted the authority given to this book. Undoubtedly pseudonymity here raises far more problems than it solves.[4]

(iv) *John Mark.* There would be no need to mention this proposition had it not been referred to by Dionysius,[5] although he does not seem to have been impressed by it. Indeed, he rejected it on historical grounds because Mark did not accompany Paul to Asia. But on linguistic grounds it has nothing to commend it, while Mark gives no indication in his Gospel of possessing the prophetical qualities of the author of the Apocalypse.[6]

d. Conclusion

To extract a conclusive or even satisfactory result from all this mass of conjecture seems impossible. The most certain line of evidence is the early tradition and there would seem to be some excuse for taking refuge in this for want of a better alternative. At least, if this is the true solution it at once explains the rise of the tradition, which none of the

[1] Cf. e.g. T. Henshaw, *op. cit.*, p. 417.

[2] So A. Farrer, *op. cit.*, p. 23.

[3] The earlier disputants of apostolic authorship resorted to this theory. Beckwith (*op. cit.*, p. 345) cites Semler, Volkmar, Scholtau and more recently Weizsäcker, Wernle, Bacon.

[4] Practically all modern scholars reject this solution. Cf. R. H. Charles, *op. cit.*, II, pp. 43ff.; F. Torm, *Die Psychologie der Pseudonymität im Hinblick auf die Literatur des Urchristeniums* (1932), p. 29.

[5] It has been held in modern times by Hitzig and in part by Spitta (cf. Zahn, *INT*, III, p. 434, n. 2).

[6] Cf. the criticisms of Zahn, *op. cit.*, III, pp. 428, 429, and Swete, *op. cit.*, p. clxxvi.

others satisfactorily does.[1] But many prefer to leave the authorship an open question.[2]

III. DATE

An examination of the problem of the date of this writing raises many problems which are by no means easy to solve, and several different hypotheses have been proposed in an effort to provide a satisfactory solution. Although the main purpose of the book may be considered apart from the question of date, this question is not unimportant in the quest to ascertain the precise historical background, nor is it entirely irrelevant for arriving at a satisfactory interpretation of the book. The most widely held view is that this Apocalypse was written during the reign of Domitian, more precisely towards the end of that reign, i.e. AD 90–95, and reasons for this dating will first be given. After this alternative theories will be considered.

a. Arguments in favour of a Domitianic date

(i) *Emperor worship.* Even a casual reading of the Apocalypse is sufficient to impress the reader that the background is one of conflict between the ruling powers and the Christian Church (see further discussion on p. 282). The great representative of the opposing party, the Roman Empire, is personified in the figure of a Beast, who is evidently meant to represent the reigning emperor. The main focus of attention wherever this Beast is mentioned is his demand for universal worship (cf. xiii. 4, 15f., xiv. 9–11, xv. 2, xvi. 2, xix. 20, xx. 4) and his insistence that all should bear his 'mark'. These references can be interpreted only by reference to the imperial cult. But does this in itself help us to place the background of the Apocalypse in its right place in the development of this cult? This is clearly an important question in relation to the date, for if it points to a fairly well defined period it will greatly assist in answering other problems.

That the idea of emperor worship arose even before the rise of Christianity cannot be disputed. Julius Caesar claimed divine honours

---

[1] A. Schlatter (*Die Briefe und die Offenbarung des Johannes*, 1950, p. 127), who accepted apostolic authorship for all the Johannine writings, pointed out that no other apostle has given so complete a presentation—faith in the Gospel, love in the Epistles, hope in the Apocalypse. The same idea was emphasized much earlier by C. E. Luthardt, *Die Lehre von den Letzten Dingen*[2] (1870), p. 167.

[2] Cf. Boismard in Robert-Feuillet's *Introduction à la Bible*, II, p. 741.

and, although Augustus was not so forward in encouraging this, there
were temples in his and Rome's honour in some of the provinces.
Caligula made a demand for the universal worship of his statue, although whether any effort was made to enforce this is very dubious.
No evidence of it has survived, but the order for Caligula's statue to
be placed in the temple of Jerusalem is some indication of his own mad
schemes in this direction. What would have happened had he lived to
insist on the carrying out of his project cannot be foreseen. But at this
period in the development of the cult there is nothing to correspond
with the situation reflected in the Apocalypse. It is the period from
Nero to Domitian which saw the rapid development of emperor
worship into an official policy of imperial politics. Not all the inter-
vening emperors took their divine honours seriously. Vespasian was
an example of this, but Domitian determined not only to treat it
seriously, but to enforce it. What is not certain is the method he adopted
to deal with any who were disinclined to offer him homage. No knowledge of any rescript or edict has survived from the first century which
enforced emperor worship. The earliest official pronouncement belongs to the reign of Trajan.

If there are lacking official records of the enforcement of emperor
worship, there is ample evidence to show that the attitude of the State
in this matter was bound sooner or later to clash with the Christian
Church, and this much is abundantly clear from the Apocalypse. The
issue has become a challenge between homage to Christ and homage
to Caesar. But does this represent a development which could not
have been reached before the time of Domitian? Many scholars[1]
believe that it does, although there are some who have maintained
that the book contains no details which could not have obtained
during the time of Nero (see discussion below).

Before passing on to the closely linked problem of the persecution
background, it is well to recognize that, although the emperor worship presupposed in the Apocalypse would well suit the later period
of Domitian's reign, there is no conclusive evidence that it could not

---

[1] So Charles, *op. cit.*, p. xciv. 'There is no evidence of any kind to prove that
the conflict between Christianity and the imperial cult had reached the pitch of
antagonism that is presupposed in the Apocalypse of John before the closing years
of Domitian's reign.' Cf. similarly, Moffatt, *ILNT*, p. 504; I. T. Beckwith, *op.
cit.*, p. 201; H. B. Swete, *op. cit.*, pp. civ, cv, all of whom consider the evidence to
be quite conclusive on this point.

have occurred earlier. In other words the evidence based on emperor worship would not of itself be enough to close the discussion on the date.

(ii) *Persecutions*. Of greater importance is the identification of the persecution which has either just commenced or is immediately impending, for the book itself furnishes more data for deciding this problem. It is well to cite these data first and then to discuss their significance against the known historical background of imperial persecutions.

1. The writer himself appears to have been in exile on the island of Patmos, because of his Christian profession (i. 9). But it is not quite certain that he is still there.[1] And in any case there is no definite reference to an imperial action which resulted in this exile. It might quite easily have been a local proconsular decision.

2. In the church at Pergamum a Christian named Antipas had been killed, presumably some time previous to the writing of the letter addressed to that church (ii. 13). This would appear to be an isolated instance of persecution, for there is no hint of a general outbreak in this district.

3. The church at Smyrna is warned of imminent imprisonments (ii. 10), which suggests a rather more widespread and organized threat. There is a possibility of the death penalty, for the Christians are urged to be faithful unto death.[2]

4. Some have already suffered martyrdom according to vi. 9, for the writer sees their souls under the altar and wants to know how long they must wait to be avenged. But the description here is notably general, embracing 'those who had been slain for the Word of God and for the witness they had borne', which is wide enough to include the Old Testament martyrs as well as Christian martyrs. All that can certainly be deduced from this is that at some previous time certain people had been martyred for the sake of their testimony. It tells us nothing about how many were involved, nor how widespread was the persecution, nor indeed whether these martyrs belonged to the same district as the readers. In all probability they did not. The statement may, in fact, be a reference to those who were victims of Nero's infamous outrage against the Christians in Rome, which would not

[1] Cf. Michaelis, *op. cit.*, p. 317.
[2] Michaelis (*loc. cit.*) supposes that the instigators here are Jews and not the imperial officials.

greatly assist us in arriving at a date for the Apocalypse, apart from its requiring a date subsequent to that event.

5. In the message to the church in Philadelphia there is a reference to 'the hour of trial which is coming on the whole world, to try those who dwell upon the earth' (iii. 10), which would certainly seem to refer to more than local actions against the Christians. Here we seem to be in the presence of a threat which could only come from the emperor himself, with power of enforcement through the whole world. At the same time this world-wide 'trial' may be intended in an eschatological sense of the troublous time expected immediately before the *parousia*,[1] in view of the statement of iii. 11. The trial has apparently not yet begun.[2]

6. In certain passages regarding the great harlot (i.e. Rome) there are statements about her being drunk with the blood of the saints (xvii. 6, xviii. 24, xix. 2; cf. also xvi. 6, xx. 4), which suggests a period of widespread persecution, although since these references occur in visions it is not possible to be certain that such persecutions had actually begun. On the other hand fierce persecution was obviously to be anticipated in the not too distant future.

The next question which arises is whether this persecution situation fits best into the Domitianic period. The majority of scholars would answer in the affirmative. But whatever the final decision on this matter may be, the evidence is not as conclusive as many suppose. As pointed out in discussing 1 Peter (pp. 105f), data about the Domitianic persecutions tend to be elusive. This emperor put to death his relative Flavius Clemens and banished his wife on a charge of sacrilege (ἀθεότης),[3] which strongly suggests that it was on the basis of their Christianity, since the wife, Domitilla, is known from inscriptions to have been a Christian. In addition to this, Clement of Rome contains a vague reference to 'sudden and repeated misfortunes and calamities',[4] which had recently befallen the church in Rome. Since Clement's Epistle is generally thought to belong to the time of Domitian this

---

[1] Cf. Swete, *op. cit.*, p. 56.

[2] Michaelis (*op. cit.*, p. 316) considers that the references in the letters to the churches do not reflect a position in which the State is definitely the persecutor, and a Domitianic date is, therefore, too late. Charles (*op. cit.*, p. xciv) agreed with this type of approach, but considered that these references are to material earlier than the main book and that they have been re-edited.

[3] According to Dio Cassius, *Hist. Rom.* lxvii. 14.

[4] *Clement 1*, i (K. Lake's translation, *The Apostolic Fathers*, 1912, p. 9).

could refer to the outbreak of persecution. But the identification is by
no means certain for there are few data in the letter to enable the date
to be fixed without dispute. Several later Christian writers speak of a
Domitianic persecution of Christians, as for instance Eusebius[1] and
Sulpicius Severus.[2] Two writers, Tertullian[3] and Hegesippus (according to Eusebius[4]) mention that Domitian stopped the persecution.
One writer only, Orosius, who tends to make extravagant statements
in other respects, mentions widespread persecutions.[5] It would seem a
fair conclusion from this evidence that Domitian persecuted some
Roman Christians, but that no definite evidence of any persecution
outside Rome is forthcoming. But this does not necessarily mean that
it did not happen, and if on other grounds the Apocalypse must be
dated during this period, the evidence of the book itself would be
sufficient to show that persecution had in fact spread to Asia. The
strength of the Caesar-cult in Asia and the fact that a new Caesar-
temple was erected in Ephesus during Domitian's reign[6] would make
some persecution there in his time highly probable.[7]

(iii) *The background of the Nero myth.* Many scholars assume that behind
Revelation xiii and xvii lies the widely believed myth that Nero would
return to Rome and, since this form of the myth did not develop until
after about AD 80, it is supposed that the book must have been issued
after this. According to Charles[8] the development shows a modification of the earlier form of the myth, in which it was thought that Nero
was not really dead but had escaped to the East (a belief which by this
time had had to be abandoned) and this idea was combined with current theories about Belial and Antichrist. But does the Apocalypse itself really demand this? The Beast with the mortal wound which has
now been healed (xiii. 3) may be illustrated by the current Nero myth,
but in its later forms that myth involved Nero returning at the head
of a Parthian army to recapture his lost throne,[9] with the consequent
destruction of Rome. Yet there is no reference to Parthians, either in
chapter xiii or xvii. The Beast represents the embodiment of evil, a

[1] *HE*, iii. 18. 4.   [2] *Chronicle*, ii. 31.   [3] *Apology*, v.   [4] *HE*, iii. 20.
[5] Cf. Hort, *op. cit.*, p. xxiv, for the quotation.
[6] Cf. Feine-Behm, *op. cit.*, p. 286.
[7] Moffatt (*ILNT*, p. 504), who adhered to the Domitianic date, admitted
the paucity of evidence for a general Asiatic persecution, but suggested that the
few drops of rain (i.e. the few cases of hardship and persecution) warned of an
approaching storm.
[8] *Op. cit.*, I, p. xcvi.   [9] *Ibid.*, II, p. 81.

conception quite comprehensible without recourse to a Nero myth, which, according to Tacitus, had become a 'joke' (*ludibrium*) by Domitian's time.[1] Moreover, since the Apocalypse represents the Beast as returning from the dead, this could only refer to Nero after a period when he might conclusively be considered dead (i.e. after AD 100, in which year Nero would have been 63 years old had he lived).[2] If then an allusion to the Nero myth is still maintained as underlying the language of Revelation xiii and xvii, it must be regarded as extremely inconclusive for a Domitianic date. The most that can be said is that it may possibly point to this.[3] But if, on the other hand, the Nero-myth background is denied, the allusions to the returning 'king' will furnish no information for purposes of dating.[4]

(iv) *The condition of the Asiatic churches.* Here we are on firmer ground, for the letters to the seven churches (chapters ii and iii) supply certain positive indications of internal conditions. In some of the churches there has been a marked deterioration (e.g. Ephesus, Sardis, Laodicea). It is significant that this has happened in the two churches known to be Pauline and it is thought, therefore, to indicate a considerable interval since the foundation of the Church.[5] All the letters, in fact, give the impression that the churches have a history behind them. But it is difficult to assess the length of time needed for deterioration to set in. All depends on the spiritual standard of the original church. That all the apostolic churches were not equal in this respect is abundantly clear from the Pauline Epistles themselves. Spiritual decline and heretical ideas take little time to develop in fertile soil, and some caution is necessary before concluding for a later date on these grounds.[6]

But Charles' argument[7] regarding the church of Smyrna would seem

[1] *Hist.* i. 2; cf. C. C. Torrey, *op. cit.*, p. 73.

[2] Cf. Zahn, *INT*, III, p. 444. Cf. also C. Clemen, *ZNTW*, 2 (1903), pp. 109f., 11 (1910), pp. 204f.

[3] Swete comments, 'The legend has been used by St. John to represent the revival of Nero's persecuting policy by Domitian "portio Neronis de crudelitate"' (*Tert. Apol.* v) (*op. cit.*, pp. 163, 164).

[4] It is significant that Augustine was the first Christian writer to speak of Nero returning from the dead (*Civ. Dei*, xx. 19. 3), but does not connect this with the Apocalypse.

[5] A. Ramsay (*The Revelation and the Johannine Epistles*, 1910, p. 5) considered the omission of any mention of Paul in the Ephesian letter to require an interval of a full generation.

[6] Feine-Behm, *op. cit.*, p. 287, are very cautious on this point.

[7] *Op. cit.*, I, p. xciv; followed also by Moffatt, *ILNT*, p. 507.

to have considerable weight, for he maintains that this church did not
exist until after AD 60–64. His evidence for this is drawn from a statement in Polycarp's letter to the Philippians,[1] in which he implies that
the Smyrnaeans[2] had not known the Lord when Paul wrote to the
Philippians. From this Charles concludes that the letter to this church
could hardly have been written earlier than AD 75. But Torrey[3] challenges this interpretation of Polycarp's statement, maintaining that
what Polycarp means is that Paul boasted about the Philippians among
the earliest established churches of Asia and Europe, but that this could
not have included Smyrna. In other words, Smyrna had not such a long
history as Philippi. But that does not require a post-Pauline date,
although it might suggest it.

Another factor which might be more conclusive is the reference to
the Nicolaitans, who have been active both in the church at Ephesus
(ii. 6) and in the church at Pergamum (ii. 15). They are introduced in
such a way as to suggest an established and well-known sect which
needed only to be referred to by name. Although mention is made of
such a sect by Irenaeus, Hippolytus, Tertullian, Clement of Alexandria
and others, little is known of its tenets or of its origin. In the time of
Irenaeus its adherents were supposed to have been followers of Nico-
laus, mentioned in Acts vi. 5, who was assumed to have turned heretical. If this tradition is correct (and the fact that it is most unusual for
any Christian mentioned in the New Testament to be later associated
in tradition with heresy suggests that it may be true), the formation of
the sect must have been in the early period. Yet it is still impossible to
say how soon it affected the church at Ephesus. Perhaps Paul saw the
danger threatening at the time of his address to the Ephesian elders (Acts
xx. 29, 30).

In spite of the fact that each of the grounds which has been examined
from the internal conditions of the churches could be disputed as a
pointer to a Domitianic date, it must be admitted that a date towards
the close of the century would allow more time for the conditions to
develop. The Lord's strong revulsion at the state of the Laodicean

[1] *Ad Phil.* xi. 3. 'But I have neither perceived nor heard any such thing among
you, among whom the blessed Paul laboured, who are praised in the beginning
of his Epistle. For concerning you he boasts in all the churches who then alone
had known the Lord, for we had not yet known him' (Lake, *op. cit.*, p. 297).

[2] Polycarp was bishop of Smyrna, and the 'we' presumably means his church.

[3] *Op. cit.*, pp. 78f.

church would certainly become more intelligible after a considerable interval.

(v) *Arguments deduced from the relationship of the Apocalypse to other New Testament writings.* It is probable that our author used the Gospel of Matthew and perhaps also the Gospel of Luke.[1] If the widely held dating of these books is correct (i.e. AD 80–85), the Apocalypse would need to be dated subsequent to this, which would support a Domitianic date. But since this dating of the Gospels is conjectural and may very well be wrong it would be precarious to base any argument upon it. Moreover, the parallels may be drawn from oral tradition or even first-hand acquaintance where the teaching of our Lord is paralleled.

(vi) *The traditional dating of the book.* Undoubtedly a strong argument in favour of a Domitianic date is the fact that the earliest and the weightiest external witnesses attest it. Irenaeus[2] is quite specific that the Apocalypse 'was seen no such long time ago, but almost in our own generation, at the end of the reign of Domitian'. Since Irenaeus' own

---

[1] Charles (*op. cit.*, I, p. lxxxiii) gives a detailed list of parallels, the most notable of which are as follows. Parallels with Matthew: Rev. i. 3, Mt. xxvi. 18; Rev. i. 7, Mt. xxiv. 30; Rev. i. 16, Mt. xvii. 2; Rev. iii. 2, xvi. 15, Mt. xxiv. 42, 43; Rev. iii. 5, Mt. x. 32 (Lk. xii. 8); Rev. vi. 4, Mt. x. 34; Rev. vi. 12, 13, Mt. xxiv. 29 (cf. also Mk. xiii. 24, 25, Lk. xxi. 25); Rev. xi. 15, Mt. iv. 8; Rev. xiii. 11, Mt. vii. 15; Rev. xvii. 15, Mt. xx. 16, xxii. 14; Rev. xix. 7, Mt. v. 12; Rev. xxi. 10, cf. Mt. iv. 8. The Lukan parallels are less numerous but the following are worth noting: Rev. i. 3, Lk. xi. 28; Rev. v. 5, Lk. vii. 13, viii. 52; Rev. vi. 10, Lk. xviii. 7, 8; Rev. vi. 15, 16, Lk. xxiii. 30; Rev. vi. 17, Lk. xxi. 36; Rev. xi. 3, 6, Lk. iv. 25; Rev. xii. 9, Lk. x. 18; Rev. xiv. 4, Lk. ix. 57; Rev. xviii. 24, Lk. xi. 50. Many of these parallels are no more than verbal echoes and may not indicate literary dependence. They may do no more than indicate the author's acquaintance with the oral tradition.

E. F. Scott (*The Book of Revelation*,[4] 1941, p. 30) maintained that the author was so familiar with the apocalyptic section of the Synoptic Gospels that he used it as a framework for his own prophecy. Scott suggested that he found it in Mark's Gospel. But this supposition is dubious, although it would not be surprising if our Lord's apocalyptic teaching had deeply influenced the author's mind. But there is no evidence that he *consciously* modelled his own book on it.

J. Oman (*The Book of Revelation*, 1923, p. 29) raised the question whether John would have possessed any MSS of other New Testament books in exile and thought that any parallels with other books would more likely be due to memory than to literary dependence.

[2] *Adv. Haer.* v. 30. 3. F. H. Chase (*JTS*, VIII, 1906, pp. 431–435) disputed that Irenaeus was referring to the Apocalypse. He argued that it was John and not his writing that 'was seen'.

connection with Asia Minor and acquaintance with Polycarp in his youth would give him a good opportunity to receive reliable opinion on this matter, this evidence must be treated seriously. Yet it is, of course, possible that Irenaeus made a mistake.[1] Later tradition mostly supports Irenaeus' testimony,[2] although there is some evidence for the time of Nero[3] and even one witness for the time of Claudius,[4] but this was no doubt an error for Nero Claudius. The testimony of this external evidence is so strong that even Hort,[5] an advocate for a Neronian date, concluded, 'If external evidence alone could decide, there would be a clear preponderance for Domitian.' On the principle that a strong tradition must be allowed to stand unless internal evidence makes it impossible, which is certainly not true in this case, the Domitianic dating must have the decision in its favour.[6] But some brief indication of the arguments for an earlier date must be given in order to stress the need for caution against being too dogmatic.[7]

[1] Hort (op. cit., p. xxxii), who preferred a Neronian date for the Apocalypse, thought that Irenaeus' statement may have been a mere guess.

[2] For details, cf. Swete, op. cit., p. xcix; or Charles, op. cit., I, p. xciii.

[3] So the Syriac Apocalypse and the apocryphal Acts of John.

[4] Epiphanius, Haer. li. 12. 233 (probably based on Hippolytus).   [5] Op. cit., p. xx.

[6] An attempt to reconcile the tradition with an early date was made by H. B. Workman, Persecution in the Early Church (1906), p. 46 n. 3. He suggested that the letters were sent separately in Nero's time, but the entire work was not published until Domitian's reign. He also held to composite sources (p. 358).

[7] No reference has been made to arguments for a late date based on three minor points: (a) the reference to the 'Lord's day' (i. 10); (b) the apparent liturgical purpose of the book (cf. i. 3); and (c) the supposition that the angels of the churches represent monarchical bishops. The third point is definitely open to challenge, while the other two indicate nothing regarding dating. How early the first day of the week was called the Lord's Day we do not know, neither do we know enough about early Christian liturgical practice to place i. 3 in its true perspective (if indeed it is to be understood liturgically!). Cf. the comments of Michaelis, op. cit., p. 317; and Feine-Behm, op. cit., pp. 287, 288.

Another incidental corroboration of a Domitianic date is suggested by the reference in Rev. vi. 6 being understood as an allusion to Domitian's edict in AD 92 for the regulation of crops (cf. Moffatt, ILNT, p. 507, and Exp., VII, vi, 1908, pp. 359–369). Torrey (op. cit., p. 79) rejects this theory, originally proposed by Reinach in 1901, while Michaelis (loc. cit.) calls it 'quite uncertain' (ganz unsicher).

It has not been thought necessary in the discussions on date to comment on the critical analytical views of such scholars as Völter, who maintained a date as late as AD 140 for the addition of chapters i–iii, which, he considered, combated Cerinthianism (Das Problem der Apocalypse, 1893, pp. 375ff.). But see p. 287 for a review of compilation theories.

b. Arguments in favour of a Neronian date

(i) *The identification of the sixth king of Rev. xvii. 10.* In view of the mention of the seven hills in verse 9 there can be little doubt that the primary reference[1] in verse 10 is to the sequence of Roman emperors. Since five have fallen, the sixth must be the reigning emperor. Now the identification will depend on whether calculations commence with Julius Caesar or Augustus. The latter is the more natural since he was the first to be proclaimed emperor, and he would have had particular significance, in view of the fact that it was during his reign that the Christian Church commenced. In this case, Nero was the fifth emperor and it may be supposed, therefore, that the Apocalypse belongs to the time of his death and the period immediately following. There is some doubt about the sixth, but advocates of the earliest date would suppose that he was Galba.[2] It may at least be said in favour of this method of calculation that it avoids the necessity for ignoring altogether the three minor claimants for the throne in the year following Nero's death, viz. Galba, Otho and Vitellius, in order to make the sixth king Vespasian. But it may reasonably be objected that these three emperors would have no importance for the provincials, who would naturally enumerate only the settled heads.[3] At the same time, if John is actually writing before the collapse of Galba, the position would be different, but the fatal objection is that the eighth king cannot be identified with Vitellius, who reigned for only a very short time. Some advocates of the Domitianic date, on the other hand, make the sixth king to be Vespasian and the eighth Domitian, but this is difficult because the eighth is said to be one of the seven returned to reign. The only solution is to regard Domitian as a kind of reincarnation of Nero, because he continued the persecuting policy of his predecessor. But even then the vision comes in the reign of the sixth king and not the eighth. Perhaps the seer received his vision earlier than he published it,[4] or perhaps we have here a

---

[1] This is not to exclude the possibility that it may have a secondary futuristic reference in common with Hebrew prophetical method.

[2] This is strongly argued by C. C. Torrey (*op. cit.*, pp. 58ff.) who dates the book in AD 68 just after the Neronian persecutions and the emperor's death.

[3] So Moffatt, *ILNT*, p. 506. Hort (*op. cit.*, pp. xxviii, xxix) considered the year of anarchy should be treated as an interval on the strength of Suetonius' comment (*Vesp.* i) (cf. also Lohmeyer, *op. cit.*, p. 143).

[4] W. Sanday (*JTS*, VIII, 1907, pp. 489ff.) thought that what had been written at one time had been adapted to another, hence the confusion.

genuine prophecy. This latter supposition, which is in full harmony with the book's own claims to be a revelation, would necessarily date the book before Domitian, in the early years of Vespasian (see below). Or even more probably, perhaps, the numbers of the kings should be regarded symbolically.[1]

(ii) *The identification of the number 666* (Rev. xiii. 18). Many attempts were made to interpret this symbol in ancient times, but not until recent times[2] has it ever been calculated on the basis of the Hebrew transcription of the name Nero(n) Caesar, which in Hebrew enumeration makes a total of 666. But there are some insuperable difficulties here. Irenaeus[3] discusses the identification, but assumes without question that the calculation must be done in Greek, although he comes to no satisfactory conclusion.[4] It is true that a textual variant arose in early times which read 616,[5] which might possibly refer to Gaius Caesar (the mad Caligula) or else Nero Caesar (i.e. without the Hebrew letter 'n'— a distinct advantage). But the variant reading witnesses to early perplexity over this number. Another reason for rejecting the above-mentioned hypothesis is the fact that the author would hardly expect his Asiatic readers to understand a Hebrew cipher, unless, of course, Torrey's view that the book was originally written in Aramaic be accepted.[6] It seems better to suppose that the key was well enough known to the original readers, but that it soon became lost in the sub-

[1] So Lohmeyer (*op. cit.*, p. 143), who treated the number as typical of apocalyptic tradition. Lohmeyer maintained that the 'eighth' is symbolical for a superhuman form and considered that the 'five' bear an apocalyptical unity. Even if Lohmeyer's comparisons with Mandaean parallels are open to challenge as a basis for interpretation, yet his rejection of the literal historical method of interpretation is worthy of careful consideration (cf. *ibid.*, pp. 145–147 for his excursus on this). Cf. also M. Kiddle, *The Revelation of St. John* (1940), pp. 349–351.

[2] According to Zahn (*INT*, III, p. 447 n. 4) it was Fritzsche (1831) who first proposed this identification.

[3] *Adv. Haer.* v. 28–30.

[4] It should be noted, however, that the idea of enumeration in Hebrew and the significance of numbers attached to ancient personalities was familiar to Jewish exegetes. It was valuable in maintaining the validity of the Law as, for instance, when Moses married an Ethiopian, it was discovered that her name totalled 736, which was also the total for the phrase 'fair of appearance'. The offending alien was thus conveniently explained away (cf. Carpenter, *op. cit.*, p. 137).

[5] This alternative reading is mentioned by Irenaeus and was known by the Donatist Tyconius (see Zahn, *op. cit.*, p. 448, for details).

[6] Cf. his comment on this cipher, *op. cit.*, p. 60.

sequent history of the book.[1] It is hardly a safe guide in chronological discussions.[2]

(iii) *Supposed references to the pre-siege conditions in Jerusalem*. In xi. 1ff., there is a description of the measuring of the city of Jerusalem, with special reference to the temple. Does this refer to a time, therefore, when the temple is still standing? It might well be so, but this would date it before AD 70. Against this it should be noted that there is no need to interpret this description literally of the temple of Herod, although its form is no doubt suggested by that temple.[3] Moreover, Clement of Rome also refers to the temple in the present tense and no-one would suppose because of this that his writing must be dated before AD 70. Yet there is point in Torrey's contention that the absence of any reference to the siege of Jerusalem is difficult to imagine in a Jewish book after AD 70. The only problem is to be sure that we are dealing with a Jewish book. But if we are, this argument must be allowed some weight. Nevertheless, some who acknowledge a pre-siege date for chapter xi resort to a theory of sources to explain it away from any considerations of date.[4]

This evidence as a whole, while suggestive, cannot be regarded as at all conclusive, and indeed, in view of the strong external evidence for a later date, must be regarded as doubtful. It would be strange, if the book really was produced at the end of Nero's reign, that so strong a tradition arose associating it with Domitian's.

[1] In a recent article E. Stauffer makes the plausible suggestion that the number should be calculated in Greek from the official title of the reigning emperor. He believes that emperor to be Domitian, but suggests the calculation should be made from the abbreviation of the full title Αυτοκρατωρ Καισαρ Δομετιανος Σεβαστος Γερμανικος (i.e. Α. ΚΑΙ. DOMET. ΣΕΒ. ΓΕ, which totals 666). Abbreviations were usual on coins, but this form is uncommon and would have been chosen for greater security (see article '666' in *Coniectanea Neotestamentica*, XI, 1947, pp. 237–241). But other suggestions have been made which appear to be ·equally plausible (cf. W. Hadorn's argument for Trajan according to his surname ULPIOS, which in Greek totals 666; *ZNTW*, 19, 1920, pp. 11–29).

[2] It has been more generally recognized that a safer procedure is first to fix the date and then to decipher the number. There are more indications of the former than the latter.

[3] Cf. Swete, *op. cit.*, *ad loc*. Cf. A. Feuillet (*NTS*, 4, 1958, pp. 183–200), who calls the temple reference a pure symbol.

[4] Cf. Beckwith, *op. cit.*, p. 208; Charles, *op. cit.*, I, p. xciv.

c. Arguments for a Vespasianic date

A dating during the period AD 70–80 has been favoured by some,[1] largely owing to the identification of the sixth king with Vespasian, which then allows any time during the full period of his reign as possible for the production of the book. But there are some fatal objections. Vespasian did not take seriously the idea of kingly divinity and as far as is known was not a persecutor of the Church. Moreover, the period of his reign was marked by comparative calm and would not well fit the tumultuous background of the Apocalypse. Charles[2] has maintained that the background of the letters to the churches belongs to Vespasian's reign, but that the writer has re-edited them in Domitian's. Editorial theories[3] of this sort vitiate the argument which depends upon them, for whatever does not agree with the point of view maintained is too easily got rid of by editorial ingenuity or stupidity. If this method must be rejected, the fact remains that the text of xvii. 10 would seem most naturally to point to Vespasian as the reigning emperor and it is not satisfactory to resort as Charles[4] does to relegating xvii. 10, 11 to earlier sources. It would be much more reasonable in view of the impasse which seems to follow all historical attempts to interpret this statement, to regard it symbolically,[5] and so leave it out of calculations of date.[6]

IV. PURPOSE

Assuming that the first three chapters form an integral part of the book (see the discussion on Unity, pp. 287ff. below), we may at once say that it was designed for a specific group of people with specific needs. The main portion of the book (chapter iv onwards) appears to be prepared on a much broader canvas, but nevertheless the more local purpose is not lost sight of, as xxii. 16 shows. Evidently the writer originally intended his message to be read aloud in the churches to

---

[1] Moffatt (*ILNT*, p. 503) cites B. Weiss, Düsterdieck, Bartlet, C. A. Scott as maintaining this opinion.

[2] *Op. cit., loc. cit.*

[3] M. E. Boismard seems to favour some such theory (cf. his comment in Robert-Feuillet's *Introduction*, II, p. 742).

[4] *Op. cit.*, I, p. xcvi.   [5] Cf. Michaelis' discussion, *op. cit.*, pp. 316, 317.

[6] A. Feuillet (*NTS*, 4, 1958, pp. 183ff.) considers that the book was published in Domitian's reign but issued as if in Vespasian's, a process which he calls 'antedatation' and supports from Jewish apocalyptic usage.

whom it was addressed (i. 3), in which case it may well be described as a circular letter.[1]

The letters to the seven churches reveal much about the internal conditions of these churches, which helps us to fix with some accuracy the writer's purpose. As a true prophet he must record the challenges he has received from the Lord of the Church and must pass them on as he has been commanded (i. 11). The Lord has some things to commend but also many things to condemn. There is a manifest tendency towards spiritual deterioration. Some churches are being subjected to the pressure of immoral environments. Some are affected by false teachers. In most of the churches there is need for the call to repent, while in at least one church, Laodicea, material prosperity has resulted in spiritual decline to such a degree that it has caused revulsion to the Church's Lord. Yet, in spite of the words of criticism, for most of the churches the dominating theme of the letters is encouragement. Whoever is prepared to listen is invited to do so, as the formula at the end of each letter shows. Moreover each message ends with a promise. A remarkably practical note is thus struck at the very beginning.

Beyond the need to challenge the churches is the problem of the increasing opposition between the Church and State. But all this was to be viewed against the background of the end time and this leads John to contemplate in the Spirit the consummation of the ages. He paints in vivid colours the various judgments which are to fall upon those whose activity is motivated by the spirit of Antichrist. Throughout the book there are hints at coming triumph, but it is not until towards the end that the final overthrow of the Beast and of Babylon (the Roman Empire) and even of Satan himself is portrayed. This belief in the ultimate triumph of Christianity over all opposing forces brought a remarkable optimism at a time when the Roman Empire was increasing its power and when the Christian Church in proportion was pitifully small. The whole book is, therefore, a message of hope particularly adapted to those who are passing through, or who know they may soon be called to pass through, fierce temptation.

But it may well be intended to forewarn those who were indifferent to the coming threats and who would not be prepared for the storm when it broke. They needed to be told the true nature of the imperial

---

[1] By the end of the book the writer almost seems to anticipate that the book will have a wider public (xxii. 18) and that it will be of vital importance to ensure its integrity. Cf. Swete, *op. cit.*, p. xcviii.

power, particularly when the titular head of the empire demanded divine worship. No-one who had heard this book read could be in any doubt about the issues involved and any compromise was out of the question.

Because it portrays the triumph of right over wrong and all is brought into subjection to God, Charles[1] called the book 'the Divine Statute Book of International Law', and there is aptness in the description. In an age of political intrigues this book succoured the conviction that all true government proceeds from God and is upheld by God. Its basis is the certainty of the ultimate triumph of divine justice.

V. DESTINATION

It is not difficult to decide on the immediate destination of the book, for it was obviously intended for the churches of Asia mentioned in chapters ii and iii. It is not, however, addressed to all the Christian churches of the province, for there were certainly Christians at Troas (Acts xx. 7ff.), Hierapolis and Colossae (cf. Col. ii. 1, iv. 13, 16) in the first century and almost certainly at Tralles and Magnesia, since Ignatius addressed letters to them in the early second century. What then was the principle that John used in his choice of churches? It was definitely not their civic importance, although the first three are in order of civic dignity, for the inclusion of such small towns as Thyatira and Philadelphia to the exclusion of much larger towns sufficiently disposes of this.

W. M. Ramsay[2] supposed that the choice of churches was governed by the great circular road which linked them all and which, therefore, provided a convenient network for the distribution of the letters throughout the whole province. The order of mention would then represent the route which the messenger took in delivering the book. There is much to be said for this suggestion. But it must not be lost sight of that John is recording his messages as direct communications from the Lord of the Church and it may, therefore, be supposed that these were the churches which were especially under his care and for which he had been particularly burdened before the Lord. It has been suggested that the itinerary is an imaginary one, since the letters are addressed to the 'angels' of the churches[3] and not to the churches

[1] *Op. cit.*, I, p. ciii.   [2] *The Letters to the Seven Churches of Asia* (1904), p. 183.
[3] Elsewhere in the book the word 'angel' is always used of spiritual beings and it is reasonable to suppose that 'guardian angels' are here meant in accordance with current belief. But it is strange to find the guardian angels so strongly condemned for the misdeeds of their churches (cf. Swete, *op. cit.*, pp. 21, 22).

themselves, and this in such a book would not be altogether surprising. Yet the messages are so definitely linked to the historical circumstances that it is impossible to suppose that John did not intend each church to take special note of its own message.[1] Indeed, as Ramsay has clearly shown, each message not only suits the needs of the churches but also reflects the geographical background.

It would seem, therefore, that in the book as a whole the writer thinks primarily of the immediate needs of his Asiatic churches, but that he foresees that the message of Christian triumph over the adverse forces of evil would have a much wider relevance. It is difficult not to feel that he envisaged the distribution of the book to a wide Christian public beyond the seven churches named. The early attestation for the book shows, at least, that such wide distribution actually occurred.

VI. SOURCES

In common with every other book in the New Testament, the Apocalypse has been subjected to the source-critic's analysis and it will be necessary to give a brief indication of the results.

The most obvious source of ideas and mental images is the Old Testament. The author has drawn most from the books of Daniel,[2] Ezekiel[3] and, to a lesser degree, Zechariah, which have supplied the forms to express new apocalyptic revelations. But his mind was also saturated with other parts of the Old Testament, particularly Isaiah (whose words are reflected more than any other), Jeremiah, Joel and Exodus (in the parallels with the plagues). Indeed so basic is the Old

---

[1] Oman (*The Book of Revelation*, 1923, p. 28) suggested that John on Patmos knew that he would be unable to communicate with the outside world and therefore addressed the message to the 'guardian angels', who he believed would be able to communicate with the churches.

[2] Most notable are the reminiscences of the persecuting Antiochus Epiphanes (Dn. vii; cf. Rev. xiii. 1ff., xvii. 12, xx. 4) and the figure of the Son of man coming in judgment (Dn. vii. 7–13, 22; cf. Rev. xiv. 14, xx. 4, 12).

[3] Cf. such common ideas as the initial throne-vision (Ezk. ix; Rev. iv. 1–11); the scroll written on both sides (Ezk. ii. 9; Rev. v. 1), and the eating of a scroll (Ezk. iii. 3; Rev. x. 10); the four products of the fourth seal (Ezk. xiv. 21; Rev. vi. 8); the marked foreheads (Ezk. ix. 4; Rev. vii. 3); coals of fire thrown from heaven to earth (Ezk. x. 2; Rev. viii. 5); an assembly of birds as a symbol of judgment (Ezk. xxxix. 17f.; Rev. xix. 17f.); Gog and Magog (Ezk. xxxviii–xxxix; Rev. xx. 7–10); the messianic Jerusalem (Ezk. xl–xlvii; Rev. xxi). For a concise table showing how Ezekiel dominates the structure of the Apocalypse, cf. P. Carrington, *The Meaning of the Revelation* (1931), pp. 64, 65.

Testament to the writer's mental concepts that out of 404 verses in the entire book there are only 126 which contain no allusion to it.[1] Yet it should be noted that nowhere does the writer quote from the Old Testament, and even where his language echoes the Old Testament he rarely uses the *ipsissima verba*.[2] There is no conscious attempt to construct a mosaic from Old Testament materials. Rather has the language of the Old Testament so moulded the author's thought that he cannot write without reflecting it. As Swete[3] remarked, it is as though his 'words and thoughts arrange themselves in his visions like the changing patterns of a kaleidoscope, without conscious effort on his own part'. It is important to recognize this fact, for it means that the book is more than a dramatic compilation; it is an experience under the control of the Holy Spirit (i. 10).

Many scholars have considered the Jewish apocalypses to be a more certain source for the author than the Old Testament, but it is because this notion must be rejected that the Old Testament background has been considered first. The apocalyptic form which our book possesses may certainly be paralleled from the Jewish pseudepigrapha. Apocalypses were in vogue and were generally written in the name of some such ancient worthy as Enoch, Abraham, Ezra or Baruch, who was made to predict the history of the Jewish people from his (the assumed author's) time up to the real author's time, and to include in the same vein an extension of the history into the future. The idea was to use the past history to give confidence in the future predictions. While the style used has many similarities with the Apocalypse of John in that imagery is used to symbolize events, yet there are some vital differences which suggest that, although the writer was acquainted with the Jewish works, he is independent of them and cannot be considered as a continuation of them.[4] To begin with, he does not use a pseudonym, but writes in his own name. Secondly, he does not focus attention on past history, but concentrates on the present and future. Thirdly, he is more in alignment with the Old Testament prophets in the denunciation of evil and in the moral exhortations to nobler living. And finally,

[1] From the list of citations in Westcott and Hort's text. See Swete, *op. cit.*, pp. cxxxix ff., for a selected list of the most important examples; or Charles, *op. cit.*, I, pp. lxviii ff., for a more exhaustive list.   [2] Cf. Swete, *op. cit.*, p. liii.

[3] *Loc. cit.* Lohmeyer speaks suggestively of the Old Testament as the Seer's 'Atmosphäre' (*op. cit.*, p. 196).

[4] Cf. the article by G. E. Ladd, 'The Revelation and Jewish Apocalyptic', *EQ*, XXIX (1957), pp. 94–100, for a discussion of the differences.

the spiritual grasp of the writer is far removed from the pedestrian and often gloomy approach of the apocalyptists. It is no wonder that the books of the latter were never even considered for canonical status, while the work of the former, in spite of its many obscurities, was recognized from earliest days as having the stamp of inspiration upon it. Nevertheless, this is not to say that John does not reflect any of the apocalyptical writings. Charles[1] has listed eighteen passages where he thinks there is dependence, or at least parallel thoughts. The force of the evidence will appeal differently to different minds, but in the present writer's judgment, there is little to conclude for the dependence of the Apocalypse on these Jewish pseudepigrapha. Almost all the passages are from 1 Enoch, and for the author's acquaintance with this book there is certainly something to be said, but the others are more doubtful.[2] To give two examples of the influence that Jewish apocalyptic is supposed to have exerted, in iv. 6 the description of the cherubim, according to Charles,[3] owes more to such literature than to Ezekiel, to which it is also clearly indebted. Moreover, in vi. 11 the idea that the world would end when the number of the martyrs is complete is paralleled almost exactly in 1 Enoch xlvii. 3, 4.[4]

The sources so far referred to are those which affected the author's background of thought. Some comment must now be made on the theory that our author has used literary sources which he has incorporated in his own work. Charles,[5] for instance, found such sources behind vii. 1–8, xi. 1–13, xii, xiii, xvii, xviii and perhaps xv. 5–8, of which some are reckoned to be Greek and some Hebrew. But Charles' grounds were wholly subjective and for that reason must be regarded with caution. At the same time he did not, as did many earlier interpreters, infer from the use of sources the disunity of the book (see discussion below). Yet if the author is presenting what he claims to be a direct revelation from God in the prophetic manner, it is impossible to think of him editing literary sources as carefully as Charles' theory supposes. This type of critical analysis can carry no

[1] *Op. cit.*, I, pp. lxxxii f.
[2] Charles (*loc. cit.*) includes the *Testaments of the XII Patriarchs*, the *Assumption of Moses*, the *Psalms of Solomon* and *2 Enoch*. Lohmeyer (*op. cit.*, p. 196) admits the parallels but thinks they point to tradition, not necessarily to books.
[3] *Op. cit.*, I, pp. 117ff.
[4] Other parallels mentioned by Charles (*op. cit.*, I, pp. 178f.) are 4 Ezra iv. 35, which appears to have been indebted to our apocalypse here, and 2 Baruch xxx. 2 similarly.   [5] *Op. cit.*, p. lxii.

conviction among those who treat the visions of the Apocalypse as genuinely ecstatic.

VII. UNITY

Because some scholars have supposed that the book contains incongruities and adjacent passages which are unrelated to each other, various theories have been proposed which involve compilation from one or more sources, which have later been edited. It is possible here to give only the briefest indication of these theories, which were mainly in vogue at the turn of the century and are now largely discounted. For the sake of clarity they will be classified under three main types.

a. Compilation theories

There have been several hypotheses which suppose that an editor (or editors) has taken over some independent sources and welded them into a unity.[1] Some (Weyland, Holtzmann, de Faye) supposed the combination of two Jewish sources, while others (Schmidt and Spitta) maintained three sources, either all Jewish or a mixture of Jewish and Christian, which were later adapted and modified by an editor. Other forms of this type of theory were the two-source theory, in which one was Jewish and one Christian (J. Weiss) or both were Christian Hebrew sources (Bruston). A more complicated theory (propounded by Völter) supposed that the basic apocalypse was written by Mark, who added an appendix (AD 68), and then a revision was made by Cerinthus in Vespasian's time and a later revision in Domitian's time. Two considerations are sufficient to dispose of this type of theory. First of all, the impression of unity which the Apocalypse gives, both in form and content, would have to be attributed to the skill of the compiler, which is most difficult to concede. Secondly, the linguistic peculiarities in the Greek, which have already been mentioned, run throughout all parts of the book and must therefore be attributed to the author and not to an editor.

b. Revision theories

This type of theory assumes one basic source which has been worked over. E. Vischer's[2] is the most notable form of this hypothesis, for he

[1] Details of these theories may conveniently be found in Beckwith, *op. cit.*, pp. 224ff.; Moffatt, *ILNT*, pp. 489ff.; Bousset, *op. cit.*, pp. 108ff.

[2] 'Die Offenbarung Johannes eine jüdische Apokalypse in christlicher Bearbeitung', *TU*, II, iii (1886). Others who have advanced similar theories are Harnack, Martineau, S. Davidson and von Soden (cf. Moffatt, *ILNT*, p. 490, for details).

postulated that the original was a Jewish apocalypse and that an editor has adapted this for Christian purposes. He accounted for the impression of unity by supposing that the editor, who appended the Christian additions, was also the translator of the Jewish work. But the whole theory was based on the insecure supposition that there were irreconcilable elements (Jewish versus Christian), which were due more to the proposer's faulty exegesis than to the real facts of the case. Moreover, the final editor must have been wholly blind to these supposed contradictions. Such differences as are found (e.g. in the presentation of Messiah) are certainly not evidence of different authorship, but of changes of emphasis within one mind.[1]

c. Incorporation theories

Many scholars, who are convinced of the unity of the book, but who at the same time consider sources to have been used, have proposed an original apocalypse in which are incorporated various fragments of Jewish apocalyptic writing. This was first suggested by C. von Weizsäcker[2] and has been followed with many variations in the precise delineation of the incorporated material.[3] The contention in this kind of theory is that when these portions are extracted a basic unity of plan is revealed. But would any author encrust his own original pattern with the accretions of several other fragments? It is difficult if not impossible to believe that he would.[4]

---

[1] W. H. Simcox (The Revelation of St. John the Divine, CGT, 1893, pp. 215–234) gave a very balanced criticism of Vischer's theory, but was not convinced by it because of the unity of style throughout. M. G. Glazebrook (The Apocalypse of St. John, 1923, p. 16) accounted for some of the inconsistencies by assuming that the book records the author's experiences over some twenty years and by assuming that the disorder of the xx–xxii section was due to an abrupt cessation of the work before final revision could be made. This is, at least, a more probable revision theory than Vischer's, but assumes some stupidity on the part of the final editor.

[2] In his Das apostolische Zeitalter der christlichen Kirche[3] (1902), pp. 486ff.

[3] Others who have maintained similar theories are Sabatier, Schön, Pfleiderer, Bousset, Jülicher, McGiffert, C. A. Scott, Charles, Moffatt (cf. ILNT, p. 490).

[4] Charles gets over this by importing into his account of the origin of the work an unintelligent editor, who was a disciple of the author. But he is confident of the unity of the book, on the grounds of the basic similarity of grammar in all its various parts. He uses this also as a criterion for his reconstruction (cf. Charles, Lectures on the Apocalypse, Schweich Lectures, 1922, pp. 11ff.).

d. The traditional theory

This denies that any sources have been incorporated and supposes that the author is directly responsible for all the material in the book. This has the great advantage of accounting most adequately for the unity and of dispensing with any arbitrary methods of distinguishing sources.[1] It accounts for the alleged differences in the different parts of the book as due to normal variations in literary productions of an apocalyptic kind, although it does not deny that the author's mind has been influenced by the thought-forms of earlier material.[2]

VIII. STRUCTURE

So many and so varied have been the theories of the plan of this book that it is quite impossible in a work of this kind to give an adequate account of them. What will be attempted, therefore, is to give a brief survey of the main types of theories and to give sufficient indication of where the student interested in further enquiries may find the detailed analyses.

The majority of interpreters of this book assume that the action is not intended to be continuously described, but rather that successive groups of visions each portray similar events in different ways. By this means the recurring allusions to the approaching end of the age become intelligible. Yet under this general category, which may be termed theories of recapitulation, there have been numerous different theories of the structure of the book. On the other hand some theories are based on the assumption that the visions are in a continuous sequence throughout. These different theories may roughly be summarized as follows.

a. The patchwork theory

In this type of theory, which regards the book as a compilation but not necessarily by a mere editorial process, it is useless to look for a development of thought, for the author has been too deeply influenced by his sources to weld them into a closely-knit whole. Moffatt's[3] plan for the

---

[1] Moffatt (*ILNT*, p. 491) admitted that most of the above theories are handicapped by what he called 'Overprecision and arbitrary canons of literary criticism'.

[2] Advocates of this theory do not, of course, maintain that the book contains no obscurities, but rather that the obscurities are not necessarily due to the use of different materials or of derangements.

[3] *ILNT*, pp. 485–488.

book illustrates this, for he postulated what he called 'intermezzos' to form the sutures between the various visions (e.g. vii. 1–17, x. 1–xi. 14, xiv. 1–20). Yet the whole has certainly the appearance of a unity which the author himself has impressed upon the material. Moffatt referred to 'the kaleidoscope of visions' in the book and this well sums up his view of its structure.[1]

b. The poetic theory

Kiddle[2] rejects the idea of treating the book according to any strict chronological scheme and in this respect his theory is somewhat akin to the preceding. But he considers that John has so mastered his material that it is useless to regard the work as a compilation. The author himself is not a calculating and careful arranger of vision-materials, but a visionary prophet and poet. To expect a logically worked out plan is, therefore, irrelevant. The poet aims to build up an impression and is not at all concerned about repeating himself, or arranging his material in a design which would pass the mechanical demands of many literary critics. Thus the recurring themes are all part of the total impression of the inevitability of coming judgment, each repetition of the theme adding some new colouring to the whole picture. There is much to be said for this kind of approach, for it avoids the forced attempts to reduce the book to a clearly defined plan of development.[3]

c. The symbolism theory

Closely allied to the last is the interpretation of the author's design by reference to the symbolism underlying the book. This type of theory has had many advocates, but has been given a new impetus recently through the work of Austin Farrer.[4] This writer traces three

[1] Carpenter (*op. cit.*, p. 28) refers to separate sketches rather than to a coherent order between the scenes. M. E. Boismard (*RB*, LVI, 1949, pp. 507–539) has a similar theory, for he finds two sets of visions, one in Nero's time and one in Vespasian's or early in Domitian's time. The two were later combined and the letters added. At the same time Boismard does not regard it as necessary to dispense with unity of authorship. See also Robert-Feuillet's *Introduction*, pp. 122ff., for Boismard's doublet theory.

[2] *Op. cit.*, pp. xxviiff.

[3] This idea of a poetic purpose is in line with the poetic form which many scholars have noted (e.g. Lohmeyer, *op. cit.*, pp. 185f.; Charles, *op. cit.*, pp. 41ff.; N. W. Lund, *Chiasmus in the New Testament*, 1942, pp. 321–411).

[4] *A Rebirth of Images* (1949).

successive symbolical threads in this book which furnish the key to the interpretation of the whole—the number seven, the Jewish liturgy, and astrology (the signs of the zodiac).[1] It need occasion no surprise that Farrer manages to fit all the complexities of the Apocalypse into his scheme, for the pursuer of symbols can see them wherever he chooses.[2] There is bound to be much manipulation with the plain meaning of the words and it is difficult to imagine what the original readers of the Apocalypse would have made out of Farrer's interpretations. He anticipates this objection[3] and maintains that they 'would understand what they would understand, and that would be as much as they had time to digest', which nicely side-tracks the difficulty. If this theory does not appeal to less symbolical minds, Farrer has made some provocative suggestions which may at least in some measure illustrate the subconscious images in the author's mind, even though they hardly seem convincing as an explanation of the main structure of the book. An author who had a burning message to proclaim may be expected to put it in a form more readily understood than this theory supposes.

d. The drama theory

Even more recently an American, J. W. Bowman,[4] has proposed that the book should be regarded in its entirety as a drama designed after the pattern of contemporary dramatic productions. Hence it consists of a prologue, a seven-act play and an epilogue. Between each of the acts are passages which serve to introduce the following act, in a way comparable to the stage-props of contemporary drama. In this scheme Bowman regards chapters i. 5–iii as Act I of the drama and considers that only i. 4–6 and xxii. 21 have been appended to give the work the appearance of a letter. He argues that since the number seven figures so largely in the book, it is reasonable to suppose that it provides the key to its structure (compare the next theory considered). The so-called 'stage props' (e.g. i. 9–20, iv. 1–v. 14, viii. 2–6, xi. 19, xv. 1, 8, xvi. 1, xvii. 1, 2, xx. 4–6) are paralleled by the habit of dramatists in intro-

[1] Farrer was not the first to connect the twelve houses of Israel with the signs of the zodiac (cf. C. E. Douglas, *JTS*, xxxvii, 1936, pp. 49–56, who nevertheless thought that John was using ancient traditions).
[2] Cf. T. W. Manson's criticism in *JTS*, L (1949), pp. 206–208.
[3] *Op. cit.*, p. 21.
[4] 'The Revelation to John: Its Dramatic Structure and Message', in *Interpretation*, IX (1955), pp. 436–453.

ducing gods to give information necessary for the audience. On the other hand, Bowman suggests that in these sections John is thinking more of the imagery of the temple than of the theatre.[1] There might be something to be said for this as far as the author's own conception of it is concerned, but the stage-prop idea must surely have been far from his mind.

e. The sevenfold design theory

It is, of course, clear that the number seven held a particular fascination for the author and all scholars would acknowledge this. But few have carried this to such lengths as Loenertz and Lohmeyer, who have both maintained that the number is the key to the whole structure of the book. The former[2] recognizes a distinct break at iii. 22 and consequently treats the book in two main visions, which together comprise seven groups of seven. The latter[3] goes even farther and finds seven-structures in strophes and sometimes in the divisions of strophes, much as he does in the First Epistle of John. The theory is worked out very ingeniously, but the impression is inescapable that if Lohmeyer is right the author of this book has developed his literary technique to such a degree that he must have concentrated more on the form than on the content. Yet a reading of the book does not give one the idea of a literary artist so much as of a prophet whose burning messages would transcend mere literary devices. At the same time, Lohmeyer has drawn attention to an important aspect of the relation of this book to the other Johannine literature in that all this literature contains similar sevenfold patterns.[4]

f. Transposition theories

All the preceding theories have assumed that some of the series of visions recapitulate on the previous series, but there have been attempts to treat the visions as strictly consecutive. It is significant that two lead-

[1] In a suggestive article on the influence of the Greek drama on the Apocalypse of John, R. R. Brewer maintained the opposite view, even finding the counterpart of the altar in the Dionysian altar before the throne in Greek theatres (ATR, xviii, 1936, pp. 74–92).

[2] The Apocalypse of St. John (Eng. tr. by H. J. Carpenter, 1947).

[3] Op. cit., pp. 185f.

[4] Archbishop Benson held a theory between this and the preceding, for he considered the book was like the relating of a drama, yet was not a drama. He made much of the seven choric songs which divided the action into seven parts (op. cit., pp. 37ff.).

ing exponents of this view, Charles and Oman, have both achieved their end by means of textual rearrangements. Charles[1] considered that the concluding editor was not only stupid but morally culpable. Many interpolations were introduced (e.g. i. 8, viii. 7-12, xiv. 3e-4ab, xiv. 15-17, xxii. 18b-19). Charles arranged the visions in three continuous series, and to get over the difficulty of the repetitions, some of these visions are described as 'proleptic' (e.g. vii. 9-17, x.1-xi. 13, xiv). Whatever the merits of Charles' reconstruction, its considerable demerit is that continuity of plan is achieved only at the expense of quite arbitrary excisions or adjustments, a subjective procedure which cannot commend itself as being in accordance with the principles of scientific criticism.

Oman[2] differs from Charles in that he conceives of the derangements as being accidental and not intentional and he endeavours to produce an explanation of the present state of the text. Oman still, however, postulates some editorial additions,[3] which became necessary when the editor had arranged the sheets (although incorrectly) in the order which seemed right to him. The striking thing about this theory is the claim that the book naturally falls into sections of almost equal length in the Greek text, calculating on thirty-three lines for each papyrus sheet. The resultant rearrangement is considerable.[4] Moreover, some of the editorial glosses are not obvious and appear to be assumed more to make the text fit the theory than because of internal probability. In addition Oman admits that two sections are of different length and must be treated as exceptions. It would seem easier to imagine a writer carefully constructing a sevenfold structure with numerous sevenfold substructures than to conceive an author laboriously fitting his

[1] *Commentary on the Revelation of St. John*, I, pp. 1ff.

[2] J. Oman, *The Book of Revelation* (1923).

[3] In a second book, *The Text of Revelation. A Revised Theory* (1928), Oman considers these additions to be doublets, which the first editor repeated from his author.

[4] Oman's revised order is as follows: i. 9-iii. 22, xxii. 10-12, x. 1-11, xi. 1-13, xii. 1-14, xii. 14-xiii. 11, xiii. 11-18, xiv. 6-12, xv. 5, 6, xvi. 2-16, viii. 6-11 (+ other insertions from viii), xix. 11-15, xiv. 19, 20, xix. 16-21, xvi. 17-xvii. 9, xvii. 9-xviii. 6, xviii. 6-19, xviii. 19-xix. 9, i. 7, iv. 1-v. 2, v. 2-vi. 1, vi. 2-17, vii. 1-17, viii. 1-5, xvi. 4-7, viii. 6-13, ix. 1-7, ix. 7-21, xi. 14-19, xiv. 1-5, 13, 14, xiv. 14-19, xv. 1, 6-xvi. 1, xv. 2-4, xxi. 9-24, xxi. 24-xxii. 5, 6, 8, 9, xvi. 15, xxii. 14-17, 20 (+ insertions from xix. 10), i. 3-6, xx. 1-10, xx. 11-xxi. 1, 3-8, xxii. 18, 19, 21. McNeile-Williams (*INT*, p. 259), while admitting that this revised text reads more smoothly, yet rightly point out that it involves even greater manipulations.

sections so accurately to his papyrus sheets. In any case, Oman maintains that some of the original sheets contained passages which are now
found in various parts of the Apocalypse, and it is impossible to see how
they came to be so distributed. A misplacement of whole sheets is
intelligible, but a redistribution of fragments of any one sheet is surely
highly improbable.[1]

g. The liturgical pattern theory

The presence of many liturgical features, particularly the numerous
hymns, has recently led to the theory that behind the structure of this
book is to be found a primitive form of the Paschal Vigil. The main
exponent of this view is M. H. Shepherd,[2] who has suggested that the
Seer has adopted the liturgy as a general framework for his book. Thus
he holds that i–iii represent the Scrutinies, iv–vi the Vigil, vii the
Initiation, viii–xix the Synaxis and xix–xxii the Eucharist. Several
interesting parallels occur, but these cannot prove that the structure of
the book is indebted to the liturgical pattern, for the evidence for the
latter is not sufficiently early for us to be certain of its primitive form.
This is a difficulty which confronts all liturgical theories for New
Testament books. Yet it is not impossible that some of the hymns may
have been in common use and that the writer's mind was well stocked
with them. One feature of this particular theory which is commendable
is its assumption not only of the unity of the book, but also of its
consecutive and logical sequence.

IX. THE PERMANENT MESSAGE

The history of the interpretation of the book does not concern us here,
except in so far as it throws light upon its permanent message. The
Futuristic school of interpretation which regards the book as in some
measure a prophetic forecast of future history down to the consummation of time can have no possible doubt about its continual value.
This view, which was popular during the Reformation because of the
identification of the power of the Roman Church with Antichrist, is
capable of great flexibility and adjustments, as the history of the interpretation of the enigmatic number 666 abundantly shows. But alongside
this school of thought has been the Contemporary Historical school
which has denied all future reference and confined the purpose of the

---

[1] Cf. Carpenter's criticisms (*op. cit.*, pp. 187, 188).
[2] *The Paschal Liturgy and the Apocalypse* (1960), pp. 75–97; cf. also E. Lohse, *Die
Offenbarung des Johannes* (1960), pp. 48ff.

Apocalypse to the immediate circumstances of the author's own day. As a consequence there was no point in attempting a full-scale exegesis of its riddles, because the key, which was well known to its original readers, has now been irretrievably lost. The logical outcome of such an interpretation is that the book might as well be discarded. It has no message for our modern age.

Obviously some combination of these two points of view is desirable if a true picture is to be attained. That the writer wrote wholly for the future is demonstrably untrue, particularly in chapters i–iii, and all attempts to turn these clearly practical letters into predictions of the successive periods of Church history are possible only at the expense of sound exegetical principles. But if, in line with the Hebrew prophets, there are both immediate and distant points of view, the historical and eschatological aspects are taken into account.

The Literary Critical method of dealing with the book, which concentrates attention on sources and grammatical form, has done very little to re-establish interest in this book in spite of its claims to have solved much of its enigmatic symbolism. Although this method has thrown light upon many obscurities, it must in the end be recognized that the abiding value of the book rests not on its sources nor on its form, but on its message.

But the problem is to discover some means of expressing this message in a form relevant for every age. This has led to the Symbolic school of interpretation which uses the imagery to illustrate spiritual truths irrespective of the original historical context, a school of thought which has had its advocates in all periods of Church history. Yet its divorce from historical background inevitably makes it more subjective, although it has not been without its real spiritual values. A surer exegesis will want rather to draw out the permanent spiritual values against the historical background. The book will then still claim its place in the Canon, because it enunciates principles which are always applicable. These principles may briefly be summarized as follows.

1. The first principle is that faith triumphs over might. This is the most obvious conviction which must strike every reader of the book. All the gathering power of antagonistic forces, whether personified in Rome (= Babylon), the Beast or Antichrist, which seem at the time of writing to be irresistible, are laid low at the end. Their evil designs and malicious persecutions may be vividly described in the body of the book, but the confidence in their final overthrow, which is glimpsed

now and then, reaches its climax when mighty Rome is reduced to dust and irrevocable judgment is carried out against Antichrist and the Beast. In the end it is the Lamb who is victorious, and this conviction has brought immeasurable comfort in all ages to those who have seemed so helpless in a time of crisis and persecution.

2. The second principle is the inevitability of judgment. Although closely linked with the first principle, this should be separated from it because of the frequency with which it has been overlooked, particularly in our modern age. The idea that sin and evil in all its manifestations in a materialistic age is doomed to final judgment is not palatable for our easy-going society. But the idea of judgment is integral to Christianity. It was emphasized by our Lord and by all the apostles. If John's imagery sometimes appears to be crude and even horrific, and if his spirit seems to be vindictive it must not be forgotten that judgment is a fearful theme for a poet's pen. He was attempting to describe the indescribable, and if he used current apocalyptic terms to assist him, his fundamental message of judgment must not be allowed to elude us because our modern literary tastes find the apocalyptic forms abhorrent. Judgment is an idea which no amount of sophistication will ever make attractive and John has grasped that more fully than his modern denigrators.

3. The third principle is that the Christian approach presents the true philosophy of history. John looks at the present in the light of the future, as well as in terms of the past. If it be objected that the future is unknown and his method is, therefore, invalidated, it must be recognized that the Christian view of history assumes an onward movement to a final satisfactory consummation. Without this confidence there seems no ground for anything but pessimism and this was never truer than in a nuclear age. This book with its powerful assurance that there are ultimate values which far outstrip the claims of pure materialism has a particular relevance for today.

The book is, therefore, a book of encouragement and exhortation. To those who combat the great forces of evil with apparently little success, the book brings particular inspiration. And to those who are inclined in any age to forsake their faith because the odds against them seem to be too great, the book issues a powerful challenge to endurance.[1]

[1] Cf. H. H. Wernecke, *The Book of Revelation Speaks to us* (1954), pp. 32, 33, who is a lucid exponent of the symbolic method of interpretation. Cf. also A. Burnet, *The Lord reigneth* (1946).

CONTENTS

I. THE PREFACE (i. 1–3)

John calls his book both a revelation from God and a prophecy which is to be read aloud.

II. THE SEVEN LETTERS (i. 4–iii. 22)

a. The introduction (i. 4–20)

The writer sends a general greeting to the seven Asiatic churches. This is followed by an introductory vision in which he is commanded to write what he sees for these churches, and by a majestic vision of Christ in the midst of the churches.

b. The letters to the churches (ii. 1–iii. 22)

Each message is intended to meet a specific internal condition and each ends with a promise to those who are victorious.

1. Ephesus is a church with a fine past, but a loveless present (ii. 1–7).

2. Smyrna is subjected to special attack from Satan, and Christians who are faithful in the midst of it are promised a reward (ii. 8–11).

3. Pergamum is another church placed in a satanic environment, and some, who have been drawn away towards false teaching, are called on to repent (ii. 12–17).

4. Thyatira is affected by immorality, but those who have not been deceived are urged to hold on to what they possess (ii. 18–29).

5. Sardis is described as a dead church, with a few only who have not become soiled by their environment. The advice to these people is to wake up (iii. 1–6).

6. Philadelphia receives warm commendation for its past loyalty and is promised special protection in the coming world-wide trial (iii. 7–13).

7. Laodicea is condemned for compromise, but is still given the opportunity to repent (iii. 14–22).

III. VISIONS INTRODUCING THE PROPHECY (iv. 1–v. 14)

a. The vision of God (iv. 1–11)

The writer records vividly a scene in heaven which is dominated by the throne of God and the worship which is offered to Him.

b. The vision of Christ (v. 1–14)

The scene is still in heaven but now the focus is on the Lamb, who is alone worthy to open the seven-sealed scroll which He holds in His hand. Again the worship is described, and several groups join in the responses.

IV. THE SEVEN SEALS (vi. 1–viii. 1)

a. The first six seals opened (vi. 1–17)

After each of the first four is broken, a rider on a horse appears, representing conquest, war, famine and death. On the opening of the fifth seal, the cry of the martyrs is heard and they are told to wait a little longer. Immediately afterwards, terrible calamities come into focus as the sixth seal is broken; this is the Lamb manifesting His wrath.

b. The sealing of God's people (vii. 1–17)

In contrast to this awful scene of wrath is the moving description of the sealing of God's people, represented by twelve thousand from each tribe. Following this ceremony is another vision of the Lamb being worshipped. A conversation between one of the elders and the writer results in an explanation of the great multitude of worshippers.

c. The seventh seal (viii. 1)

This leads to the revelation of the seven trumpets, but only after half an hour of silence.

V. THE SEVEN TRUMPETS (viii. 2–xiii. 18)

a. The trumpeters introduced (viii. 2–5)

The scene is in heaven as the seven trumpeters prepare to blow their trumpets. They wait for an eighth to fling a censer down to earth, which results in violent disturbances in the natural order, a clear hint at what is to be expected when the trumpets are blown.

b. The first four trumpets (viii. 6–12)

Hail and fire, volcanic eruption, a poisonous star and a darkening of the sun, moon and stars follow the blasts on these trumpets.

c. The eagle's warning (viii. 13)

An eagle's expression of woe from mid-heaven heightens the expectation for the next three trumpets.

d. The fifth and sixth trumpets (ix. 1–21)

The former of these shows a glimpse into a bottomless pit, which is presided over by Apollyon (the Destroyer). It is a place of torture (ix. 1–12). The latter shows four angels whose mission is destruction, and again the description is one of dreadful power to hurt; yet in spite of it those unaffected refuse to repent (ix. 13–21).

e. The little book eaten (x. 1–xi. 2)

In the midst of a thunderstorm, John sees an angel with a scroll and hears him announce the seventh trumpet-blast at which God's mystery is about to be completed. John is commanded to eat the scroll, following which he is told to prophesy and to measure the temple.

f. The two heavenly witnesses (xi. 3–13)

Still the trumpet-blast must wait until two witnesses have prophesied for three and a half years. But they are opposed by the Beast from the pit, are killed but rise again and return to heaven.

g. The seventh trumpet (xi. 14–xii. 17)

Before the woe is announced a vision is seen depicting once again worship in heaven, but the emphasis is now on God's wrath. To the accompaniment of thunderstorm and earthquake the scene changes and there appears a pregnant woman who is molested by the appearance of a dragon (xii. 1–4). A child is born but is at once taken to heaven and this is the signal for a war between Michael and his angelic hosts and the dragon (xii. 5–9). Victory is proclaimed in heaven, but the dragon resolves to attack the woman and her children who witness to Jesus (xii. 10–17).

h. The Beasts (xiii. 1–18)

The character of the opposition is now more clearly described. A Beast emerges from the sea having a terrifying appearance and yet is the object of worship (xiii. 1–4). It is blasphemous in its speech and tyrannical in its power (xiii. 5–10). Another Beast emerges from the earth, who has particular power to deceive by miraculous actions and who compels all to receive his mark, the mysterious 666 (xiii. 11–18).

VI. VISIONS OF THE WORSHIPPERS OF THE LAMB (xiv. 1–20)

a. The purity of the martyrs (xiv. 1–5)

In contrast to the last description, the scene now shows those marked with the Lamb's mark and their song of adoration is heard.

b. The angels' announcement (xiv. 6–11)

Three angels announce the dawn of the judgment hour, the doom of Babylon, and the condemnation of the worshippers of the Beast.

c. The martyrs commended (xiv. 12, 13)

Blessing and rest await those who die in the Lord.

d. The harvest of wrath (xiv. 14–20)

In two visions the Son of man and an angel, both with sickles, reap the earth (xiv. 14–20).

VII. THE SEVEN BOWLS (xv. 1–xviii. 24)

a. Introductory scenes (xv. 1–8)

Three successive scenes prepare the way for the pouring out of the bowls. Seven angels are seen holding the last plagues (xv. 1); those who have gained victory are seen praising God (xv. 2–4); and the angels come forth from the heavenly temple holding the seven bowls of God's wrath (xv. 5–8).

b. The bowls of wrath (xvi. 1–21)

In quick succession these are poured out at the command of a voice in the temple. The first produces ulcers, the second pollution of the sea, the third pollutes rivers and springs to look like blood, the fourth produces scorching heat, the fifth darkness and anguish, the sixth the drying up of the Euphrates and the appearances of frog-like fiends and the seventh the dramatic announcement of the end as 'Babylon' falls to the accompaniment of terrible upheavals in the natural world.

c. An explanation (xvii. 1–xviii. 24)

'Babylon' is first described and her great sins enumerated (xvii. 1–6). This harlot is then more precisely identified with the imperial city

(Rome) (xvii. 7–18). In spite of the dominion it exercises the Lamb will overcome it. Then follows a description of the fall of 'Babylon' (xviii. 1–3), a comment from heaven upon it (xviii. 4–8), lamentation on earth over it (xviii. 9–20) and a parabolic illustration of the finality of its destruction in the casting of a great stone into the sea (xviii. 21–24).

VIII. FURTHER VISIONS OF WORSHIP (xix. 1–10)

a. Hymns of praise in heaven (xix. 1–8)

First is heard a hymn to God for His avenging of His martyred servants and then follows the marriage hymn of the Lamb.

b. John is also commanded to worship God (xix. 9, 10)

IX. VISIONS OF THE LAMB'S JUDGMENT (xix. 11–xx. 15)

a. The appearance of the King of kings (xix. 11–16)

In the description of the 'word of God' there are echoes from the introductory vision in chapter i. But now He comes forth in wrath.

b. The destruction of the Beast, the false prophet and their followers (xix. 17–21)

The resultant carnage is vividly described as God's feast for the birds of heaven.

c. Satan bound for a thousand years (xx. 1–3)

d. The reign of Christ (xx. 4–6)

This is described as the first resurrection.

e. The final destruction of Satan (xx. 7–10)

His fate is to endure ceaseless torture.

f. The last judgment (xx. 11–15)

The present natural world disappears and the second resurrection takes place as death and Hades are cast into the destroying fire.

X. VISIONS OF THE NEW ORDER (xxi. 1–xxii. 5)

a. A new creation (xxi. 1–8)

This takes the place of the old order and is dominated by the descent of the New Jerusalem. It is a place without death or evil.

b. The splendours of the new Jerusalem (xxi. 9–xxii. 5)

Its twelve gateways, its measurements (also in multiples of twelve), its jewelled foundation stones, its glory and purity, its Tree of Life with its twelve fruits, and its ceaseless light, are all described.

XI. CONCLUDING EXHORTATIONS (xxii. 6–21)

a. An angelic endorsement (xxii. 6, 7)

b. John's own exhortation (xxii. 8)

c. Christ's message (xxii. 9–16)

There is an echo here of the introduction to the book. The whole is clearly designed for the churches there addressed.

d. The Spirit and the Church's invitation (xxii. 17)

e. A concluding warning (xxii. 18–21)

A severe penalty is threatened for all who tamper with the book, which then closes with a brief prayer and benediction.

GENERAL BIBLIOGRAPHY

Abbott, E. A. *Contrast: or a prophet and a forger*, 1903.

Alexander, J. P. *A priest for ever*, 1937.

Alexander, W. *The Epistles of John (Exp. Bib.)*, 1901.

Alford, H. *The Greek Testament*,[4] 1871.

Allen, W. C. and Grensted, L. W. *Introduction to the Books of the New Testament*, 1918.

Allo, E. B. *L'Apocalypse de Saint Jean (EB)*,[3] 1933.

Appel, H. *Der Hebräerbrief ein Schreiben des Apollos an Judenchristen der Korinthischen Gemeinde*, 1918.

Archer, G. L. *The Epistle to the Hebrews: A study manual*, 1957.

Ayles, H. H. B. *Destination, Date and Authorship of the Epistle to the Hebrews*, 1899.

Bacon, B. W. *Introduction to the New Testament*, 1900.

Badcock, F. J. *The Pauline Epistles and the Epistle to the Hebrews in their Historical Setting*, 1937.

Barclay, W. *Hebrews (DSB)*, 1957.

Barclay, W. *Letters to the Seven Churches*, 1957.

Barnett, A. E. *Paul becomes a Literary Influence*, 1941.

Barnett, A. E. and Homrighausen, E. G. *The Second Epistle of Peter (IB)*, 1957.

Barnett, A. E. and Homrighausen, E. G. *The Epistle of Jude (IB)*, 1957.

Barrett, C. K. *The Gospel according to St. John*, 1956.

Bartlet, J. V. *The Apostolic Age*, 1907.

Bauer, W. *Die katholischen Briefe des Neuen Testaments*, 1910.

Bauer, W. *Rechtgläubigkeit und Ketzerei im ältesten Christentum*, 1934.

Beare, F. W. *The First Epistle of Peter*,[2] 1958.

Beckwith, I. T. *The Apocalypse of John: Studies in Introduction*, 1919.

Behm, J. *Die Offenbarung des Johannes (NTD)*,[6] 1953.

Bennett, W. H. *The General Epistles (CB)*, n.d.

Benson, E. W. *The Apocalypse: structure and principles of interpretation*, 1900.

Bertholdt, L. *Historischkritische Einleitung in sämmtliche kanonische und apokryphische Schriften des alten und neuen Testaments*, 1812–19.

Bieder, W. Grund und Kraft der Mission nach dem ersten Petrusbrief, *Theologische Studien*, 29, 1950.

Bigg, C. *The Epistles of St. Peter and St. Jude (ICC)*, 1901.

Blackman, E. C. *The Epistle of James (TC)*, 1957.

Blenkin, G. W. *The First Epistle General of Peter (CGT)*, 1914.

Boismard, M. E. *L'Apocalypse (Sainte Bible)*, 1950.

Boismard, M. E. *Quatre Hymnes Baptismales dans la première Epître de Pierre*, 1961.

Bonsirven, J. *L'Apocalypse de Saint Jean (Verbum Salutis)*, 1951.

Bornhäuser, K. *Empfänger und Verfasser des Hebräerbriefes*, 1932.

Bornkamm, G. *Studien zu Antike und Urchristentum*, band 28, 1959.

Bousset, W. *Die Offenbarung Johannis (KEK)*,[2] 1906.

Bowman, J. W. *The Drama of the Book of Revelation*, 1955.

Brandon, S. F. D. *The Fall of Jerusalem and the Christian Church*,[2] 1957.

Brooke, A. E. *The Johannine Epistles (ICC)*, 1912.

Brown, D. *The Structure of the Apocalypse*, 1891.

Bruce, A. B. *The Epistle to the Hebrews*, 1899.

Bruce, F. F. *Biblical Exegesis in the Qumran Texts*, 1960.

Bruce, F. F. *The Acts of the Apostles* (Greek Text), 1951.

Bruce, F. F. *The Speeches in Acts*, 1944.

Büchsel, F. *Die Johannesbriefe*, 1933.

Bultmann, R. and Soden, H. von, editors, *Festgabe für A. Jülicher*, 1927.

Burch, V. *The Epistle to the Hebrews, its sources and message*, 1936.

Burkitt, F. C. *Christian Beginnings*, 1924.

Burkitt, F. C. *Jewish and Christian Apocalypses*, 1914.

Burnet, A. W. *The Lord Reigneth*, 1946.

Cadoux, A. T. *The Thought of St. James*, 1944.

Candlish, R. S. *The First Epistle of John*, 1866.

Carpenter, J. E. *The Johannine Writings*, 1927.

Carr, A. *The General Epistle of St. James (CGT)*, 1896.

Carrington, P. *The Meaning of Revelation*, 1931.

Carrington, P. *The Primitive Christian Calendar*, 1952.

Carrington, P. *The Primitive Christian Catechism*, 1940.

Chaine, J. *Les épîtres catholiques (EB)*,[2] 1939.

Charles, R. H. *Commentary on the Revelation of St. John (ICC)*, 2 vols., 1920.

Charles, R. H. *Studies in the Apocalypse*, 1913.

Charles, R. H. *Lectures on the Apocalypse* (Schweich Lectures), 1922.

Clogg, F. B. *An Introduction to the New Testament*,[3] 1948.

Cox, S. *The private letters of St. Paul and St. John*, 1867.

Cranfield, C. E. B. *I and II Peter and Jude (TC)*, 1960.

Cranfield, C. E. B. *The First Epistle of Peter*, 1950.

Cross, F. L. *I Peter: A Paschal Liturgy*, 1954.

Cross, F. L., editor, *The Jung Codex*, 1955.

Cullman, O. *Peter: Disciple, Apostle, and Martyr*, 1953.

Dale, R. W. *The Epistle of James and other Discourses*, 1895.

Davidson, A. B. *The Epistle to the Hebrews*, n.d.

Davies, W. D. and Daube, D., editors, *The Background of the New Testament and its Eschatology*, 1956.

Deissmann, A. *Bible Studies*, 1901.

Deissmann, A. *Light from the Ancient East*, 1927.

Deissmann, A. *The New Testament in the Light of Modern Research*, 1929.

Delitzsch, F. *Commentary on the Epistle to the Hebrews*, 1868 (German edn. 1857).

Dibelius, M. *A Fresh Approach to the New Testament and Early Christian Literature*, 1937.

Dibelius, M. and Greeven, H. *Der Brief des Jakobus (KEK)*,[10] 1958.

Dodd, C. H. *The Apostolic Preaching and its Developments*,[2] 1944.

Dodd, C. H. *The Johannine Epistles (MC)*, 1946.

Dods, M. *The Epistle to the Hebrews (EGT)*, 1910.

Douglas, C. E. *The Mystery of the Kingdom*, 1915.

Du Bose, W. P. *High Priesthood and Sacrifice*, 1908.

Easton, B. S. and Poteat, G. *The Epistle of James (IB)*, 1957.

Ebrard, J. H. A. *Biblical Commentary on the Epistles of St. John*, 1860.

Ebrard, J. H. A. *The Epistle to the Hebrews*, 1853.

Edmundson, G. *The Church in Rome in the First Century*, 1913.

Edwards, T. C. *The Epistle to the Hebrews (Exp. Bib.)*, 1888.

Eichholz, G. *Jakobus und Paulus: ein Beitrag zum Problem des Kanons*, 1953.

Eichhorn, J. G. *Historische-kritische Einleitung in das Neue Testament*, 1812.

Elliot-Binns, L. E., *Galilaean Christianity*, 1956.

Eltester, W., editor, *Judentum Urchristentum Kirche (Festschrift für Joachim Jeremias)*, 1960.

Eltester, W., editor, *Neutestamentliche Studien für Rudolf Bultmann*, 1954.

Erbes, K. *Die Offenbarung Johannis. Kritisch untersucht*, 1891.

Fairweather, W. *The Background of the Epistles*, 1935.

Farrar, F. W. *The Epistle to the Hebrews (CGT)*, 1888.

Farrer, A. *A Rebirth of Images*, 1949.

Feine, P. *Theologie des Neuen Testaments*, 1936.

Feine, P. and Behm, J. *Einleitung in das Neue Testament*,[11] 1956.

Feret, H. M. *A Christian Vision of History*, 1958.

Findlay, G. G. *Fellowship in the Life Eternal*, 1909.

Foakes-Jackson, F. J. *Peter: Prince of Apostles*, 1927.

Foerster, W., editor, *Manet in Aeternum, Eine Festschrift für O. Schmitz*, 1953.

Frost, B. *To the Hebrews*, 1947.

Gaugusch, L. *Der Lehrgehalt der Jakobusepistel: eine exegetisch Studie*, 1914.

Gebhardt, H. *The Doctrine of the Apocalypse and its relation to the doctrine of the Gospel and Epistles of John*, 1878.

Giet, S. *L'Apocalypse et l'Histoire*, 1957.

Glazebrook, M. G. *The Apocalypse of St. John*, 1923.

Goodspeed, E. J. *A History of Christian Literature*, 1942.

Goodspeed, E. J. *Introduction to the New Testament*, 1937.

Goodspeed, E. J. *New Chapters in New Testament Study*, 1937.

Goodspeed, E. J. *The Key to Ephesians*, 1956.

Gore, C. *The Epistles of St. John*, 1920.

Grafe, E. *Die Stellung und Bedeutung des Jakobusbriefes in der Entwicklung des Urchristentums*, 1904.

Grant, F. C. *The Epistle to the Hebrews in the King James' Version with introduction and critical notes*, 1956.

Grant, P. W. *The Revelation of John*, 1889.

Green, E. M. B. *2 Peter Reconsidered*, 1961.

Griffith Thomas, W. H. *Let us go on: The Secret of Christian progress in the Epistle to the Hebrews*, 1923.

Grosch, H. *Die Ectheit des zweiten Briefes Petri,*[2] 1914.

Gunkel, H. *Schöpfung und Chaos in Urzeit und Endzeit* (on Genesis i and Revelation xii), 1895.

Guthrie, D. *New Testament Introduction: The Pauline Epistles*, 1961.

Guthrie, D. *The Epistle to the Hebrews in Recent Thought*, 1956.

Guthrie, D. *The Pastoral Epistles* (*TNT*), 1957.

Hadley, J. *Essays Philological and Critical*, 1873.

Hadorn, W. *Die Offenbarung des Johannes*, 1928.

Harnack, A. *Die Chronologie der altchristlichen Literatur bis Eusebius*, 1897.

Harnack, A. *Das Neue Testament um das Jahr 200*, 1889.

Harnack, A. *The Origin of the New Testament*, 1925

Harris, J. R. *Side Lights on New Testament Research*, 1908.

Hart, J. H. A. *The First Epistle General of Peter* (*EGT*), 1910.

Hauck, F. *Die Kirchenbriefe* (*NTD*),[8] 1957.

Hauck, Fr. *Der Brief des Jakobus*, 1926.

Haupt, E. *The First Epistle of St. John. A Contribution to Biblical Theology* (Eng. tr. by W. B. Pope), 1879.

Heard, R. *Introduction to the New Testament*, 1950.

Hendriksen, W. *More Than Conquerors* (Tyndale Press edition), 1962.

Hengstenberg, E. W. *The Revelation of John* (Eng. tr. P. Fairbairn), 1851.

Henshaw, T. *New Testament Literature in the Light of Modern Scholarship*, 1952.

Héring, J. *L'Epître aux Hébreux* (*CNT*), 1954.

Hewitt, T. *The Epistle to the Hebrews* (*TNT*), 1960.

Higgins, A. J. B., editor, *New Testament Essays. Studies in memory of T. W. Manson*, 1959.

Holtzmann, H. J. *Einleitung in das Neue Testament*, 1885.

Holtzmann, H. J. *Die Offenbarung des Johannes*, 1908.

Hort, F. J. A. *The Epistle of St. James* (part), 1909.

Hort, F. J. A. *The First Epistle of St. Peter* (i. 1–ii. 17), 1898.

Hort, F. J. A. *The Apocalypse of John, i–iii*, 1908.
Hoskier, H. C. *Concerning the text of the Apocalypse*, 1929.
Hoskyns, E. and Davey, F. N. *The Riddle of the New Testament*,[3] 1947.
Hudson, J. T. *The Epistle to the Hebrews*, 1937.
Hunt, B. P. W. S. *Primitive Gospel Sources*, 1951.
Hunter, A. M. *Interpreting the New Testament, 1900–1950*, 1951.
Hunter, A. M. *Introducing New Testament Theology*, 1957.
Hunter, A. M. *Introducing the New Testament*,[2] 1957.
Hunter, A. M. and Homrighausen, E. G. *The First Epistle of Peter (IB)*, 1957.
Huther, J. E. *Petrus und Judas Briefe (KEK)*, 1877.

Jacquier, E. *Le Nouveau Testament dans l'Eglise Chrétienne*, 1911.
James, M. R. *The Apocryphal New Testament*, 1924.
James, M. R. *The Second Epistle general of St. Peter and the general Epistle of St. Jude*, 1912.
Jelf, W. E. *A Commentary on the First Epistle of St. John*, 1877.
Johnson, S. E., editor, *The Joy of Study*, 1951.
Johnston, C. N. *The Seven Churches of Asia*, 1916.
Jones, M. *The New Testament in the Twentieth Century*, 1924.
Jülicher, A. and Fascher, E. *Einleitung in das Neue Testament*,[7] 1931 (Eng. tr. from 3rd edition, 1904).

Käsemann, E. *Exegetische Versuche und Besinnungen*, 1960.
Käsemann, E. *Das wandernde Gottesvolk, Eine Untersuchung zum Hebräerbrief*, 1939.
Kenyon, F. G. *The Chester Beatty Biblical Papyri*, 1936.
Kenyon, F. G. *The Story of the Bible*, 1936.
Kepler, T. S. *The Book of Revelation*, 1957.
Ketter, P. *Hebräerbrief, Jakobusbrief, Petrusbrief, Judasbrief (Herder's Bibelkommentar)*, 1950.
Kiddle, M. *The Revelation of St. John (MC)*, 1940.
Klostermann, A. *Zur Theorie der biblischen Weissagung und zur Charakteristik des Hebräerbriefes*, 1889.
Knopf, R. *Die Briefe Petri und Judä (KEK)*,[7] 1912.
Knowling, R. J. *The Epistle of St. James (WC)*, 1904.
Kühl, E. *Die Briefe Petri und Judä (KEK)*, 1897.
Kümmel, W. G. *Das Neue Testament*, 1958.

Lake, K. and S. *Introduction to the New Testament*, 1938.
Lake, K. *The Apostolic Fathers* (The Loeb Classical Library), 1912.
Law, R. *The tests of life: a study of the First Epistle of St. John*, 1909.
Leconte, R. *Les épîtres catholiques (Sainte Bible)*, 1953.
Leighton, R. *A Practical Commentary upon the First Epistle of St. Peter*, 1831.

Lenski, R. C. H. *The Interpretation of John's Revelation*, 1935.

Leonard, W. *The Authorship of the Epistle to the Hebrews*, 1939.

Lewis, G. *The Johannine Epistles (EC)*, 1961.

Lias, J. J. *The First Epistle of St. John, with expository and homiletical treatment*, 1887.

Liebermann, S. *Hellenism in Jewish Palestine*, 1950.

Loenertz, R. J. *The Apocalypse of St. John* (Eng. tr. by H. J. Carpenter), 1947.

Lohmeyer, E. and Bornkamm, G. *Die Offenbarung des Johannes (LHB)*,[2] 1953.

Lohse, E. *Die Offenbarung des Johannes (NTD)*,[8] 1960.

Loisy, A. *L'Apocalypse de Jean*, 1923.

Lowe, J. *Saint Peter*, 1956.

Lowther Clarke, W. K. *Concise Bible Commentary*, 1952.

Lund, N. W. *Chiasmus in the New Testament: A Study in Form-geschichte*, 1942.

Lütgert, W. *Amt und Geist im Kampf*, 1911.

Luthardt, C. E. *Die Lehre von den letzten Dingen*,[2] 1870.

Maier, F. *Der Judasbriefe*, 1904.

Manson, W. *The Epistle to the Hebrews* (Baird Lectures), 1951.

Martin, H. *The Seven Letters. Christ's Message to His Church*, 1957.

Martin, R. P., editor, *Vox Evangelica*, 1962.

Martindale, C. C. *St. John and the Apocalypse*,[2] 1958.

Marty, J. *L'Epître de Jacques (Etude critique)*, 1935.

Masterman, J. H. B. *The First Epistle of St. Peter*, 1912.

Maycock, E. A. *A letter of wise counsel; studies in the first epistle of Peter*, 1957.

Mayor, J. B. *The Epistle of St. James*,[3] 1913.

Mayor, J. B. *Further Studies in the Epistle of St. James*, 1913.

Mayor, J. B. *The Epistle of St. Jude and the Second Epistle of St. Peter*, 1907.

Mayor, J. B. *The General Epistle of Jude (EGT)*, 1910.

McDowell, E. A. *The Meaning and Message of the Book of Revelation*, 1951.

McGiffert, A. C. *A History of Christianity in the Apostolic Age*, 1897.

McNeile, A. H. and Williams, C. S. C. *Introduction to the New Testament*,[2] 1953.

Meinertz, M. *Der Jakobusbrief und sein Verfasser in Schrift und Ueberlieferung*, 1905.

Meinertz, M. *Einleitung in das Neue Testament*,[5] 1950.

Ménégoz, E. *La Théologie de l'Epître aux Hébreux*, 1894.

Merrill, T. *Essays in Early Christian History*, 1924.

Meyer, A. *Das Rätsel des Jakobusbriefes*, 1930.

Michaelis, W. *Einleitung in das Neue Testament*[3] (with Ergänzungsheft), 1961.

Michel, O. *Der Brief an die Hebräer (KEK)*,[11] 1960.

Milik, J. T. *Ten Years of Discovery in the Wilderness of Judaea*, 1959.

Milligan, G. *New Testament Documents*, 1913.

Milligan, G. *The Theology of the Epistle to the Hebrews*, 1899.

Milligan, W. *Discussions on the Apocalypse*, 1893.

Milligan, W. *The Book of Revelation* (*Exp. Bib.*), 1898.
Milligan, W. *The Revelation of St. John*, 1887.
Mitton, C. L. *The Epistle to the Ephesians*, 1951.
Moffatt, J. *Introduction to the Literature of the New Testament*,[2] 1912.
Moffatt, J. *The Epistle to the Hebrews* (*ICC*), 1924.
Moffatt, J. *The General Epistles* (*MC*), 1928.
Moffatt, J. *The Revelation of St. John the Divine* (*EGT*), 1910.
Moulton, J. H. *A Grammar of New Testament Greek*, Vol. I, 1908.
Moulton, J. H. and Howard, W. F. *A Grammar of New Testament Greek*, Vol. II, 1929.
Munck, J. *Petrus und Paulus in der Offenbarung Johannis*, 1950.

Nairne, A. *The Epistle to the Hebrews* (*CGT*), 1917.
Nairne, A. *The Epistle of Priesthood*,[2] 1915.
Narborough, F. D. V. *The Epistle to the Hebrews* (*Clar B*), 1930.
Nauck, W. *Die Tradition und der Charakter des ersten Johannesbriefes* (Wissenschaftliche Untersuchungen zum N.T.), 1957.
Neil, W. *The Epistle to the Hebrews* (*TC*), 1955.
Nineham, D. E., editor, *Studies in the Gospels*, 1957.

Oesterley, W. O. E. *The General Epistle of James* (*EGT*), 1910.
Olivier, A. *L'Apocalypse et ses enseignments*, 1955.
Oman, J. *The Book of Revelation*, 1923.
Oman, J. *The Text of Revelation. A revised theory*, 1928.
Oxford Society, *The New Testament in the Apostolic Fathers*, 1905.

Palmer, F. *The drama of the Apocalypse in relation to the literary and political circumstances of its time*, 1903.
Parry, R. St. J. *A discussion of the General Epistle of James*, 1903.
Peake, A. S. *A critical Introduction to the New Testament*, 1909.
Peake, A. S. *Hebrews* (*CB*), n.d.
Peake, A. S. *The Revelation of John*, 1920.
Perdelwitz, R. *Die Mysterienreligionen und das Problem des ersten Petrusbriefes*, 1911.
Philippi, F. *Das Buch Henoch, sein Zeitalter und sein Verhältniss zum Judasbriefe*, 1868.
Phillips, J. B. *The Book of Revelation* (translation), 1957.
Pieters, A. *Studies in the Revelation of St. John*, 1954.
Plummer, A. *St. James and St. Jude* (*Exp. Bib.*), 1891.
Plummer, A. *The Epistles of St. John* (*CGT*), 1886.
Plumptre, E. H. *The General Epistle of St. James* (*CBS*), 1878.
Plumptre, E. H. *The General Epistles of St. Peter and St. Jude* (*CBS*), 1879.

Porter, F. C. *The Messages of the Apocalyptical Writers*, 1905.
Preston, R. and Hanson, A. T. *The Revelation of Saint John the Divine (TC)*, 1957.

Ramsay, A. *The Revelation and the Johannine Epistles*, 1910.
Ramsay, Sir W. M. *Luke the Physician and other studies*, 1908.
Ramsay, Sir W. M. *The Church in the Roman Empire*, 1893.
Ramsay, Sir W. M. *The Letters to the Seven Churches of Asia*, 1904.
Reicke, Bo., editor, *Coniectanea Neotestamentica XI in honorem Antonii Fridrichsen*, 1947.
Rendall, F. *The Epistle to the Hebrews*, 1883.
Rendall, G. H. *The Epistle of James and Judaistic Christianity*, 1927.
Rendtorff, H. *Getrostes Wandern*, in *Die urchristlichen Botschaft* (editor, O. Schmitz),[7] 1951.
Reuss, E. *History of the Sacred Scriptures of the New Testament*, 1884.
Riddle, D. W. and Hutson, H. H. *New Testament Life and Literature*, 1946.
Rigaux, B. *Les Epîtres aux Thessaloniciens (EB)*, 1956.
Riggenbach, E. *Der Brief an die Hebräer (Zahn's Kommentar)*, 1913.
Rissi, M. *Zeit und Geschichte in der Offenbarung des Johannes*, 1952.
Rist, M. and Hough, L. H. *The Revelation of St. John the Divine (IB)*, 1957.
Robert, A. and Feuillet, A. *Introduction à la Bible; II, Nouveau Testament*, 1959.
Robertson, A. T. *Studies in the Epistle of James* (ed. H. F. Peacock),[2] 1959 (original edition 1915).
Robinson, J. A. T. 'The New Look on the Fourth Gospel' in *The Gospels Reconsidered*, 1960.
Robinson, T. H. *The Epistle to the Hebrews (MC)*, 1933.
Robson, E. I. *Studies in the Second Epistle of St. Peter*, 1915.
Roller, O. *Das Formular der paulinischen Briefe*, 1933.
Ropes, J. H. *A critical and exegetical commentary on the Epistle of James (ICC)*, 1916.
Ross, A. *The Epistles of James and John (NLC)*, 1954.
Rothe, R. *Der erste Johannis Brief praktische erklärt*, 1878.
Rowley, H. H. *The Relevance of Apocalyptic*, 1944.
Russell, D. *Preaching the Apocalypse*, 1935.

Salmon, G. *Introduction to the New Testament*,[6] 1892.
Sanday, W. *Inspiration*, 1893.
Sanday, W. and Headlam, A. C. *The Epistle to the Romans (ICC)*, 1895.
Schammberger, H. *Die Einheitlichkeit des Jakobusbriefes in antignostischen Kampf*, 1936.
Schelkle, K. H. *Die Petrusbriefe, der Judasbrief*, 1961.
Schlatter, A. *Das Alte Testament in der johanneischen Apokalypse*, 1912.
Schlatter, A. *Der Brief des Jakobus ausgelegt*, 1932.
Schlatter, A. *Die Briefe des Petrus, Judas, Jakobus, der Brief an die Hebräer*, 1950.

Schlatter, A. *Petrus und Paulus nach dem I Petrusbrief*, 1937.

Schlatter, A. *Die Briefe und die Offenbarung des Johannes*, 1950.

Schmauch, W., editor, *Lohmeyer Gedenkschrift*, 1951.

Schnackenburg, R. *Die Johannesbriefe*, 1953.

Schneider, J. *The Letter to the Hebrews*, 1957.

Schneider, J. *Die Kirchenbriefe* (NTD),[9] 1961.

Schoeps, H. J. *Theologie und Geschichte des Judenchristentums*, 1949.

Schonfield, H. J. *Saints against Caesar: the rise and reactions of the first Christian Community*, 1948.

Schütz, R. *Die Offenbarung des Johannes und Kaiser Domitian*, 1933.

Schweizer, E. *Der erste Petrusbrief* (Prophezei: Schweizerisches Bibelwerk für die Gemeinde),[2] 1949.

Scott, C. A. A. *Revelation* (CB), n.d.

Scott, C. A. A. *The Book of Revelation*, 1905.

Scott, E. F. *The Book of Revelation*,[4] 1941.

Scott, E. F. *The Epistle to the Hebrews*, 1922.

Scott, E. F. *The Literature of the New Testament*, 1932.

Selwyn, E. C. *The Christian Prophets, and the Prophetic Apocalypse*, 1900.

Selwyn, E. G. *The First Epistle of St. Peter*, 1946.

Shepherd, M. H. *The Paschal Liturgy and the Apocalypse*, 1960.

Simcox, W. H. *The Revelation of St. John the Divine* (CGT), 1893.

Smith, D. *The Epistles of John* (EGT), 1910.

Smith, H. M. *The Epistle of James*, 1914.

Snell, A. *New and Living Way. An Explanation of the Epistle to the Hebrews*, 1959.

Soden, H. von, *Der Brief an die Hebräer*, 1899.

Soden, H. von, *Die Briefe des Petrus, Jakobus, Judas*, 1891.

Souter, A. *The Text and Canon of the New Testament*, 1913.

Sparks, H. F. D. *The Formation of the New Testament*, 1952.

Spicq, C. *L'Epître aux Hébreux* (EB), 1952.

Spitta, F. *Der Jakobbrief* in *Zur Geschichte und Literatur des Urchristentums*, II, 1896.

Spitta, F. *Der zweite Brief des Petrus und der Brief des Judas*, 1885.

Spitta, F. *Die Offenbarung des Johannes*, 1889.

Spörri, T. *Der Gemeindegedanke im ersten Petrusbriefe* (Neutest. Forschungen II. 2), 1925.

Stauffer, E. *Theology of the New Testament*, 1955.

Stibbs, A. M. and Walls, A. F. *The First Epistle General of Peter* (TNT), 1959.

Stonehouse, N. B. *The Apocalypse in the Ancient Church*, 1929.

Strachan, R. H. *The Historic Jesus in the New Testament*, 1931.

Strachan, R. H. *The Second Epistle General of Peter* (EGT), 1910.

Strathmann, H. *Der Brief an die Hebräer* (NTD),[7] 1956.

Streeter, B. H. *The Primitive Church*, 1929.

Swete, H. B. *The Apocalypse of St. John*,[2] 1907.

Synge, F. C. *Hebrews and the Scriptures*, 1959.

Tasker, R. V. G. *The General Epistle of James* (*TNT*), 1956.

Tasker, R. V. G. *The Gospel in the Epistle to the Hebrews*, 1950.

Taylor, V. *The Atonement in New Testament Teaching*, 1945.

Tenney, M. C. *New Testament Survey*,[2] 1961.

Thiessen, H. C. *Introduction to the New Testament*,[4] 1956.

Thyen, H. *Der Stil der jüdisch-hellenischen Homilie*, 1955.

Torm, F. *Die Psychologie der Pseudonymität im Hinblick auf die Literatur des Urchristentums*, 1932.

Torrance, T. F. *The Apocalypse To-day*, 1959.

Torrey, C. C. *The Apocalypse of John*, 1958.

Usteri, J. M. *Commentar über den ersten Petrusbriefe*, 1887.

Vaughan, C. J. *Lectures on the Revelation*, 1882.

Vaughan, C. J. *The Epistle to the Hebrews*, 1890.

Völter, D. *Das Problem der Apokalypse*, 1893.

Völter, D. *Der I Petrusbrief—seine Entstehung und Stellung in der Geschichte des Urchristentums*, 1906.

Völter, D. *Die Offenbarung Johannes keine ursprünglich jüdische Apokalypse*, 1886.

Vos, G. *The Teaching of the Epistle to the Hebrews*, 1956.

Wand, J. W. C. *The General Epistles of St. Peter and St. Jude* (*WC*), 1934.

Weiss, B. *Die katholische Briefe* (*KEK*),[6] 1900.

Weiss, B. *A Manual Introduction to the New Testament*, Eng. Tr. 1887.

Weiss, B. *Die Johannes-Apokalypse*, 1882.

Weizsäcker, C. von. *Das apostolische Zeitalter der christlichen Kirche*, 1886.

Welch, A. C. *Visions of the End: A Study of Daniel and Revelation*,[2] 1958.

Wendland, P. *Die urchristlichen Literaturformen* (*LHB*), 1912.

Wendt, H. H. *Die Johannesbriefe und das johanneische Christentum*, 1925.

Werdermann, H. *Die Irrlehrer des Judas- und 2 Petrusbriefes*, 1913.

Wernecke, H. W. *The Book of Revelation Speaks to us*, 1954.

Westcott, B. F. *On the Canon of the New Testament*,[4] 1875.

Westcott, B. F. *The Epistles of John*, 1892.

Westcott, B. F. *The Epistle to the Hebrews*, 1889.

Westcott, B. F. *The Gospel According to St. John*, 1887.

Wickham, E. C. *The Epistle to the Hebrews* (*WC*), 1910.

Wikenhauser, A. *Der Sinn der Apokalypse des hl. Johannes*, 1931.

Wikenhauser, A. *New Testament Introduction*, Eng. tr. of 2nd German edition, 1958.

Wilder, A. N. and Hoon, P. W. *The First, Second and Third Epistles of John* (*IB*), 1957.

Wilson, R. M. *The Gnostic Problem*, 1958.

Windisch, H. and Preisker, H. *Die katholischen Briefe* (*LHB*),[3] 1951.

Windisch, H. *Der Hebräerbrief (LHB)*,[2] 1931.
Wohlenberg, G. *Der erste und der zweite Petrusbrief und der Judasbrief (Zahn's Kommentar)*,[3] 1923.
Wolf, C. A. *Ein exegetischen und practischen Commentar zu den drei Briefen St. Johannes*, 1881.
Wood, H. G., editor, *Amicitiae Corolla*, 1933.
Wordsworth, C. *St. Paul's Epistles*, 1872.
Workman, H. B. *Persecution in the Early Church*, 1906.
Wrede, W. *Das literarische Rätsel des Hebräerbriefes*, 1906.
Wurm, A. *Die Irrlehrer im ersten Johannesbrief*, 1933.
Wuttke, G. *Melchisedech, der Priesterkönig von Salem* (Beihefte *ZNTW*), 1927.

Zahn, T. *Die Offenbarung des Johannes (Zahn's Kommentar)*, 1924–26.
Zahn, T. *Geschichte des neutestamentlichen Kanons*, I, 1888; II, 1890
Zahn, T. *Introduction to the New Testament*, 1909.

CLASSIFIED BIBLIOGRAPHY

In the following lists commentators and writers of special studies on individual books are mentioned by name and date only. The full title of their writings may be obtained by reference to the General Bibliography.

HEBREWS

Commentators: Alexander 1937, Archer 1957, Bruce 1899, Davidson n.d., Delitzsch 1868, Dods *(EGT)* 1910, Du Bose 1908, Ebrard 1853, Edwards *(Exp. Bib.)* 1888, Farrar *(CGT)* 1888, Frost 1947, Grant 1956, Griffith Thomas 1923, Héring *(CNT)* 1954, Hewitt *(TNT)* 1960, Ketter 1950, Manson 1951, Michel *(KEK)*[11] 1960, Moffatt *(ICC)* 1924, Nairne *(CGT)* 1917, Nairne[2] 1915, Narborough *(Clar B)* 1930, Neil *(TC)* 1955, Peake *(CB)* n.d., Rendall 1883, Riggenbach 1913, Robinson *(MC)* 1933, Schlatter 1950, Schneider 1957, Scott, E. F. 1922, Snell 1959, Soden 1899, Spicq *(EB)* 1952, Strathmann *(NTD)*[7] 1956, Vaughan 1890, Vos 1956, Westcott 1889, Wickham *(WC)* 1910, Windisch *(LHB)*[2] 1931.
Authors of Special Studies: Ayles 1899, Bornhäuser 1932, Burch 1936, Guthrie 1956, Käsemann 1939, Klostermann 1889, Leonard 1939, Ménégoz 1894, Milligan, G. 1899, Synge 1959, Tasker 1950.

JAMES

Commentators: Bennett *(CB)* n.d., Blackman *(TC)* 1957, Carr *(CGT)* 1896, Chaine *(EB)*[2] 1939, Dale 1895, Dibelius-Greeven *(KEK)*[10] 1958, Easton and

Poteat (*IB*) 1957, Gaugusch 1914, Hauck (*NTD*)[8] 1957, Hauck 1926, Hort 1909, Knowling (*WC*) 1904, Leconte 1953, Mayor[3] 1913, Moffatt (*MC*) 1928, Oesterley (*EGT*) 1910, Plummer (*Exp. Bib.*) 1891, Plumptre (*CBS*) 1878, Robertson-Peacock 1959, Ropes (*ICC*) 1916, Ross (*NLC*) 1954, Schlatter 1932, Schneider (*NTD*)[9] 1961, Smith 1914, Spitta 1896, Tasker (*TNT*) 1956, Windisch-Preisker (*LHB*)[3] 1951.

Authors of Special Studies: Cadoux 1944, Eichholz 1953, Grafe 1904, Marty 1935, Mayor 1913, Meyer 1930, Meinertz 1905, Parry 1903, Rendall 1927, Schammberger 1936.

1 and 2 PETER

Commentators (An asterisk indicates 1 Peter, two asterisks 2 Peter, and the absence of either 1 and 2 Peter).

Barnett and Homrighausen** (*IB*) 1957, Beare*[2] 1958, Bennett (*CB*) n.d., Bigg (*ICC*) 1901, Blenkin* (*CGT*) 1914, Chaine (*EB*)[2] 1939, Cranfield* 1950, Cranfield (*TC*) 1960, Hart* (*EGT*) 1910, Hauck (*NTD*)[8] 1957, Hort* 1898, Hunter and Homrighausen* (*IB*) 1957, Huther (*KEK*) 1877, James** (*CGT*) 1912, Knopf (*KEK*)[7] 1912, Leconte 1953, Leighton* 1831, Masterman* 1912, Maycock* 1957, Mayor** 1907, Moffatt (*MC*) 1928, Plumptre (*CBS*) 1879, Rendtorff*[7] 1951, Schelkle 1961, Schlatter 1950, Schneider (*NTD*)[9] 1961, Schweizer*[2] 1949, Selwyn* 1946, Soden 1891, Spitta** 1885, Spörri* 1925, Stibbs-Walls* (*TNT*) 1959, Strachan** (*EGT*) 1910, Usteri* 1887, Wand (*WC*) 1934, Windisch-Preisker (*LHB*)[3] 1951, Wohlenberg[3] 1923.

Authors of Special Studies: Abbott** 1903, Boismard* 1961, Cross* 1954, Green** 1961, Perdelwitz* 1911, Robson** 1915, Völter* 1906, Werdemann** 1913.

THE JOHANNINE EPISTLES

Commentators: Alexander (*Exp. Bib.*) 1901, Brooke (*ICC*) 1912, Büchsel 1933, Candlish 1866, Cox 1867, Dodd (*MC*) 1946, Ebrard 1860, Findlay 1909, Gore 1920, Haupt 1879, Jelf 1877, Law 1909, Lewis (*EC*) 1961, Lias 1887, Plummer (*CGT*) 1886, Rothe 1878, Schlatter 1950, Schnackenburg 1953, Smith (*EGT*) 1910, Westcott 1892, Wilder and Hoon (*IB*) 1957, Windisch-Preisker (*LHB*)[3] 1951, Wolf 1881.

Authors of Special Studies: Lütgert 1911, Nauck 1957, Wendt 1925, Wurm 1903.

JUDE

Commentators: As for 2 Peter, except Strachan, for whom substitute Mayor (*EGT*) 1910; add Plummer (*Exp. Bib.*) 1891.

Authors of Special Studies: Maier 1904, Philippi 1868, Werdermann 1913.

REVELATION

Commentators: Allo (*EB*)[3] 1933, Barclay 1957, Behm (*NTD*)[6] 1953, Boismard 1950, Bonsirven 1951, Bousset (*KEK*)[2] 1906, Bowman 1955, Carpenter 1927, Carrington 1931, Charles (*ICC*) 1920, Douglas 1915, Feret 1958, Glazebrook 1923, Grant 1889, Hadorn 1928, Hendriksen 1962, Hengstenberg 1851, Holtzmann 1908, Hort 1908, Johnston 1916, Kepler 1957, Kiddle (*MC*) 1940, Lenski 1935, Loenertz 1947, Lohmeyer-Bornkamm (*LHB*)[2] 1953, Lohse (*NTD*)[8] 1960, Loisy 1923, Martin 1957, Martindale[2] 1958, McDowell 1951, Milligan (*Exp. Bib.*) 1898, Milligan (*Baird Lectures*) 1887, Moffatt (*EGT*) 1910, Olivier 1955, Peake 1920, Pieters 1954, Preston and Hanson (*TC*) 1957, Ramsay, A. 1910, Ramsay, W. M. 1904, Rist and Hough (*IB*) 1957, Russell 1935, Scott, C. A. A. (*CB*) n.d., Scott, C. A. A. 1905, Scott, E. F.[4] 1941, Simcox (*CGT*) 1893, Spitta 1889, Swete[2] 1907, Torrance 1959, Vaughan 1882, Weiss 1882, Welch[2] 1958, Wernecke 1954, Wikenhauser 1931, Zahn 1924–26.
Authors of Special Studies: Beckwith 1919, Benson 1900, Brown 1891, Charles (*Schweich Lectures*) 1922, Charles 1913, Erbes 1891, Farrer 1949, Gebhardt 1878, Giet 1957, Gunkel 1895, Hoskier 1929, Lund 1942, Luthardt[2] 1870, Milligan 1893, Munck 1950, Oman 1923, Oman 1928, Palmer 1903, Porter 1905, Rissi 1952, Rowley 1944, Schlatter 1912, Schonfield 1948, Schütz 1933, Selwyn 1900, Shepherd 1960, Stonehouse 1929, Torrey 1958, Völter 1886, Völter 1893.

WORKS OF INTRODUCTION

Allen and Grensted 1918, Bacon 1900, Badcock 1937, Clogg[3] 1948, Dibelius 1937, Feine-Behm[11] 1956, Goodspeed 1937, Heard 1950, Henshaw 1952, Holtzmann 1885, Hoskyns and Davey[3] 1947, Hunter[2] 1957, Jacquier 1911, Jones 1924, Jülicher-Fascher[7] 1931, Lake, K. and S. 1938, McNeile-Williams[2] 1953, Meinertz[5] 1950, Michaelis[3] 1961, Milligan 1913, Moffatt[2] 1912, Peake 1909, Reuss 1884, Riddle and Hutson 1946, Robert-Feuillet 1959, Salmon 1892, Scott, E. F. 1932, Sparks 1952, Tenney[2] 1961, Thiessen[4] 1956, Weiss, B. 1887, Wikenhauser 1958, Zahn 1909.

AUTHOR INDEX

SUBJECT INDEX